From the high seas through to the 'coincidental' meeting of her Guru and beyond, Robyn Catchlove has lived an unconventional life. As a jack of many trades, she has managed a used car yard, done the travelling salesman gig, sold Lightning Ridge opals, and been the promotions officer of a race club. She holds a Master Grade 4 enabling her to skipper certain trading vessels in all Commonwealth waters.

Such a life has been lived across Australia, California, New Zealand, India, Nepal and Tibet and now in Sydney, where she resides in a garage fully decorated with 1970s 'stuff'. Robyn constantly listens to funk, blues, kurri and classical music, plays drum, and always greets the unexpected with great delight.

She is a Tibetan Buddhist practitioner, writes poetry, short stories and political rants and these days is learning the blues harmonica and dabbling in the art of lino printing.

ROBYN CATCHLOVE

SOMEWHERE DOWN A CRAZY RIVER

MACMILLAN
Pan Macmillan Australia

First published 2010 in Macmillan by Pan Macmillan Australia Pty Limited
1 Market Street, Sydney

National Library of Australia
Cataloguing-in-Publication data:

Catchlove, Robyn.

Somewhere down a crazy river : a spirited life catching fish,
love and wisdom / Robyn Catchlove.

9781405039802 (pbk.)

Catchlove, Robyn.
Fishers—Queensland—Biography.
Women—Queensland—Biography.

799.1092

Typeset in 12.5/14.5 pt Granjon Text by Post Pre-press Group, Brisbane
Printed by McPherson's Printing Group

Papers used by Pan Macmillan Australia Pty Ltd are natural, recyclable products
made from wood grown in sustainable forests. The manufacturing processes
conform to the environmental regulations of the country of origin.

To my extraordinary Mother and Father,
with unceasing love.

Contents

Maps   x
Acknowledgements   xiii
Prologue   xvii

CHAPTER 1:   The Gateway of Escape   1
CHAPTER 2:   The Man   10
CHAPTER 3:   Our Boat   16
CHAPTER 4:   Life and Death   25
CHAPTER 5:   New Friends and an Intruder   34
CHAPTER 6:   A Rude Blow   39
CHAPTER 7:   Flush with Luck   45
CHAPTER 8:   The Coral Sea   50
CHAPTER 9:   Cooktown   56
CHAPTER 10:   The Old Man and the River   65
CHAPTER 11:   Showdown   76
CHAPTER 12:   Sacred Rituals   82
CHAPTER 13:   Parting Company   92
CHAPTER 14:   Get Ready, Set, Go   98
CHAPTER 15:   Going to the Top   103
CHAPTER 16:   Whacked by a Storm   106
CHAPTER 17:   A Funny Way to the Top   112
CHAPTER 18:   Thursday Island   116
CHAPTER 19:   Workin' Girl   122
CHAPTER 20:   Goodbye to Our Crew   127
CHAPTER 21:   My Goddess of the Sea   132
CHAPTER 22:   Surprise, Surprise   137

CHAPTER 23:   The Seed of Change   141
CHAPTER 24:   Bramble Cay   145
CHAPTER 25:   Last Days at the Cay   154
CHAPTER 26:   Richard's Joss Stick   159
CHAPTER 27:   Our Pot of Gold   162
CHAPTER 28:   A Night Intruder   165
CHAPTER 29:   The Pearl Diver and the Decathlon Champion   170
CHAPTER 30:   Snake God   177
CHAPTER 31:   Weipa   184
CHAPTER 32:   In the Swill   198
CHAPTER 33:   Reunion with the Mulligans   205
CHAPTER 34:   Lost at Sea   215
CHAPTER 35:   Waiting for Barra   223
CHAPTER 36:   The Deep Pain Within   234
CHAPTER 37:   A Harbinger of Fortune   240
CHAPTER 38:   Outlaws on the Sea   247
CHAPTER 39:   Aurukun Mission   264
CHAPTER 40:   Taking a Stand   274
CHAPTER 41:   Trapped in the Love   288
CHAPTER 42:   Losing It   300
CHAPTER 43:   A Hardening Resolve   308
CHAPTER 44:   Game Over   314
CHAPTER 45:   Sailing on Pain   321
CHAPTER 46:   Myriad Turns for the Best   332
CHAPTER 47:   Awakenings: Rude and Otherwise   343
CHAPTER 48:   From Tinsel Town to Tibet and Back   359
CHAPTER 49:   The Best Bit   371

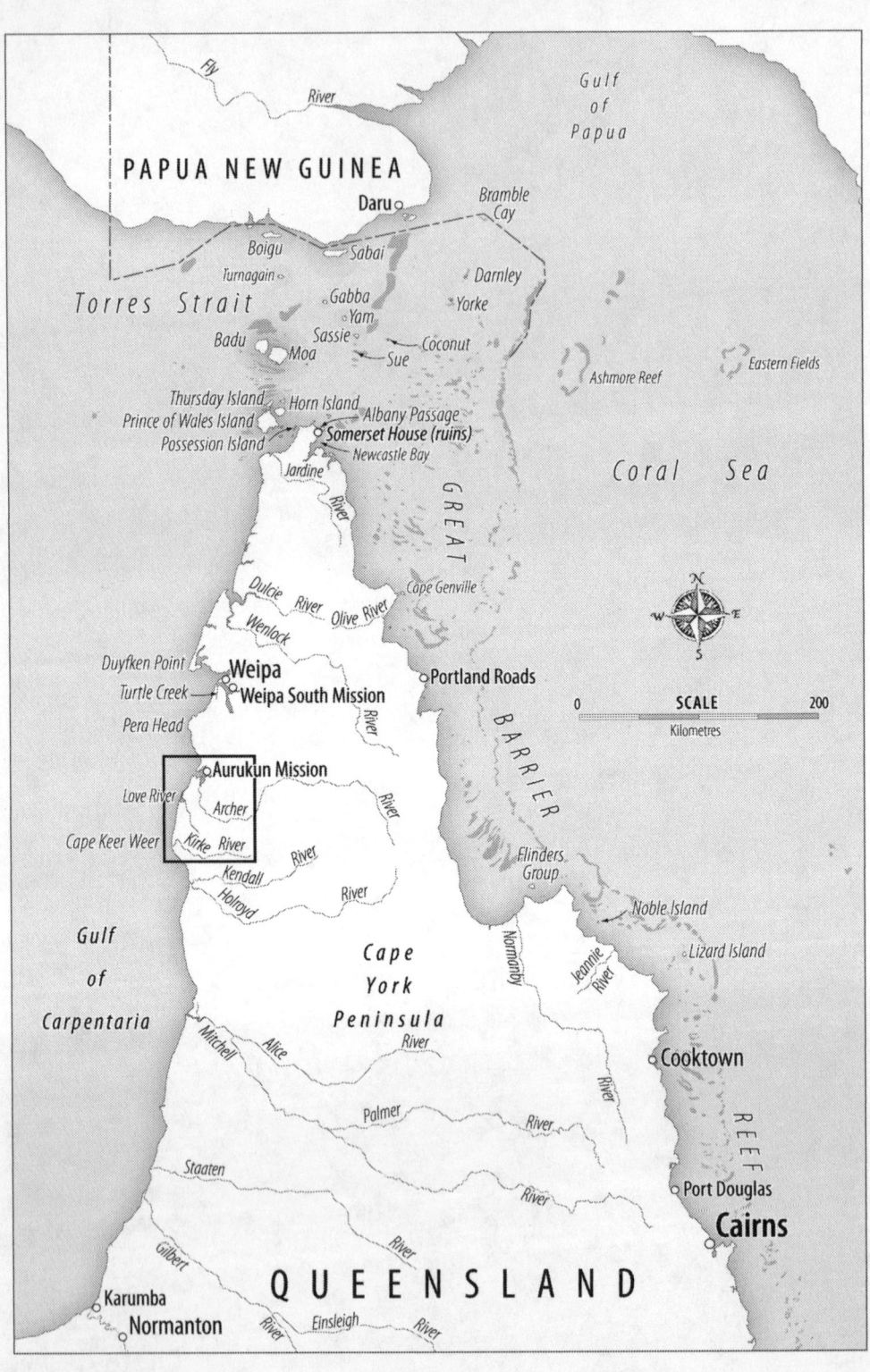

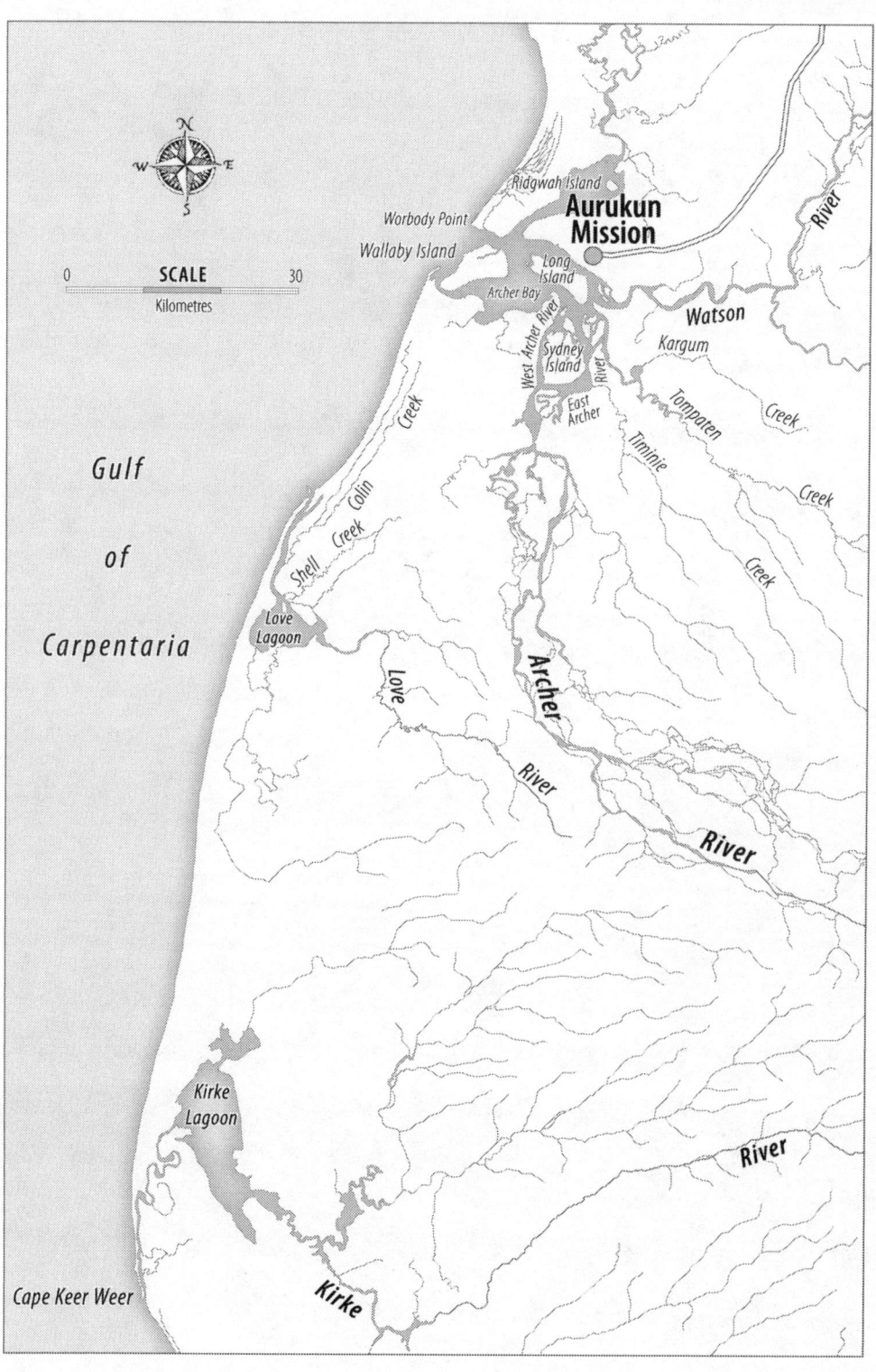

Acknowledgements

Considering that life is a profoundly unexplainable imperma-
nence, thanks seems not enough, so I want to pay homage also
to all those who have played any part in my life (including Tim), to
my past, present and future teachers, especially my Rinpoche, and to
all the water, land and sky animals whose lives have been sacrificed
along the way; and to the magic ones, Pippa, Alex and Emma.

We are the people we are waiting for.

– Ancient Hopi Indian proverb

Prologue

*W*ho says children aren't capable of murder? Certainly, I'd well and truly had enough of the furtive yet regular bullying by my brothers when, as a little kid, suddenly I lunged out of the bath, turned on the youngest one and coldly delivered the following deadly sentence: *'I'm gunna kill you, David. Right now!'* After all, they had both been relentlessly harassing me for years and, since Mum and Dad weren't listening to me, this looked like the only way to fix things.

As the sound of gushing water revives this early childhood memory, I decide that swimming upstream in my mother's vagina has been the easiest part of my colourful life so far. It is 28 August 2007 and I have just arrived at the famous 'women only' Ginseng Baths, at the back of Kings Cross in Sydney. Coincidentally, the full moon, the earth and the sun are performing a spectacular lunar eclipse, so not only is the night very intense, it makes me feel different too. Stripped naked, the surrounding full-length mirrors fully highlight the scars on my body that came from all my years on the sea. Internally, I can feel the invisible scars stirring up, trying to reach the surface. I mean it was a pretty tough way of life and please don't get me wrong, it wasn't all bad – but still, I wouldn't wish what I went through on anyone else, especially not as a woman.

Floating face-down in the bubbling spa, I let the warm water rock me this way and that. It feels so womblike and safe, and makes me think how very different my own birth must have been – probably I drove out in an eight-cylinder Holden, enthusiastically snatched up a packet of fags and a bottle of cheap whisky and blindly headed for the most exciting adventure I could find. Born with boundless, passionate enthusiasm, how could it have been so misread by others, especially the one I gave the most to? Tears spring up at the memories . . .

So, back in the mid 1950s as my brattish brother skittled away, I dashed to the kitchen, snatched up the nearest knife and, like an Olympic javelin thrower, bolted down our home's narrow full-length hallway and with almighty force thrust the silver blade into the bottom of David's tender young spine, and ripped it upwards. God, it felt good. My brother fell onto the shiny linoleum floor and let his piercing scream fill the entire neighbourhood – then he looked up at me, gave a trickster wink and continued the naughty hullabaloo until Mum and Dad arrived. As luck would have it, the knife I'd plucked for David's demise would not have cut through melted butter so he wasn't dead or even badly bruised for that matter, but he sure made it sound that way. Of course, on the surface, Mum and Dad saw that this was all my doing, so once again I was showered with verbal splatter and sent into shameful solitude. If only someone out there would listen to me.

By lunchtime the next day, in what was already a habit, I had wagged school and was at home preparing a cigarette. Liberally sprinkling Lipton's tea-leaves onto a page of Adelaide's daily newspaper, I rolled a very large, loosely wrapped cigarette, lit it up and took a drag. Smoking helped me think. It had been a rough week and a few things started to dawn on me. Even though Mum and Dad were loving, intelligent parents, both worked full-time and ran a very busy household, so no matter how hard I tried, I was not being heard. And now that David had survived my assassination attempt, it meant that he would continue to torment me even more heavily. Then there was me being a girl with a surname like Catchlove – I'll leave you to imagine how incessant the cruelty of the boys at school were around that! Even though wagging school relieved some of that pressure, plus allowed me to avoid the absolutely dull, colourless lessons called education, I was still without answers to my main dilemma. What was it with the double brother standover tactics? Why did Roger and David spend their time making life hell for me? Why did everyone make me being a tomboy kind of girl so difficult?

As the end of my fag flamed up and started creeping toward my face, I stomped it out and realised that already I was an outcast, what in those days was known as being the black sheep of the family. Perhaps I was just too smart for my own good, I mean whiz-kid I may have been, but I was eight years old and already things did not look good.

Back at the baths, I roll over, take a deep breath and hear the soft titter of women's voices echo around the hallowed, mist-filled spa. The tiled walls above me depict a time when women were women, you know that typical ancient Roman bathes scene with voluptuous, big-breasted, thick-hipped, proud Mona Lisa-like women languishing around in various stages of undress – and I notice that they are all smiling quite readily. Yet here we are a few hundred years later and we're all – including me – still swimming around bare and exposed, searching for true love, desirable beauty, a real hero and good sex. Of course there was the fateful moment when I did find the love of my life, which was followed by a stormy and passionate affair at the end of which, eight years later, I was left with unfathomable pain and he a stranger to me. There were others after that, but I am still alone and in that sense, unfulfilled. Was this all there was? Was life just a fickle fling with time, as quick as a flash of lightning, and without any prize? It certainly felt like I had missed something crucial on the run-through. With eyes closed and floating aimlessly, for the first time in a long while I let the old memories flood in and naturally tears spill into the healing waters.

Eventually my recollections pass, and feeling pure and crinkled like a newborn baby, I step out of the baths and prepare to head for the outside world. In the change room, someone tells me that after a quarter-century of service, the baths are just about to be torn down. 'Oh really, how sad,' I comment in a voice sounding unlike mine, and as this sinks in I think maybe it is time, maybe this is a sign to tear down the walls surrounding my own inner conflict. The grief comes on again, and I feel the prickle of tears in my soul.

Driving home to Marrickville, the intense clarity of the evening sky, the powerful light of the full moon and the unusual baths experience make me feel so open that I realise that on a day just like today, at some second of the cosmic clock, I will die – so why not let it all go, why not tell my heart's story? Then my favourite radio station butts in and says that tonight is the closest the moon has been to our little planet for hundreds of years. Fair enough – this is probably the closest I've been to honestly getting in touch with my own feelings too. After all, from birth until death, no matter who we are, love drives everything – it's just how we are around it, right? Along with the strong urge to start writing comes the hope that I and whoever reads my tale will understand a little more about why this is so.

CHAPTER 1

The Gateway of Escape

*I*t was 1948 when I shot out of Mum's womb in a souped-up Holden and I must have taken a wrong turn because I ended up in the painfully conservative city of Adelaide. Not my style really, and the boondocks suburb we came to live in was so raw that I can remember seeing sheep grazing in the nearby paddocks of the yet-to-become next subdivision. If I made a mistake in choosing my place of birth, I couldn't have done better when choosing my parents. Mum and Dad loved each other well, and were happy, accommodating parents, but other than that it was a battlefield out there.

Apparently being the only girl in our half-built street meant all the little boys gave themselves the right to cowardly close ranks, deliberately casting me out and forever thereafter always keeping me at arm's length. In the already well-developed male model of the day, they thought nothing of abandoning me way too far from home, nor did they care how or whether I made it back. And whenever it pleased them, just for entertainment, they belted me up, so from the beginning, operating in survival mode was a definite necessity – it was me against them, and therefore me against the rest of the world.

At the tender age of five, even the first day of school was a bit of a shocker. It wasn't just the being-a-girl thing but it was then that I realised that having a surname like Catchlove was an unchangeable burden I'd have to bear and which would call for fisticuffs on a daily basis. From then on, defending myself against school bullies never stopped, and nor did fending off my two brothers' nasty attacks, or me having to thump the standover boys who lived all around me. Apparently being a mere female also meant I should meekly submit to their authority or else whammo. As if that was ever going to come to pass! And you could hardly call what was happening at school an education – oh no, it was more like a monotonous regimental brainwashing assault on the intelligence of us school kids. Not that I would have been able to describe it that way at the time but you didn't have to be the dux of the school to realise how unimaginative and senseless most of the lessons were.

For a while I stuck at it and then in a bid to relieve the drudgery tried the classroom clown routine, but that meant even more pain from being sent to some stranger they called the headmaster who would whip my young soft hands with a cane which always left raw, very sore stripes. I sorted that by hanging off a fence to make my palms look badly red, so by the time I got to him it looked like I'd already been caned. What draconian people ever thought up the barbaric practice of caning kids? I mean when are we ever going to get that physical punishment never works? Certainly not on me. Taking all this in my stride, I learned to throw really effective punches and run so fast that none of the kids could catch me, all the while yelling the lie that my dad was a cop and he'd be over to arrest them soon. Still, it didn't take long before I decided that if you weren't wagging school, you just weren't healthy.

The only peace I could find was in being alone, so by lunchtime each day I stole home, smoked a tea-leaf fag, then like some intrepid explorer in search of unknown parts I'd pedal off into the horizon on my bicycle until late afternoon. With trusting parents working full-time, it was easy not to be found out. I suspect this modus operandi became the template for my life – fighting with the impossible and running away worked for me then, and probably did for way too long after that.

It wasn't that I suffered from loneliness, but it looked like I was going to have to make my way unaided and I certainly felt alone against the tide of others. Seems like even then, I was an avid reader, not just of books but of life itself. Anyway, from the beginning, these things made me different, an unusual kind of kid, and as I grew, so too did my restless, rebellious spirit, from which was born a life very much unlike that of others and with it my outsider fate.

Of course suburban high school was about as enlightening as a nuclear bomb, so without too much effort on my part I made sure to do only enough to pass my grades. However, three things did change. I took up sport, gave up smoking and got my periods. Sport was a godsend which I excelled at easily, smoking just went out the door, but it was that later event which altered everything! With the buds of womanhood appearing, instead of being in charge and beating the crap out of boys who taunted me with cruel names derived from Catchlove, I started blushing and turning away in humiliation.

Then, just as my tomboy days drew to a close, to the frenzied delight of teenagers throughout the planet, the 1960s burst onto the world stage. Yes, there it all was, including Elvis looking like a smouldering man angel, scurrilously gyrating his hips *and* singing suggestive love songs, the British pop bands turning us into screaming, hysterical fans, and fashion gurus leading us girls into wearing skirts shorter than the Fab Four's so-called 'long hair'. *How dare we!* Even though all the parents hated it, across the world frenetic teenagers with unstoppable gusto began turning their backs on stuffy convention and started asking unthinkable questions *out loud*, like, 'Why shouldn't there be sex before marriage?', 'Why not make peace instead of war?', and, quite frankly, 'Why couldn't there be a lot more of all of the above all of the time?' It's paradoxical really that it was the young who were the vanguard of such a brand new frontier, and as we began reclaiming some sense from the common nonsense, although none of us knew it then, rock and roll was here to stay and brought with it irrepressible change.

Well, revolution was certainly in the air, but saying 'fuck' was still something the pretentious Adelaidians did only after the lights went out. In fact, my home town was so puritanical that the ruling Methodists took conservatism to new heights by banning *Hair,* the newest, worldwide, 'smash hit' stage play, merely because the 'F' word was said openly onstage. Not to be outsmarted, most of us young'uns just drove across to Melbourne for the weekend, watched the 'offensive' musical there, loved it, then turned around and drove back – that generation had no fear and knew it had plenty of options.

The swingin' sixties scene felt intoxicating and I took to it like a natural, worked a well-paying day job and, at 21 years of age, even won Best and Fairest player for the South Australian Basketball Association. Life was a ball and then for a moment I took my finger off the pulse and thoughtlessly accepted a wedding proposal – you'll see why I say thoughtlessly soon enough. My husband to be, Ron, was like my dad – a decent, stable, caring man who had in mind security, a nice three-bedroom home, 2.5 children, a dog, a cat and a car-towing-caravan holiday every second year. What's more, our life together was going to be as happily unruffled as both our parents' lives were.

Mmm – just like the 'hip' generation were all trying to 'find' themselves, maybe I should have stepped out of the hotted-up Holden I was born driving and taken some time out to see who I really was, and just how fast I was going. But, truth be told, right then all I really wanted was to be able to make love somewhere other than the uncomfortable back seat of Ron's four-door sedan. The 'me genera-tion' were cool cats, but 'living in sin', as it was absurdly called, was as big a no-no as getting a divorce, so the only plausible method of being with one's lover seemed to be marriage – that terrible signed, sealed and delivered lawful contract of no return. I've always won-dered at what part of the ceremony the minister actually turns into a legal rep, or why, if you don't like the wedded state, you can't just return the contract to the minister/legal rep concerned!

So in the early seventies, there I stood at the entrance to a Meth-odist church in the full-length white gown and traipsing veil, in the centre of a classic wedding. Suddenly it felt like I was becoming con-scious after a coma. *Oh no!* Facing me was a rather large crowd of smiling, familiar faces, while behind me, all lined up and ready to go, stood the four spruced-up, beehived bridesmaids in typical match-ing ensembles. *Bloody hell!* With my suited-up dad on one arm and a bunch of fresh flowers in the other, the wedding march struck up and hesitantly I set off down the red carpeted aisle toward my intended. *Oh my God!!* Some people call them watershed moments, but I wanted to do more than cry when at that precise moment my lack of belief in marriage, particularly Christian marriage and its institutionalised commitment obligations, struck me more loudly than the church bells that clanged from the outside steeple.

Maybe the practice of covering the bride's face with a veil does have some purpose after all because, as *'Fuck. How the hell am I ever going to get out of this?'* ran through my mind, at least it gave me some momentary privacy By then there was no turning back, and the unexpected reality of this truly alarming situation shocked me so much, I don't remember taking any vows or much more about the whole dizzying event – other than that by the time the reception was underway, already I was thinking I needed a clever plan to escape from this stifling, typecast arrangement.

It wasn't just Adelaidians, all Australians had been handed down a whole load of nonsense about life and how it should be lived – including the whitewashed propaganda of our historical past which failed to even acknowledge the existence of the Aboriginal race, let alone the part we had played in their ferocious genocide. Obviously the landed gentry were hell-bent on perpetrating the dishonourable actions of the conquering British and some of our first colonialists. And women too had been taught to marry because it protected us from giving birth to 'bastards', the cruel yet legal name assigned to all children born outside of wedlock. I don't mean to sound harsh, so such moral dilemmas aside, we all knew that the Christian God loved Australians and that we were all very fortunate little vegemites to be living in the 'Lucky Country'.

But while God and the good-hearted Aussie folk wallowed around in the Great Australian Dream, I did not. Yes, to the casual onlooker everything between Ron and I seemed fine and dandy. He was well-liked, a successful accountant and loved play-ing Australian Rules footy, and I, a rising public servant, had good friends, loved fashion and played plenty of basketball and squash: and together we appeared to settle contentedly into the suburbs of so-called wedded bliss. Every Saturday night we partied with the gang and most nights made regular, satisfying love. Yet under-neath the urban veneer, my heart wasn't in it. Not that I didn't have some kind of love for this gentle and honest man, but hell, at the ripe age of 24, wouldn't you be worried about the door of sensuality slamming closed forever? It was that silly Christian obligation to never experience another lover until 'death do us part' which disturbed me so much. And his family were good, kind people too, but there I was stuck with the clunky, untrue label of 'Mrs Someone Else', the wearing of the telltale gold ring plus all the other disturbing associated connotations including the of loss of identity. Marriage was such a common arrangement and it was assumed that all women would obey the rules written centuries beforehand by a few monk blokes. All it did was make me feel repressed and stuck, and so I struggled almost daily with the unreasonableness of such feelings. You know, if most women were happy with the antiquated ritual, why wasn't I?

Ron definitely deserved to be happily married for 'ever after', but one thing seemed sure – it was not going to be with me. Now I had the safety net of an adoring husband, it was unbearable. Holding a secret like that only helped it grow more rapidly, until I felt trapped by the unadventurous tedium of what looked like my tidy lot in life. Ironically, sometimes I hoped he would hit me so there would be some rational reason for me to up and leave. That was being gutless, and besides, I should have been more careful about what I wished for.

Quietly, I became paper-thin, almost stopped eating altogether and made sure that no one knew. As I craved to break free I pined away to a shadow. There was no name for it then, but today it's called anorexia. Why did I feel such an inexplicable sense of loss and entrapment? With hindsight, it all seems so predictable that any observer, including me, should have seen that I was not going to be happy with an easy ride. Unconsciously I must have decided to do it the hard way, and having already cultivated a strong rebellious streak, it looked like the edgy, challenging side of life was the only place I would find my answers. Or perhaps it was all just unfolding as it was meant to.

The answer to my dilemma finally came in 1973 when Ron's company suggested we transfer interstate. What a relief that was. I saw the wide open road as the breakaway I'd been desperately praying for, so despite the fact that we were being sent to a little-known country outpost called Cairns, I started packing our bags almost on the spot. Who cared where, just let me out of the closet, I thought. Deep down inside, my heart told me that by putting a good distance between us and our loving families, the flight from marriage would be easier and unhindered by well-meant intervention.

Within the month my innocent husband and I, in our heavily laden family sedan, had driven 5000 kilometres up the meandering, two-lane No 1 Highway to the gateway of the Great Barrier Reef, and straight into the ripening Age of Aquarius. I had also acquired a secretarial job and a new friend – a local Cairnsite called Aileen.

When she invited me over to her place, I went. While we sipped awful instant coffee and talked with zest about the dynamic new vibe which was on everyone's minds, Aileen put on a Bob Dylan record, lit up a long, thick, hand-rolled 'cigarette', took a puff, and casually mentioned that it was marijuana. The times might have been a-changin' but thinking that at any minute the cops would burst in, make an arrest, then toss us into jail, I leapt to my feet, screamed, 'What the hell are you doing?' and fled home. Ah, how quickly that naivety was to change.

Still, Aileen was really only showing me a part of that which I was seeking, and so although I didn't smoke the stuff, our friendship grew. Then at her home one day a hippie with plaited hair down past his shoulders sucked in some of the good gear, and in a breath-held voice squeaked, 'So what's your name man?'

Ready to flair up, I replied defensively, 'Robyn Catchlove!'

He just smiled really warmly, handed me the joint and said, 'Oh wow man, what a beautiful name man.'

This was the first time in my life that anyone – let alone a man – had said such a kind thing about my surname so I rallied without hesitation, 'Hey, thanks man,' and immediately reasoned that whatever he was smoking was definitely worth a try, so I accepted the lumpy, smouldering fag and took a puff myself.

With Flower Power in full bloom, wisely every man and his dog was into peace, the Rolling Stones and $30 scrunched-up brown paper bags stuffed with sticky purple heads. And the more joints I puffed, the more my mind expanded to the birth of this enticing, wildly innovative world that was exploding before my eyes. The straight life was over.

Any obligation to be as my family had wanted was easy to shed from so far away, and so was my marriage: it just washed up on the rocks while I hung out with my new friend Aileen, listened to the brilliant rock music explosion, and got educated into this new irresistible way of thinking: about lifestyle, politics, art and sex. Having kept up appearances so well in Adelaide, this turn of events sent unexpected waves of shock and disappointment through friends and families alike. Really, none of them had any idea why our relationship was over – and if you had asked me to elucidate clearly, I couldn't have. Maybe this means that each life is already written and it's just how we respond to it that makes the difference.

As the stockings, high heels and the straight-laced office outfits peeled off, out went the nine-to-fiver steno-secretary girl and in cruised the nature-loving, sarong-wearing chick – and the only thing my shattered, well-intentioned husband could do was stand by helplessly and watch me completely transform. Certainly Ron's powerless grief was plain to see, and I felt pretty selfish about that so I cut the ties and shifted out. Whatever was driving it, when he tried desperately to win me back, the poor man didn't stand a chance. Ron was the wise one and, being a responsible bloke, kept going to work every day until eventually he remarried and went to live in Western Australia. A couple of decades later, we did find each other again. By then I knew what I had done and badly wanted to apologise, but he wouldn't hear a word of it, putting it all down to our restless youth. I think he let me off very lightly!

Maybe the rumbling of the sea was already making itself heard within because even though those around me all deserved a better explanation – I'm not sure I even listened to how anyone else even felt – nothing could stop my relief at regaining the freedom and passionate confidence which came from all that I thought life would bring. With what was about to sail my way, I would need all of that and a whole lot more. The future might have looked like a bed of red roses, but I forgot that all roses have thorns which not only pierce the skin but draw blood too.

By now I was in my mid-twenties, more the black sheep of the family than ever, and absolutely ready to tune in, drop out and turn on to the good vibes. At about 157 centimetres tall, with coppery-auburn tresses which sprung untamed around my freckled face, I was slim, athletic and although not beautiful, had natural loveliness.

If the sixties had been about shedding the old values and getting hip, historically the 1970s were equally unparalleled – the philosophies, fashion and mind-altering style of life was so refreshingly unpredictable, clever and tempting that the entire rising generation was drawn to it like bees to honey. You would have had to have been in a trance not to want to get with the scene – and what better place to do that than in the green, green tropics of north Queensland.

CHAPTER 2

The Man

*I*n the code of true hippie-dom, overnight I became a vegetarian, stopped drinking alcohol and turned to sampling the best weed in the southern hemisphere bar none: you know smoko, scooby-do, marryijahootchy, sweet, thoughtful marijuana – Kuranda Green, that is, with its coast-to-coast blast-off reputation, and the probable truth in the saying that there was at least half an hour of genius in every joint. Those were the days when some enlightenment briefly shone down on the planet, and even society and politics changed by the sheer force of popular attitudes. In fact for a few brief seconds in the history of mankind, it felt like everyone might even have been on the same profound page.

It sure seemed like that as we tried to live in harmony with nature rather than by conquering it, made love without attachment and successfully shared our food and money with others, without fear or expectation – all seekers of the way were in the thick of it, including me. Up in the velvet brown soil of the rich, lush north Queensland jungle, growers and smokers alike just tossed the lovely herb's seeds into the sky and grooved on by. Behind us, more marijuana grew and more hippies sprang up to pluck the vine. So the beat went on. And hey, let's give credit where credit is due here and not forget that the all-important Green Movement of today was born from that first hippie generation.

They say once a hippie, always a hippie, but before long the 'wow man', 'far out' and 'dig it' scene started getting passé, and I was restless for a new horizon. One day a girlfriend called Skye and I came down from the fecund, hillbilly tablelands of Atherton to Cairns to collect some essential supplies. As we strolled past a hotel on the main street, the balmy tropical breeze unexpectedly rustled up a change because an odd thirst came over me, and on that whim alone I suggested we duck into the pub for a beer.

Slipping on past the dense, semi-lit pool room with the cues all racked up like violinists' bows, I heard the rasp, rasp, rasp of white chalk passing across the player's tip and the clock, clunk, doosh, dotch – that expert clinking of balls connecting on the green cloth as the nicotine-ish smoke swirled up past the eyebrow level of the low over-table lights. We two must have been an intriguing sight for the jaded midday drinkers as we happily perched on bar stools and, oblivious to their stories, sipped and chatted on.

That's when the stranger with plenty of bravado tapped me on the shoulder, and made his bizarre request. Even the way the man did it made me feel like he'd been standing there, waiting for me and the chance to open our door of fate. It sure as hell was an approach I'd never seen before.

'Er, excuse me,' he said politely, 'but er, can I have your permission to do something I've never done before to anyone?' Honest – that was his opening gambit!

I laughed at that, and attempted to get a feel for the nuggetty, grinning Aussie bloke with the sea-swept face. Refreshing, I thought, at least he wasn't a hippie; but then there were the scruffy stubby shorts, the ragged navy blue singlet, the faded visor cap – all of which screamed no, so maybe it was the glint in his ocean-blues eyes or some hint of the unknown that captured me, because I agreed.

Without hesitating, the stranger reached over, delicately angled my face to one side, and with uncommon finesse softly ran his tongue along those very fine, tiny fairy hairs that grow along the bottom bridge of everyone's nose. True! Now that's different, I thought, little knowing that this was the moment the arrow was shot, that this was the very action that would change my world forever. After more light conversation, I quaffed the final dregs, wiped away the beer moustache and brushed casually past him. 'You don't know it yet lady, but we're meant to meet again,' he murmured in my ear, 'mark my words.'

Coincidentally that evening, Skye and I walked down to the wharf where the then small fleet of marlin boats quietly lapped beside it, and on one corner an old colonial style two-storey pub called the Pacific Hotel stood overlooking the waterfront. It was filled to over-flowing with rowdy, happy drinkers whose rhythmic clapping got the better of us, so we went over to see what was happening.

Because the jam-packed front bar broke out in maniacal whis-tling and cheering when we entered, I joked that I felt like taking a bow, and then my friend said, 'Look up man, look up.'

Following her gaze, surprise surprise if my eyes didn't meet the same blue eyes of the man who had licked my nose just hours before – only this time he was doing a tidy soft-shoe shuffle along the top of the bar and, it should be added, was totally nude!

'Les was the only one who was willing to do this to help raise money for the kids at our local orphanage,' explained the ruddy-faced cook still wearing the chequered splat pants and dorky hairnet, as she cut across our path, asked us to give generously and pointed to an upside-down hat propped on one corner of the bar. Later I would understand why this man had every reason to support orphaned kids, but then, as we quickly threw cash into the cowboy hat, I was too busy flashing my eyes appreciatively over his, er, 'well propor-tioned' frame and whispering to my hippie friend, 'Well, now I know a couple of things about him, plus his name!' With the Friday night pub crowd well into their cups, the chanting did its job and the hat didn't take long to overflow with donations.

We stayed amongst the happy-go-lucky crowd until the intrigu-ing man, now shaven, shampooed and wearing clothes came our way. He might have taken the trouble to sharpen up but he was still pretty cocky. 'Told ya we'd meet again,' he announced, and possessively took a seat beside me. Cheeky though he was, I liked it, and his manliness.

To say that all-consuming, passionate romance sprang up is a universal understatement. The 'meant-to-be' stars must have had a major collision when romance swirled around us, and Les and I began the most fantastic love-match of our lives – something we still agree upon today. With eyes only for each other, and captured by such intense feelings, we became inseparable. This meant mooning around reading aloud to each other from the latest fad book, *The Lord of the Rings*, swimming all night in moonlit private pools – one night even dancing naked at a party where others were dressed – and both sighing over Neil Young's twangy confession when he sang about needing someone to love the whole night through. And we did that too. In the exquisite passion of sweet surrender, our love-making was like nothing either of us had dreamt possible. It was soul mate love, and we made it wherever and whenever we could.

Les was 33 years of age and with both arms covered in tattoos, I was so taken by this tough, spunky fellow – he was strong, uninhibited and earthy – in short, the very opposite of Ron. There, all in one, stood my hero and hopefully the adventure I'd been waiting for: the man was so unlike any I had ever considered as a partner before, that even those from my past were bowled over. Again I completely dropped the old life and fell in with his friends – a naughty bunch of innovative scallywags mostly from interstate who all knew that laidback Cairns was not only an undiscovered nirvana but which was also rich with work opportunities.

Very soon – in fact within a fortnight – the two of us were winging our way to New Zealand so that Les could take up the job that he had accepted before our fateful meeting. And because there was no letting go of each other, there was no question as to whether I should or shouldn't go, I just went. At Auckland airport we hired a car, drove up to the Bay of Islands and while I settled back, Les, playing deckhand to a wealthy charterboat patriot, helped pull sterling black marlin in from the clear abundant waters.

Of course I could have been way more delicate in explaining my latest dramatic change in circumstances to Mum and Dad. New Zealand was not only an overseas country, but a very long way away from Adelaide, so it must have been quite a shock to receive an unexpected small postcard from there written by their only daughter confessing her naughty living arrangements. It read:

Dear Mum and Dad,
As you can tell by this postcard I am living now in New Zealand. I
am also living with a man and am very happy.
Love to you both, Cheers Robyn.

Fortunately, they were liberal thinkers and always insisted that my brothers and I had the right to choose our own way in life, and that whatever made us happy was how it was meant to be. Dad wrote back:

> *Dear Robyn,*
> *Thanks for the card. We are however most concerned. Will this man take care of you? Will he love you forever?* [Uh-oh, there's that all-pervasive Christian marriage question again.] *If so, love, you have our blessings. Nice to hear that you are happy. Please stay in touch. Love Mum & Dad.*

New-age parents in the mid-seventies were a rare and handy commodity, and their blessings on our union important, yet there was nothing much they could do but agree because I would not have changed anything for the world.

When marlin season was over, we moved to much more dubious accommodation at a Methodist boarding house in Auckland where, it's fair to say, the other patrons had probably not heard such persistent thrusting in their lives before. We both got work, drank nightly at the dingy nearby boozer where we played darts with the local chapter of Hell's Angels and happily let our unfolding love lead the way. Ah, life's glorious embrace made all appear as it really should be all the time.

Finally one mid-Saturday afternoon, after making love to our favourite tune, 'Bolero', Les proposed that we leave New Zealand behind, return home, meet each other's folks, then whiz back up to Cairns where, after building a boat, we would, he whispered romantically, 'live on the sea happily ever after'. I must have been dreaming not to have picked up on that fairytale 'happily ever after' ending.

Now despite having never ever been on the sea, let alone knowing whether I'd get seasick or not, this sounded perfect to me. It felt like Les and I could do anything we set our minds to, so impetuously I upped the ante by adding my divorce property settlement into the equation, a house sitting on two and a half acres of land in the Adelaide Hills from which there was a clear view of the ocean. 'How about I sell up and we use the profit to build the boat?' I suggested.

This time such spontaneous generosity was the right thing to do, but later in life I did this when it was not deserved. Being unintelligent around one's assets doesn't leave much in the escape fund, I assure you.

Now that such a fabulous trousseau had been thrown into the union, we flew posthaste back to Australia. On the run through, Les gave me a chain from which hung a gaggle of five silver marlin. The finely designed pure silver fish swam between my breasts, constantly making different configurations. It was a troth, a thing of beauty, and never meant to leave my young neck.

Conveniently both our families were native Adelaidians. My family called Les a rough diamond because he was less academic than they, but still took to him easily. Whereas Les's dad, King Coles, never really trusted me, but then he had good reason not to trust women – you see way back in the early 1940s, with Les only just born, Kingy's wife, without warning, had up and left him to raise five kids alone. Imagine the guts it would have taken to do that.

Still Adelaide was a very happy time, and my property in the hills sold effortlessly and for the right price to the people already renting it. Within the month it was time to go, so we bought a one-owner, low-mileage, very tidy little Volkswagen, and with copious bundles of money in the bank, split for the land of boat-building.

In later years Mum confessed to grieving each time I disappeared over the horizon, fearing that she might never see me again. Most times I was too self-absorbed to be aware of that. 'Thanks for having us,' I remember sending back on the wind as we sped north, up the east coast, only stopping to make love off-road, in the bush, by the banks of uninhabited, babbling brooks, or in the little Volkswagen right beside the busy highway.

Somewhere on a calm blue afternoon, perched high on a mountain ridge above the bustling world, he laughed, and we sought each other out. Listening to the rhythm as he took me, desire from its natural source pulsed as though there was an umbilical cord between us. I couldn't help thinking that perhaps our purpose came from another time; that with such exquisite love, maybe our souls had been mated previously? In an immenseness almost too great to bear, I felt a love that so few ever get to experience.

CHAPTER 3

Our Boat

*C*airns was like an uncut chunk of emerald perched on the edge of the vast, sapphire-blue Coral Sea, and everyone who lived there did the Queensland crawl. This was not a swimming style nor was it the slow-motion, dawdling pace at which we all walked, it was the way everyone lived up there in the 1970s. Think of the fast pace of life today, divide it by a thousand and you're on the money. That's why all the southerners who happened to stumble upon Cairns stayed and made it their home. Les and I were no exception, and as soon as we arrived back in the tight-knit, mischievous little town, we set about finding the right location to build our dream. It didn't take long.

The locals knew it as Old Rosenfeld's but from the start we called it the Big Shed. Positioned on the periphery of Cairns city proper, the enormous ex-timber warehouse was at least 100 metres deep and had layered shelves that ran 25 metres back along each side wall. Looking out through the seven-metre high, thick-planked front roller doors, we saw that Mount Budda Baddu was watching over us.

The massive building faced the train yards, was close to town, and just down the street from most of the marine suppliers. Insisting that it was made for us, Les checked that the overhead gantry worked, pointed out that the saw doctor in the next bay would come in handy, and noted that with the biggest front doors in town there would be no drama getting the boat out at the time of launching.

Additionally, the industrial zoning meant we had council permission to not only work but make noise 24 hours a day. Being a mere half-mile away, Smiths Creek was so close we could almost see it – and it ran straight out into the bay which meant that when the boat was complete, it would be a piece of cake to drop her into the water and drive straight out to sea.

His excitement was infectious, but still, there was one unanswered, important question: 'Yep, it feels great, but where do we sleep and eat?'

'Just watch us,' my young bloke confidently predicted.

And with that, we were in like Flynn.

By the first week's end, we had cut into the wall shelving on one side and built a cosy living alcove including a table with plank seats, a cutting bench, a set of shelves with a primus stove sitting on top, an op-shop fridge and a kitchen sink. Well, specifically, the kitchen sink was a cold-water tap with a plastic bucket underneath it. Our two-man tent, the love bubble, got pitched above all of that, on the top shelf. This meant we would literally step off the tent platform and straight onto the deck of the boat – when 'she' was built, that is.

Then Stevo, a longstanding buddy of Les's, generously swapped our little Vee Dub for his barely used, second-hand one-tonner. The sale was sealed in typical Queensland style – on a handshake. The truck was just right for our purposes, so we raced to the local dump which kindly coughed up a surprisingly good stereo system, a few half-decent old lounge chairs, enough rusty tools to get started with, and a frippery of doorway pot plants to greet the gawkers, nosy parkers and any of our mates who came by. Later, when our two dogs came to stay, the solid dirt-packed floors made it easy to live around them, like natural companions.

The boat we planned to build was to be a 30 by 11 foot beam, fibreglass vessel powered by a four-cylinder Bedford diesel engine, complete with fo'c'sle, wheelhouse, sleeping and living quarters and built in below deck would be the fuel and water tanks – plus, of course, a real kitchen sink! And rather than using timber or steel, innovatively we turned to fibreglass, a medium still very much in its commercial infancy then. It was the most efficient, cheapest medium for both of us to master quickly, so although all the boat aficionados shook their heads despairingly, that's what we decided on. Then, after shelling out significant cash on sufficient 44-gallon drums of polyester and epoxy resin and massive rolls of specific density fibreglass material, we proceeded to wax down and lay up the hull.

I relished in the fact that Les never treated me like an incapable woman. He just assumed I was up for it, handed me the chainsaw, electric drill, grinder or whatever, taught me how to use it and left me to it. Same as the natural prowess I had with the beautiful 1908 Winchester pump action rifle Les gave me that year as a birthday present. In turn I gave him and our boat everything there was to give. So learning on the job, we laid glass, sanded, welded, set the main shaft, hooked up the steering, pitched the prop, and kept on going. We did the lot, and were happy to be there. Young and thrilled with the challenge, sometimes we'd chase each other vertically up those big front doors, bound onto the top shelf, sprint halfway down the shed, leap easily down onto the dirt floor, and get back to the job at hand. Being in love and defying gravity was easy. Not so in the money department though, which was tight from the start. To help compensate, I wrangled the tax department into giving us total sales tax exemption on everything, even though technically we were not, at that stage, a commercial venture. Every possible minute was spent working on the boat, plus one of us often went out to a paying job.

They used to say if you put a bean in a jar every time you made love in the first year of a romance, and then every time you made love after that you took a bean out, you would never empty the jar. Certainly we would have needed a bloody big bean jar in that first year, which is not to say it wasn't a feisty relationship or that we never had words with each other – but at that stage, Les never demonstrated even the slightest hint of wanting to use physical harm to get his way, we just lived in healthy accord.

Living next door to the one and only brothel in Cairns turned out to be a harmonious bonus too. In a status befitting her profession, the madam always sported a perfect beehive hairdo, a great deal of classic, top quality gemstone jewellery and long fingernails immaculately painted in proper fire engine red. Miss Maxine was not without influence in the growing town and also made us a proposition too good to refuse, the upshot of which meant that with one press on her under-the-counter buzzer, an alarm bell rang in our shed. At this, Les would up and burst next door like Flash Gordon, all ready to sort out any would-be troublemakers. This killed a few birds with one stone: we made some quick cash on the side, the working girls got instant protection, and it kept the madam in bed – so to speak – regarding the industrial noise and our living arrangements.

Perc, the saw doctor in the next bay over, was a softly spoken New Zealander from Wongerea. He loved companionship, anything marine, was an innovative designer, a great listener and turned out to be a very handy source of knowledge, machinery and timber. Once, after watching me weld a few freezer pipes, then bevel some timber using his deadly spindle-moulder, Perc swore blind he'd take me on as an apprentice any day. He reckoned I was better than most men simply because I listened closely, and didn't have any preconceived ideas on how to go about things. Genuine praise and such unpreju-diced encouragement of a woman was almost unheard of then. Not that I was cleverer or any different than the men at all, but I really appreciated being treated as though I had equal intelligence.

There was never a moment of doubt between us about whether the project would be completed, but of course the churlish local busybodies with nothing better to do came soon enough. Les called them the green gills and reckoned that while we were keeping them tantalised, they weren't bothering anyone else. Enviously they'd peer in, laugh dismissively up their critical sleeves, all the time hoping that we'd tip upside down. So it was par for the course that rumours floated around our venture, and even came back to us – things like: *'Those two will never finish it . . . Yeah, it's a total waste of money . . . Nah, it'll never get off the ground . . . It's hopeless, they'll never get past the hull . . . He's got no idea . . . She'll never stick it out . . . Of course, it'll never float, eh but!'*

Funny things, Queenslanders, with their local lingo habit of putting 'eh but' at the end of almost every sentence. For example, at birth they were likely to say, 'You're my mum, eh but.' This was not a question, but more of an affectionate sign-off. Additionally, when any person was parting company to go elsewhere, Queenslanders spontaneously said 'Hurray'. This was not a form of cheering but rather an endearing goodbye. For example, at death, it's likely they'd utter, 'Oh well, see ya then, hurray, eh but!' Search me, but they were tenaciously proud of how different they were to anyone outside their own borders. Anyway, having none of the nitpicking deriders, we turned our backs on them and painted our own life picture by successfully building a strong, seaworthy boat from scratch.

Most of our money was spent buying the bulk materials or had been set aside to purchase the main engine, so what remaining cash there was needed stretching, and then some. To offset this, each Sunday morning we religiously dashed off to 'work' at the dump where practical treasures like unused paintbrushes, reasonable tools, boxes, chunks of chain, tins, rope, and even the boat's first steering wheel were all waiting to be rebirthed. It was so much fun fossicking at the best shop in town where everything was free that Les used to joke, saying, 'Don't say I never take you shopping.' You name it, we found it, took it home, used it, gave it away, or took it back to the dump the following Sunday and got more of the same to take home. Being there was like reading 'The People's Guide to the National Economy': good times equalled good dump pickings; when times were bad, the quality and amount of 'stuff' declined, and the more dump rats there were competing for the pickings.

Late one moonless night, we even snuck down to the silty edge of Smiths Creek and snaffled – er, borrowed . . . er, extracted – a loose-planked, beached-up, abandoned small fishing dory. It wasn't really that salvageable, but the challenge and fun of retrieving it spurred us on. Life felt like that. Besides, the dory came in handy as a big rag bag.

Even though non-paying help rarely came, nevertheless we built away the days and at night, with our favourite music filling the Big Shed, our passion continued to sparkle and sizzle. Wrapped up in fun and infallibility, we decided it was baby-making time. At Les's instigation, I dutifully trundled off to a gynaecologist for a check-up who, without much of a proper internal examination, all too quickly announced that I did not ovulate. He said not to worry, though, because the very latest drug company invention would fix that. Called the fertility drug, this, the doctor declared, was guaranteed to bring results. Instead of giving the doctor a healthy argument, I swallowed both his story and the wonder pills as though they were favourite lollies.

Each evening, we'd down tools and lounge around out the front of the Shed amongst the dump furniture and pot plants. As an occasional train carriage shunted past, and Mount Budda Baddu bathed us in her caring gaze, Les and I contentedly sipped beer and plotted and planned the next moves. By then we were about twelve months into the project, but before the roof could go on, the main engine had to be dropped inside from the overhead gantry. It was time to go and pick up the big engine from the Bedford Depot in Townsville. Because there were a few good rivers on the way down, Les reminded me to chuck snorkels, goggles and towels into the truck.

'So tell me, what'd your last slave die of, overwork?' We both chuckled away at that, but I had just laboured for a full day, finished weeding the sprouting veggie patch weaving its way along the front wall, and was inside lighting up the big 44-gallon drum. Burning all the timber off-cuts and sawdust from each day's productivity got rid of rubbish, kept the mozzies at bay, and also lent welcome warmth to our open home.

Following a predawn start, by mid-morning the next day we had already snorkelled naked in the Herbert River, torn off a knee trembler, devoured a few chunky sandwiches, had a cup of tea, rolled up in Townsville and proudly taken possession of our brand new four-cylinder diesel engine – which was all checked over, systematically strapped down, and waiting patiently on the truck's backboard while the moleskinned sales rep gave us a spiel about why ours was called a Wednesday engine: 'By its markin' the engine's been built in the middle of the week, when the factory workers are over the previous weekend's partying and not yet gearin' up for the next weekend, so it's the time when they're most focused. This means that it should be a real beauty. In our industry, we call it a lucky engine.'

Looking up at the grim overhead sky, I told Les to cut the chit-chat, that it was time to get back on the road. As the trusty truck charged up the sugar-cane highway, in silent concentration we both focused on driving, while above us the accumulating nasty black clouds gathered pace – thereby confirming my bad weather prediction. By the halfway-home mark, thunder clapped at full volume and wilful, furious rain blinded our view of the cruddy, single-lane, zigzag mountain pass that we were climbing. Only the random zaps of lightning that crisscrossed the heavens helped illuminate the dangerous way.

'Shit, this is hard fuckin' work,' Les yelled above the crashing rain.

I turned to shout back some encouraging words but suddenly a big, ugly mother of a rock bounced smack-bang into the windscreen, instantly shattering it into an unsolvable jigsaw of thousands of pieces – all of which then cascaded down on us in brittle chunks of pointy glass. Les yelled more expletives, kept the whole show barrelling forward, and insisted I grab both sets of goggles. 'Shove 'em on,' he urged, 'it's the only way we'll be able to see any bastards comin' from the other way!'

With spitting rain stinging our faces, and hearts pumping more blood than the truck was using petrol, we crashed head-first through the tempest like Olympic sled-barrellers shaving the edges. This was our element. As we wound, up, up and over that dark, squally mountain pass and rumbled down the other side, my man even challenged the godforsaken storm by breaking out into a song or two.

Finally the cracked bitumen road levelled out, the blizzardy rain stopped and up in front we saw a backed-up, bunched together crowd of caravan combos, four-wheel drives, family wagons chocked with kids and dogs, a couple of 'travelling salesman' sedans – and sure enough, right at the end of the traffic jam, the obligatory hippie kombivan all a swirl with flowers and peace slogans painted down both sides. Weaving through ban-the-bomb symbols was written: *THE 'A' MUSING MUSIC MACHINE TROUPE. For Bookings call Blossom* and a fading phone number.

We surfed the one-tonner to a screaming halt, and with the engine still racing, Goggle God Les leapt feet-first into the stack of anxious travellers who were clutched together beneath the bullying storm. The boggle-eyed crowd broke circle and let out a collective gasp. With a blanket of splintered glass shards falling away from his body, Les didn't mince words either. 'What the fuck's goin' on here?' Everyone's jaw dropped open as they stared from him to goggle-faced me, back to Les, back to me, and all silently nodded in unspoken confirmation of the obvious – yep, both had the goggles on; yep, both were grinning happily; yep, both looked like drenched underwater comedians. Me beaming and waving through the non-existent windscreen probably didn't help matters.

Of course it was the hippies who got it, and one broke the ice straight away: 'Like you two are far out man, but it's the river man, like, it's way too high to cross and still rising man, so it looks like an overnight thing before it like . . .'

The long-haired, caftaned man's sentence drifted away when Les cut to the heart of the matter and stormed straight into the quick-rising stream that appeared to be impeding everyone's journey. The water dashing over the highway was on its own frantic way to reaching the equilibrium of the ocean, so Les sloshed into the centre of the flood and let it flow and whirl around his chest. As he peered intently this way and that, whipped the goggles off, lobbed a quick dollop of spit onto the lenses, rinsed them in the raging creek and snapped them back onto his face again, the stunned mob watched with open fascination. With streams of water and glass shards still falling away from him, like the original iceman he emerged, bounced back into the driver's seat, cranked the one-tonner into first gear, and plunged boisterously into the gushing river.

The man was unafraid, and so spontaneous. When the water rose above the truck floor and into the cabin, I let out a whoop. 'Yee-haaaaa. Let's go to the ends of the universe together, Lesy, and if we die along the way, at least we'll be having an adventure!'

Soon we surfaced at the other end of the flash flood, and pressed on through the countryside, not giving up until we reached home. Effortlessly, I tore apart the big doors, he reversed the truck with its precious cargo inside and with that, the task was complete.

'You know I love you like the storm we just plunged through. Let's hit the cot, you beautiful woman.' That sounded romantic enough to me and the tent air felt like the eye of a cyclone – all charged up with fierce intention, as was Les when he clasped me firmly and made the stuff of love babies.

The main engine was also about to be bedded down because at dawn the following morning, four of our buddies were pounding on the front doors. By the time the last sip of their first morning coffee was over, the glossy green Bedford hovered from the overhead gantry, right above the boat's central keel area.

'Thanks for comin' fellas because I can't lift this thing all on me own,' Les said, as he positioned the men and issued instructions about how he wanted things done.

For a while the big men grappled and wrestled that heavy diesel engine around unsuccessfully, and I stood by, ready at any instant to do whatever I was told. No matter how hard the team tried to nurse the precious engine into position, and the unoiled, cranky gantry chains jangled up, down, up, down, up, down, somehow it was all too difficult. That meant the swearing became more artistically profuse, the deep gutsy grunting became more laboured and the tempers grew hotter than the muggy, tropical summer day that brewed outside until finally Les blew his stack.

'Drop the engine down and step aside. Get back all of you.' My man's dead quiet voice, the tone of it, commanded obedience.

We must have known that something special was at hand because without a word, everyone did as he had said. I reckon you could've heard a pin drop when Les wrapped his frame around the massive bulk of steel like he was going to squeeze the bejesus out of a grizzly bear. Then there was this deep guttural growl that demanded his own supernatural strength shift heaven, earth and the bloody fucking Bedford diesel engine. In one movement he snatched up the impossible weight, straightened, took two steps forward, and like a lover completing the final pleasure stroke, he thrust the engine forward and down onto the timber beds. Hearing the comforting clunk of something landing in its right place told us that our Wednesday engine was bedded into its final resting position, the boat's inner ribs. I'm still a firm believer that if you're on the right track, divine intervention is never more than a primordial roar or two away.

CHAPTER 4

Life and Death

While we knuckled down and the boat progressed, the town's curious fascination dwindled. Gradually, Cairns began agreeing that the whole fiasco might just be a goer, so they only bothered passing by the Big Shed as part of their traditional Sunday afternoon drive – you know, for light entertainment.

Then, too early one morning, in hustled our next-door neighbour. Maxine was without makeup, and her red, pointy fingernails ominously beckoned Les. 'Barb's on the phone, says she's your sister from Adelaide and reckons it's real urgent.'

She bustled back out just as smartly, only peering back through her untamed silver-white tresses to further urge Les: 'Drop the tools, love. Come on!'

His sister's news was a bombshell: their dad, Kingy, the only parent who had stuck with them through thick and thin, lay in hospital, dying. By dusk that same day, we had rumbled the front doors shut, Miss Maxine was in charge of the Shed, and inside our boat sat waiting while both of us flew above the outback, South Australia-bound.

Les tried to explain, 'Maxine's lent me the money . . .'

I squeezed his hand, 'Hey, there's nothing to say. I know how important your family is to you and I'm there for you all the way. Oh, and don't be too disappointed but my period has just started, so there's no baby this month.'

My man gazed out of the plane's porthole into the never-ending cloud mountains and absently replied, 'It's probably better that way for now.' I could tell that he was far, far away, probably back in the days when his family, the Coles, had been more than poor; when they had nothing and his dad had been his only saviour. And tougher than tough would have been life on the wharf in the 1940s down Port Adelaide way – and Les's dad had a ruthless reputation so the other wharfies left him right alone and Kingy liked it that way. The man was all muscle and as wide as he was tall, so being 193 centimetres there was a fair bit of weight behind the legend. He was known as a hardworking, teetotalling loner who rarely spoke and it didn't pay to mention Kingy's family situation either because the man was a king-hitter and was known to go berserk. That was because the fifth child had only just been born when his wife disappeared completely, not to be seen nor heard of ever after. After that, the King never mentioned her again. Besides, he had a calamity on his hands because although the four older kids went to school each day while he worked, Les, the new-born, had been forced to spend his babyhood lying all day alone in a crib. So each lunchtime, Kingy bicycled home, changed the kid's nappy, poured food into his forlorn belly, packed him tightly back inside the crib fence, then pedalled double-trouble back to work: the wee baby left all alone again until his dad clocked off in the late afternoon.

Ultimately this led to Les being the one who was taken away from the family by the government and placed in a state institution. By the age of about thirteen or fourteen, he was doing juvenile detention in a boys-only correctional reformatory, and later even ended up doing some misdemeanour time in Yatala jail. In these primitive places he saw way more than a young one should, and not enough of his brothers and sisters. Around his early twenties, Les came to his own senses and broke away from that life by going on the road, a road that eventually led him to me.

No one likes hospitals, but when Les and I arrived in the car-park we could hear King's screams and knew there was no mercy in the cancer that pervaded every cell of his 81-year-old body. Inside, the five reasons which he'd lived and fought so tenaciously for, now parents in their own right, nestled around him and watched as the illness rained blows of pure torture onto his mortal form. With so much pride, Kingy's iron will turned against him and so as his pain-wracked, withered frame took up the foetal position in preparation for rebirth, the man screamed out against the death that was trying to whisk him away. And so, the sad days blurred on by. In the end, thank heavens, he wrenched himself into the beyond. All the mourning had been over and done with so there were few tears when his deeply relieved sons and daughters stood quietly at the sombre, desolate funeral on an unpredictably grey and windy summer's morning.

There is nothing unusual about death – in fact it is the only certain thing that we know about life. And whether you like it or not, the only thing we don't know is exactly what day, month, year or second that death will come for us. Even the period of time it takes for death to descend and birth to arrive rests with whoever it is that's getting ready to go in either direction. Life is such an unpredictable, sometimes even random event, that we should live every second like it is the last, shouldn't we? Looking at it that way, what choice do we have? I mean, even then what none of us knew was that as sure as King Coles's death had been written on the outgoing tide, there was another unlikely death rising on the incoming.

As a goodbye gesture to Les and me, the next Saturday night both our families gathered together. As we all chatted on, how were we to know that the persistently turbulent weather was not the only uncharacteristic event that was to occur that evening. Suddenly thick, deep maroon splotches of blood gushed down my legs and splattered onto the back porch floor. Abruptly, I paled and slumped into unconsciousness. When I came round, my man was hovering above me and we were in the back of a kick-butt, siren-screeching ambulance clanging noisily toward hospital.

'Listen Les, what with all the pain around Kingy's death and your family never being far from his bedside, I just didn't want to give you anything else to worry about,' I managed to whisper. The truth was that by the time I realised that my prolonged scatty bleeding was not just an unusual period but instead a slow, untapped haemorrhage, I wasn't thinking straight anymore. Quietly I had been bleeding to death and no one had noticed. Unfortunately, some pretty serious complications were about to come about because of that.

'Don't talk, Robby,' he muttered worriedly, 'save your strength.' As I lapsed in and out of consciousness, Les held my hand and confided words of love.

When I came to the following morning, a myriad of upside-down plasma and blood bottles hung above my crisp white bed like a newly born baby's giant toy mobile. Suddenly a tanned face wearing black-rimmed glasses and a white coat appeared – a doctor, I presumed. While I was still trying to come to grips with exactly where I was, the doctor trotted past and nonchalantly dropped a bolt from the blue, something about a curette in the late darkness of the night before.

'A what? What are you saying? I mean who are you? Was I pregnant?' It felt like a glass baby rattle had fallen onto the unforgiving, sterile floor and smashed apart.

Oblivious to my feelings, the lab-coated man blurted back perfunctorily, 'Look, we've performed a curette. That's a clinical procedure which totally scrapes out the womb so you're definitely not pregnant now. Everything's just fine and dandy.'

On its own, the diagnosis was a jolt, but delivered like that it was an even bigger shock to the system. Even so, there was enough fire left in my belly to yell after him, 'I'll give you fine and fucking dandy!' With a distanced, superior look, he shrugged carelessly and was gone.

Les hustled in a couple of hours later, and though still shaky, by then I was sitting up and had philosophised the whole experience into a healthy level-headed understanding. Besides, time was pressing on and we still had a boat to get in the water, and naturally the urge to get on with it lay heavily upon us both.

'It's better this way, so don't hold on to it,' I explained. 'This is nature's way of telling us that the kid wasn't ready for us.'

Look, we were young, you know, young and sure-fire, so traumas weren't so difficult to let go of. Nor was it too hard to believe in our own hype, because when I asked how much money was left, we both laughed when Les answered, 'What's 50 per cent of nothin'?' Taking life by the balls like that meant there was no turning back, and unspoken though it was, we just assumed that the Gods would turn events in our favour: actually they did, but who would have thought the wand of providence could get us to stand out on such a slim limb?

'Anyway, things will be right in a flash,' I said brightly, and told him to arrange our send-off party for the next Saturday, and rebook the flight for the day after that. 'Now please get me out of here.'

Being with Mum and Dad was the best medicine in the world, and figuring that all was on the mend, I embarked on the standard health-kick diet of 'made in South Australia only' specialties: lemonade manufactured from spring water, a classic vanilla ice-cream, thick slices of fritz sausage with red sauce and Dad's celebrated specialty, home-baked Cornish pasties. Since my parents lived by the beach, most days we spent underneath the gnarled old willow tree, breathing in the sweet seaweedy air.

'Here, Bird's Nest,' – Dad's private nickname for his little boy-girl – 'have another slice of pasty. It's good for you.'

Although everything felt a bit tender, there was a heightened clarity to the world, an intangible preciseness, so when Dad used his endearing nickname for me, it suddenly triggered a dormant childhood memory from about the time I started smoking, wagging school and roaming away from home – something Dad had said as we slowly prowled the streets of Adelaide with me clinging on to him from the back of his buckety old Harley Davidson motorbike. I remembered peeking up around Dad's leather jacket as he explained, 'I want you to always remember that you are equal to anyone else in the world, Bird's Nest, and that you have the right to accomplish anything you want to. Don't let anyone ever tell you any different.'

Wise, albeit idealistic words, especially from a man in the 1950s, and I believed him totally. Little did I know that taking his advice into the wider world was going to prove so troublesome.

The next Saturday, with a few of Dad's pasties packed for the plane, everything was ready for the following morning's flight when the phone rang.

It was the surgeon-in-chief from the Queen Elizabeth Hospital. 'So glad we caught you in time. Don't be alarmed, but we do need you to come back in . . . as soon as possible.' Straight away feelings of a wispy, inner fear stirred and I deliberately tried to brush him off. 'I mean today,' he insisted.

Adding our half-built boat to our nine-tenths empty bank balance meant that now was not the time so I insisted back, promising to see the doctor in Cairns as soon as. This was a lie, but I hoped it would be a good enough ploy to get rid of this interference to our well-laid plans, and lamely went on to invite him to our party – but his ominous intention sliced through the phone and fell into my heart: 'I'm afraid you won't be going to any party tonight, Robyn.'

The change of tone, his use of my first name and the having to come immediately started to scare me, so swallowing a gulp of fear, I asked why not, and got a shocking reply: 'Because if you get on that plane tomorrow, Robyn, you could die on the flight.' That's when I felt an awful raw, chaotic flash of alarm flutter wildly in my belly. 'Miss Catchlove, unfortunately this is no joke. It's a Saturday morning, I've had to cancel my weekend for this, and I'm waiting here for you. Now!'

We dropped everything and raced to the hospital where the doctor explained that according to blood tests taken *after* the curette, I still appeared to be pregnant, and that 'they' were going in to 'fossick' around as soon as I was prepped. That statement alone was enough to scare me silly but, really, having no time to think was a bonus because within the hour I lay stretched out at the head of the operating theatre's waiting line. Ripped to the eyeballs on the hospital happy gear I may have been, but still I had enough smarts to refuse to hand over my medical files to anyone but the main man.

When the masked chief surgeon loomed overhead, I gave him my best grin, and saw his eyes grin back. 'Pleased to meet you again,' I said. 'This name-tag here on my wrist, and me, we all go with the file in my hand. After all, I'm trustin' you with my life.' As I went on, others, the faceless ones, started plying me with the ether of goodbye and good luck. 'Just making sure there's no good news, bad news jokes. I don't want the bloke in the next bed buying my slippers.' One of his eyebrows raised quizzically, so the joke had worked and somehow that helped me feel safer . . . So I started the icy countdown . . . *99, so play your cards right . . . 98, and you can come fishing . . . 97, up in God's own . . . 96 . . .'*

My mother says that our lives are already mapped out before we're born, written in the sand, so to speak. Certainly, every living second carries the full range of life's potential from birth and delight to death and the limbo states in between. Every day we busily engage until the sun falls over the edge. Every night we gladly enter the country of dreams. Meanwhile, the sea laps, the tides whisper their way in and out, and stars gleam. The cosmos is so profound we cannot possibly understand.

Coming out of the operation, as my eyes opened an indifferent male voice cut through my hazy consciousness. The tone was cold and detached, but I still assumed that it was most likely a doctor. Yet whoever it was seemed to be using a megaphone because he was booming out for all the ward's ears to hear: 'You know you lost the baby, and the right fallopian tube, and the adjoining ovary, don't you? And of course, you'll never ovulate again.'

Chopped into quarters through the iron bed's bottom frame, I saw the offender's floating white-coated body scuttle past, and picked up on the stark sterile mood. It felt like I had been dragged backwards through a dense, clogged-up cyclone but knew nothing about what, when, or for how long. Still, my internal fire needed no stoking, and thinking the jerk wouldn't get away with it this time, I rose angrily up from the pillow. 'Listen here fella, I might not know what day it is, but I'll bloody have you. You're a goner!'

I meant it, and with that swiped away the grey blankets and crispy sheets, then swung my legs to the floor. This caused all the needles plastered into my hand and arm to start tearing away from my veins, and alarm began to register on the doctor's face. Immediately, too, a tremendous stinging, searing pain, like a freshly honed Samurai harakiri sword had severed my body in half, tore across my gut and I collapsed backwards feeling sure that my insides had started to spill out and puddle onto the clinical, flatline lino floor. And that's how it felt inside my heart too: like a knifing.

Later, I got the story of blood and death, of a burst fallopian tube and cysts, and major emergency, double ethers, with me being held under while nightmarish specialists were brought in from the outside. There had been hours of clots, more blood everywhere, double transfusions, infusions of plasma and bloody bloodiness – all because a tiny soul had gotten trapped in an impossible pocket of my body. The baby was now gone and this was not the end of the world but internally a miraculous quiver cord had been severed, a tender life gone. Being so unprepared, it was pretty shattering all round.

Torn between his love for me and our other baby, the boat, which was crying out to be born too, Les was relieved and grateful when I insisted he go back north before me. So he held me close, said, 'There's plenty more of them in the pipeline,' and was gone in the blink of an eye. Honestly, it was the best thing to do because I needed some 'alone' space, some time to dwell internally.

Once again, my prized mum and dad hovered around intelligently as I submitted to the forces. Occasionally we told old jokes and kind stories from the past, and time went by. More importantly, they honoured my solitude. Every day, I sat gratefully swathed in blankets under the swishing leaves of the craggy willow while the desolate wind and ever-shifting clouds spun overhead. Can birth be any less than a miraculous event? I mean a soul, a being, a holographic blueprint manifests from the ether, willingly entering this physical plane through such sensuous energy. Like a spark plug, a *specific* being bursts instantly into a visible electrical pulse and then at some immaculate nano moment connects and arises through the rich, pulsing energy of two precise beings. How astonishing.

Whether it helped my heart-healing process or not, being outside in the elements felt important – but within, I was invoking the purest intrinsic bloodline of all ancestry, that 'women only' lineage of giving human birth. You see, in whatever gender the extraordinary seed of new life gets planted, in the human species only women enter the profound experience of giving birth. It's the reason why men will never really understand. Deeper and deeper into the weeping blood I forged, and wove my own philosophy around the events. Of course I had changed inexorably. Already my womb had begun listening out for the tiny child set adrift.

Such a traumatic loss could have lingered on and on, but I saw in every second a new world taking shape and let my feelings flow in accordance with that – there was still the journey of my life calling and the ever-evolving knowledge of all things once again being possible. That certainly sounds terribly clever, but really, who can hold back the dawn of tomorrow?

Naturally I never took the fertility pill again, and since conception had come only after taking the drug of promise, rightly assumed that without it pregnancy was impossible. Despite this, I never ceased to revel in the vital, vivid red flush of enthusiastic blood that came every month to signal my femaleness.

The little fellow was lost forever, and whether it was healthy or not, Les and I never spoke of it again.

CHAPTER 5

New Friends and an Intruder

*A*fter Adelaide, it was heads down and bottoms up as we went hammer-and-tongs on the job and the Big Shed once again filled with the tangy, sharp aroma of fibreglass resin, the sound of constant instructions and the millions of sawdust particles drifting through the sunbeams. While the two of us raced up and down ladders in and out of the boat everything buzzed: drills zipped, paint slapped, music bopped and we ate enough food to satisfy five Yugoslavian bricklayers. The reward was seeing our boat start to take obvious shape, a fair bit as we had intended.

Lucky us, when some thoughtless ignoramus unceremoniously dumped your 'usual' black-and-white-spotted bitch pup with your 'usual' beautiful heart close by; and she came from across the railway line and into our place looking for a drink. We understood the significance straight away, and told her not to worry about seeking other accommodation, that she could stay with us. We named her Jacky and she moved straight in.

Our other dog, Theo, must have had good plucking karma too. You see he just appeared in the back of the truck one day when Les picked me up from paying work, and pretended that Theo wasn't there. 'So is that a hairy monster in the back, or am I hallucinating?'

I asked. Les just looked straight ahead, thunked the truck into first gear and charged off, sheepishly replying, 'He's Happy's dog and we're just babysittin' him for a while.'

A lot of our friends had clever nicknames, and while none were called Happy, the big dog pressed up against the back window looked pretty pleased, so when Les strategically suggested we visit Big Red, I let it be. Helen, or Big Red as she was known, was my closest girl friend, and a number one supporter of our project. Les knew how to pull my strings and this was not the last time he'd use Helen to win me over.

As luck would have it, Theo had been plucked from death row at the dog pound just in time, and standing nine or ten hands high, was a princely, well-proportioned, mongrel dog with the loveliest of natures. He and Jacky travelled everywhere with us and, like most wild-bred dogs, were quick, intelligent and only had to be taught any skills and manners once.

With all the pieces of the puzzle now slotted together, the boat – that is, the *Jean King* (Jean for my mum, King for Les's dad) – really started to blossom. By then we were adept fibreglass-workers so all the moulding, decks, water and fuel tanks, all the edges and curves had been laid up, her shaft was sitting in place, plus the prop was pitched, bolted on and ready to spin. There was just a freezer to build, and the interior left to do. Everything was possible.

The shed doors were never locked, only ever drawn together, and when the tilly lantern in the tent boudoir was snuffed, only the dogs got to hear us whizzle and splutter in undisturbed sleep. Then early one morning we were woken by the rumbling sound of our front door being very slowly rolled open. After checking it out, Les pushed his head back into the tent, indicated 'Shh' silently with his fingers and, buck naked, stood noiselessly and, like an appari- tion passing through a sunbeam, snuck softly along the top shelf and down the back ladder. Through the tent slit, I saw down below a skinny, pimpled teenage lad bent on extracting our latest dump find, a fish-casting net. Sure, the net was full of gaping holes but nailed on the shed wall we fancied it was an Aboriginal wall hanging, a paint- ing of string knots.

As I watched, Les silently came around the side of the boat with the fingers of one hand shaped to look like a cocked and pointed .44 pistol, and had that sitting on the wrist of the other hand like he was steadying the aim of a gun. Without a sound, he snuck up behind the boy and, one menace to another, snarled threateningly, 'Stop or I'll shoot!'

The frightened kid spun around to see a totally naked, growling ball of muscle whose early-morning hard-on and imaginary pistol were both pointing right at him – a man, his secret weapon and his barbaric weapon = three menaces. The young thief uncoiled like a spring and shot up to about tent level where he pirouetted then bounced back to earth. Being caught in such a compromising situation, the kid was too busy protesting to notice the truth of Les's fake gun, and with his own hands clasped in prayer, splurted out, 'Fuck' – naturally – 'fuck!' he screamed to the gun-toting stranger. 'Please don't shoot me mister. Me name's Jason and I'm just a kid.' Nice plea, I thought. 'I'm innocent and I'll do anything, swear I will.' Another clever call.

Maintaining his straight-faced cop stare, the straight dick and the straight 'gun' position, Les said a few heavy words, then turned his free hand palm up, told the young bloke it was a Bible and got him to put one hand on the nonexistent book, raise the other in the air, and made him repeat, 'I swear that I will never steal again, so help me God.' Even though the young bloke was now successfully scared and fully repentant, there was still more to come.

'Furthermore,' the nude man demanded, 'I want you here, in the shed, workin' for me all next Saturday. Now don't bullshit me, son, I know your dad.' Les followed through with a harmless ear clout, and shoved him out of the semi-open door.

Kids steal. Don't know about you, but I did. I mean, didn't we all have to have a go at that? And it wasn't what he had tried to steal, or about a day's work, but we hoped that if he did turn up the next week, we might be able to put someone who was new to life into the real picture intelligently – so in that sense, it was our privilege. Ah, those were the good old days of principle and no nonsense, where apt punishment spoke loud and clear – and through that process, the possibility of self-respect had an opportunity to rise.

Repentance Saturday came, and there was Jason waiting for us to roll open the doors. The three of us toiled at a good pace that day. Afterwards, the lad confessed his appreciation of how we had dealt with him, even suggesting that he come back the following Saturday.

As Les explained to him, 'Instead of taking, next time you ask first. The less you steal, the less you'll get stolen from.' Jason consumed several massive sandwiches and guzzled a few gallons of cold milk, then decided it was time to go home for dinner, so my man said, 'I'll let yer dad know what a good worker you are, and here, we reckon you've earned this.' Jason face was prize enough when we handed over the cast net, and he left, whistling his way off down the railway track.

As we watched I leant back on my bloke. 'So who is his dad, anyway?'

'Buggered if I know.' He grinned, slapped my rump, beelined to the boat and started to slap another coat of glass onto the water tank.

Hell, I loved this bold, quick to defend, powerful man with all my heart.

The fishermen used to say that a seaworthy vessel was just an excuse for pouring endless amounts of money into a bottomless hole surrounded by a sea of empty beer stubbies. Not meaning to harp on about money, but that's what it felt like. Paying for work was out of the question, and although we asked for help often, mostly friends forgot to come. However, we did make the acquaintance of a lean and very sprightly 84 year old, one Wally Kebbel, who we had found hustling pool at the local pub. Upon learning of our endeavour, he became a daily visitor. So besides it keeping him away from the dens of iniquity, Wally possessed very sound boat-building acumen which helped us tremendously. He told us that not only had he been declared the World Snooker Champion in Bombay in 1933, but that in the old days he had also been a slave-shifter and moved black people (Kanakas) to and fro across the Pacific in his yacht. Frosty, another mate who in later years became a well-recognised Australian bow-hunter, also spent many unpaid days helping us toil.

In what Les used to called 'refuellin'', when it all got to be too much, we'd head for the uncluttered shoreline, sniff in the ocean, poke around in the flotsam and jetsam and let the fine salty spray enliven us. And that's how our destiny to become fishermen was sealed; the time we 'obtained' the *Jean King*'s first freezer, when a quaint, sodden dory beached itself just for us. In the stern sat a most unexpected prize: a battered but still intact 400-pound fibreglass freezer complete with all the copper keel cooling ensemble! The timing could not have been better. We wrestled the gifted freezer up and out, heaved it onto the truck and strapped it down tightly. Another bit of our legend had been sown, and it also left quite a few more bucks up our sleeve.

Strolling on into the setting sun's rays, Les reflected on why we called the planet Earth, since 70 per cent of it was water. Then I noticed at the sea's edge a wee, bright pink plastic heart lying just under the frothy sea suds. Pointing to it, I jokingly replied, 'Planet Plastic's gotta be more like it.'

Les whistled, grabbed the petite heart up from the ocean's treasure chest and pocketed it, so I laughed, saying, 'It's just some cute plaything a little kid's dropped.'

He told me I was wrong: that in an old mariner's tradition for good luck, the little pink heart would be sealed under the main bowsprit. 'Call it superstition, but I reckon the sea's givin' her blessings to the *Jean King* and all those who sail the high seas on her.' He held out a gallant hand, 'Are you game, my lady?'

There was no question about that. I bowed, and took his offered hand. 'Blood oath, I am. What good would it be without you?'

To borrow from the Taoists' view, union makes one and division makes two – a number from which our remarkable partnership would eventually become nothing. But there was still oceans of water to go under the bridge before that happened – the signs were good, and we were one, then.

CHAPTER 6

A Rude Blow

*Y*ou can tell how well everything was going – not just with the boat but with our relationship. Still, even at the best of times, everyone needs a break, and we had been working non-stop for weeks on end so one night we got the urge to go out on the town. This just happened to coincide with the standard end-of-work week event, the Friday night drink-a-thon – yes, the one and only enduring ritual Australians called their own. Let's face it folks, the only ceremony we identified with was a horse race event, the legendary Melbourne Cup, an event that never ceased to bring the entire nation to a standstill and even after that five-minute affair we all went off and got on the drink anyway.

Really, what respectable Aussie knew the words to their own national anthem, let alone the tune? *But,* we could all do chook raffles, kick footies, munch pavlovas, eat burnt chops and at the same time swill beer like it was going out of fashion. Aussies, the white ones that is, didn't have a ritual to bless themselves with – no historic costume, no traditional dance, no ancient symbolic chant to the Gods – so getting drunk at local pubs across the sunburnt land was the next best thing. Oh, and as a sacred offering, only on Friday nights, along the edge of every chatty bar on the Australian pubscape quaint bowls of steaming hot saveloys (finger-size sausages wittily referred to as 'little boys') and pots of red sauce would appear. Unglamorous? Sure. Part of the great Australian way of life? Absolutely.

Up in Cairns, the pumping pub strip was fondly known as the Barbary Coast, a well-deserved namesake inherited from the town's 1940s heyday, when the place had literally swarmed with wharfies. And the strip hadn't lost any of its charm because no one ever missed this weekly cultural event. Inside the crowded pubs, inebriated punters passionately drank beer, talked at top volume, and occasionally slipped out the back to share in a joint – and there was certainly plenty to say after a deep toke of Kuranda Green. Ah, the mystical tropical paradise at its intellectual height, the only occasion when everyone talked at once and everyone knew what each other was saying.

So off into the fray we ventured to do a rare spot of mingling. Heaven knows, we had earned it! About halfway through the night, to be heard above the peaking din, Les hollered in my ear that someone had a swag of 'borrowed' (that is stolen) external hull paint for sale, and that the price was right because 'instead of taking cash, he'll swap it for my .303 rifle'.

I yelled back that it sounded like a good deal, and asked, 'Didn't your dad give you that gun?'

He winced slightly, nodded and responded casually, 'True. But money we don't have, and the paint's that top Navy stuff.'

Instead of talking above the crowd, we both nodded in agreement and turned back to the idle chatter floating around us.

Eventually we pulled ourselves out of the madcap fringe and back to the semi-lit Shed. From somewhere inside the boat's hull, I could hear our little portable radio stridently belting out the *Clockwork Orange* theme. Both swaying unsteadily beside the propped-up boat, an argument sprung up about who should turn the music off.

Les seemed unusually narky but still, it was straight out of left field when our babbling argument turned into incoherent threats and I began paying some attention and heard '. . . and that's the only thing Dad ever gave me . . .' The bad tone was new, but I was inebriated and still thought he was just prattling on, '– it's your fault we're givin' away my dad's gun . . . you've never given anything of yours away.'

'Is that right?' I bluntly snapped back. 'So handing over the entire

$25,000 bloody profit from my house does nothing for ya, mate!' From as far back as the eighteenth century, one of Australia's most famous female writers, Miles Franklin, had advised women that it didn't pay to show blokes how smart they were. On the other hand, she hadn't been out imbibing on a tropical Friday night because there I went a hundred years later being way too smart for my own britches.

Under the shadowy light, the man I loved stumbled a bit, then loomed closer, and brandished his hand in an intimidating bully's threat. In disbelief and with drunken impetuousness I lay on our dirt floor, smirked and goaded him on. 'Hang on there, Les, why don't you kick me while I'm down?' The act was such a mindless challenge and I was so cocksure. 'Go on, have a go, you bloody mug. Have a go!'

So he did! Kerthud! As such, technically speaking, the first blow was really a kick which not only landed in my stomach, but got me right in the guts, if you get my drift. What words can describe how it feels when your love gets violated: disbelief, shock, shame, humiliation, unknowingly harmed too far into the future – that should do for starters. And the physical pain was only half of the stifled bovver-boot thud. It was all over nothing and that hurt too. It goes without saying that should have been the end of the liaison right there and then but in that classic choice of 'fight or flight', the one time when I should have taken flight, instead I stayed.

Although folded over in pain, I leapt up and sprang away. It might as well have been Halley's comet crashing through the roof, I was so astonished. His face filled with shock too. It was so unbelievable I think we even reached out and touched each other for a second or two.

Laying the blame on being drunk is often used as the excuse for committing such damaging acts. This helps let the perpetrator pretend they are not really responsible, while relieving them from feelings of guilt – but to my mind alcohol only heightens the anger that's already there, just waiting for an excuse to act.

Les fell to his knees, wrung his hands together in repentance, and anxiously swore that he'd never done anything like that before – whether this was the truth or not was anyone's guess. There was the love of my life, my hero, begging forgiveness and promising that such a thing would never happen again.

Sleeping was out of the question so we sat around awkwardly in the dark silence not at all sure what to do next. When light came the next day, things were equally uncomfortable. We were just so ashamed that we couldn't even look at each other let alone think about working on the boat. Anyway what was the point if we weren't going to stay together? At night the two of us lay at opposite sides of the bed tent, recoiling at any accidental touch, both wide awake and filled with anguish. Although neither of us was counting it went on like that for the next few days.

Outspoken women were only just on the rise then, and Australian men were not used to being challenged. How could I have known that when men ran out of reason, some of them resorted to violence? Being so uninitiated in the game of hitting your own lover, what was I to do? And although my mum had taught that love could overcome all, she'd never been around violence and I don't think she meant even being booted by my own man. Yet it was undeniable that milestone experiences had come to pass in the previous eighteen months: on top of the grinding nonstop work, there was his dad's death, our lost child, my own brush with death and the now serious lack of money. Maybe, just maybe, this eruption was simply a spillover, I thought, and fooled myself into believing that love would prevail. While this decision seemed courageous and wise, in reality I was simply not strong enough to let go of my own desires. Whatever it was, one strike was not enough to wipe out the love I felt, so whether it would happen again was a gamble I was willing to take.

Finally Les was so desperate to recover ground he suggested we shut up shop and head for the back mountains, intelligently volunteering not to take any alcohol. John Lennon reckons you can't hide when you're crippled inside – I'm not sure he's right there, at least not in the short term, because the breakthrough was such a relief I agreed. So we went out and spent most of what little hand-held cash there was on food, flopped our whole tent bedroom across the back tray of the one-tonner, and rumbled the sturdy big doors closed again. By the time Les whistled Theo and Jacky up into the truck, they were already halfway through the air. Who said dogs can't fly, or talk for that matter?

Feeling mightily relieved, we turned our backs on the half-finished dream, and on the friends who never came to help, and wound up the open highway into the uninhabited gold-rich mountains just west of the coast. Along the road, from a country curiosity shop we spent the last drop of cash on an old gold sluice jigger. After spending a day in a knee-deep tributary, tussling with the rowdy, mud-only spewing sluice, the both of us tossed the fossicked handful of flaky gold shavings into the limitless sky and laughed raucously. Fools with gold, gold made fools, who gave a right royal? This was us and we had the best gold – alchemy gold. So up in the rarefied atmosphere of Goldsborough, in an attempt to get ourselves back, we let go of everything. Simplicity is such a relief, but why is it so elusive?

Surrounded by nature, amid the early nineteenth-century mining fields, we just hung around like neighbourhood bosom buddies. It was perfect in another way too because there wasn't another person within miles. All the supplies and gear ended up inside the tent, and we naturally gravitated outside to live and sleep right next to the deep, steady flowing river. Every morning, the icy water shocked our naked bodies into wakefulness; all day we wandered through the bush, investigating the old gold trails and afterwards, feeling hot billy tea in the pit of our bellies, we'd lie under the night heavens, beside the camp fire with our dogs. Out there, it was easy to talk about what was on our minds, feel nurtured by the harmony of it all and give the elemental forces free rein to flow around us, to fully cleanse our souls.

Little Jacky's coming on heat had gone unnoticed until we heard her piercing wail and saw that she had mated with Theo. At least this way it was all in the family, we agreed, and both saw it as a sign of new things to come, of growth and rebirth.

Still I needed some space, so three or four times that week, always with Theo, I set out and stayed a few hours up on the mountain ridges, alone. Crossing the chilly, quick-flowing river while keeping my .22 single barrel rifle and my body above the waterline was a bit of a splutter, but I wanted to be away from Les's influence, and being alone helped me to regather and look at what had happened rather than being in it. Les understood all of this, in fact encouraged me to go, and I knew that he was doing a fair bit of soul-searching of his own.

Going bush like that was the best way for us to get untangled, and as the love-dance between us rekindled, nature did the rest. It took a week before I got back onto trusted, solid ground, and before he got game enough to pull me close. When he did, I smelt his salty aroma and felt the power of his spirit weave back into me.

'There's somethin' I've never told you but just before we met, I asked the sea for a wife. They gave me you, Robyn, so I'll love you till after I die. Don't go, please. Give me another chance, please don't go.'

Of course how it would all turn out was a risk, but there was no doubting his sincerity, and, feeling his strength beside me, the answer came. 'Yes, I know, and I'll love you till we don't see stars in the sky.' So when his ready shaft slipped into my body, we both knew that the troth was true, and that our love was undeniable. Trust is one thing, and no one gets through life unscathed, so why get hung up on that which has gone before and let it affect the rest of your life?

As we packed up to leave, Les summarised our quandary, saying that we just had to surrender to the thing we had going, and that 'if we walked away, we would never forget not finishing the boat, and regret that all of our lives'. When he said, 'Listen, woman, we're coming down the final stretch. All we need's another ten to fifteen thousand and we're home and hosed. Promise, on my honour, I'll get it somehow,' I knew that he loved me, and loved the sea, and that our boat was calling and that it was destined to float. I knew too that him hitting me had been a once-only thing. As we spoke, a full rainbow shone over the entire Goldsborough Valley. Well if that wasn't another good sign, what was?

While the four of us cheerfully thundered along the merry-go-round mountain and down, down, down into the moist, vivid wetland plains, Les and I were already mentally in the Big Shed, building, scheming and doing. The time had ripped past faster than a galloping stead, it was Friday, and we were back on the case again.

Many would have us believe that the world is a three-dimensional affair, but look for yourself at the sky and tell me where its border ends. Perhaps I was idealistic enough to believe I could have a borderless life and love – maybe that's why I gave him the benefit of the doubt.

CHAPTER 7

Flush with Luck

*F*riday it may have been, but in boat-building land it was the same old, same old: money bloody money, and the severe lack thereof. No matter how financially powerless we felt, the fact that ours and other people's lives would depend on the quality of boat we built, meant no economic short-cuts could be taken. Only fools and wankers did otherwise. So where was the final chunk of magic money going to come from? Well, we did come up with a plot – I call it that because it was silly, risky and incalculably improbable. Couldn't call it a plan because it had no intelligence about it whatsoever. A plot which, by lunchtime on the Saturday, found me carrying a shoulder-bag discreetly stuffed with all the cash we owned in the world, and us giving it our best shot at 'the' major event in the annual race calendar: Cairns Amateurs Race Day. If life is about the odds, we were the longest shots on the track.

Yep, as the drums rolled, the red carpet unfurled and the major trump in north Queensland racing events was up and running, there we two stood at the racetrack of dreams and promise: a track crammed with the usual swathe of the highly ambitious shonks, duckers, weavers, jocks and trainers, mums, dads, criminals and poncy politicians. What hope did we have of winning $10,000 at the races? Bugger all. Yet there, surrounded by the giddy-up, festive crowd of fancy high-flyers, knee-deep amongst the players, was Les, yelling his head off.

'GO you little beauty GO,' he screamed, 'git up, ride like a demon, YES, YES, YES!'

On such a preposterous mission, we were backing each other heavily so I urged him to go and collect the winnings and to double it up on the next race. Oblivious to the scrambling crowd and deaf to the lure of 'beginner's luck', the first few bets did fall our way. This early form made the rest of the day look as promising as a bowl of magic mushrooms. By mid-afternoon, however, the racetrack could have been an effervescent bottle of champagne, but with our pot of gold now in the saddlebags of unrelenting bookies, things were very grim in the *Jean King* corner.

'Jesus H Christ, there's nothin' amateur about the way the bastards snap up ya bloody money,' Les worriedly moaned as he put an arm around my shoulder and led the way to an empty bar, far away from the happy, fun-filled crowd. 'There's only enough left for a beer each, then we're outta here.'

Putting on my best face I nodded and lied that everything would turn out in the long run.

Right then we ran into our good buddy Stevo who enthusiastically introduced us to Harry the Handbag (handbag a nickname for the one who carries the money purse). 'These are the two I was tellin' you about, the ones buildin' the boat in Rosenfeld's shed.' With sinking hearts, being the centre of attention or even being nice was the last thing either of us wanted. Thankfully Stevo prattled on, 'I'm pretty right financially these days,' saying that he only worked for a bookie on Saturdays for a bit of fun. He laughed and beckoned to the bartender: 'Here, the shout's on me.' With Stevo buying the drinks, at least we didn't have to walk home, I reasoned.

Stevo had sold us the truck in the beginning, and had always been one of the few generous enough to help us out over the last couple of years, so without owning up to anything, distractedly we chatted on until Les accidentally blurted out, 'Yeah, things are pretty tough right now.' This was a proud way to say that we were in deep shit.

Harry quietly leant into the group, paused, then posed a question to Stevo: 'Ya trust these two, eh?'

With one hand over his heart, Stevo looked unblinkingly into Harry's eyes, 'I kid you not mate, they're one of ours.'

Sharp Harry slyly glanced this way and that, then turned back to face us, 'Then youse had all better gather closer in now and lend an ear.'

As we scrunched up closer together, Les and I shrugged at each other, silently intimating, *Why not? We've got nothin' to lose.*

'I've heard all about ya Les, and I trust Stevo straight up and down, so I'm gunna do youse two a big favour.' Harry let the words slip, gangster-like, from one side of his mouth as he explained that there was a plunge going down late in the day, 'after all the mugs' money' had been lost. Though our hearts still told us there was nothing doing, we leant closer so as not to miss a thing. Apparently there was a certain country horse (let's just say it was from Wagga, and call him Battler) running at ten to one 'and driftin' out', said Harry, his eyes shifting this way and that, 'and trust me, it's gunna win. Trouble is, everyone down south knows me, so I've come up here especially for the race.' Like a giraffe reaching for the best buds on a branch, Harry peeked up and looked around then let his smoke-ravaged, gravelly undertones keep the naughty news coming. 'So while everyone's on the drink and had enough of racin' fer the day, we're gunna put the big money on this nag in the last, here in Cairns. Look, everything's sweet, and if youse are smart cookies youse'll bet your boat on it.' With that, Harry the Handbag was gone.

I knew nothing about horseracing, even less about odds, and Harry could've been talking in Swahili for all I understood of what he'd just said, but I got the drift that something big was in the offing. The only problem was that we had five parts of sweet FA, which in layman's language was not even enough for a short cab fare, let alone sufficient funds to make a quick killing on a shonky horse race. As I was thinking along these lines, Les and Stevo went off to one side and had a pretty serious chat. That's when the plot thickened significantly, when Stevo conjured up $5000 cash and lent it to us. *Boom boom* – just like that, once again in typical Queensland style, all on a handshake. I'd also be lying if I said that it took much longer than a short half-head nod for me to agree. Who wouldn't? Caught up in the moment, now we had everything riding on plenty of nothing, and still had plenty to lose. Is everything and nothing the same thing? This would all depend on how the dice fell.

By the time the last race went down, the crowd – and most of the revellers' wallets – had thinned out considerably, and all the party animals were heading off to bars, to winners' parties or home to count their losses. With the show just about over, only the crafty punters, those in-the-know and desperates like us, were left in charge. Even the blue sky had begun to pack away its sunny frock, and the race-caller had had enough for the day because he was calling only the leaders of the pack when the frothing horse herd thundered intently toward the dimming finish line: '. . . and there's not much left to go in the home stretch ladies and gentlemen, and it's God's Choice, it's Battler, it's God's Choice . . .'

As the dappled greys, the browns and blacks, and the whipping jockeys came racing past us, Les shifted his focus to God in all his/her forms. 'GO, sweet Jesus, GO!' he pleaded when the mount from Wagga stormed into the straight, second from the leader. The race surged on in a dreamlike adrenalin, and I prayed harder than when I was a reluctant bride searching for a way out. My man even stopped swearing so I turned and yelled, 'This is the most painful fucking everything I've ever not had.'

With dirt clods pinging up through the rails like big bouncing hailstones smacking bitumen, the galloping steeds' ears pricked, their noses frothed and bubbled, their haunches poured with sweat, and their necks stretched toward the winning post: 'It's Battler, neck and neck, it's God's Choice out front by a nose, a half-nose, it's Battler, racegoers, and with only metres to go . . .'

The skinny crowd still hollered last-minute instructions to the nags and jockeys or, in our case, to God. 'It's Battler all the way, she's got the take here . . . hold ya britches, look at God's Choice go, now both jockeys are standin', and on the whip, as they hit the winning post. It's not God's Choice, ladies and gentlemen it's anyone's choice in a photo finish to finish off the Amateurs, it's too close to call, just a whisker between 'em . . . just waiting now on the photo . . .'

It wasn't the Melbourne Cup so it hadn't stopped the nation but it stopped us in our tracks – and if things turned out right, our cup was just about to overflow with money nectar: or it would just make the proverbial bottomless hole into which we were pouring money so large we could be well and truly fucked (to use the vernacular). Ouch!

Funny how many minutes one can stay alive while barely breathing. When Les started crunching up the betting tickets and whispered anxiously, 'I thought this race was fixed,' it was just about too much to bear. 'Yes ladies and gentlemen, the judges have reached a decision, and the winner of the final race in the Annual Amateurs Race Day of Far North Queensland for this year is, by God, the Battler!'

Being the last in the deserted grandstand, he and I cheered from the emptiness into the sky gone beyond, quickly dashed to various bookies, collected the massive winnings and went to pay back the outstanding debt. Whoever was it that said never mind the bribery, just give me the corruption?

Stevo took the cash graciously, smiled and commented, 'Nice doin' a spot of business with youse two.'

Clapping his shoulder, Les waxed on, 'You only do certain things once in ya life. This is one of them. You're a conjurer alright, and we sure as hell owe ya, Conj': a name which, for a select few, was to stick with Stevo for many years after.

Agreeing that cabbing it back into town seemed not unreasonable, we sped toward the Big Shed. Tucked under Les's protective arm, I let him explain while I discreetly stroked the shoulder-bag, the lovely money jar chocked with the twenty-seven and a half big ones, the 27 grand, the 27 gees. Apparently, the odds had not drifted out but rather the margin had narrowed down to five and a half to one. Whatever that meant, I understood the upshot was that we had won $27,500 plus our initial bet of $5000 which we had paid back to Conj. (Just to keep the record straight, in those days, bookies were more benevolent and used to pay back the initial bet on top of the winnings.) 'We deserve it, woman of the sea, we do,' he insisted.

What better way to get a grip on that which had just gone down other than to stop off and lash out on some fresh prawns and ritzy champagne before whizzing home? Extravagantly we even got the cab to keep his engine running while we did just that. Mount Budda Baddu was waiting and must have had a chuckle or two herself that night watching Les and me lounge around out the front with the dogs munching, laughing, drinking and talking a lot. In short, we dreamed on.

The next day it was work as usual.

CHAPTER 8

The Coral Sea

Not long after, the old wooden dory-cum-ragbag we had salvaged from rotting death in Smiths Creek played a very different role when our dog Jacky lay in it and shot out five bagged up, motley puppies. While the father stood by quivering, Les and I hovered around giving encouragement to the little dog people who had arrived. They were all keen, sharp-looking ankle-biters who staggered bravely underfoot, brawled healthily and gnawed on knuckle bones, work boots and anything else they could sink their baby teeth into.

By inheriting Theo's unusual features, the distinctive pups were easy to give away and went to good people. Les felt this much more than I did. One night, before they were all gone and the funny little balls of fur were stumbling all over our feet, he reached into the puppy pond and plucked the smallest one by the loose skin at the back of its neck. 'We're takin' this one with us, and we're callin' her Stryder, aren't we Strydy girl?' Appropriately, a wizard's name for a magic companion.

I gazed at the horizon where dusk was doing its 'usual' spectacular thing. Everyone should make a practice of stopping to watch dusk: it's full of surprises, and is the only time of every day when the world entirely changes colour. Same as life actually, iridescent and always unpredictable.

*

Just before launch day, without any proof of identity or suchlike paperwork, we walked into the State Fisheries Department, filled out the straightforward one-page form, handed over $30 and were given on-the-spot legal boat driving *and* fishing licences. Whatever happened to the simple life? And as the days dwindled down unarranged, both of the older dogs seemed to go away, naturally: friends asked for Jacky, and Theo, without a backward glance, leapt into a kombivan filled with hippies. Hippies are nature's Buddhists, and in the 1970s it seemed like there were as many hippies as there were straight people – if only the same balance existed today.

Boydie Lee was the right man to christen the boat; being a living relic of Queensland maritime history, his boat-building knowledge had also proved invaluable to the *Jean King*. He was a bit hippie-like too, being a loyal old drunk whose personal living arrangements usually found him in nightly residence either right opposite the Pacific Hotel along with the chattering tides beside the tall, swaying palms of the esplanade park, or with us discovering him camped below the *Jean King*'s keel the next morning. A man of few words and less money, Boydie had managed to 'tie one on' ever since anyone could remember. By then, even though alcohol had the fading fellow well and truly in its dogged grip, the wrinkled-up sailor always acted with unexpected grace: so like some ancient, skull-and-crossbones mariner with landed gentry manners, his already small, now-shrunken frame was draped in Shar Pei puppy skin, all of which balanced precariously on spindly, unsteady legs. The dear man was a great treasure in our midst. So it was an honourable request to one of the oldest salts in the whole of the northern sea quarter when we asked the Boydman to baptise the boat. Tears trickled down his crumpled-up weather-pickled face, he beamed, came to attention and nodded acceptance.

Finally, the day of days. One early dawn, armed with written permission from the invisible City Fathers and with Boydman's trashcan pushbike tottering up front leading the way, the *Jean King* was tractor-towed down to the wharf and ceremoniously entered into her natural element. Heads shook in wonderment – friends, the doubting Thomases, drifting Aboriginals, the seagulls, Mount Budda Baddu – all of them were there as Boydie momentarily stopped swaying, rocketed the champers cork up to the heavens, took a big swig of the froth and bubbles then poured the rest across her bow. His speech was short but compassionate. 'May all those who sail on the *Jean King* always be fuckin' safe.'

Insightful enough, I thought, as the goodies, the baggers, the few early risers, innocent strollers, dogs, cats, wharf rats and others whistled, cheered and thudded each other's backs in congratulation, as though they had built the boat themselves, all the while mumbling lines like, '*Always knew those two would do it, definitely had it in 'em . . . Yep, never a question . . . I was there from the start, you know,*' etc.

Seeing that our clever boat actually floated, all attention turned to Wednesday, the lucky Bedford engine. When it faithfully kicked over first go too, I'm told I did a full victory salute and repeatedly shouted out, 'She works! She works!' With the formal proceedings over, triumphantly the three of us drove off upstream. Unlike some of the adventures ahead, the *Jean King* slipped effortlessly along on the calm, glassy waters of the Coral Sea.

That first night out on the anchor, the moon seemed extra bright, the ocean lapped soothingly in our ears, and the she-oaks from the nearby mudflat sent aromatic blessings that tingled our noses. With chilled champagne in our vegemite jar glasses, we toasted to all of that, and requested the sea to give her blessings too. In a time-honoured tradition, we put a note inside the empty wine bottle, recorked it and pitched it through the sky, far out into the star-mirrored sea. The handwritten message read:

> *There are dreamers and there are doers.*
> *If you're a dreamer, keep dreaming.*
> *If you're a doer, never ever give up.*

Sure, Les and I were young and free; the thing is, we had expressed it in such a creative way.

And so, in nautical radio talk, '**off**' we '**O**scar **F**oxtrot **F**oxtrotted'. Yes, out into the blinding twilight of high sea adventure we and our little puppy plunged – without a contact radio, or lifesaving jackets, or dinghy, safety flares, first-aid kit or any money, or any real plan for that matter. Naturally, we had plenty of tobacco, food and drink.

It was about then that I learnt Les did not really know the way either. Did it matter? Not at all. We just kept on celebrating with the few remaining bottles of launch bubbly, dipped blindly on, accidentally turned north and made sure to keep the coastline on our left-hand side. Now, anyone who tells you that they have never been lost or scared out at sea is lying. Not that we got lost. We got chucked around a fair bit, wallowed around like an abandoned Tupperware bowl in a busy public swimming pool actually, but lost – no.

Almost immediately the weather became a nasty taskmaster, a bitch in fact, who took advantage of us nouveau navvies and threw the boat straight into the arms of a sid-vicious storm. She, the sea that is, did us a favour! How else would we have learnt to sharpen up and get with the safety program? Trapped in a spewing ocean spa, we churned around helplessly like a new duck dinky toy. To stop from going down the big plughole in the sea, Les had to drive the newly launched vessel head-first up mountainously high, frothing-at-the-top waves. Here the frightened boat, precariously unsupported, swayed around hysterically in thin air: it's called yawing. Then Les had to yank the rev stick back, thus letting the boat drop off the wave top, bang, down into the sloppy swirling ocean valley below, immediately fighting the storm to get the boat's nose straight and facing head-on into the next crashing wave – then he'd flat throttle her up the next 15-footer, then *boom* down again into the next wallowing basin, every which way, rip up again, *boom blat* down again, up again, down again, up again . . . Not that we could see much anyway, but at the bottom of the gigantic waves there was no horizon at all, just massive wave mountains foaming threateningly above us.

The pup was all jelly and eyes, and got rudely wedged into a chunk of bed pillows on a corner of the lounge. She made not a sound, nor did she move; she passed the litmus but we humans certainly had not – amongst the safety measures we didn't have the brains to be carrying, the lack of life jackets started to feature largely in my mind. To keep a grip on my rising fear, and totally untrained, I desperately tried to read the one sea chart which by sheer fluke we had somehow managed to pack. While we pale, speechless warriors rode the precocious gale for our lives, the boat we built never let us down.

Many hours later, like a lifetime or so, I'm not sure whether we managed to navigate the Endeavour River or whether the naughty sea slapped the rocking and rolling *Jean King* right into its broad entrance. Fortunately, it was a deep river that lent generous protection from the brutal outside forces, plus just upstream on its banks sat Cooktown, so named after the famous Captain Cook himself. And just quietly, it looked like the modest town was doing some rock and rolling of its own. 'Thanks for nothin', including swearwords, the ever-eloquent Les blurted out gratefully, and noted that it seemed like the entire Queensland fishing fleet was in port.

Sure enough, the little three-boat country-town wharf was literally creaking under the stress of umpteen boats all being tied precariously to it. This included a dozen or so trawlers, a few shallow-draughted barramundi boats and a couple of open sea, atlas-wandering yachts. The storm's strength had even forced one of the Mason's Shipping Line's large coastal barges in for shelter. Now safely harboured in out of the storm, they were all straining at the bit like jerking jack-in-the-boxes. As the massive tide flushed through the rich abundance of mangrove and kept the undercurrents ripping about, the chaotic wind played very careless touch footy through the lot of them. And the wharf looked busier than Hong Kong Harbour on their annual water festival day. Apparently overnight, the storm had turned Cooktown into a boomtown.

Well, it had been a rough honeymoon voyage what with all the bucking, and with us very nearly becoming well and truly unhitched. It had been bloody hell out there and I was anxiously keen to get myself back on land. With lots of luck and Les's unflinching albeit raw skill, we were very much alive – and without saying so, I fancied a drink or two straight away. Still looking scared shitless, Les turned my way and said, 'We need a few stiff drinks to get back on our feet again.' This may have been a clever joke but I didn't laugh, I just nodded eagerly.

To the simple town folk, the untameable wildness born on the sea made the fishing fraternity appear like insatiable ravagers from outer space. The simple folk were on the money. Les and I were no different, and both thinking 'beer', clumsily hitched our ropes to the last boat in the row. That made us five boats away from the wharf – and all the boats were dancing around so much it looked as though they were still outside riding the storm. Les, like a practised tightrope walker, lit out across the erratic, jumpy mooring ropes that held the row of jaunty boats together. Without hesitation Stryder followed by leaping overboard and dog-paddling to the shore. Realising that there was no other choice, and backed with the fear of falling into the rushing current, I without fault followed suit. Later, with a few drinks under the belt, and a few above it – actually up to the hilt – the dancing from boat to boat over the unpredictably swaying ropes got much easier. All seafarers have a bit of ballerina in them; it must be a genetic thing.

CHAPTER 9

Cooktown

So, after years of effort and still not enough cash to bless ourselves with, there we were stuck in a small historical settlement brimming with eighteenth-century buildings, and probably fewer than 200 inhabitants. Intrigued, I joined the library and read up on the local history (and delved around in my other interests, which included politics and things esoteric).

Apparently in the mid-1700s, Captain James Cook had, also after wicked weather, sailed into this very port to lay up his British ship, the *Endeavour*. The local black chaps, the Guyu Yimithirr tribe in a civilised manner welcomed, even offered gifts to the English visitors, but were rudely rebuffed by the arrogant intruders. James Cook, according to all the history books, had been a brilliant sailor and was the first to discover Australia: of which the latter statement is definitely not true, but yet another handy example of British propaganda. Still, some time after he left Cooktown to sail further north, 35,000 white men surged though Cooktown's surrounding dense jungle with only one purpose in mind – to pan the Palmer, the river of gold. It was up there in 1873 that the most significant gold rush in Australian history began. Overnight, a tent town pitched itself on the steamy mangrove shores of the Endeavour River and men and women of every nation jostled through the crowded streets filled with banks, brothels, pubs, gambling dens – you know, all the great necessities in life – oh, and not to forget the food suppliers. Within months, Cooktown was the second-busiest port in Queensland, and with 22,000 Chinese in residence too, in business houses across Asia, the north Queensland town was spoken of as the 'Canton of the South'.

Looking through the library window across the modest town, I tried to picture how it must have been 100 years earlier with 77,000 opportunistic seekers surging through it as the Palmer River feverishly yielded hundreds of tonnes of the alluring precious metal and the men who found it spent it like there was no tomorrow. Stupid bastards. Horses got shod with gold, nuggets were wagered on flies crawling up bar-room walls, and decent chunks of it danced between hall girls' tits in fitting payment for Australia's very first striptease shows. As the rugged frontier surged with gold fever, the yellow metal kept the balance by making others pay the ultimate price. Hundreds died of starvation, from mysterious fevers, from speeding bullets or from spears flung by angry Aboriginals. It was truly the last of the old-style rushes. Then even more hastily it faded away, and the men and the Palmer gold were no more.

I saw this history reflected in the cache of century-old bottles carelessly lying in heaps on the banks of the Endeavour River, and in the glass case displays of the unsung museum that sat atop the hill, just down the road from the country hospital, itself colonial in design and encircled with a broad, old-fashioned veranda. Given the multitude of previous-century rustic hotels that littered the main street, it should have been called Pubtown, not Cooktown. They too were remnants of the gold-rush days, and they too were all under siege again – fishermen's siege.

With prolonged cyclonic conditions playing havoc outside, a very big drink was on the cards. Like thirsty travellers who luckily had stumbled upon an idyllic oasis in the middle of the Nullarbor Plain, more rum with less coke flowed through the pint-sized town, hundreds of jugs of iced cocktails, alcohol by the cascade, cartons of the stuff, all flooded down the fishermen's insatiable throats.

We joined in, quickly became mates with the seamen, and spent plenty of hours in each other's wheelhouses sharing knowledge, stories and drinks. There was none of that girlie stuff like wearing clean clothes, shaving or combing hair. They all seemed to wear stubby shorts right-side out for a week or so, then turn the shorts inside out and wear them the other way for another week or so – give or take a week or so. That way the cardboard shorts could stand clumped beside their bunk (think sculptured, sawn-off elephant feet) next to the scrubby thongs and the essential tobacco pouch, ready for action at any hint of emergency, or on the half-chance of a drink happening without warning. For the same reasons, it seemed that even as they slept, the sailors' cruddy, weather-worn hats stayed glued to their sun-dyed, sea-swept heads. As I observed it, on those rare occasions when the seamen weren't gripping either a drink or their dicks, a touch to the faithful cap made them feel safe.

And fishermen's breakfast: that consisted of a few hot cups of extra-strong bitter instant coffee, a quick look-around and a few roll-your-own fags. Cannily, they'd all appear simultaneously on their own back decks, honk big wads of snot over the side, scratch their scrotums, do mooring rope adjustments, and lunge from boat to wharf, on up to the pub. The only thing missing was the right music to go with it. Looks are deceiving, don't you think? Certainly there were plenty of daggy-looking wild men, none of whom appeared capable of finding fish anywhere at all in the vast unmarked ocean, let alone of running the million-dollar fishing operations apparently under their control.

Certainly it was a much easier lifestyle than the gold diggers had in Palmer in the 1800s. Back then, after some poor bastard's frantic gold-mining finally paid off, the fellow's troubles had just begun. Immediately he would abandon the strike and head for Cooktown, galloping bareback past Aboriginal camps where Chinese coolies hung by their pigtails from trees in batches of half a dozen or more, ready to be knocked on the head, roasted and eaten.

Still, avoiding the restless natives was much easier than avoiding the cunning opportunists waiting in Cooktown's main drag. All that glittered was not gold, particularly the shonky gambling dens, the lantern-lit Chinese opium parlours and the beady-eyed hoteliers who offered free lodgings, free drinks, free anything really, including perfumed ladies of the night (and day) just for the opportunity to lock the lucky miner's gold in their safe. Men, as we all know only too well, are just human, and most being blinded by the vast array of wonderful vices on offer usually lost their newfound wealth faster than the speed of an illegally balanced roulette wheel. Not having enough gold to buy their way onto the next eastbound sloop sailing for 'civilisation', the profiteering hotelier would generously refinance (typically including interest) the poorer bastard's return to the jungle of gold. Yes folks, if you think only a fool and his gold are easily parted, try walking down the street of promise and come out the other end intact yourself.

Despite the fact that by the mid-1970s Cooktown had not one brothel or opium den – surprise, surprise, nothing else had changed. The seamen, bulging with cold hard cash, careered intently through the quiet coastal settlement splashing the legal tender everywhere. And like the gold miners of old, they too were also flat-out making it down to the wharf at night with any money left. The locals may not have liked the newly arrived visitors but the constant jingle of cash crossing their palms improved the unsure smiles they wore.

There was no going anywhere, so the days oozed hazily on as the angry, capricious storm sulked just off the coast, gaining more than its original momentum with every weather report. As without, so within: the Cooktown drinking rage went unabated, so both forces smouldered and I too was becoming annoyed.

Sitting on the back deck together one morning, I reminded Les of our promise to pay back, just as soon as possible, the people in Cairns we owed money to: those small players who had been kind enough to let us sail on the strength of our word.

'Don't go makin' sense this early.' Les had a hangover and swigged gladly at his mug of coffee. 'The party's just warmin' up and you know it's not on for us to just steam out willy-nilly into the bloody blue yonder. Jesus Christ, we just had a taste of that, didn't we just?' His bloodshot eyes grinned vaguely.

Looking up into the heavy black clouds, the flock of frigate birds still hovering over the land lent further confirmation that any change to the wicked outside conditions was not coming soon. So I put it to him that we'd now been in port for more than two weeks, and that I was not going up the pub every day anymore – that we had no money when we hit the town, and that anything we were borrowing from our newfound mates also had be paid back. 'Anyway, when was drinking money we don't have a good idea?'

He knew I was right and capitulated easily. Without a car, the dump was too far away, and two visits to the museum was enough, so we got curious and took to wandering around the outskirts of town where a few abandoned, lovely pre-century homes caught our eye. One day, in a gleam of mischief, Les suggested we slip inside and check them out. 'No one's been living in these places for at least half a century so no one will mind.'

Knowing we had no intention to do harm, I agreed. Respectfully we prised open the ornate, probably handmade garden gates and just the way the age-old cottage door fell open at a touch of the doorknob made us feel like we had permission to enter. Inside, surprised geckos and spiders scurried away while the large caretaker carpetbag snakes coiled about the place did not even bother to stir – not even at the pup. More reason to feel less like gatecrashers and more like guests. With simple delight we spoke in reverent whispers, as though not to disturb those who were long gone.

And oh, what a bonanza of pristine vintage treasures awaited us inside the 30-centimetre thick walls: an old burnt black combustion stove, antique wardrobes, tall Jacobean cupboards, mint condition crockery, and in one cobwebbed corner even a huge pile of very early *Women's Weeklys* on top of which sat a bundle of strung-together handwritten letters dating from the 1920s. Amongst the backyard junk we tripped over early miner's camp ovens, timber crates stacked with 100-year-old glass bottles complete with stone lids, and perched on some bricks even one fully original Model-T Ford with a weed floor. We kept our game secret, each day returning to let the untold stories reveal themselves, were both amused, and had stopped squabbling – unlike the threatening black skies.

The famous mateship that built Australia had almost disappeared by then – but not on the sea. You just never knew when you might need each other, besides our fraternity proudly boasted the upholding of this important tradition – and anyway, you'd be a fool to stop listening and learning. Like it or not, mateship is born from necessity, so staying on side with experienced fishermen was a smart move. I had also realised that beneath their reckless disguise, seamen were quietly brilliant jacks-of-all-trades, a title that underestimated the extraordinary breadth of self-taught knowledge and skills they had to possess to survive at sea. This included advising, fixing and inventing parts for all brands of diesel and petrol engines, freezers, props, radios, compasses, etc.

We still joined the pub throng of a night to sip cold beer with chasers of the Queensland-made Bundaberg rum – Bundy – and that's where we first heard mention of a bloke reverently called the 'Old Man', aka Dave Mulligan. Gossip had it that in addition to being the best fisherman on the coast, he was also the meanest, gun-totin' son-of-a-bitch there was. Leaving the others to their drinking, the two of us would gladly cut through the rattled wind and rain with Stryder in tow, back to our water home. The *Jean King* still sat on the outskirts of the trawler-rim, so reaching her each night took substantial skill – not *just* the dancing across the jerky ropes, or manoeuvring across the group of unfamiliar bridging boats, no, the skill was to avoid being lured into lonely, drunken skippers' wheel-houses. Easier said than done.

To fill in time, and without asking for money, Les and I spent a few days cleaning out an old-timer's big freezer, so one night when he invited us in for a drink it was hard to say no. After all, this Second World War immigrant had a reputation too, and was none other than the legendary German Jack – he who had trapped, captured and shot crocodiles and fished barramundi from there to New Guinea since the 1940s onwards: a man so recognised for his accurate field knowledge of crocodiles as to be known worldwide. He also knew by heart the lay of the reefs, islands and all the waters right up to the top – this was 'the' Jack Kiell, the only man I ever knew who was totally fearless about his own death.

Easily seduced by the dimly lit, chart-strewn cabin, we swapped yarns and sipped from our cups. From outside I heard tall timber masts wail softly to each other and the tarty ocean slap itself up against Jack's boat, the *Banshee*. The excitement I felt for this life was more than I had dreamed of. After a while, Jack asked where we intended to go once the infernal storm had abated, and Les's response lit up his eyes.

'Heard a few things about Davey Mulligan, up Princess Charlotte Bay way at the Normanby River. Sounds like a bit of a bad bastard, with plenty of know-how. Reckon I might go up and see him.' My man glugged down the last drop of rum, scooped Stryder into his arms and turned to shake Jack's hand – a hand with two fingers and a thumb missing, his lost digits being somewhere up a river in New Guinea in a crocodile's belly. 'See ya Jack, I've got a good woman wanting to go home.'

Even with just a two-fingered hand, the tough man had Les in a bull terrier grip, and the info he gave us proved to be life-saving, especially about rum and the man we intended dropping in on.

'There's shallow mudflats runnin' out each side of the Normanby River entrance, so be real careful goin' in. Now the Old Man's set up camp 'bout a good mile upstream and he's pretty possessive about what goes in and outta the place. It's one of the best fishing grounds north of here and Davey's got good reason to think he owns the fuckin' river. If anyone talks barramundi, it's him.'

Les stopped, straightened up and listened intently.

'Just look out around the Old Man, a straight shooter he might be but I'm warnin' you, don't ever cross him. Anyway, if he likes ya, it'll be sweet. If not, just turn around, and get the hell outta there real quick. Oh yeah, he carries an M1 around like you wear a hat, and he's big on the Bundy. Likes a drink, the Old Man.' (And for those who don't know, an M1 is a semiautomatic carbine repeating rifle.) German Jack finished off by saying that in payment for the work we had done, the small beaten-up dinghy, outboard and anchor which had been sitting over on the shore was ours. Anything we got for free was a bonus, but the wrathful storm had control and everyone was very edgy.

The next day over at our secret house-snooping playground Les stumbled across a real treasure-chest find. This was the only time we ever stole from the abandoned cottages and when you know what it is, I'm sure you would have done the same. Easily smuggling the treasures in a bulging duffle-bag back through town and past the locals down to the boats, we had something new to show so everyone quickly gathered on the wharf. The goodies' bag was filled with what were obviously the forgotten leftovers from some previous Cooktown parade – cut-out and painted timber pirate swords and daggers, coloured cardboard pirate hats, black buckled belts and eye-patches, everything but wicked wenches. Inspired by the contents, the mob decided to have a pirates' party that night: a night which, historically speaking, was to go down as 'That Night We Fucked Cooktown'.

In a storm of our own, straight away everyone began to cook up a banquet fit for the Gods, kings, queens and scallywags of the sea. With seafood just newly taken from the ocean, amazing aromas swirled around the wharf: crayfish, Morton Bay bugs, prawns, barra, coral trout, snapper, mackerel, mussels and turtle meat, all of which was being grilled, sautéed, poached, baked, boiled, curried, and even sashimied. By late afternoon, the prawn trawlers' back decks had music amps strapped high into their masts and were lit up brighter than the clouded sun which was falling across the chaotic sky and into the ocean.

Les had been missing all afternoon so I wandered through the boats looking for him and sprung one of the skippers, Big Eddy, in his cabin reading a shabby old Bible. With 1970s rock music belting out of his amps and a beer in his hand, it all seemed a bit odd. Anyway, when the northern twilight gathered, finally Les reappeared, and with every single one of us tarted up, we flowed up onto the wharf and into the unsuspecting town. God help it. Might have been 30 of us all up, counting skippers, deckhands, cooks and Stryder: all decked out with swords in buckled belts, eye-patches, neck scarves, real fishnet stockings, torn split-leg skirts, knee-high rubber boots and the rest – it looked like we had risen from another century. Being totally loaded up with the precious gold of the twentieth century and ready to rock, I swear Cooktown fleetingly slipped back a century to the throbbing boomtown it had once been. And we pirates did drink the town under the table and got ripped and rowdy, until finally still yelling for more, all of us surged like a king tide toward the drinking hole closest to the wharf.

Stryder must have been the only sober player when knee-deep in the wild and incoherent rabble Les stood up on the bar and talked the crowd down from a dull roar to an excited buzz. Not the first time I'd seen him from that angle, but his proposal knocked me out. Yes folks, with the intelligent timing of about quarter to nowhere, Les asked for my hand. 'Lady, be mine forever, marry me, my woman of the sea, marry me now. Marry me tonight!'

The delirious pub held its collective breath so I sucked in a lungful of the magic smoke, passed the nice thick joint on and leapt up to join him, and to one and all, and to the wrathful skies above, declared: 'My oath I will Lesy. You're my man.'

With that the crowd went to pieces, cheering until their throats got husky and more drinks were needed. That was when the naughty gang sliced back to our impatiently waiting ships, and got into the real swing of things.

Everyone was as high as the royal storm above, so someone cranked up the volume on 'Greetings from LA' and let Tim Buckley, in sweet surrender, beg for more. Just as a bunch of ruffled frigate birds settled in a row along the wharf shop roof to stand witness, the huge black clouds split asunder to reveal the Milky Way and, there amongst the pirates and wenches, Big Eddy shaped up to us, whipped out his battered old Navy Bible and began. 'Jesus H Christ, and dear buccaneers,' he roared, 'we are all gathered under the stars to join these two mad bastards together . . .' So while the irreverent congregational throng looked on, in amongst the swell of rollicking boats, down onboard the *Jean King* we, with Stryder in attendance, both agreed: 'Yes mate, I do, mate,' and tied the wedded knot. Romantically, Les slipped onto my finger a trochus shell ring he had fashioned that afternoon. Amongst the madness, I tried to remember that my man was not an ordinary man.

By now everyone was on talking terms with the heavens, so we surrendered to the feeling too, and played the game swashbucklers play. As agile as you like, the whole gang pirouetted around the rigging – slash, slash, lunge – up and down, under the masts, scaling the heights, in between the ropes, parried and thrusted from one sorting tray to the next, here and there leaping deftly over thrusting couples, we fucked along with the rest of the galaxy. And why not? This was our territory and, after all, we had just fucked with the weather, hadn't we?

Interestingly enough, by early the next morning the town-altering storm transformed into her mirror opposite and within hours the raucous, untameable mob had merrily dipped out to sea. While the fishing fraternity all reckoned it was the healthiest vibe Cooktown had felt for an age or two, the township was glad to untangle its nightie, count its money and I'm sure mightily pleased to see the back of us.

CHAPTER 10

The Old Man and the River

*T*he malarkey was over for now, and fully revived from our first jaunt, the *Jean King* crew was more than content to be chugging at five knots up the coast. The sea was still choppy but all the hard yakka started to pay off: in the moment, a happy marriage.

What had happened in the Big Shed when Les kicked me seemed a million surrealist miles away from how far we had come. When something made sense, we influenced each other easily and apart from the normal spit-for-spat things, life was carefree. We owned the boat outright, there was always plenty of food in our freezer, and I trusted him implicitly – and trust was essential because there weren't any taxis or phones where we were going next.

Slipping along the Great Barrier Reef, we gazed through a 24-hour kaleidoscope which reflected all the goodies and the baddies of the underworld water realms: poisonous sea snakes, all species of fish brimming with colour, including 450-kilo baby blue marlin, painted crayfish and the incorrectly damned crown-of-thorn starfish.

Les sat on the boat's roof and I, with one foot inside the wheelhouse steering the way, stood beside him, excitedly pointing out another passing island. 'That's Noble Island, the prettiest of 'em all,' he said, describing it as having coconuts, fresh water and a reef bursting with fish. Seeing that the Jeannie River was not far away, he suggested we turn back and get some shelter for the night by anchoring up inside it.

With shaky sea legs, I was glad when we dropped anchor in the safety of the river's inlet. Straight away, the three of us leaped into our newly acquired dinghy and went investigating. The creek's silty mudflats were so filled with Cooktown orchids that it was breathtaking. Seeing them all flailing around in the whipping salt wind prompted Les to yell over the engine noise, 'Thought orchids were supposed to be delicate bastards!' as we whizzed past hundreds of the purple flowers growing on everything including rocks.

The watercourse was lined with mangroves weaving in between each other's roots – the whole place could have been a virtual reality art gallery when, suddenly round the next bend, lo and behold if we didn't run straight into a den full of saltwater crocodiles, a croc crop – in number, probably upward of 25 or so. Who was counting? And even though there were all sizes, the majority seemed to range from 10-foot up to maybe 25-foot long, which was way bigger than our eight-foot dinghy. Some, with heavily armed jaws cracked wide open, were snoozing, but most were lounging around like lazy lizards and looked like fallen tree trunks. What's more, the herd of 'salties' was just way too close, like within arm's reach. When the dinghy swished in amongst them, naturally they became agitated and stirred. Whether they had ever seen human beings before I don't know, but it was the first time either of us had seen a live crocodile, let alone a mob of them. Pale with fear and holding on to the side of the boat for grim death, I let out a shocked scream.

Trying to take the scene in, we wallowed around in the millpond for too long, and unexpectedly one of the 20-footers got up on his back legs and scuttled, very bloody fast, toward the river, which also meant he was racing toward us. At the water's edge, with one powerful swish of his tail, the crocodile simply vanished into the drink. That move provoked the rest of the herd into instant action, and suddenly the once peaceful waterway became a churning whirlpool of jaws, claws and lashing tails. This included one very fastly exiting dinghy, and us both yelling incoherent commands of escape to anyone in the universe who would listen.

Leaving on the tide the next day, on we intrepid adventurers glided past Cape Melville, into the Flinders Island Group and through Rattlesnake Passage. There ran the Normanby River.

Rattattta tat, rattatta tat, rattata tat.

When the M1 bullets whizzed right across our bow, I hoped that the burly old bloke whose fuzzy grey hair was madly waving out through the brim of his beleaguered captain's hat had made a bad mistake. He was a nasty-looking kettle of fish.

Rattatta tat, rattatta tat, rattata tat . . .

Didn't look like a mistake when the repeating rifle let out another burst – this time close enough to the *Jean King*'s hull to put the fear of death into us. Who noticed the stained and torn, nearly dead singlet, the crunched-up, daggy stubby shorts, and the neanderthal bare feet as they pounded fiercely up the homemade wharf? A crusty affair, and a right cranky fella stood before us carelessly waving around the loaded repeater as though it was a magic wand. Two naked little tackers clung around the man's hairy, knobbly knees.

'Er, sorry, I thought it was a shark!' the bristly bloke yelled angrily. Shark my arse, I thought, and strategically moved in behind Les, whispering urgently, 'You got us in here, so you betta pull one outta the hat, real quick.'

So Les – leading with the two large bottles of Bundy – stepped bravely from the wheelhouse onto the rickety wharf. The gummy bloke gnashed for a bit, allowed a stealthy, semi-grin to escape, and relaxed the M1 until it pointed somewhere between the rum bottles and the venerable side of our brand new boat.

'Dave, no shootin' us till you get to know us. Hell knows, you might even like us. Besides, we haven't had a drink together – yet.' Les's ambush trickery needed to work. 'Here mate, one's for you.' He stepped toward the cranky rogue and said, 'Nice ta meetcha,' and extended the rum toward him. 'And one's for us to drunk, er drink, right now. German Jack sent us, mate.' Nice balls, I thought.

The wild man guffawed. 'That's the best offer I've had all fuckin' day. Rae, Rae,' he yelled backwards, spinning the taller leg-clinger away back up the wharf. 'Harry, git up home, 'nd git your mother down here.'

Seeing Dave, or the Old Man as we got to call him, drop his guard like that left at least a slim possibility of us getting out alive. Then Rae came waltzing toward us. She was tall, very young, had shining chestnut hair flowing to her waist and, although it was hard not to notice her missing front teeth, her smile was fully genuine. The woman might have had the earth-mother look but the last thing I ever saw her do was babysit the two littlies. Rae, in fact, was the camp mechanic, and did a decent job with any of the numerous engines, mains, outboards, freezers etc. She had grimy, oil-packed, torn fingernails, muscly male type arms, and a few face hairs, and was not to be messed with. She also caught fish, shot things and was unafraid. All necessary, given that the shirty, unpredictable old scoundrel we'd just temporarily massaged into reasonableness was her lover. Oh, and one last demographic: Rae was in her early twenties, and the Old Man in his mid fifties.

Dave immediately set us straight on his life, his universe and everything. 'Me God is the M1, the single side band radio, and me family.' And level pegging always worked, what with the equaliser he still had in hand, so Les and I both listened intently. That day he put us to work – that is, right after we tossed down enough quick, straight rums for the first bottle to be an empty vessel, and had gone 'up home to have a feed'. As he led us up the garden path to 'home', the wild-looking man issued instructions to his woman, the mechanic. 'Rae, we've got engine trouble with the main freezer, and there's a couple a tonne of fish snapped down, so can ya look into that right now – thanks, luv,' he said kindly. With a freezer that size, it sounded like quite a big land-based operation and Dave seemed polite, mannerly and 'in charge'. If you think you can read a person's character from first impressions you're bound to go wrong, as I did that day. Dave was not what I had guessed – I just hadn't seen him get mad yet.

While we sat under the iron lean-to and tucked into a tasty, abundant spread of leftover roast beef and vegies, talk turned to business quick enough. 'Robyn, yeah, nice name that.' The Old Man's eyes were rum-glittered by then. 'With you bein' the new chum, better if you just stick around the camp with the kids, eh but. Keep 'em away from the crocs while me and Les sort a few nets out.'

Shit! Mozzies as big as medium-sized glider planes were soaring around drinking my blue blood by the beer jug, so the crocs should be pretty easy to spot, I thought. At least now I knew how to pick out a croc, but how did one protect the kids, nay oneself, against the infamous munchers – wrestle the bastards bare-handed? I let a nervous giggle escape.

By then the morning's rum intake had hit the spot so Les proposed they crack open a camp-made beer. 'Guffaw, guffaw,' went the Old Man, but he was not distracted, issuing further instructions, this time to the same little boy he'd sent spinning off to get Rae. 'Cow turds, Harry, we need cow turds. Quick love, grab a big bucket and take Robyn over the back paddock.'

Harry, who was about four, skilfully led me through the grassy junkyard of any working man's paradise. Surrounded by a fence of ragged fishing net, the pickings included engine bits, bobs, nets, weights, anchors, ropes, crab pots, foam buoy balls, upturned dinghies, kids' bikes, wheels, props, shafts, kids' toys – plus a few fat, slithering snakes. Just like having an untidy office desk yet still knowing where everything is, up there *nothing* ever got wasted or tossed right out: it might not have looked like it but every piece was strategically dotted around the place, all within reach. Harry also enlightened me: apparently, dried smouldering cow turds smoked out the gigantic mosquitoes, the fishing net fence prevented the wild pigs from raiding the veggie garden, and he too was gunna be a fisherman when he grew up.

Returning from the poo run, I tried to take in this strange new world: gutters from the lean-to directed rain water into a few 44-gallon water drums, so fresh water was on tap. There were also a couple of dozen clucky chooks scratching up the patch, and the outdoor toilet was panoramically positioned so one could keep one's eye on the whole place.

Since we're on the subject, there may well have been some contention as to the ownership of the beef just heartily consumed, however there was no question as to who owned the lean-to we had just dined in, even though it was situated on a cattle property. Warts and all, the Old Man was a bush lawyer born with more than his share of smarts – and had specifically established the shack approximately 55 links (an old British measurement) above the highest, verifiable king tide water mark. This meant that according to Queensland State maritime law the place was legally his. Although dissatisfied, the owners of the cattle station upon which the shack sat could do nothing about it.

'You sure we're not dead?' one of us moaned the next morning. Sniffing out the fresh new southern blood in the camp, the dawn mozzies were on to us in a frenzy.

'Les, git up,' Davey called into our wheelhouse. 'Bring a gun. We're going upstream to bang a beast.' Given that the closest butcher was a two- or three-day journey to the south in Cooktown, taking the occasional cow or steer roaming the cattle station was deemed necessary.

Sleeping with one eye open was a prerequisite when living on a substance as unpredictable as the ocean, so Les and I snapped up and into action as quick as lightning. There beside the *Jean King* in his 16-foot punt stood the Old Man. With a tidy .308 resting across his lap, he had gotten the jump on us. The ageing hobo was wearing last week's scungy duds and an excuse for a T-shirt, but he was sharper than a nasty catfish spike piercing your foot. His big, aluminium punt was very broad and had been purpose built to accommodate four 44-gallon drums, a couple of large sacks of flour, rice and spuds, a spare outboard, crab pots piled on each other, and a few people all in one hit. Clever that.

'Reckon you could hold a good-sized square dance in this thing,' I commented as I swung over the side and squeezed in between the blokes. I didn't want to miss out on anything and was also less than keen about wrestling crocs away from my own mum let alone two little fellas I hardly knew. Stryder wasn't getting left behind either – besides, taking a dog into the bush made a lot of sense.

'Don't drop these then, eh but!' Davey shoved a steel, a stone and a couple of intensely sharp, mid-sized knives toward me. Being way out there in the ignorant backwaters, it seemed ironic that neither man minded me, a woman, being part of the action. The Old Man said, 'I've left me only pair of glasses back at the camp. Couldn't see me arse if I was scratchin' it,' and indicated that Les take over the driving – and we were off.

Right from that very first time Les and I were bewitched: the Normanby River was so rich it felt sticky and smelt musky and its every gesture was provocative, so unexpectedly vibrant it was irresistibly enticing. All around us flocks of amazing birds whipped up a full operatic aria, and the fabulous, weaving limbs of mangroves jived through the thick oozy mud of these exquisite everglades. So pivotal were the mangroves that without them there would be no river fish. The place was luscious, so much like the gardens from the dawn of time must have been that I couldn't help muttering, 'Dr Livingston's gotta be around here somewhere.'

Both blokes shrugged, raised their eyebrows quizzically and kept flying upstream until Dave pointed out the spot. Les killed the engine and we slid in, tied the dinghy up, and stealthily forged into the lush river plains. We were rustlers on the hunt, looking to kill and slaughter some beef on the hoof.

'Pssst. Up front. The young cow strayin' from the rest.' As we quietly sidled toward the unfortunate animal, Davey growled, 'Don't let 'em smell ya on the breeze and make sure you git him with the first bullet. We don't want 'em suffering, or goin' off and dying needlessly.' Cattle, while notoriously short-sighted, can still smell a vegemite sandwich at 500 paces.

Les cocked the .308, levelled it to his eye, aimed, breathed in to still the line of fire and pulled the trigger – boom. A shocked cry, an earthy thud and the job was done. We were to do this a few times, and once, when Dave and he both fired at cattle at the same time, a bullet just grazed Les's cheek. There were a lot of unattractive words said about it, but generally speaking we relied on each other to act intelligently, remain alert and stay 'relatively' intact and sane.

Davey cut the cow's throat, slit open the belly and expertly sliced out and inspected the liver and the lungs, explaining, 'Always, always check for disease.' He tossed the dead beast's kidneys to Stryder, severed the hindquarters, carved out the meat roll from across the backbone, the heart, then ribs. On his hands and knees carving away, constantly sharpening the knives and keeping his eye out for unwelcome interlopers, the Old Man grinned up at me and said, 'Lucky us, a young tender thing, and only about ten minutes' walk from the dinghy.'

Oh yeah, that's right, we had to lug the bloody thing back. Les hauled a bleeding hindquarter onto my shoulder, then one onto his and off we set. Stryder, without being told, took the lead up front with eyes peeled for any pigs or crocs that might be lurking in the spongy swamp we had to cross. I scaled fallen logs, surged through a small stream, cursed the jumbo-jet mozzies taking advantage, and dashed forward as fast as I could. Halfway there, I backed up against a tree, lodged the carcass's weight against it and rested. After a few deep breaths, my mate, hauling the other quarter, came tripping through the virginal green bushland. This, I realised, was our back-yard. Using the standard outback call, I crowed 'Cooo-eee!' shoved my shoulder in under the leg, straightened up and ran at the boat again. Once there, I bent over and shrugged the bleeding leg into the punt. The tucker was in the bag.

Arriving back onboard the *Jean King*, Davey got Les to slit the cow's Achilles tendon, pass a rope through it, and hang the hind-quarters from the back canopy's crossbeam. And to repel blowflies, he taught me to plaster pepper over the open flesh. Then to make the haunch nice and easy to carve up the next morning, we left it to gel overnight.

Back at the shack, sitting at the huge wooden table, we ate a meal large enough for two sumo wrestlers coming off a fast.

Ever on the prowl, Les asked hopefully, 'How's about we have a quick rum?'

Already at the camp oven which hung over the shack's open fire, Davey was busily sorting out the next meal. He squared off to Les and snarled softly, 'That's mine, son. You've got plenty of work to do yet.'

Yes, the Old Man was legendary: a highly unattractive bastard, like King Coles only more deadly, his reputation definitely preceded him up and down the coast, yet he was to give us everything. Even on that first morning he handed over a reliable outboard attached to one non-leaking (relatively speaking) large dinghy, some half-reasonable nets with anchors and buoys to go, plus the first short commentary on the hows, where and why of setting fish nets.

'Here's a bit of gold for you blokes,' Davey said pointing to a 44-gallon drum of petrol. 'Just make sure to replace it when we share the first load's profit.' Outboard fuel: another God, for without it, the business was not possible. The Old Man read the language of fish, he was the river. Incredible. He must have been a good judge of eager young'uns too, because we stuck by this extraordinary man who in time would teach us, directly from his mind's library of fishing, an unwritten and matchless knowledge.

It was all of 7.30 in the morning and yes, we were in.

There's an old adage which says that fools go where angels fear to tread. Well we did, and had fallen on our feet and in harmony with the Mulligans. And there was no doubt or complaints whatsoever about who ran the show: the Old Man was the tribal elder, and had very operational brain matter. Only his ageing body could not do the unforgiving, back-slogging net work so he blasted out commands, herded the little people around and daily cooked excellent meals. For Rae, there was more machinery repair and maintenance work than she could keep up with, so Les and I got relegated to do all the fishing. This involved setting, clearing and repositioning nets day and night, then filleting, cleaning, weighing, packing and freezing the fish down as we went.

From before dawn every day until just before dusk we worked diligently, ate like starving dingoes and read the river. And while the fish ran there was no such thing as a break. So with one hand protected by a steel glove, and in the other an extremely sharp knife, there we'd be standing on the back deck carving up the fish and loving it. Les reckoned doing ten to fifteen barra trays a day was a 'piece of piss for trained jungle fighters like ourselves'. With a pump that continually flushed creek water over the filleting tray or through the bucketed, skinned fillets, and a proper weighing dish hung from the back deck canopy, our professional product was presented as standard weight per carton to buyers.

It was a unique livelihood and barramundi, with their brilliant, silver flashing coats, unmistakable iridescent rabbit-pink eyes and finely shaped bodies, were beautiful to watch as they sprinted through the clear waters. So remarkable was this fish that they knew when there was an imbalance between the sexes, and then just enough of them would metamorphose from male to female to rebalance and ensure the species' survival. What a good trick! Too bad the human species doesn't have that same capacity to walk a mile in each other's shoes every now and then.

Naturally, the shack, colloquially 'up home', was the true heart of the operation. Built from local wood, the three-walled construct's open side faced down to the river. Beside one wall, wedged under an open-cut window, a shroud of mozzie nets covered the four-poster bed, a single bed and a cot. Scattered here and there stood a few desperate-looking wardrobes and clothes-swollen cupboards. With no electricity, why a defunct old stove slumped contentedly in another corner was a mystery, but there were plenty of mysteries up there. The four-metre long, thick wooden-planked kitchen table served many masters. The edge closest to the junkyard was always filled with a half-stripped motor of one sort or another, circled by a newspaper-spread of nuts, bolts, tools, oily rags and grubby engine instruction books, mail order catalogues and grease-encrusted sea charts. Here and there drifting along the tabletop were the inevitable piston ash-trays, the tomato sauce, white sugar, and the big red Saxa salt tower, mustard, pickles, country newspapers and tall brown beer bottles. Finally, a small, wind-protected external fire lived in the back right-hand corner. Strung above it hung a smoke-tarnished camp oven in which a damn fine stew or soup perpetually bubbled. Above that was usually strung a hock or two of slowly curing wild pork stuffed with pockets of bacon and garlic.

Talking about cooking, there was a famous old outback saying that a man is not a good bush cook unless he can make tasty soup from a pair of old socks – or was it jocks? Anyway, turning some-times scanty ingredients into a tasty food fest is not everyone's caper, but I guarantee that the Old Man was the Iron Chef of the bush. While we tucked into our second helping of creamy-smooth mashed potatoes and lightly sautéed fish roe fresh from the morning's run, he hooked the heavy cast-iron pan above the permanently licking flame and grunted, 'The trick is to get the previous meal's leftovers to roll over into the next meal, that way there's no waste.' Good advice, and the next meal following on from roe was a big favourite: fish patties. Suddenly the Old Man's schizo bully voice erupted, his teeth gnashed and his darting eyes went searching through the hut. 'Where's me fuckin' mug? By the livin' jeez, if anyone touches it, I'll kill 'em,' he threatened, snatched it up and took a decent slug. The enamel cup was always close at hand, and right then I realised that it was always filled with alcohol. As nice as pie once again, Davey turned to me: 'Just duck out to the veggie patch. I need a bit'a basil and parsley, love.' The wrath had dissolved and his smile felt open enough but the M1 rifle was always lurking within arm's reach. I had my secrets too. Just quietly I was still pretty wary – actually quite scared – of this all-night roaming, all-day grog-sipping volatile bloke, and was always glad to get some distance between us. How could you trust someone like that when it always felt like some heavy physical harm was about to erupt at any minute?

Stryder, rising a year now, followed me out to the fertile veggie patch. It was another world. With knees sunk deep into the rich-smelling brown clump, my fears evaporated so I repacked the broken dirt surrounds, tugged weeds to help the water channel flow freely, and relaxed. My dog, with one ear cocked, spread out under the closest water tank and watched.

'You're a pretty good all-rounder, girl.' Davey had come up behind me, but instead of jumping in fright, I kept gardening. Men used to say that if you told a woman how good she was, she'd get big-headed, so this was unusual praise.

He picked some herbs then looked at me. 'Seriously, Robyn, alcohol's another one of me Gods. It's a stabiliser, ya git me? It helps keep me pain to a minimum, keeps me steady.'

Bloody hell, I thought, so far Dave had been about as stable as a category 1 cyclone, so 'unstable' was going to be plenty of fun.

'Besides,' he winked, 'the M1's got the fishing inspectors fooled. I just want to be left alone, you with me there, girl?' Better not to speak than to say something ridiculous so I nodded politely and weeded on. 'And by the way, I never speak badly of the dead. And when it comes to business, I make it a policy never to deal with women or cripples; they'll outsmart ya every time.'

The hairs on the back of my head rose. Shit, I truly was stuck up shit creek without a paddle surrounded by a bunch of yokels. Is this what love was about?

CHAPTER 11

Showdown

*A*lmost too innocently a few days slipped quietly by – that is, until after smoko one morning when all of us were inside the hut admiring a very large, very rare black orchid spray freshly plucked from the river's fringe on the early net run.

'Come on, Rae,' Les hassled, 'let's go untangle the big hammerhead shark from the net before the wind turns on us.'

With the .303 in hand, the pair strode away and I heard the dinghy sprinting off downstream. Stryder lay at my feet under the table, and I casually chatted to the little ones who were sitting inside cardboard cartons, playing cars. Then came another outburst, its ferocity almost tangible.

'Where's me hammer? Who's stolen me fuckin' hammer? Where's the bastard gone?' The Old Man was virtually frothing at the mouth as he screamed, 'Ahhhhhhhhhh!' He grabbed his beloved enamel mug in one knobbly hand and with the other, snatched the unfortunate hammer, stormed outside toward the little boys, stumbled over some junk and stopped short at a flat slab of timber. Stryder and I were on our feet and ready to bolt. The frenzied man squatted down. 'Aahhh!' he screamed again as the hammer came pounding into life and loudly beat the hell out of his apparently no longer precious mug. Finally, the murdered mug, now all scrunched up into a clown's grin with its badly twisted handle pathetically hanging down like a loose ear, lay at rest.

Still in escape mode, I realised that the slaughtered mug looked just like him, and accidentally chuckled. Coolly he looked over my way, and my heart pounded so loudly I was sure he would hear it. 'Fuckin' cup had a rusty hole in the bottom and the last of my grog just leaked away. Fuckin' mug!'

I'll leave you to decide just who the real mug was, but the little boys barely blinked an eye before driving off into junkyard land once again. There were still a few beers on the *Jean King*, so I volunteered to go get them. Without waiting for his reply I called up Stryder, 'Come on Stryd,' instantly turned heel and was gone.

Phew! Getting out of his eyesight felt much safer; besides, there was still some green at home – a thick sprinkle on top of a rollie would settle my nerves. Normally getting high was just a bit of fun; this time I really appreciated it. Davey's moodiness was part of the landscape and so when he got like that, we learnt to say less, tread more quietly and avoid him as much as possible.

Living on the river also meant that frenzied mozzies attacked at dawn and dusk. The only way to avoid being eaten alive was by letting the dried cow turds' smoke saturate the cabin just before sundown. This made such a dense smokescreen that it was nigh on impossible to see anything including each other, so normally we were in bed under the mozzie net as the sun dipped below the horizon. Strategically, this also meant we could enter into the enduring companion love which had developed between us. Ever since being in the Normanby we were really happy together, and had become stalwart mates.

The weeks moved along and Davey's madness kept taking its toll on everyone. Then one morning he was ranting on at full volume again, this time about his lost glasses. 'Who's stolen me fuckin' glasses? Rae, get me glasses. I'm sick and tired of lookin' for 'em. I'll kill whoever's got 'em, Rae. Rae? Where are you, Rae?' His threats were nerve-racking and ear-splitting and the busy camp always responded to his furious, livid mouth by obeying instantly. Everyone would drop whatever they were doing and run around like chooks with their heads chopped off, placating him, scared of where and what the anger would do next, and knowing that by this stage all the alcohol had finally been drunk made the situation even more combustible. The Old Man with the mad M1 in hand was haunting everyone, and getting more adamant, more het up by the second. 'Ya can't trust anyone, turn ya back, the lying bastards'll thieve ya only pair of fuckin' glasses. I've had a gutful!' he screamed at full bore.

And there was no escape because with all the morning's jobs done, Les, Rae and I were halfway through pressing homemade sausages out of the old mechanical mincer which was screwed down onto the table. We must have all felt a bit screwed down too because the snags were coming out like painful, sprung coils, and looked tense enough to block up your foofer valve for weeks: uptight mood equals uptight snageroonies. As the beef churned through, we unhappy chappies hurled in handfuls of crushed garlic, grated cheese, chillies or whatever else happened to be close to the grinder. With him in top stride, we'd probably chucked in a rusty spanner or two by then because it felt as though the invisible sky seams that held the whole show together were about to burst. Grind, crunch, grate: all of it, too much.

Without warning, even to myself, suddenly I kicked the chair from under me for a six and jumped up. This was showdown at the Not OK Corral and since I was the only one in the whole god-forsaken camp who wore glasses, a big, non-adjustable screwdriver was about to be chucked into the churning mix. '*You've* had enough! Yeah well, I've had a fuckin' 'nuf too, enough of your nasty, loud, abusive mouth . . . you, you arrogant, bullyin' old bastard.' Stryder's back hair bristled like a razor cut, her teeth set and she snarled. The bitch took up a stance between the two of us and did not flinch.

I'd laid a big one on him alright, and the Old Man instantly crouched like a cranked-up grizzly bear. All and sundry froze, including the crocs living close by, and even things in the grass stopped slithering. Even the two little blokes, who were used to this kind of thing, took a break from chasing snakes and looked on with gaping mouths. When Les moved toward me protectively, I let loose again, and with that some more of my hidden fear came bursting out.

'Don't come any closer, Les. No one, no one has ever called me a thief or a liar and I won't cop it.' Everyone's eyes went from him to me then back to him. I could feel my legs go wobbly, and my

heart was noticeably sitting in my big mouth, but there was no turning back, so I let rip. 'I'm the only one who wears glasses in this
jumped-up circus and I haven't stolen your crappy, stupid glasses,
and if ya don't believe that, get out the back and have a go, ya fuckin'
standover merchant.' So saying, up went my closed fists in the old-
fashioned boxing stance, and I shuffled around a bit. What the hell
was I doing? I mean, in anyone's language, them there were fighting
words.

With nothing to lose, I didn't give a fish tit. 'And while we're
at it, *mate*,' I threatened, 'stick your nets, your dinghy and your precious petrol right up your arse, you cantankerous son-of-a-bitch. You
might be big but ya don't scare me. Carn, let's do it.' Was anything
ever going to be the same again?

As the Old Man's squint narrowed for a second or two, time
seemed to get acutely long. Then I saw the gun fall onto the bed,
with the barrel pointing away from us, and him sink onto the nearest
chair in howls of rowdy, tearful laughter. 'Oh fuck me,' he laughed,
gasping for breath through the mirth, 'oh dear and most beautiful
woman. Come here, sit, sit on me knee,' he motioned. 'Let me hold
you, you thing of beauty. Jesus Christ, I love women, Les.'

I gratefully did sink onto his lap, the crocs got back into lounging, the invisible sky seams relaxed and the stalwart lean-to felt safe
to be in once again. No one had spoken like that to the Old Man and
lived to tell the tale so Les and Rae, using hysterical laughter as a
pretext, let a lot of pent-up feelings go too.

Tenderly, Davey's wizened hands turned my face toward him.
'Didn't mean to scare the bejesus outta you, love. It's just me monster
taking me for a walk. Apologise I do – no really, from the cockles of me
barnacled.' He meant from the bottom of his heart, the zombie wolf
did. 'Now listen here.' Well, who wasn't? 'I'm bein' serious. Never
think for a minute that I would harm you or yours, ever.' Whoops,
another turn for the books: him apologising. Dave turned and, jabbing
his busted-up fingers at Les's heart, insisted, 'A damned fine woman
here, fella. She's a bewdy. Don't ever go losin' the plot and lettin' her go
mate. Ain't no more where she come from, I'm tellin' ya.'

'That's my tiger,' Les said, beaming proudly. He loved me
proudly for standing up for my rights.

Then and there I fell into undying love for the Old Man, a love that never faded.

Still, in the fishermen's scheme of things, every day was a day of work and this one was no exception, so for the rest of the day work continued as normal. That evening when the sun ducked off to light up someone else's life and the little boys went chasing dreamland, we four friends wolfed down roast beef, spuds, pumpkin, patch-fresh spinach, peas and the big favourite – Yorkshire pudding covered in juicy gravy. This time there was none left for the following morning's bubble and squeak. The Old Man knew the way to our hearts was through our stomachs, so his humble pie won us over easily.

Our close-knit mateship and the flickering Tilley lanterns gave the night a soft, sensuous glow, so following the sumptuous meal, we were quietly yarning away and sipping kettle tea when the Old Man popped the $64,000 question: 'You're a pretty smart girl, Rob, so I wanna ask you somethin' real personal. Rae's been naggin' me about it 'nd I'm fucked if I know.' He looked uncomfortable, and shoved his captain's cap around a bit, so the silver-grey wizened curls sprang out. 'Er, thing is, I just dunno how to put it.' Rae nudged him, nodding him on. 'But well . . . exactly what is "coming"?'

I sat up in surprise, and immediately suspected that they were deliberately pulling my leg but no, vigorously shaking their heads, he and Rae kept on insisting.

'You know how you shoot sperm up into Rae, right?' Nodding, his eyes now remained lowered under the privacy of the hat beak. 'Well, that's an orgasm, and women have orgasms too.'

His woman let out a satisfied sigh, saying, 'See, I told ya so, Dave.'

'Yeah, but she's on me back about it, so why do I have to be knowin' about all that stuff and how it works, Robyn?' Him using my full first name further indicated that this was a serious enquiry: and even though Rae had egged Dave on, it looked like they both wanted more intimate detail so I obliged.

'Just touch her on the clitoris. I mean caress her and don't press too hard; it's a beautiful and delicate thing.'

Across the table from me, Davey shrugged and shuffled restlessly. 'Yeah but . . . why can't she just sort that stuff out . . . herself?'

Seeing him stuck for words was priceless and it also helped me understand that neither of them knew exactly where the cloaked lotus blossom hid, that it was birds and bees time in tropical paradise. Flickering fire, whirling smoke swirls, the rich roast-soaked atmosphere, the occasional croc roar, us all being out there as the little people snored softly and the stars looking down, my Les, Stryder at my feet – it was so intoxicating, this intimate spaciousness. I knew I would never forget it and naively presumed that this piece of Australia would be my home forever.

When I pulled the Tilley lanterns closer, dropped a fair wad of saliva onto my free hand and dipped a willing finger into it, they all hunched over excited, as on a cleared space in the middle of the big table I explicitly drew an A3-sized layout of the woman's most exquisite button, the clitoris and its surrounding terrain. Women go to bed with love in mind, men go to bed with sex in mind. Women go to sex with love on their minds, men go to sex with sex in mind.

As we two strolled home down the garden path, Les passionately bit my neck and crooned the only bit of poetry he knew: 'When a woman is with wanting and her pulse begins to race,' he whispered, tearing my clothes in half and tossing the shreds to the ground, 'you can tell it's the night, the night of the silver lace.' I felt his bristly sandpaper beard brush my tenderness and the night's fine mist tamper with my exposed skin, as pressed up against the vibrating freezer wall, one-handedly my man took me. I sure was somewhere down a crazy river . . .

CHAPTER 12

Sacred Rituals

*B*uilt with a 1.5-metre draught, our vessel did open ocean, coastal and river work like a breeze and we, by staying sharp and abreast of local offshore wind and tide movements, slipped in and out of rivers like a homing fish. And while the Wet and Dry seasons of tropical splendour kept an all-year-round green vibrancy in the jungle, regularly Les and I steamed south, back to Cooktown a few times. There we'd offload barra, stock up on important depleted stores, refuel various things, mix with the locals and have a few drinks. Still, it never took long before we would be pining to get back up to the gossipy river and the Mulligan tribe.

Return supplies included a mandatory carton of Bundy rum for the Old Man, a few whizzbang toys for the beaut little people, and a pretty blouse for the mechanic – and always a few cartons of Forex, or Yella Peril as the home state beer was fondly called. Forex was also the fishermen's clear and proven favourite, mainly because when dropped drunkenly overboard, instead of sinking, the full cans floated.

The second we arrived, the Mulligan tribe swarmed over the back deck. First there'd be beers all round and for Rae, the non-drinker, renewed tobacco supplies, then opening up the months-old mail, clucking around overdue engine parts, sampling of fresh fruit and chatting. All of it – the splendid river, our tribe, the pleasure of rubbing good quality tobacco across the palm, rolling it, lighting up, feeling the deep taste in your lungs, followed by the ceremonious coughing when its distinct texture ripped at your tonsils – all of it was well intentioned and lots of fun.

Rae and I also came to create a ritual that ran deeper than even we could know, when occasionally we would head upstream alone. One esky would be filled with shampoo, conditioner, brushes, razors, nailfiles, scissors, face masks, moisturisers, tweezers and pluckers, towels, and so on. In the other esky went grilled barramundi wings, a flask with more rum than coffee plus the short-nose .22 pistol. In what was absolutely secret women's business, by the crisp first light of day, she and I, all set up in the square-dance punt, would cruise at a leisurely pace to our private freshwater sanctuary.

Our haven wasn't that far away in river miles, but was undoubtedly a planet or two away from the camp when amongst dappled sunlight in the untainted, fresh river water the two of us stripped off, bathed, swapped luxurious back scrubs, and partook of sips and nibbles. After the preening, I'd brush my friend's waist-length mane until it shone and we would speak of our private dreams and share secret confessions, laughing wholeheartedly at the funny side of life, like when Rae explained how she'd won a fight once by knocking the Old Man unconscious with a plank of four by two timber. She also confessed to having once thrashed the little boys with such a fierce anger that it had scared the daylights out of her. Rae made it clear that she loved them deeply, but after that learnt to be a mechanic and left the kids' upbringing to Davey. Sometimes laughing until we cried, less often crying until we understood, we both always knew that something important had taken place. It was a very sassy moment in the jungle, and other than the animals of land, sea and sky who happened to be passing by at the time, it was for our eyes, ears and hearts only.

I realise now that this was not just a girlie thing, it was us responding naturally to the feminine call, and the cyclic purification of our souls. Whether it was in that secluded outback creek or at the Ginseng Baths of the red-light district of Sydney, women across the world have been evoking the ritual of purification for centuries. Perhaps the visible blood of menstruation helps women acknowledge the call. But please don't tell me that this is a rite for women only – surely the same sacred call comes for men, a call they have yet to hear. And as sure as women have 'periods', that is a monthly cyclical rhythm, men must also have the same 'periods', something that so far, they flatly deny – who knows why?

Every year, Rae held birthday parties for the two little people. It was such fun when, waking unsuspectingly one sun-up, Graham and Harry were immediately pressed into taking an *early* morning bath – in other words, get a good scrub while dunked into one of the big plastic bins. And as if this uncustomary event wasn't enough, next thing on would go their only set of 'best' clothes and shoes too. Must have thought they were off to Mars. The little ones' only friends were the four of us so after the big table was spread with the best of everything we could conjure up. Much to their amazement out would come party hats, whistles, balloons and streamers, and away we'd go. Harry and Gray-Gray were such beaut kids, it was a gift to witness their innocent joy.

The Normanby River wilderness stretched way up until it birthed a pristine lake that spread across the land like an ocean. Occasionally flood water broke over the riverbanks so Les and I would drive across the submerged fields now afloat with flowering waterlilies. Where the earth had once been, suddenly a stunning pond with uncountable, orange-winged, delicate dragonflies hovered above it – being a species about 180 million years old, the dragonfly is way more ancient than the croc. While the rainbow-winged creatures shimmered just above the silky water's surface, and yellow and black-striped tiger wasps carrying bugs larger than themselves buzzed this way and that, ducks flew overhead and fish plopped around us lazily – all undisturbed by each other. The richness of that headland – the variety of nature amicably responding each to its own purpose, the remarkable tranquillity of that country – was so moving that I always felt like I was in some kind of Gondwana Origami Land.

Having such freedom from the normal world did not escape us.

Sometimes we'd just let the dinghy meander around by itself, and make love on top of the barra nets: or Les would easily pull me on top of him so we would both be looking upward. Put it this way, the privilege of being the only two human beings up in the astonishing headwaters was just about indescribable.

Often the sky and the swollen river expanse mingled into the blue infinity, and even time seemed to stop ticking and everything just 'was' – without beginning without end. Then, with one hand dangled over the side, my own finger and its mirror reflection touched each other and rested on the border between realms. In such a world, it even felt possible that human beings might be able to live in harmony. Les thought my idealistic way of thinking was strange and used to say that too much thinking sent people crazy.

And sure, Les and I debated plenty, but then it was never serious and always made us ripen to each other. In the Normanby days there was no deep verbal or physical abuse and we made love just like the rich musky jungle around us did: to own each other – or to be distinct from each other, in a word, naturally.

Just for a change we took the *Jean King* upstream for a month or so, and over the radio used a code to tell the gang back at camp how many fish we were catching. But one morning, the Old Man came across the wavelengths like a bull at a gate, raving about having troubles and us having to come 'fuckin' right away'. It was uncharacteristic, as the Old Man never swore over the air.

At first we assumed that Dave was complaining about the lack of fish down his way and started giving him our secret radio code, the gobbledygook fish tally, of how many caught and how many trays. But he brushed it all to one side and kept insisting we come back downstream, on the double. Having caught plenty of fish, we were reluctant to change matters but Davey sounded oddly alarmed. Could it be one of the kids? A serious freezer failure? Definitely sounded like an emergency. Besides, the radio was one of the Old Man's Gods and swearing on it was frowned upon so seriously that the authorities could cancel your licence, so there was no mistaking the tone or the seriousness.

Mates always backed up mates, no matter what. And mateship asked no questions so we seized the nets, battened down the hatches, tied the dinghy on the back and headed downstream. It only took a couple of hours before we pulled up at the makeshift wharf. The unfamiliar dinghy tied up there barely rated acknowledgement what with the surprise intro and the bombshell standing righteously on the wharf, haphazardly waving a loaded .44 like an unsuccessful fly swat. It and the M1, same jumpy disposition.

'Me name's Whitcock, Sergeant Whitcock. I'm from the Brisbane Drug Squad.'

Les whispered out of the side of his mouth, 'Looks like we've got a couple of real sloppy, nasty sharks here, girl. Keep ya wits about ya, talk all the time but tell 'em nothin'.'

Having just drifted in from the backblocks of hillbilly land, it felt like Dr Who must do when he magically drops in on a bunch of extraterrestrials.

When the tall, uniformed, pock-faced cop went to shake hands, Les reneged. With that, the stranger audaciously black-booted it, uninvited, onto our vessel. Out in the yard, I spied Rae, Davey and the little ones all huddled up together under the intense midday heat with another uniform talking insistently at them. He looked like a nasty streak too. Having two arrogant cops gripping loaded pistols way up in no-man's-land was deadly serious.

'It's Robyn, and Les, yeah. Mr Coles, you're the captain, I believe. I'm here to have a few words with you and Robyn, separately.' Out in the back of tropical paradise, the straitlaced outfits, chequered stiff hats, heavy-duty Gestapo boots, the dry welded guns all smelt of maximum tension. 'So let go hands and go out on the back deck till I've finished with Miss Catchlove.'

I gripped my man's hand tighter. Les, on the other hand, stood blocking the back deck and eyeballed the cop.

'Yeah, I'm Les Coles,' he murmured, and forced Whitcock to shake his hand then. It made the cop drop his guard. 'And I'm not leavin' me woman alone till you get some manners about you. We're of the one blood, her and me.' It seemed impulsive but fear has its own vibration. 'We haven't broken any laws, so back off and put that .44 back in ya pocket.' Les's own unflinchable authority was a force to be reckoned with.

With that, the pug-like young boofhead holstered his cannon, a move that tidied up the atmosphere somewhat. Bulky, and heavy, .44s were quite silly weapons in the bush, especially in the blundering hands of city cowboys. Either of the unarmed fishermen could have had them for breakfast, but where would the grey matter in that have been? Like Jacky Chan doing battle with Clint Eastwood. Remember too, at that time Queensland politicians had a notorious reputation as white-collar criminals, and similarly the police force for being their dirty-collar enforcers. So there we bushies were, staring down the barrel of two rotten eggs who had permission from the highest possible authority.

Whitcock asked me for a rundown on my previous – that is, whether I had a criminal record. 'Whatever previous means, me, I'm just a poor fisherman, scratching out a livin'. You and I, Constable, we need a cuppa . . .' I smiled innocently and fussed around at the stove trying to keep the cop on the boil while the water heated.

He cut in impatiently, 'It's Sergeant. So what's your relationship with Dave and Rae, and how long have you known them?' I deliberately made him a bad cup of tea, handed it over and purposefully remained standing.

'Real friends. Best in the world those two. Helped us when we were down, got us on our feet. Yep, do anything for them . . .' He sneered cynically. 'We've known them a year or two, forever really. Trust them with me life, I would . . .'

He changed tack and asked how long we'd been upstream.

'Don't really know. A week or two, a month – out there you lose track of time . . .'

The cop was hot, sweaty and looking for trouble, and asked why we went upstream.

I could feel Les listening from the back deck and responded lightly. 'Hoped the fish might have gone up there too but no such—'

Peacock cut back in, dropping the shocker. 'So, d'you believe that they'd ever deal drugs?'

'You mean Dave and Rae? No way! The Old Man doesn't even smoke cigarettes and Rae never drinks. Don't reckon either of 'em would even be able to recognise drugs, Captain.' He didn't correct that one. Anyway, I meant what I was saying. 'Nah, no one'd ever convince me they knew anything about drugs, let alone use—'

'So what's with the code you were usin' on the radio?' he snarled suspiciously.

Smiling was not Whitcock's custom so his lips curled falsely as his eyes tried to read me like braille. The cop told me they heard us talking code that morning, and insisted that it was a disguise for drug talk. It took me a minute to add it all up. 'Oh that! Yeah, well, that means every fisherman on the coast must be dealing in drugs, Captain, because you'll hear codes like that every day from dawn to dusk.' He slumped a bit so I kept talking, trying to gain his trust. 'No, hell no. That's just a way of stopping the rest of the fishermen from coming over and stealing your thunder, you know robbing . . .'

Whitcock was like a hawk, like the ugly customer he'd been trained to become, and tried to bluff me by threatening to search our boat. Relieved that the last of the green had gone weeks before, it felt as easy as falling off a log so I opened my arms and waffled on, 'Go for your life, Captain. Honest, I'm a good girl.'

Whatever this curious showdown was about, instead of ransacking our home, the bully broodily turned his attention to Les, and as the two strode off up the garden path into the stinking hot sun, my man gave me a pointed look. I read it, stayed put on board and silently melded into the background. Just like crocs' eyes do, one eye stayed on Les while the other shrewdly moved along with the bizarre goings-on. Out of sight, I loaded the .303 and held it cocked. With Stryder beside me, we listened vigilantly. Meanwhile, the hatless Mulligans stood out there burning, thirsty and afraid.

'Fucked if I know what this is about,' my man said and stepped amongst them, gesturing Harry and Graham to him, 'but I bet you blokes have got kids. These two little tackers are innocent and need water so I'm gettin' 'em some. Come on, loves.' The little kids might not have understood but they instantly flocked to him.

A few minutes later he, the hatted littlies and a much cooler cop came back into the open. Les handed around more hats, water, and tobacco for Rae. This action made the fierce grip on the circle loosen and the police and the fishermen split apart, whispering urgently amongst themselves. What I heard didn't help.

'The copper briefed me. Dave, what's . . . ?'

The Old Man was grey but still. 'Yeah, it's true, I've got the stuff alright, that's another story, but I want reassurances. That's what the fuckin' stalemate's about, mate.' This was bloke stuff at the coalface.

Les shook his head in disbelief and took command. 'The game's up, Old Man. Go and get it and give it to 'em and don't pull any stunts. These coppers are jumpy greenhorns and not up for any fuckin' nonsense, Dave. They're out of their depth up here on their own, and both armed.'

They looked back over at the two gunsters who were look-ing back over at them. The worrying difference: the cops, holding deadly shooting rods, were cooped possessively around Rae and the children.

'Listen here Les, the pricks are threatenin' to fly me and Rae back to the Cooktown cop shop right now and just leave young Harry and Gray-Gray abandoned out here on their own, so I know the fuckin' score, alright.' Dave scratched his balls and snarled on, 'I'm just try-ing to get a bit'a safety net goin' so there's no comeback later, mate.'

Nursing a loaded rifle and ready to pull the trigger if needed, the dense concentration was so thick I could almost touch it.

'Jesus H Christ.' Les's face drained of colour as he realised that the whole homestead's back was against the wall. 'This is a right fucking can of worms, you old rogue, whatever possessed . . . ?'

The Old Man gnashed his jaw and sliced up the question. 'Trust me, Les, there's only one way outta this. Peacock's gotta hand over a signed letter saying that me and Rae are totally innocent and that the drugs I haven't got were handed over to him. Then I'll give the low-life the drugs. You get me drift there?'

Les shook the Old Man's hand. 'No worries, I'll back ya up. Just sort it out quick-smart, and get rid of the stench.'

Apparently, the cops had searched the camp with a vengeance and found nothing. That was because the drugs had been secreted under the defunct, rusted hotplate lid of the cobwebbed old electric stove which, with its oven door partially open, had stood neglected yet above suspicion in the darkest corner of the shack. Okay, what the hell was an electric stove doing where there was not a rumour, not a coil nor suspicion of electricity? Right now off the top, search me, but there it was.

Within 30 minutes, the nasty business was done and everyone was happier than if Snow White had turned up with the seven dwarfs. So after all had been given and received, or nothing had been found but taken, or whatever, after all that, Les escorted the sweltering, uniformed boofs to their waiting dinghy. They then tore off downstream faster than a silver bullet. By radio, we heard later that the cops had gone up the next river to a private landing strip, hopped into the anxiously hovering light aircraft and lit out for Cairns. Whether the two-kilo bag of pure heroin that travelled with them ever ended up in the official department of confiscated goodies or in the pocket of some official or other suchlike habitual of the street, is another story in the naked city.

Wiser now, the Old Man's shaking hand grasped a shoddily handwritten, unconditional reprieve from being guilty of something that he hadn't had but had handed over . . . Get it?

No two ways about it, Davey and Rae – who were ignorant about hard drugs – had learned the tough way about the ruthlessness of the game just played. Apparently, while we'd been upstream, a cold, thuggish-looking customer just lobbed out of the blue insisting the Mulligans help locate two mysterious packets with unrevealed contents that had been air-dropped just behind the Normanby in the Jayne Tableland. The tough cookie also promised $1000 cash for each packet found. On the surface it looked like good pay for a day's work so they went searching. The quandary arose when only one packet was found and the stranger split without leaving any cash.

'He was a mean son-of-a-bitch, carrying a piece too, so I wasn't gunna argue with him. Then he pissed me off, comin' in and upsettin' us, and after leavin' nothin' for our trouble. I reckoned he owed us.'

Davey didn't realise the underground figure had left big trouble. Call it crafty, call it stupid, or call it both, the Old Man guessed that the other packet, whatever the contents, must be worth a bomb.

'I'm an old man with two little kids and a young wife. It could have been us outta here, plus the kids' education to boot.' More like an education in the slammer. Enough to say that he'd brooded like a clucky bush turkey until it seemed like a genius stroke to go and find the missing packet. The web had easily gotten tangled in the grapevine after Len started communicating over the radio to a couple of well-known, nefarious characters of his acquaintance. Bush telegraph travels quicker than contriving cops on the prowl so when the legal crims got a whiff of the lost white powder it all came swirling around faster than a dark storm arriving from the north. Greed has its habits.

Although several – in fact a few several – loud, harsh words passed between Les and the Old Man behind the shack, the collective sigh of relief was far greater. And after a scare like that, for the rest of that day until the cool of night put us to bed, we all hunkered down like a team of scrum buddies.

CHAPTER 13

Parting Company

*J*ust where the barramundi went around the middle winter months was the mystery of every season. It was a guessing game. The fish simply vanished into thin air, into denser water perhaps. While out-thinking the fish was a very tricky affair, considering that every barra boat on the entire Queensland coast made it their business to eavesdrop on what every other boat was saying over the radio, outsmarting the other fishermen was a necessary art form. Therefore lying and speaking in code was a blatant practice, otherwise every fisherman and his dog would come bearing up your river and muscle in on your fish.

When the pickings got slim the following year, Les and I took the *Jean King* downstream for a few weeks to test out a barra theory or two. Other than that, the best part of each day was doing the dawn net run. And judging by the gorgeous colours in the first-light sky, it looked like another day in the river of plenty as I unhitched the dinghy and from over the top of the churning outboard, called out to Les: 'I'll do the net down the mouth first – bye,' and roared off.

Back on my words came his call: 'Watch out for the croc at the mouth.'

I hated being patronised and still flair up when it happens. After all, I had a few years' experience tucked under the belt, my body was strong, supple and as quick any athlete's – so just because

I was a woman didn't mean I needed reminding that staying alive demanded being alert 100 per cent of the time. Flying downstream, I let the nets tell their tale. If the net corks bobbed up and down erratically, there were fish below. Fish in net one, yep, net two, net three, a rolled tangle with a shovel-nose shark snout fouling it up, yep net four, net five a dragged anchor, then at the mouth of the river, yep, plenty of fish but the net was snarled around a mangrove root at the bank. The croc Les had reminded me about had been hanging round on the opposite bank for the last couple of weeks, but this day he was nowhere to be seen. In a quick summation, the whole process looked like a bit of a cinch. At that, I spun the dinghy in, cut and lifted the engine and from the midstream end got stuck into reefing fish from the net – all the while working myself in toward the bank and the tangled net mess. When you get too smart for your own good, it's easy to miss important details.

The choppy cross-current, the incoming tide and the unusual early morning breeze made the dinghy bob this way and that, so I tackled the opposing rhythms in a tai chi kind of way, balancing on top of the seat panels. As I worked away, a big flock of curved-beaked white ibis effortlessly winged across the wayward sky, shrill bickering galah squawks filled the air and beside me pelicans and wee shags competed for their own share of the schooled-up bait fish gathered just below the surface.

Finally at the river edge, I reached out over the side to separate the tangled mesh from the wild mangrove root, and the swirling salty mudflat tang captured my attention. In that second, the slippery, fish-bloodied dinghy floor jolted, jerked, lifted and speared forward, my feet slipped up and I was spiralling out and into the treacherous waters. Like a flashing neon light, instantly the word 'croc' lit up in my mind. There was no time for previous life movie shows to be orbiting the psyche, just the shocking four-letter word, then time tumbled into itself and darkness came.

Hands. Mine. Touching, me, my skin. Checking, I felt my clothes. How could they be dry? Down below sat the empty dinghy snagged in a mangrove root with the net still trapped under it. Yet my eyes were seeing from a distance above, down onto the full colour scene. Not trusting my vision, I could hear nothing either, not even my heart. As the eerie silence magnified and my perception intensified, I looked for some reference point, some lucid sight. My feet, find my feet, I thought – yes, there they were! And I was standing on a mangrove bough about three metres above the river. 'Oh . . .' The expulsion of relieved surprise came spontaneously as I swayed, reached out and grabbed – no, hugged – the sturdy tree's trunk. The experience didn't defy anything; just the powerful energy of fear had overcome gravity and by necessity, I had flown. With that my head fell back and I looked between the restless dashes of cloud beyond into the never-endingness, and a joyous, pure chant of thanks in a language older than the world bubbled out.

Hearing my heart settle into a fast rhythmic chatter, I scaled down the guardian mangrove, bounced the dinghy's nose off the tree roots and swiftly pulled myself along the net into midstream. As the outboard motor kicked in, instinctively I looked across to the other side. Sure enough, there was the croc, a big one too, back on the other side, watching, waiting, being. 'Nice try, buddy,' I called. After all, it was no more my country than it was the croc's, it was both of ours.

Being a professional, I cleared the rest of the nets – very bloody quickly, but I did do them. Like we used to say, the freshest a fish can be is straight after it's been caught – a statement that was meant as basic respect for the dying fish and for the person fortunate enough to enjoy eating it. Speeding back to the *Jean King* I couldn't help thinking that if humans didn't kill everything in their pathway, they wouldn't be considered trespassers. Nature isn't a perfect heaven, it simply responds perfectly at every opportunity. This had just been the case for the croc and me.

One way or another, between the four of us the books had balanced up a bit. We owed the Mulligans big-time so there would always be plenty of unpayable gratitude. Still, we were hard workers and after a couple or so years of work, both families' pockets were squared away and we had upgraded to our own fishing gear. Bearing in mind that a little bit of trouble is a good thing, Les and I had done well.

The Wet was clearly on its way once more when finally mangrove buds, knowing nothing of calendar months, started bobbing past our bow on their way to the coast where they would lodge in the soft silty shoreline. My man and I were ready to slip down the coast to the bright lights of Cairns, on through to Brisbane, then home to Adelaide to celebrate our success and Christmas with our families. How extraordinary we had become: cashed up, unowned by convention, and no idea of just how alive, strong and clear-headed we were.

In preparing for the holiday run, Les was in the throes of crafting a two-metre long, homemade esky ready to stack it full of frozen whole barramundi, mudcrabs and barra wings when the Old Man piped up: 'The Annual Boat Show's on in Brissy so me and Rae wanna pick up a few things. Ja mind runnin' us in at Cairns, mate?' Silly question. We would have taken them to the ends of the earth.

Ruddy-faced and wickedly happy, we must have looked like a bunch of unwinding circus clowns as we steamed down south to Cairns. It happened again then, just as it had at the headlands of the Normanby, only this time on the Earth's vastest lake. The sky and the ocean flowed so seamlessly into each other that there was no horizon, just this magic spherical mirror, a space galaxy without differentiation. Curiously, all the sea creatures must have felt the same because they just lay around on the surface of the translucent subtle sea skin. Even the perpetually coy greenback turtles gave us permission to reach down and touch their barnacle-encrusted shells. Having picked up on a rhythmic splatter-splash, splatter-splash on the horizon, one day we watched the movement for hours while a turtle twosome drifted down the current, passed us and went on to the opposite horizon, the whole time making love without cessation. It looked like an Underwater Labour Day holiday when countless dolphins, with front flippers tucked casually under-head, basked on the surface and fish lazily spiralled out of the silver blue plasma and splonked back in. The only sign of the fish pirouettes was the faintly heard resonant echo of their impeccable motion and the perfect series of ever-increasing soundless sea circles which caressed the *Jean King*'s effortless wake. The spectacular event went on for a week.

With the *Jean King* docked at Cairns, as usual, Les and I took a few fresh whole barra to the businesses who had supported us through the boat building years, quickly installed a caretaker on the

Jean King and left Stryder at a friend's. The next day the six of us cabbed it out to the airport.

'Rae, where's me fuckin' tin?!', the Old Man kept grizzling as he tightly squeezed the little people under one arm and crushed the large Nestlé's full-cream powdered milk tin under the other.

Laughingly, Les pretended to wrestle the dented tin away, but the Old Man growled like a disturbed croc, so he let up.

That morning, Rae had headlocked Dave and the little people into a half-nelson to get them truly spruced up, so what with our slightly manic country looks, the brand new T-shirts ripped that very morning from stiff plastic encasings, and the virgin stubby shorts, there we sat happily ensconced in business class. Gawky-looking nomads we may have been, but we felt unbeatably good, what with necks and shoulders rippling with muscle and arms and legs like weight-lifting champions.

The Old Man winked across the aisle at me, leant over and whispered, 'Ya fancy a drink, Robyn love? Just name it. Anything ya want.' Without his frazzled skipper's cap, the Old Man seemed much lighter. 'Why don't you 'nd Les go top shelf. It's my shout.'

So I ordered a bottle of Bollinger for us, a couple of hip-flasks of brandy for Dave, a pot of tea for Rae and a soft drink each for the hair-combed, spotlessly dressed little chappies.

The heavily made-up air hostess took one look at us, smiled like she was a bloke with scrotum squeeze, and through masked disdain condescendingly suggested that the order was going to cost a lot more money than it looked like we could afford.

Rae leaned forward, gave the young piece her best toothless grin and asked the woman if she wanted the cash upfront, and nudged Dave. 'Give her some money, love. G'won, that's how they do it up here.'

With that, the Old Man tenderly prised open the milk tin and out sprang a healthy 50,000 smackeroonies, waving around like ripe marijuana shoots just out of jail. He grabbed a fist full of the greens and stuffed them into the sophisticated, now blushing hostess's hand.

Davey's crinkled face split apart. 'Give us a hoy when you've run out love, there's plenty more where that comes from, eh but,' and spanked her all-too-skinny butt and laughingly finished up with, 'at

least with a buxom girl you can get a decent grip of her love handles.'
Sounded like my earlier 'lotus blossom' coaching instructions had
paid off.

At the Brisbane airport we parted company. And you had to give
it to him, the Old Man had style. 'Now yas are goin' off to the Big
Smoke, so listen up.' It felt like a private matter when Davey looked
over one shoulder, then went on: 'Don't go drinking water from taps,
don't trust the air you breathe down there, and believe nothin' ya
read in the newspapers!' The Old Man didn't look like your average
clairvoyant, but his wise advice still stands today.

One of us volunteered, 'Thanks for the leg-up, we don't know
how to—' but he cut in and hugged us both.

'She's apples,' he murmured softly, 'yas are family, family.' At
that the dear man turned, gathered in the little ones, Rae and his tin
of cash and left without looking back. No wonder I loved the Old
Man.

Money had never been our God but now we were awash with
the bloody stuff. With no crocs, no dawn runs, no dramas and air
tickets to distant parts, we had an excellent kick-start. Being so tipsy
with life, we set out to celebrate and share our good fortune, so away
we sped flat-chat like a busy dinghy, down to Adelaide.

Ironically – I say this in advance – it was the feisty pug in Les
that delighted both my family and me. That Christmas Day he came
to Mum and Dad's sporting a black eye and two skinned knuckles,
earned, he reckoned, after sorting out a dud bloke at his old suburban pub. My brothers loved his fearless style and unquestionable love
for me.

In a mini-cyclone of nothing but the best for friends and family, confidently we toasted to our love lasting a lifetime. Splashing
cash around willy-nilly like returned heroes soon left us with totally
empty pockets. You might say that was hardly astute, but what on
earth was there to worry about? We had return tickets, the *Jean
King*'s fuel tanks were topped up, and there were still plenty of fish
in the sea.

CHAPTER 14

Get Ready, Set, Go

*A*fter living the flash life of Riley, who wants to go back to the grindstone? Our holiday had been so grand that only a clever shock tactic would put us on a roll again. Back in Cairns, being skint meant nothing because there were plenty of rascal publicans picking their mark, lending ready cash to reliable players like us. With a good source of excellent weed and generous acquaintances, returning to work became a tussle of wills. This caused a few arguments, tit-for-tat things, which went glossy when the next round of drinks did their warm and fuzzy thing. As Les's daily drinking, then blundering home bollocky drunk every night with buddies in tow gathered pace, it really started getting to me.

That's not to say I wasn't part of it, but eventually the whole scene had that Cooktown deja vu feeling about it. Besides that, all the congratulations and questions about our boat and fishing life went to Les, so it was very obvious that I was viewed as a mere woman and therefore knew nothing. It was such an arrogant assumption that the men's persistent attitude stole my joy and quietly I harboured the resentment of not being recognised for what I'd contributed. Finally came the night when Micky, one of the local men, made a comment something like, 'Jeez, Les, you did a good job building the boat.' I saw red, barged right up to the tall, well-built man, tore him verbally to pieces then tried my hardest to bully him into a fight out the back of the pub. Although he fled from the place and always stayed at arm's length after that, it wasn't me who scared him, but what my man would have done if any harm had come to me.

One day after doing some business in town, I found Les at our favourite pub sitting on 'his' stool surrounded by a sea of all-too-familiar drinking faces. With a sleazy fag in his mouth, Les stared nonchalantly at me from across the bar and rudely blurted out, 'Ja get the fuckin' jobs done?'

I did the same, and snapped back: 'What do you reckon! Get me a Bundy.' I then leant on the beer-soaked Forex bar towel and slumped all too comfortably into the familiar seedy surroundings.

'You're a big girl. Get it ya self,' he sneered and casually tossed a borrowed $100 at me, and turned back to the bloke circle.

In a flash insight, I saw how hard and unconscious he had become, and how thin, nervy and way too shrill I was. Our success was turning into big-headed laziness. And I didn't like what I could see reflected from the wall mirror behind the bar either: same as the blokes I wore grimy grubby shorts, a creased T-shirt, no shoes, and my hair hung limply around a scrubby peak cap. It was 11.30 on a Tuesday morning. Alone, unsmiling, in a hollow bar, propped up with a stiff drink and a half-smoked fag, there was a fair chance I'd be standing in the same spot, in the same outfit at 11.30 that same night. Things were crook alright.

And one glance over at my lover told me that he looked the same – like crap. Bloody hell, I thought, he's lost it and I'm going there too. With one slurp the Bundy went down, and in the unspoken language of 'no more drinks thanks' I turned my glass upside-down on the bar and exited the pub door. On the other side, Les did not even look up. From having everything, we had swung to the other extreme.

The following morning, alone on the back deck, a renewed me sniffed in a deep nose of the seaweedy air, of the pungent, tangy oceanness. With a new haircut and a new attitude, everything smelled so alive: the lingering aromas of coffee, diesel, tobacco (both brown and green), fish being sizzled for breakfast, and so on it went. It was first light at the wharf, it was the best. A full-size moon still graced the daybreak sky, masts jangled and chimed, wharf ropes pinged and twanged, and the tide slip-slapped the boats awake. Squabbling seagulls decibelled out over a lousy crust of burnt toast while half-empty – or was it half-full? – tall tanned bottles of ale leant idly against posts along the wooden jetty. Balloon-necked pelicans, tubby shags, wee grey gerbers all chitter-chattered about nothing, a few dinghies – the collie kelpie of the sea – occasionally percolated past; and imperative little mud skippers born as fish but with two front legs and probably more ancient than even dragonflies, scurried bossily up and down the shiny, smooth creek slurry bank. Mud larks. All being themselves in between the higher and lower realms. Everything was at one in Smiths Creek, the daily goings-on as per normal.

When the sound of Les spitting, spluttering and letting forth with some foul-mouthed language shattered the good space, I knew he had tried to drink from an open beer can and found it had billy tea in it instead – a harmless joke I had done for a bit of fun. Irately, he tossed the can at the sea. I reminded him that we never chucked rubbish into the ocean like that, grabbed a crab pot hook, and plucked the crumpled yellow can off the ocean surface. Unperturbed, I dragged the heavy water hose down from the wharf into the wheelhouse and encouraged him to unscrew the water tank lid. Instead Les sulkily flung himself onto the side lounge and wallowed around in a fuggy hangover, moaning, 'Jesus H Christ, can't a man rest in his own home?'

Try as I did not to get caught up in our usual bad habits, as the pulsing fresh water gushed into the 200-gallon reserve below deck, his edgy tone got to me easily.

'So how come you're bouncing around like a fuckin' fairy?' he grizzled.

'Can you give me a break on the swearing, please? And by the way, you're giving the drink a fair nudge these days too, Les.' That went right over the top, so I asked if he'd go into town and pick up certain spare parts for the boat.

'Can't today. Me and the boys wanna check out some hootchy up in Kuranda and we'll be gone at least a day or two.'

Of course the green 'weed' was lovely to smoke, scientifically astounding, medically excellent, and a wonderful herb, but wheeling and dealing in the stuff was a definite no-no. Besides, the big boys, those above the law, did not appreciate little players sticking their interfering noses in, and if the cops got even a whiff of it, Les and I would be goners.

Pointing the awkward water hose into the tank and keeping it steady was child's play compared to trying to control my rising ire. 'I'm serious, Les. It's time we got outta here. Gettin' caught with hootchy means losing our fishing licence, confiscation of our boat, and loss of our livelihood!' Yes, Queensland state laws were that draconian in the 1970s and '80s, and probably still are. The final straw came when I told him I had released the live 2.5-metre long, perfect conch shell we'd had hanging in the water off the back – a thank-you gift from a fisherman for some work we'd done.

Les, his puffy face getting angrier by the sentence, spat out that there was a bloke coming down to buy it. 'Where's anyone gunna get something like that, for Christ's sake?'

'So money's ya God now, is it? Like the conch shell would look good collecting dust on some wanker's cocktail bar. I'm glad it's gone!' As we sat in the heavy stalemate atmosphere, I heard an internal echo saying, *and I'm gone too.*

In ancient times one of the conch shell's duties had been as a proclaimer, a natural sender of significant news, so maybe I should have been blowing a tune direct from the shell itself because obviously my deaf young lover was not getting the message.

Petulantly, Les humped off the boat, mumbling the old standard, 'Women! Fucked without us, goin' nowhere and knowin' nothin'.' Blokes then, they still had it coming.

Disappointed that I'd let him hit a few soft spots again, spontaneously I called his bluff. 'You better get a jump on yourself Les Coles because I'm gone first thing in the morning with or without you, so be here.'

He straightened a bit, scratched his daggy three-week-old beard and lit a fag, almost hearing what I proposed, but instead sniggered, 'Yeah right. As if.'

Obliviously my man drifted off to Kuranda in a smug smoke trail, leaving Stryder, in the half-eye-opened, one-ear-cocked position on top of the freezer. Not that she could take over the steering but the way it looked, the good dog would be my only companion on the solo trip.

Although fear was not one of my hang-ups, neither was taking up 'challenges' just for the show of it. Who needed that? It was much simpler: I just reasoned that if everyone else could do it, obviously so could I.

The die was cast and so in the early shadow of predawn, under a very full moon and the watchful morning star, alone and in command, I took the *Jean King* out through the heads. Winding north up the coast with my faithful hound, I felt liberated by my actions, and by the inexplicable fascination of the sea.

CHAPTER 15

Going to the Top

Up Cooktown way, a week or so later, it was definitely a new bloke who stepped on board the *Jean King*. Now sporting a short back-and-sides haircut, Les was clean-shaven and looked as sharp as all get-out. Stryder grinned and wagged her tail in welcome, but the freedom run had cleared my mind so I wasn't giving in that easily.

'You're a gutsy girl, my woman – that's what I love about you. Fuck, never thought ya had it in you.'

Bent intently over the wheel, studying a sea chart, I winced. 'Oh, gidday. You might've come here lookin' like a million quid, but you don't sound that good. Seriously, the swearing has to go.' And I turned my head back to the map.

Being put on the back foot like that kept the man guessing. 'Look, sorry love. I'm here and I'm yours. I apologise, really. It's you that I want. I mean it, Robyn.'

His own particular smell, the sparkling blue eyes, the style he cut, the undead love, the fine silver marlin in his hand started doing their own thing on me, charming me.

'You're a breath of fresh air, my wife from the sea. I'm no good without you.'

Seeing that the boat move had brought about a healthy correction, I stepped away from the wheel and yanked him possessively to me. 'What took you so long to get here?'

While adding the sixth marlin to my necklace, the man continued, 'One homecoming deserves another.'

Overflowing in through the wheelhouse door stepped flaming
red locks, big golden dangle hoop earrings, thick necklaces, bangles
haloing big wrists, rings of silver and gold on chubby fingers tipped
with bright orange nails; closely followed by big tits and bubbling
laughter, all of which were squeezed into a palm tree-swaying,
Hawaiian beach sunset sarong. The explosive wench herself, my best
bosom buddy, the Big Red was in town.

'Maaaate.' Like flapping brolga wings, our arms fluttered up and
down as we squawked, 'Maaaate,' and hugged like twins knitting
together again.

Rarely known as Helen, Red's external flamboyance was a reflection of her big heart. By the standards of the day, the two of us should
have been blokes but we knew better than that. Having notched up
a few antics, danced on the odd ceiling, occasionally loved until the
end of time, shed a lagoon of love tears, and plucked each other away
from danger, ours was an exceptionally trustworthy relationship.

Later that week while Les busily installed a newfangled steering box in the *Jean King*, I handed him a present. What made this
gift really special was who had made it and what it was made out
of. Boydman, he who had christened our boat, despite being permanently drunk, had miraculously managed to carve two petite turtles
out of a dugong tusk: a relic shaping a relic. I clasped the chain around
my lover's neck, saying it was part of our totem and explained that
because Boydie had been the craftsman, how doubly special the gift
was. Turtles: more ancient than any other vertebrate animal, hopefully signified longevity of our extraordinary life together; while the
dugong, documented as the fabled mermaid of the sea, was said to
bring good luck to ocean goers.

'While we're all turning over new leaves . . .' Les grinned. 'I scored
us a really good second-hand outboard motor.' That was good news
too and just meant I had a new outboard and the new main boat gearstick to master once we left port and were anchored up somewhere.

What with the water barely settled between us, Les had pulled a
very game trick out of the bag. My darling friend was between lovers
so she, like us, was keen to steer in a new direction.

All women have balls and the quicker they own up to it and start using them, the less confused the world will be. Look, the three of us had plenty of balls so new days, new dinghy – in fact the whole new chapter – had a bit of a flavour about it.

Les was as happy as a relaxing croc in the Jeannie River, perched up on the skipper's seat with coffee in hand and us girls at his feet. 'I reckon Thursday Island sounds brand new, let's get the fuck . . . sorry, let's steam outta here as soon as.'

Good things come in small packets: silver marlin trinkets, little people, instant-milk tins; and unusual events always come in threes, especially surprises – meaning there was one more unanticipated player who was yet to turn up.

The next day when Les came on with the old 'guess who I ran into over at the pub?' line, it sounded like another cock-and-bull story, so I kidded him along, 'Er, Bjelke-Petersen?' (That was the reigning premier of state parliament, and although much loved by Queenslanders, the same man was later exposed as an incorrigible, shifty shonk . . . but more on him later.)

Les protested his innocence. 'I'm not making up a story so I can go down the pub.' Up the pub, down the pub, in the pub, at the pub, every which way the pub was a leveller.

'No, the Conj has bobbed.' Neither of us had seen Conj since the day at the races when he and Handbag Harry had arranged for huge lashings of lovely money to be dropped upon us from a great height. 'I know he's a redneck but we bloody owe him, big-time.' There was no need to sell Conj to me, or even begin to remind me of the profound result he had brought our way, besides his presence onboard gladdened both of us. 'And maybe,' Les added, 'the Conj'll bring us some luck.'

Within 48 hours, Les whistled Stryder to leap from the wharf into the boat and said. 'We're off to Thursday Island and we're pullin' the pin right now. Secure the dinghy at the back and cast the ropes.'

In a throwback from 'The Night We Fucked Cooktown' days, the little settlement no doubt breathed a sigh of relief as we happy vegemites and Stryder the Seadog chucked a sharp left at the heads. Just like that, the gang of four unanimously resolved to dip on past the Normanby River, and head straight on up north into the unpredictable events yet to pass.

CHAPTER 16

Whacked by a Storm

*T*he wind, a chatty sou'easter, talked us up the torn and ragged coastline; a scenic tour of dotted atolls, islands, sand cays, bommies and ribboned reefs that rose and fell between the tides and the skies in a rhythm beyond our control. At best, we had respect, and from the boat's roof watched in wonder at the goings-on of the biggest playground on the planet – even seeing a pod of whales propel up through the water's brim, fly into the sky then slam-dunk back down into their underwater world. The warm khaki currents obviously tickled everyone's fancy, even the young bucks'.

Late afternoonish on the third day out, a trembling cold front came from the north. The threatening blackness stole away the sky and as it raced hell-bent toward us, the gooey green sea stirred and clashed. While the frigate birds stopped making wave ribbons in the sky and sped helter-skelter toward land, hurriedly we battened down everything. Stryder, already down below, probably knew about the storm before we had woken that morning.

Les's eyes and mind were glued to the weather outside. 'Pull the chart and tell me how quick we can get into whatever the next river is.'

Taking a bearing with a slide rule and making allowance for slippage, it didn't take long to get an accurate fix on the Olive River, and to figure out that we could make the mouth before the daylight went. The bad news was that the chart showed no depth marks at the entrance, plus the tide would be receding. Still, the *Jean King* bravely fought her way closer and closer toward the river haven until finally we turned due west. Much more worrying than the excruciatingly 5.5 knots flat-out that the boat was managing was the speed at which the sun seemed to be setting – because without light at the entrance we were stuffed. In the same way that the only person in charge of your life is you, the only person in charge of a boat out at sea is, without question, the captain. This rule is particularly practical when looking up the nostrils of a furious, galloping storm.

'Conj, Red, get out the back,' Les barked. 'Hang all the buffers down each side, in case we need to bring the dinghy alongside.' High stepping the random boat-rocking like tin soldiers at the ready for any command, off they both went.

Sighting the Conj's shadowy shape on the front deck and hearing Red holler from the back, 'I dunno what I'm looking out for, but I'm lookin' hard,' told us that everyone was still safely on board. Without constant communication like that, any one of us could have fallen overboard and the others have not known until it was too late. Now with every tick of the clock, darkness was stealing away clear sight of the river's entry, and the pissing-out tide was doing its best to push back the boat's passage.

While Les tried to wrestle the boat, the gushing tide and the new steering box into submission, right beside him I did the same, mentally. Such was the timing between realms that the black sky dropped over us like a theatre curtain just as the *Jean King* attempted to cross the risky, trap-shot river mouth. As the boat surfed forward, we all listened keenly for any crunching keel scrapes because coming aground would spell disaster.

Abruptly from under the keel came a moan like a wounded whale, followed by a dreaded, gruelling crunch and the *Jean King* lurched to a solid standstill.

'Rob, take the fuckin' wheel. Do as I say!' Les gave rapid-fire instructions, rushed for the stern, and bounced into the little dinghy.

Next thing, he was driving full-bore alongside the bloody wheelhouse window, using the outboard's power to hold the big boat pointed in the right direction against numerous flows of fluid which stormed in from every direction: the sky, the ocean, the river, the tide, the current – even our own 70 per cent of body water must have been bubbling with madness. Amongst it all, outside and alongside the boat there was a bug-eyed lunatic screeching incoherent instructions at me through the window.

'Full fuckin' forward, hard down portside. Reverse. Na, na, drop the fuckin' revs, straighten up, full forward, spin her hard. Don't cha know where forward gear fuckin' is?'

No! In fact, not only was there no vision up front, but I knew absolutely sweet fuck-all about moving the new gearstick this way and that, and was just spinning the wheel blindly at Les's indecipherable demands.

'What the hell are you doin'?' Suddenly he was there, tearing me away from the wheel and flinging further commands. 'Git in the dinghy, throw the fuckin' rope over the bowsprit. I'll drive this thing while you tow her over the bar.'

The squall whipped around us, the cutting rain stung our vision, the boat was in deep shit, and I knew absolutely nothing about how to drive the bloody fucking dinghy either. Why don't I knock up a few cupcakes while I'm out there too? I thought wildly.

Fully appreciating our dire straits, I went headlong into the fury and leapt like a drenched gazelle into the dinghy. With a snappy yet clear command, Les frantically wound up the other two: 'Jump over the back of the fuckin' boat pronto, and start liftin' and pushin' this mother from behind like your bloody life depends on it' – which it did. 'We're gettin' this bastard in.'

Conj stripped off his standard Queensland bloke blue singlet, pole-vaulted over the back and got ready to heave-ho the boat's arse. Willing and able, Big Red, also without hesitation, tore off her top and fearlessly bounded over into the volatile night – both were immersed up to their fannies in the swiftly running, outgoing, crocodile-infested creek. Just with their combined weight now being off-board, the big boat lightened and the stern lifted a bit. Both were as strong as oxen, and by shouldering in underneath the bow and tipping the beached boat forward, everything should have been honky-dory. This pourin' down, pissin' out, stuck and stranded, gruntin', groanin', sweatin' and swearin', this chaotic calamity was a grave emergency, a full-scale war in paradise, and when you think about it, any sensible crocs would have been long gone.

Red gripped the undercarriage, leaned full force into the boat and started moaning and pushing for dear life. Right then Conj glanced over at Big Red, dropped his jaw and his side of the boat's bow, and just stood there goggling at her. In more like a demand than a question, she turned and screamed back at him, 'What the hell are you gapin' at and why are you doin' sweet bugger-all?'

'Jeezuz, love,' the redneck bellowed back, 'I've never seen tits as big as those,' then fell into stammering, 'in all mmmm-me bbbb-born d-days!'

Well, had he asked for it! Her eyes rolled skyward, then in frustrated anger Red dropped her side of the vessel, strode regally through the crackling, hammering storm, and delivered one almighty king slap across the redneck's jaw. 'And I wouldn't have a friend like you in a hundred fffff-f'kin' years, so pull your finger out, ya dopey dick-head, and heave!' she screamed.

With that, the ultimate all-or-nothing woman strode calmly back, cupped her bit of boat butt up and proceeded to gut-bust the *Jean King* forward, alone. What a woman! A turn of the planet later with major novas still reeling round in his nincompoop head, Conj also redug his shoulder-joint hard into the boat's backside and, doing his best, pushed like all hell, trying to nudge the *Jean King* forward.

Meanwhile, by frightened necessity, I accidentally mastered forward gear in the new outboard, splurted uncontrollably up the boat's side, bashed into the prow and let the snarly wind help hold the dinghy against the boat while somehow miraculously fastening the umbilical rope between the *Jean King* and the dinghy.

Les's plastered-down cap pitted itself against the forces, his muscly, skull-tattooed arm appeared at the wheelhouse window, his eyes stalked the depths back and front, then he upped that bloody Wednesday engine to full bore. At the same time, I opened the outboard's throttle and, rearing up on a 45-degree angle, gunned into the void. While the storm spewed and sneered like a bitch not getting her way, all I could make out was the pointy front end of the gutsy little dinghy roaring off into the black nowhere. Out the back Big Red and the Redneck, down on their haunches at about chin level deep in the gushing waters, grovelled and grunted, busting to scrunch the hard and fast *Jean King* along the sandbar.

A thunderclap louder than an exploding atomic bomb nearly propelled us all to our next lifetimes. With it came a rain-burst of avalanche density and a massive, frenzied lightning bolt that violently lit up the sky and in doing so, nature illuminated our gateway to safety. 'FFFFFFFuck!!' we – possibly including Stryder – all roared as everything shuddered with sound and fury and our vessel got bounced and tugged into the much prayed-for sanctuary.

We electrified, gung-ho little sailors nervously talked until sleep put a stop to it. And the most delicate way I can summarise what we talked nonstop about regarding the unholy event is: in the name of the son of God until Kingdom come, may the laws of hazard be forever more lenient. (NB: please imagine 'fuck' in between every second word.) In other words, when 'cripes', 'golly' and 'darn' just don't cut the mustard, the F-word is an essential force, an energy which, when used correctly, also helps lift the arse-fucking-end of 5-tonne boats.

An unscheduled week passed before the early morning scheds (that is, marine radio schedules/weather reports) and the ocean gave us permission to float upon its fickle skin-scape. By then the stores, in particular meat and tobacco, had taken a proper hiding.

'Conj 'nd me are goin' over to the shore to bang another pig, love.' With that Les took down the old .303, and started on about how if the politicians weren't careful, foot and mouth disease from the feral pigs would destroy the cattle industry. He was right – even then there were thousands of the introduced species tearing up the coast, and the government needed a kick up the proverbial for neglecting to cull them.

Knowing it was one of Les's favourite rants, Red interjected, 'So when do ya wanna get to Thursday Island, next Friday, next month or next year?'

Point taken, Les cracked the gun's barrel open, carefully hooked it over one arm, pocketed two bullets and motioned Conj to follow him, saying, 'Why don't you girls get the boat shipshape?'

'So was your last slave a woman too?' I retorted. 'Red and I are going shopping and you're dropping us off.' We girls had noticed that even though the ocean was somewhat settled, it still remembered the storm and lapped angrily at the shoreline. Therefore, we deduced, all sorts of unexpected goodies must have been washed up in the waterline wake. Stryder also leapt from the top of the freezer into the dinghy. 'I reckon she understands English,' muttered Les as we all piled in.

Sure enough, the beach was littered with macramé-plaited Taiwanese glass balls lost from illegal long-liners, tangled hemp rope, delicate shells, even a superb slim-necked, two-metre tall soya sauce glass bottle, no doubt cast away by that other feral intruder – Asian pirates down from Taiwan busily raping the Australian waters, but no one cared. The real jewel was a solid plasma embryo of baby shells, each tucked into its own pouch, all being filtered and fed constantly by the flushing sea. The sun turned richly golden and was drinking at the edge of the shimmering sea before rumbling hunger called us back home. The men's short hunting trip had bagged a little sucker, which was already carved, portioned and freezing up in front of the snap fans.

No matter how many times the *Jean King* went in and out of rivers and ports, the buzz never changed so the next morning while Red rolled tea-leaf fags all round, Conj made double-shovel coffees, and Les skippered on, telling me to take the dinghy up front and lead the big boat out in case there was any more trouble. With a decent handle on just how the new outboard worked, I purtled off up front to gauge the water depth right the way through the exit channel – that is, I tied a small lead weight to a piece of string, then dropped it into the water until it hit the bottom, and measured the boat's safe departure that way.

Red couldn't resist waving back at the haven and singing out, 'Bye and thanks for all the shelter, Olive!' Despite the men's derision, we girls took no notice and reckoned the well-meant sentiment spread right up the river and into her lagoons. As the offshore gusts handled us up, away and out of sight, I could feel that the latest escapade had knitted the four of us more closely together than mangroves to the riverbank.

CHAPTER 17

A Funny Way to the Top

*W*hether it was one of Roger Miller's crooning lullabies coming from the tape deck, or the pacifying seas, or the fact that the four of us were having a ball, Les decided to keep steaming through the night. 'It's a following sea, we'll make up for lost time, and the boat's handling this like a summer breeze,' he justified. This proved to be yet another silly – in fact, almost perilous – decision. Apparently we still hadn't realised that we knew nothing whatsoever about the unchartered country upon on which we floated.

'I'm on your side,' piped up Conj, 'besides, eatin' this wild pork all the time is givin' me the jimmies.' He meant the shits, the jimmy brits, the runs, diarrhoea, dying from the rear – dying for a beer more like it, I suspected. However, Conj did have a good point, and wasn't on his own in the runs department. Even Stryder couldn't take it anymore and had voluntarily been eating only fresh fish for the past few days. We were all smokers too, so the astutely saved fag butts had been recycled until there was nothing but the good old Lipton's tea-leaves backup left. Citing what she wouldn't do for a tailor-made cigarette and a cold beer, Red was all for Les's decision too. Tying those two desires into the deal held considerable sway over our reasoning, and so saying clinched the deal.

Consequently when darkness came that night, using a mere hand-held spotlight, our motley crew took turns to be the *Jean King*'s eyes. While one steered blindly into the unlit night, the other stood on the front deck and, with faith alone, splayed the small light this way and that over the ocean blanket. And the thin, shallow ray of torchlight is a fair description of the fat chance we had of detecting any obstacle, obscuration or, for that matter, any of the infinite, jagged, uncompassionate reefs that had their own lives to live. Needless to say, mixing the sea with inebriated thinking was a collision course in the making. While we deluded lot were drunk on hope, the sea decided to give us another kick-butt lesson. Had to! The sea wanted some respect and it looked like the only way she was going to get that was by throwing us another curly one.

By then the moonless night was more than half gone, the air precise and chill, and the boat's slice-skimming sound seemed to magnify the speed at which we were knotting. You know how red cars go faster? Well, ships in the night do the same. With the two deckhands comatose in opposing wheelhouse bunks, it was Les's turn to do the blind-steering gig while I stood at the bow, devotedly waving the spotlight beam up front. Everything out there was not awake yet not asleep and the feeling made me shiver a bit so I stepped back closer to the wheelhouse door. When Stryder appeared from below and stood resolutely beside Les I was not surprised. Did the dog need to start speaking broken English before I would read the signs that something was not right? After all, most animals have more intuition in their little toes than we two-legged ones have in our 70 per cent of water.

Still listlessly waving the light about, we chatted idly. 'I've just got the bloody willies, and it feels like we're doing about 100 knots an hour,' I said.

Speaking platitudes, Les patted my arm confidently. 'I know love, that's because the breeze has died down.' Then the keel grated, scrunched and shuddered. 'Fuck me scared, what was that?' Which was about how I felt too, sick with fear and a heart hammering uncontrollably. As though the other two hadn't been asleep at all, like electrified zombies they sprang up and were lucid all in one motion. Amid the bursting chaotic bubble, the *Jean King* scraped a few feet further, then came to a screaming halt.

'Jesus wept! We're gunna hafta stop makin' a bloody habit of this,' moaned Les, clunking the boat into neutral and, plunging around out the back, issuing orders nonstop. 'I'll keep the dinghy from bashin' the shit outta the stern. Rob, get up the front and see what the damage is. Conj, get up there with her!'

Meanwhile, Red scurried through the cabin, saving any pathetic ciggie butts, clearing the floor of splayed books, skeleton-head ashtrays, spilt coffee mugs, sea charts and other such far-flung crap.

A minute later Les ran back through the cabin to the wheel, ever ready. 'What the hell have we run into *this* time?' he bawled crossly out into the dark final quarter of the night – a question which met with hearty irrepressible hilarity. 'This is no laughin' matter. Speak up, man,' Les rightfully yelled. 'Where's Rob, and what the fuck have we hit?'

'Australia, mate!' A reply which was followed by more whooping laughter and further goaded my already irate bloke – enough to make him pound furiously toward the bow, with Red right up his alley, and bluster, 'What the bloody hell does that mean?'

'Matey,' Conj guffawed, his hands shrugging out into the dark, 'we've run into Australia, and your girl's down there, standing in it.'

Not taking that for an answer, Les angrily swivelled the spotlight's ray downward over the side, almost breaking its neck. The beaming light revealed soft beige sand and me, ankle-deep in the lapping ocean. Spanning the light further afield highlighted a few shoreline trees which substantiated the fact that the *Jean King* had been driven up onto a miscellaneous beach. After everyone's uproarious laughter abated, we shoved the unscathed vessel back off Australia, shuffled blindly back into reasonably deep water, dropped the anchor, and all got some serious shut-eye.

By morning light, as it turned out, we had lucked on a much-sought prize – salubrious oysters. Even the thought of the extraordinary small morsels of zing made our mouths water. Conj perked right up and couldn't resist mentioning that, 'Oysters put lead in ya pencil too.' 'Pencil' meaning penis and 'lead' meaning Viagra-like virility – as if either of them needed more of that!

There, almost within arm's reach and just ripe to plunder, was an untouched, mountainous outcrop of wild oysters growing on a little rocky islet which stared right into our back deck. Obviously another accident our precious boat had just missed crunching into the night before too!

While we came to grips with that scary thought, Les had a flash. 'I'm thinkin' we oughta shuck a few dozen oysters, chill 'em down and sell the lot to the natives when we hit Thursday Island!' Putting some 'walking round' cash – some spending money – in our bare pockets was, we all agreed, an excellent trick.

Upon discovering that the pristine rocky outcrop had an uncountable number of tiny sweet greys called milkies (to be eaten in their purest, unaltered state only) and juicy black-lip oysters (a larger, less refined species used in cooking) the gang set about our task intently.

Had the fateful sea been kind, or was it just our destiny not to accidentally have drowned, sunk or been marooned somewhere out there? Or was the redneck Queenslander truly a lucky charm? Not that Conj cared, as yet another flawless, spine-tingling oyster slipstreamed down his throat, and he asked, 'Does it ever get dull around here?'

Nor Les, as he replied, 'Just keep fuckin' shuckin', and watch out for any hidden pearls.'

Forty-eight hours later, when the *Jean King* made her final sprint to the tip of Australia, tucked in the freezer were many dozens of the tasty little zinger oysters, hubble-bubbling away in glistening hibernation.

In what was a break from the gamy pork, along the way we sautéed, sizzled, toasted, roasted, souped and even rissoled those oysters, the result of which, as you can imagine, meant it would be years before any of us could face eating another one again.

So although one might have all that one desires, particularly in large quantities, the tide still turns the other way. Too much of a good thing can be bad.

CHAPTER 18

Thursday Island

*T*he entire human species is born with compulsions. For explorers it is the mind-set of curiosity which sends them in waves across the galaxy. In this case, it was Torres, the great Spanish navigator, who in the early 1600s first cast his eyes upon the remarkable Thursday island group between New Guinea and Australia. The migratory 'Canoes of Legend' followed from as far away as China, Malaysia, Holland and Japan, all of them forging forward through unexposed, boat-sinking reefs, deceptive smirky shoals, and rocky outcrops spread along the newly discovered sea-highway. This resulted in shipwreck relics, like abandoned, skeletal cars stranded along a desert highway, appearing all the way across the great shipping channel now called the Torres Strait.

And they had come way, way before that persistent British skipper, Sir James Cook: he who, after freshening up in what was to become Cooktown, sailed north in the good ships *Bounty* and *Pandora*, and he who cleverly took and declared the New Country (Australia) in the name of the Old Country (Britain) – that is, for back home, for Queen, King and calculating Pommies.

Imagine this: that while Captain Cook was up there taking possession in the 1770s, also skimming the bountiful waters were natives in huge, traditional, outrigger canoes. They too were sailing hundreds of miles along the Great Barrier Reef plucking crayfish, prawns, fish, pearl and *people* as they went. Then, in what was famously declared as 'The Coming of the Light', missionary Christians soon followed Cook, and by setting their stamp firmly amongst the same native people, the cannibalism ceased.

Thursday Island was the official hub of this island group and was appropriately known as the Port of Pearls. By the 1950s, and at its zenith, the harbour was crammed with luggers, trawlers and cargo boats – up to 200 boats or more at any given time. Imagine, too, all the businesses being in royal flush mode, profits rolling in big-time, and the joint jumping with able seamen, opportunists and dodgy characters. While pearls, crayfish, prawns, oysters and bêche-de-mer proved to be sterling cash crops, the biggest money-spinner of the lot was a small reef shell, the trochus shell, which was the main ingredient used in the global pearl button industry. All was extremely well until, in the early 1960s, some bright boffin replaced the button shell with plastic and the trochus boom crashed around Thursday Island's bare feet; a momentous crash from which it never fully recovered. Still, between the shonks, the smart pearl growers, the gold-diggers, the uncontrollable fishermen, the waffling yachties and the sharp local publicans, the island did manage to keep on rocking.

Legend had it that if you were meant to go to Thursday Island, their traditional music would enchant you there. At the sight of the sultry lushness oozing from the 20-odd tropical isles, perhaps it was Thursday Island's famous singing Mills Sisters' lullabies that mesmerised us subliminally. Certainly, my mind boggled as our brave boat, surfing on the crest of an unruly southerly, shot out of Albany Passage and splurged straight into the Torres Strait.

Neither the eighteenth-century crumbling ruins of Somerset House nor the cleverly concealed Japanese pearl farm snuggled in Newcastle Bay affected our intent when, maxing out at 5.5 knots, we turned left at the pointy bit and plundered into the Arafura Sea, a sea whose treacherous currents were moving at the speed of summer lightning. Famous for 'rippin' in' and 'pissin' out' (to use the vernacular) at anywhere between 8 and 12 knots, the underlying Torres Strait current did a tango jerk combination all of its own and shoved the fishing fleet tied up at the wharf and those out at anchor around it, as though they were still in very heavy swells out on the open ocean. Perversely, that same cantankerous sea was perpetually stunning: either vivid frog-green or intense sapphire royal-blue, or even at its deep khaki-green crappiest, the colour was so astonishing I never stopped ogling it.

Finally at the wharf we said just two words to anyone who happened to be there: 'Fresh oysters.' The island grapevine did the rest, the natives came, and we loose-bowelled, delirious-for-a-drink fishmongers sold the total oyster consignment as quickly as the planned tequila shots were going to slip down my throat once the silver coins crossed our open palms. Stryder was also glad to cock a leg here and there, and particularly liked being able to sprint past the 10-metre mark and not fall into the sea.

We were at the tip of Australia, on top of the world, and within no less than about four hours at the nearest pub quaffing a few too many cleansing ales. Splashing around cash like there was plenty more where that came from, the four of us sat perched up at the bar and talked a large amount of happy-go-lucky nonsense to the bemused, laidback locals. Dogs in pubs were part of the furniture back then, and so eventually our dog came, sat beside us and kept watch.

Some time way after dark that first night, still waffling incoherently, we fumbled drunkenly back down the wharf. Stryder corralled us onto the wharf and safely up to the post where our home should have been waiting. Yet look as we might, the boat – in fact, the whole wharf fleet, and even the ocean, was nowhere in sight, gone from the horizon. Being blind drunk didn't mean our eyesight had gone too, but in the darkness of the unfamiliar wharf, our *Jean King* was not there.

By then Stryder must have been pining to get away from it all and stretch out on top of pliable, warm sand underneath the generous palms. So for the first time ever, in an attempt to show me what had happened, the clever dog nipped my ankle. Looking down to see who had bitten me, I distinguished, four or five metres below the pier, all the boats propped up on the sea's sandy floor. It looked like the fleet was holding a private corroboree. Apparently, a big tide had 'pissed' way, way out to somewhere and until it 'pissed' way back in, there was no home to go to. A sobering thought.

While all of us tried to get our shickered brains around that, accidentally Big Red stuck her neck into the darkness. 'Am I off the planet, or can I see a funny-lookin' basket wrapped around the end of a big pole?' Well, yes she was and yes she could – only correctly speaking Red had found a lookout box (technically a crow's nest) which sat on the very top of a mast of a trawler sunk down below with all the other boats.

Amongst the jibes, Les nuzzled into her bigness, 'Luvie, your blood's worth bottlin'.' Then making sure we were watching, he laughed a bit madly and stepped off the wharf's edge into the night. From the darkness Les explained about the 'funny basket', and said, 'Come over, s'perfect place to get a bird's-eye view of the town till mornin'.' He was right – it was a perfect way to while away the time, all nestled together with close friends, getting stoned, on top of the harbour at the tip of Australia, chatting away the remaining darkness.

Hours later, feeling as illuminated as the rising purply pink golden sun, some bloke's voice came up from below: 'Hey, who the hell's that up there?' Below, the owner of the crow's nest, the mast and the rest of the boat, grinned up at us. 'Thought I was hearin' things for a while there. There's coffee down here when ya ready.' He hawked the traditional wad of vibrant phlegm into the sea, farted, made some personal adjustments in the undies department, and got back to his own business.

I said something loosely hippie like, 'Oh wow man, it's been so wonderful I don't wanna go down.'

Big Red, on the other hand, took one glimpse over the side, let out a shrill-girl 'fuck' scream, staggered backwards, and gripped the side of the little box tightly. 'Dunno about not wanting to go down, but without help, I'm not gunna make it.' It's always easy getting on, but getting off is another thing.

'Red, just close your eyes and follow me, and if you slip I'll be there for you.' While my stoned statement set them all laughing about, my next comment got them down the ladder in seconds. 'Besides, I need a fag and a coffee. Catch ya.'

All things that go down must come up, and vice versa, so while we were going down, the tide was coming up, and by the time it was fully in we had the lowdown on the island from Pedro, skipper of the trawler, upon whose crow's nest we had temporarily resided. Mind, you would've been a mug not to have lent an ear, with him having fished in that country since he was a 13-year-old kid. He was also a well-built, punchy young bloke, so it looked like he could fight like a 450-kilo marlin on a 10-kilo line.

Much later that day, after a big meal of homemade rissoles, greens and gravy, Les and I sat contentedly on the balcony of one of the pubs, watching the old-gold dark chocolate people who surrounded us. 'Feels like we're in another country,' he observed, 'and the natives look nothin' like Aboriginals. And there were more dinghies on the sand last night than there are flies in the outback, but today, where have all the dinghies gone?'

Being an extensive reader, I knew. 'The difference is these people are Melanesian, not the same genetic lineage as the Aboriginals from just across the bay.'

'You're different alright, Robbie, but that doesn't explain where 30-odd dinghies have disappeared to.'

With the other two out on the town, it was just the two of us. Being alone again was a great novelty, so I told him I knew the answer to that too, but unless I was on a promise that night, I wouldn't tell.

He slipped a possessive arm over my shoulder. 'Oh, we'll be making love tonight, even if you don't tell me, woman of the sea.'

The fact was that some Social Security Department fellows from Cairns were up snooping around so all the New Guineans illegally playing funny buggers with our social service system had done a runner. 'What's more, in the 1950s and '60s, before container ships put paid to thousands of wharf jobs, this port was busier 'n Pitt Street on a Friday arvo. This was one of Australia's greatest frontiers.'

My man teased me some more, called for the bill and pointed across the dazzling bay to the other islands that made up the group: Horn Island on the left and Prince of Wales on the right. 'How 'bout we mosey on over tomorrow and poke around a bit?'

What we didn't know was even more interesting – that Horn Island, although not nearly as populated, hid a flourishing gold mine, and that as the official Thursday Island aerodrome, planes daily ran up and down its spine; that Prince of Wales was heavily wooded, home to wild deer; and that the aphrodisiacal bêche-de-mer cavorted within reach, just below the shore's edge. Yes, while every wet season brought with it oceans of rain, enough to sink ships and totally deluge the fabled speckle of islands, and the dripping, muggy humidity drove everyone to the drink, with certainty this was 'the' sunny place for shady people.

They say there is a reason for everything, even in difficult times, and looking back I'm glad fate took us to such an extraordinary destination. You might have been to Paris, you might have been to Rome or Berlin, or you might have even visited the once forbidden land of Tibet, but right here on our doorstep is an extraordinary piece of country you will see nowhere else: the alluring Thursday Island.

CHAPTER 19

Workin' Girl

*A*s it turned out, I was not to have my wicked way with Les that night. Unfortunately the nippy tide was friskier than us, so when he leapt from solid wharf to the skittish boat, my man came a cropper. The pain of a sprained ankle far outweighed the allure of making love, yet he had no difficulty reaching the boozer every afternoon thereafter. So, I didn't get laid, he got laid up, and the boat and our lives got held up in port. And it didn't take long before our 'oyster' cash had gone down the gurgler too, and it was time to dredge up my pre-Les office skills.

Judging by the Thursday Island newspaper job advertisements, local government departments were crying out for steno-secretary-type people, and the pay looked half reasonable, so onto my unaccustomed feet went the emergency 'good' shoes, and into the one set of 'good' clothes I slid. With earrings, a dash of red lippy and a ping to the curls, it was off to the end of Fig Tree Road, to the late eighteenth-century customs building and the various government departments housed within.

There, I sat with the main man, Richard Butler, and told him not only about my former skills, but about where and how I lived, and why. This fascinated him, and I was reminded of men I often spied through the wheelhouse window, those who came to the wharf every weekend and mentally tumbled back to visit yesterday's dreams, about themselves and their unrequited longing to live on the sea.

When he asked if I would stay more than three months, provided I passed the shorthand and typing test, I thought: the job's mine, no sweat. 'Yes, my word is my bond.' This was something Les and I both used to say, and mostly it was true although in this case I'm not so sure.

Nearly tubby and definitely middle-aged, Richard didn't look at all unhappy with the exam results, yet, his stalling tactics were confusing. 'Miss Catchlove, how 'bout you pop in and see me same time tomorrow morning? I just have to mention this to several people.'

The Queen's portrait hung from the wall behind his desk and her false grin made it look like her undies were way too tight. Noting that, I leant across the professionally untidy mahogany desk and did my best to win the job. 'Really? Mr Butler, I'm a quick learner. Just teach me the once, then leave me to it.'

Taken aback, he stumbled on: 'Catchlove? An old English name, isn't it?'

With a direct blood lineage that mixes aristocratic rascals like three-times prime minister of England, Lord Pelham, with the poor but wild coal-mining folk of Cornwall, there was only one answer: 'I'm a lower–upper crust cross really. Can't have one without the other, the goodies and the baddies, the richer and the poorer.' Our laughter helped relax his stiff upper lip. I knew he liked me so I insisted he call me Robyn and asked him straight up if I had failed the test.

'On the contrary, the results are excellent, and right now we definitely need someone who works without supervision.' Both his hands lay flat on the polished desk. 'It's . . . I, er, I just need to have a chat with someone first.' Mr Butler stood, led the way back out into the light of day and saw Stryder emerge from underneath a huge fig tree. I could feel him watching as together we strolled back into the frangipani-scented mainstream, in amongst the polished bronze people who were also casually trying to put some shape into their day.

Next day, same outfit, same time, same me: bright and chirpy, same bloke, but not so chirpy. The man squirmed and coughed – as you would with a collared white shirt that looked to be buttoned directly onto his choking Adam's apple. 'Well, Miss Catchlove, er, the reason . . . er, I'm in a very difficult position.'

Something had clearly changed overnight. Who cared if the job was downgraded, I was good value, and would just work my way up anyway. 'I'm over 21, Mr Butler, and please, my name's Robyn.'

'Call me Richard, Robyn. Actually, it's been a while since we had anyone as qualified. God knows we could use you, but, but . . .' He fidgeted with his Donald Duck tie.

Still thinking there was a chance, I encouraged him: 'Just spit it out, Richard.'

He blushed, coughed some more and leaned closer. 'I've had a word but they just won't let me employ you. The local policy is that if a native Thursday Islander can qualify for the job then they must be employed before you.' There was little doubt he was being apologetic. 'Unfortunately, it means we just keep training someone new every three months, who then leaves, so we never get any real work done. I'm truly sorry. We just didn't expect anyone of your calibre to apply.' His hands shrugged and he flushed again, 'Believe me, I tried my damned hardest to get you in here.'

Good bloke, nice try, poncy place, right outcome, I decided, and right away began scheming my next move. At the building's entrance I held his hand warmly. 'I get it now. It's just blackfella discrimination in reverse. I'm a woman, so I already know how it feels.' It was one of those eloquent seconds in life when one human being gives another some hard-earned empathy. 'Don't feel badly, it's just my turn to make up for some of the wrongs we lot have already perpetrated out there in the world. You're a beaut bloke, Richard. Be seeing you.'

He let me hug him and plant a kiss on his cheek, then responded, 'Be delighted to have a sherry with you one day, young lady.'

The way he spoke to Stryder as he patted her, like one real being to another, sold me on him too. Wistfully, the brightened man watched us go.

Overhead, a masked booby, a bird the size of a small superman, glided across the day: a 65-million-year-old pterodactyl shadow. 'Next,' I thought, and purposefully set out for the Esplanade and the Grand Hotel: a place which was not just an impressive example of colonial architecture, it also commanded 'the grandest absolute beachfront' panorama of the bay. Part of the new plan was that working from there, in addition to its splendiferous view, I could catch sight of our spiffy little home bobbing boldly amongst large trawlers, pearling luggers and other willing vessels as they tried to massage the cantankerous cross-currents into reasonableness.

Being already spruced up in my one-and-only set of interview garb helped, so I tripped up the broad wooden staircase to the manager's office, read the painted name title on the partly open door and knocked. 'G'day. Mr O'Reilly?'

His frazzled face lifted and his desk moaned underneath the jungle of chaotic paperwork. 'Patrick. Take a pew and be quick, love, the yard arm's coming up.' He meant for me to take a seat and tell him what I want in a hurry because the clock said it was time for his first drink. A cheeky A4 page pinned to the wall rustled as the door closed – it read:

> *I, me and meself have an arrangement with the staff.*
> *They don't talk to us, and we don't talk to them,*
> *Signed The Boss, Chief Bottle Washer and The Pay Clerk*

Nice ditty. At least here I could probably get on with the job without any shenanigans. The signs were all good, especially the Eureka Stockade Flag propped behind him, and the crookedly tilted picture of the Queen who'd already had a skuzzy handlebar moustache and a crumbling fag charcoaled onto her grimacing lips.

'What can I be doin' for ya then?' A lilting kindness still lingered in the publican's voice but it looked like two blue-grey, wrinkled hammocks had taken permanent residence below his roadmap eyes.

Straight up, I liked Paddy and the room, with its late-night card-shuffling feel, so I grasped the man's shaky, blue-veined hand and told him I was there about 'the' job.

His crumpled shirt was open at the throat, both sleeves puffed up over thin silver armbands, and a tailor-made cigarette casually poked out from behind one ear. 'What job would that be then?' His eyes laughed so this time I knew this job was mine.

Comically, my hands danced around a bit. 'Whatever one it is you need someone doing properly.'

The wheezing, rusty cackle of his laughter was another sign of his high-rolling, boozy, gambling life, of naughty women and difficult wives. Looked like Paddy had been a good catch in his day, but by now gave the air of being loner with a bit of a chip on his shoulder.

I started straight away and did bar work, counted the till cash, handed Paddy the cream off the top, and made him feel happy. Naturally, Stryder loved him and was fed better than any dog on the prowl. It felt special when she and I walked to the Grand early every morning, via the string of poinciana trees with their wind-whirling sweet-scented blossom, then along the white sandy beach which looked like it was wearing a polka dot bikini due to the multitude of New Guinean dinghies that had returned to its shores.

CHAPTER 20

Goodbye to Our Crew

*L*ike all true wanderers, home for seamen was a place you were
going to, or coming from, never a place in which you stayed
long. That's why pubs filled in the gap nicely. As the good, the bad,
the mad, the brave and the lonely men and women of the seas came
and went, we drank ourselves inside out and talked up a storm of
stories we knew to be true. This built mateships that extended across
oceans. The subject left unspoken, yet silently acknowledged, was
that oft-times there was only a slim line between life and death. That
was why we all smoked fags without fear, made love with no strings
attached and, when the joke was funny enough, all laughed raucously in public without embarrassment.

To paraphrase a line from one of the era's popular songs, those
certainly were the days, my friends, and none of us thought they'd
ever end. We weren't shallow, it was just that in the late '70s there
was nothing of huge worldly significance about which to worry – so
unlike today. Not so for me, because even though it didn't take long
for Les's ankle to mend, just as quickly his old pub habits had kicked
back in. He wasn't on his own in this department – it was simply the
way the world went around up at the top: that is, from about eleven-
ish in the morning, the rest of the daily activities went hand in hand
with alcohol.

Les and I were living everyday life like most passionate young couples do: trying to balance liking each other with trying to bend each other more to our own will – in short, doing the ordinary life not very cleverly. And my boss was a secret marshmallow, who fussed over me a bit, which was more than what my man had been doing lately. Paddy must have sensed something was not right by forever making sure I went home with a kilo of fresh bacon, or a tray of top-quality steak. As a result, a good deal of my wages went into the bank. Our fortunes had turned somewhat but with me socialising less and him drinking more, our arguments were getting painfully pointed.

In between that, even though Conj was spending more time with Pedro, the skipper of the crow's nest trawler, and Red was being romanced by a good-looking yachtie, both drifted in and out of our boat too. The five of us plus Stryder were onboard chatting over the top of each other one day when the ABC radio blared out a newsflash red alert signal which sounded like an ambulance of premonition, and was immediately followed by the newscaster's smooth voice:

In news just to hand, the Australian Navy has apprehended a 120-foot Taiwanese long-liner caught fishing illegally off the north-eastern shelf of Queensland. The eight crew members are currently being questioned by the Federal Police. It is likely they will be charged . . .

Before the announcer could finish, Pedro slammed his coffee on the table and spat out, '*Likely!* I'll give 'em *likely!* The cops ought to be arrestin' the rich long-liner owners – they know the score! Not the poor, innocent little bastards indentured to run the bloody shoddy, badly equipped, crap junks!' He was up and running. 'Shhhh!' we all went in chorus.

The long-liner is being towed into the Thursday Island harbour where it will be quarantined until further notice. And in further news, now . . . despite heavy protests, Queensland Premier Bjelke-Petersen remained firm in his resolve to demolish the national heritage build-ing situated directly opposite Parliament House . . .

One of us (not one of the Queenslanders) got on the pedestal by calling the premier a shonky bastard. I mean, the long-liner arrest was good news but using political bullying in an attempt to demolish the historical, early century building had been a very unpopular, ongoing scandal for some time. As we all hunched around the radio, Premier Bjelke-Petersen's shifty, condescending voice started shuffling the cards using his well-known pretend stutter:

Well now you, you, you, why don't you look after reporting, girlie, and and I'll, I'll run the state of Queensland. People down south don't realise that this is the best state in Australia . . .

For once, the premier was right about both: at that time, no one knew just how much the corrupt premier and his cronies were doing for corporate property developers, international robber barons and the underground crims, and Queensland beauty was yet to be recognised by the rest of Australia or the world.

In exasperation, Les flicked off the radio. 'Fuckin' dunces. The Taiwanese have only been fishin' our waters for a few years, so it's about bloody time. Trouble is the chinks [Asians] take every bloody type of fish, 24 hours a day, so the fishin' grounds don't stand a chance.' Amongst fishermen, this had been a passionate sore point for years. He recalled the time we had bailed up a long-liner on the east coast a couple of years earlier only to be told by the authorities that they didn't have the planes or men to do anything about it. Les finished by bitterly denouncing 'the pricks down in Canberra' that didn't give a stuff.

This inflamed the situation so much that Pedro sucked his cigarette with such force that his cheeks met and kissed inside. 'The yella peril are comin'! I'm warnin' ya, this is only the beginning. Next thing the damned pests will be coming down here by the drove. There'll be boatloads of the bastards. I'll give ya fucking nips [Asians], alright, I'm tellin' ya we wanna nip it in the bud. Just wait and see if I'm not right.' Pedro didn't belong to an academic think tank, but his spin on the matter was accurate to a tee.

Conj, the thoroughbred redneck, came in like a spinner, agreeing he was up to his neck with it all too. 'We might not know the national anthem off by heart, mate, but by the devil we know that low lot in Canberra are as crooked as bent lamp posts.' Queenslanders loved their backstabbing Bjelke-Petersen so Canberra always copped the blame. 'And what about them dirty commie Ruskies [Russians] . . . ?'

With them both waving the red flag around angrily, to lighten the mood I did a mock Chinese accent, and with hands clasped in prayer mode, bowed and said, 'Ah so, honourable gentlemen, old Chinese proverb: when Asia sneeze, no need to have convulsion.' Thursday Island library, like all the coastal libraries I joined, was a great resource – but I should have been studying myself with a bit more intelligence too.

Queenslanders, being different, always had issues with any person outside their own border, especially 'bloody southerners'. Indeed, many harboured an intense desire to secede from the nation, and both issues were never far from their thoughts. They also had elephant memories and were still particularly dirty on the filthy Huns (Germans), the cunning Japs (Japanese), the dirty Dagoes (Italians), all the Second World War enemies, and the crafty Slant Eyes (the Chinese) – in fact basically everyone not born in Queen's England and their own Queen's Land. This was a big part of the reason why they had earned the title of 'best rednecks in Australia'.

Back in our wheelhouse, Pedro's face screwed up like a demented sunstroked coolie as he strangled the fag to death and angrily flicked it into the ocean. 'Fuck, I've got to get outta port. All I need's a half-reasonable deckie.' This brought us back into the real world. Since Conj had loved his first taste on the high seas and was champing at the bit to get back out amongst it, that he and Pedro agreed to go off to sea together was a match struck in redneck heaven.

The two men were only gone a couple of weeks when Red pulled up anchor too. The yachtie who had been courting her must have been doing a good job because she looked like a glowing wedding reception. 'He's asked me to sail up to Darwin, then over to Asia with him,' she crooned contentedly, 'and if he's half as good on the sea as he is in bed, we'll be sailing till the cows come home – horizontally!' Red squawked. Like all switched-on women do, we swapped some essential intimate details like length, technique, method, timespan, tongue, touch etc.

I was not surprised she was leaving. 'I haven't seen you for a couple of weeks, so I figured you were practising!' Having a quiet Bundy onboard the *Jean King*, we two were looking over at the yacht and yachtie in question. I knew she was good at sea, and it sounded like he was just the goods. The yachtie was a lucky man, and I was so glad for my beloved friend.

Stopping just short of declaring that he could be 'the' one Red twittered, 'The tide's right, so we're off tonight.'

Life was there for the taking, not for the thinking, so we cooed and clucked like doves, swapped radio call signs and I dropped a delicate silver marlin into her palm. 'Good sailing, my friend, and remember: never drop your guard.'

As she rowed off into Episode 3999, Red made one last comment: 'A bit of not so nice advice – after all, that's what real mates are for. I need to tell you that Les is losin' it again, big-time.'

Her honest prod was a healthy thing and pulled my senses into gear. It was weeks since Les had bothered to meet me after work, and I suspected that he was using borrowed money again. Certainly the man spent more time at the pub's front bar than anywhere else. The next night, after work, I saw that the day's alcohol intake had once again made Les sloppy, so I cornered him, and lashed out at him with my sharp, sober tongue.

'But that's where I'm gunna get any work that's going,' Les protested blurrily.

'Well, I hate seeing you like this,' I told him and insisted he get the blokes inside our wheelhouse to leave pronto. 'I start work at six in the morning!'

He acquiesced but grumbled away in bed, and just to make sure his male pride got its way, snored at a deafening level all night long.

CHAPTER 21

My Goddess of the Sea

Not surprisingly, the outdoor sea life had turned my curly locks from auburn to startling blonde. Even when things were tough at home, to the outside world I was sun-kissed, slim, fit, and always smiling. This made the natives curious, to say the least. The lovely, woolly rascal kids, the squizzy little people with deep brown skin that had been put through a jeweller's tumbler for maximum shine, would run up, touch me, then run away, filling the air with squeals of laughter, while the tall giraffe-kneed men with wiry ringlet hair and mud-pool, ever-seeking eyes looked on with other things in mind; more privately, from a distance.

The broad black sisters with crinkled curls dotted in mother-of-pearl clasps were another ball game altogether. Often more hefty than the men, the thick-necked women displayed missing teeth and nostrils that flared like racehorses in training. Theirs was a different kind of envy. Plus they were always trying to stand right over me with their belly-sized black-brown eyes bugging right into my face. They didn't hesitate to come on with the fierce warrior caper: 'Hey, you, you got your man, don't come near ours. You white woman, you lucky. You fuck off.'

I understood. Real or not, the threats didn't get under my skin. I'd just smile, keep on moving, saying, 'No worries, sister, no problems.' Hell, those men weren't my cup of tea anyway; moreover, the one who should have been walking beside me was wild enough.

There is no such thing as 'common' sense. If there was, everyone would have it and no one would have to keep wondering why no one ever uses it. Really, such sense is a rare thing and when, as a woman, you hang around the tough edge of life, you have to make sure not to create unnecessary dramas. Aware that Les and I travelled together in 'ride 'em cowboy' country, I was always acutely conscious of being totally responsible for my own actions, and made sure not to create problems that my man might have to defend. This was no-man's-land and there were no rules when it came to fighting. In parts less influenced by civilised notions, you never knew who was running from the state, from the feds or even from international law. Some hid from broken families, plenty had outstanding alimony bills, most came with ingrained, bitter alcohol abuse and raging gambling habits; all outsiders, foreigners, strangers, and strange pieces of work: the alias tribe.

Whatever the case, from place to place the culture changed entirely, cultures we two knew nothing about, even amongst the white, er, pink people. I mean, what is it with this black–white thing? Is everybody colourblind? Looks to me like whitefellas are pinkish-red or at worst a very pale sickly jade, blackfellas are light brown to heavy bronze, and yellow fellas are beigy-tan or a pasty mustard-ivory. Hell, the only true white person I ever saw was in Cooktown: an albino Aboriginal with white hair and pink eyes. Wheels within wheels, cultures within cultures: the world is just one festering yoghurt.

Within days the Taiwanese long-liner was towed into port. At night, watching the foreign-shaped ship's silhouette lamenting in the bay was strange, like seeing a beautiful cut-out Chinese lantern hanging suspended, alone, in a gum tree.

'At least she's simple to pick in the dark.' Les cut the dinghy engine and slid up to the long-liner's southern side so the town's lights wouldn't show us up. We tied the dinghy to a chunky hemp buffer, shoved a torch into a back pocket, and scrambled up the side like show-off circus monkeys. Soft back deck lights gave just enough all-round vision to help us scuttle barefoot over the boat's deck. Inside, the aroma of sandalwood incense still wafted in the air. Below deck, fat Taiwanese cockroaches shared the cramped sleeping quarters with skimpy bamboo mats, the mattresses for the workers. 'Jesus H, the beds are so close together, they must all have to roll over at the same time.' Nearly as big as the captured little fishermen, the black crunchy cockies scuttled for cover. Above, in the wheelhouse, Les stared admiringly at the shiny white navigation equipment and let out a low whistle. 'Fuck me lucky, this is the latest sat-nav and worth thousands.' Not knowing what I was looking at, simply seeing the complexity of the equipment told me the same story. 'The nips might live below like sardines pressed in a tin, but it's nothin' but the best up here.' Upstairs, downstairs; haves, have nots – an unspoken rule which applied the world over, apparently even in Taiwan. Lovingly, he touched the big screens and spoke another truth: 'Pig's arse they *accidentally* strayed into Australian territory. By Christ, I'd like to snaffle this gear, but it looks heavier and bigger than the *Jean King*.' Les's desire for the sat-nav got the better of him, and he gripped his dick with such earnest, I thought he was going to strangle it.

Meanwhile, I had also found a most unexpected treasure, so I took him below again and shone the torch on the object of my desire: a beautiful female Buddha painted on a 2 metre x 1 metre glass pane.

Just then the chugging sound of a dinghy getting closer made Les peek through the circular porthole. Realising the porthole was made from quality stainless steel caused him to whistle low again – at least this object of desire was one he could actually extract easily enough. Already on my knees, unscrewing the painting from the wall, I begged, 'This might be a federal offence, but she needs rescuing. Please, Lesy, I'll help you "acquire" the porthole, if you help me save the Buddha.'

None the wiser, the anonymous dinghy putted past on the northern side and kept going.

'See ya later alligator,' Les muttered to it, and started extracting the entire glass porthole. 'Listen, my woman, I know I've been off the rails a bit lately, but I love you with all me life, and I'm gunna win you over again.'

I let the screwdriver drop softly to the floor and rose to him. In the filtered town lights, while Kwan Yin, the Buddha of the Ocean, looked on, I gripped that half-unscrewed porthole while my old man did what he did best. Fiercely, he whispered, 'I hope everyone in the galaxy's as lucky as I am.' Unknowingly my man had made a proper Buddhist offering on behalf of all the living beings in the world.

As karma would have it, the circular porthole was easily transported back to our dinghy and actually ended up in the centre of our bedroom's top hatch. And even though the precious pane of glass required a more skilful approach to get it safely down the side of the long-liner, from then on the Buddha took up residency in our wheelhouse.

She had a Mona Lisa kind of smile and was surrounded by blue sky, auspicious birds and good luck signs. Emanating as a Sea Goddess, the female Buddha had been painted standing barefoot on pink sea sponges, and floating upon a mirror-calm green ocean. Holding an urn in one hand, She poured endless water into the ocean, thereby controlling the weather, and by inference the lives of those who sailed upon it. Curiously, it had been painted in reverse from the back of the glass pane, so the sublime Buddha was looking out through the clear glass, seeing time and space in all directions. Every home should have a goddess.

Yes, stealing is wrong, especially a Buddha, yet I thought I was saving her. That's not an excuse or justification; it is how I clearly remember thinking of it at the time. As for the porthole, we lazily justified that by deciding that the illegal ship's rich owner didn't deserve any better.

That lovemaking and our rascally jaunt to the long-liner had been just the thing to get Les refocused, so while I worked at putting cash in the bank, he drove the boat into the shoreline sand, chocked up her sides with wooden planks, scraped off the tenacious, crusty barnacles, painted the underbelly with red lead, and slid her back off. His work meant that the debarnacled *Jean King* gunned from the 5.5 knot previous top up to a 6 knots best. The whole time, Stryder, relaxed on the silvery sand and, just like she'd been a harbour master in a previous life, kept her eye on us and on the constant comings and goings of the luminous bay.

A dream, a vision, maybe it was an unconscious wish, I'm not sure, but sometimes it even felt like a solid memory, whatever that is. Certainly, about then I experienced an ephemeral yet vivid mental picture which, with inner beckoning, would easily come and linger. There was no background, just three kids: two sandy-haired, freckled-faced white kids, and another, just a toddler. The tallest one had an arm around the other, and they stood smiling: the littlie, brown-skinned, less visible and slightly behind, had arms reaching forward. This dream lived in my heart, in the place of secrets. Having kids would have been good but I hadn't been thinking about it much, so why such a vision hung around I cannot say – additionally, as I knew only too well, the eggs of life did not hatch in my womb.

CHAPTER 22

Surprise, Surprise

*B*y six every evening on any night, the Grand Hotel rocked. Everyone in there was laughing too loud, getting the lowdown on any action, moving a bit of this and that here and there – whoosh, whoosh. Even the flies used the loud chatter for breeze. On Friday nights, the noise levels went up a treble or two, plus the traditional savoury bickies, cubed cheese chunks and steaming bubbles of orangey-pink baby savs accompanied by great farts of red sauce appeared erratically along the bar. The bar offerings weren't the only things being erratic. The boutique bar garden of tropical splendour would be packed tighter than beer bottles in a carton; the Friday night swill-a-thon was on, no worries.

Whenever one of us couldn't find the other, the Stryder whistle worked a treat so I picked up on Les straight away in the middle of what looked like a comedy minstrel show in early rehearsals. Seeing him deep in a smoky gully of smarmy white and black faces I felt a squeezy belly pang: he looked like he'd had a few, and it was still early. Les heartily threw out both arms, snatch-lifted me above the crowd, stormed out to the balcony and plonked me on the solid timber rail. I got off on his demonstrative love and let the anxiety transform and leap to my pulsing heart. He was so strong, so man.

'Mate, you want the good news first, or the good news second?' As he turned my face toward the lonely Taiwanese interloper, his

137

beery breath danced up my nostrils. 'I've just come back from Richard's office. We've got the contract!' So at least he hadn't been at the pub all day. 'See, told ya I'd get work from being in the pub at the right time.'

Leaning back, his protective arms wrapped around my waist, I was all ears.

'Just happened to be up here earlier, seein' someone' – yeah, right! – 'when he waltzed in askin' for you. Paddy introduced him to me, and we've done a deal on the long-liner. And there's a swag of good cash in it.'

As the door for us to get back out to sea swung open, excitedly he explained how the blokes (they weren't bastards anymore) in Canberra had decided to remove and destroy all the foodstuffs on the Taiwanese long-liner. Apparently all the illegal shark fin had been confiscated as evidence, but there were still a few hundred hessian sacks of rice, flour, sugar and noodles on board.

When I mentioned that we hadn't seen many sacks of food in the gantry, Les jumped the gun. 'Listen, quit makin' sense. The government never did and never will make any sense, let alone have a clue about what's really goin' on out here in the real world. So who gives a rat's arse? We pay taxes, so let's get a quick bite of the big cherry. They owe us.' So, one minute we were sticking it up them, next minute we were having a lend of them. As 'they' say, business doesn't have sides and bullshit baffles brains.

Insisting that we celebrate, he stood me back on my feet and explained that the signed and sealed contract promised to pay $100 per destroyed bag.

Later that night, by some accidental courtesy from the pub pandemonium, Les and I were invited to a locals-only Thursday Island party, our first and only one. Barefoot, we strolled to Tamwoy, the shanty side of town, where finding the right fibro pole house was easy, what with a mob of sassy little people straggling around us all the way.

Everyone at the party – except for us – was like the night itself, black and shiny. With faces that had been carved from a prehistoric quarry of another millennium, most of the Islander population was there, and they only come in two sizes: big ones and whoppers.

Christmas-tree fairy lights shone from flowering frangipanis while the banana trees clumped together on one side like Aussie blokes standing around a keg. Four long wooden planks supported by levelled-off tree stumps stretched out into a rough square, making a dance floor of the middle ground. Ambrosial flower aromas merged into the fire's smoke and a few bright, chubby kids stared and giggled with the excitement of the white strangers from somewhere-else-land being in their midst.

With frizzy hair speckled by shells and coral, three wizened toothless women rested against one of the big trees, appearing to have melded into the trunk. Each had one spindly leg slung over a deliberately dented, empty 5-gallon kerosene tin. Each was drumming a tin with a handpicked tree branch. In the background, invisible rowdy crickets, who had probably been tuning in to this genre for a few hundred centuries, played the vibes section. Together, the trio beat out a centuries-old rhythm, and like weaving witches, crooned the legends of their people. No question that they'd earned their Gods' permission to evoke historical psalms; this was something special.

Fine dust rose from the ground and swayed amongst the shadowy figures who, through dance, were interpreting the intricate story songs. Damp humidity became visible as their dark brown faces shone into the black night. When one of the mean-looking, original earth men invited me to join in the song enactment circle, I did. With Les close at hand, and being careful not to offend our newfound friends, I set myself free and let the man lead me further into each movement. We danced rowing off in a dugout canoe, off diving into the ocean, off spearing fish, we danced into the story unfolding. All hearts pump red blood, and all breathe the same air – somewhere we are all one. Lazy smoke spiralled across the midnight stars while the soft aroma of damper rising suggested that all was well. Tirelessly, the old ones kept rhythmically painting the song, and watching. Even the language sounded ancient, but how were we new chums to know?

Inspired by the night's magic, the smouldering fire flared up and licked out into the dark. Just then the large ferocious black women started circling in on me: they were jealous, and about to call my bluff, I could feel it. Without raising any alarm, I saw Les squatting in the outer circle and caught his eye then nodded casual-like back toward the town centre. 'Got that' his eye winked in reply, so I turned to my dancing partner and asked, 'S'cuse me, mind showing me where the bathroom is?'

I liked that the black man led the way: being escorted to the house by one of their own meant the women dared not touch me – yet. When we reached the kitchen stairs, he pointed. 'It's up there and to ya left, love,' and I heard Les ask loud and clear, 'Where can a man take a leak around here?'

At the top of the stairs, I glanced down to see the irate women glaring up at me, and watched as Les slipped round the dark pathway, headed for the road. At the top of the stairs, I stepped inside, locked the back door behind me and then ducked quick-smart through the tidy fibro house. Mum had always taught me to have good manners in other people's homes so whoever I flitted past on the way through were politely offered, 'Bye now, and thanks very much for having us.'

Soon by Les's side, holding his hand and laughing, we ran along the dirt avenue of palms and mango trees, past the hospital and down to the shore. On one side the ocean quietly sang the tide up the beach and on the other, 100-year-old strangler figs stood on permanent guard.

Obviously, as a couple, we had good times and bad times – and let me say that when they were bad, we argued tooth and nail, too hard in fact. But the possibility of my man being violent again never crossed my mind. Right then, the strength of our love was intact – or so I innocently thought.

CHAPTER 23

The Seed of Change

*R*ichard, I knew, had done us more than one good turn by giving us that government contract, so the next day I strolled into his office and handed over the best piece of sea art work I think I ever made: three grinning tiger shark jaws set inside each other. Framed in silvery beechwood and black coral and with row upon row of macabre teeth peeling back from the perpetual gummy grins, the piece was a stunner. The surprise really snuck up on him. 'It's such an irony, dear girl. The sharks in Canberra paying you to do Taiwanese dirty work. How many paper tigers is that?' 'Paper tiger' was a popular phrase used by western commentators to describe the shallow political jargon that Asian politicians spouted when defending themselves. I got the joke, Richard loved the gift, and we christened the long-liner appropriately. Par for the course, the bureaucratic process for us to go ahead on the Asian junk took longer than the Taiwanese had taken to sail down to Australia, fill up with illegal fish and return home. We had already been in port for way too long, and so our excitement soon became edgy impatience. A few weeks later, back on the *Jean King*, Les reflected this by sounding off once again: 'Jesus H, Canberra must have their heads up their arses. Richard reckons it'll be a while before we can get on board the bloody long-liner. They wanna pull their fuckin' fingers out before the damned thing gets ransacked.'

Didn't men at the western gates of rebirth receive a reasonable vocabulary? His constant swearing and negative attitude grated on my mind. 'Look who's calling the kettle black. Lighten up, all the paperwork's been signed,' I said patiently, and asked him to come out to the back deck. I had a surprise, something I had been dying to give him – sitting on top of the freezer was a brand new single-side band radio. With the Taiwanese contract and money in the bank, the timing seemed right so I'd secretly ordered it up from Sydney. This was a major purchase we had talked about over the years, so Les should have been thrilled – still, I couldn't pick it really, but he seemed only strangely happy about it. And when I volunteered to help him install it, he brushed me aside moodily. 'Nah, just get the toolbox and leave it to me.'

How can you tell about blokes, I thought. Maybe living in each other's pockets was a bit much so I let it go and got out of his way. Upon returning from the library a few hours later, the prized box was in, the dash lights were showing power, and everything seemed cool, so I grabbed the new mike and hammed it up a bit – 'That's a roger, roger, rubber ducky, this here's a convoy up, big buddy, romeo romeo, wherefore art thou . . .' – and began adjusting the dials as per the manual's instructions.

His stern, humourless reaction severed the fun. 'Jezuz Robyn, next thing you'll be wantin' to be the fuckin' skipper!' He swiped the booklet away. 'You're already pullin' the anchor, steamin' the boat, helpin' with the engine repairs. Be told, touch nothing! This has got nothin' to do with you.' Les snatched the mike from me and stepped defensively closer to the new communication tool. 'You're takin' a man's job, now get back!'

Being the late 1970s, it would take another 20 or more years before women were accepted, let alone appreciated, on fishing vessels. So all through those years, 99.9 per cent of the time I was the only one out there. Men weren't difficult to offend then – after all, they'd had it their way for a few centuries – and women like me were part of the new breed. So much of it was hyped-up nonsensical bravado, as it was anywhere in the world for women at that time. The way I saw it, the female and male brain were equally as functional in technical situations like this, so of course such deeply ingrained bloke attitudes always came as a real shock. And underneath their bullying and prideful manner, I'm sure they felt threatened by us. To give you some idea, men even used to say that women were asking to be hit when they spoke out. In truth, when abusive words failed to win their arrogant standover tactics, men resorted to violence – that always worked.

I knew my rights and, thanks to Dad, was passionate about that, so I snatched the mike back and quipped, 'You can't be serious.'

'Fuck off! Don't touch it, Miss Goody-two-shoes. Only I handle the radio!'

It was so preposterous, so unbelievably stupid, that I misread his mood and let my own frustration rear up too. Insulted, I snarled back, 'So, we're 25 miles out to sea, you become seriously ill, or knock yourself unconscious – if I don't do it first – and I can't dial a few silly, silent knobs to get to bloody help. That's real clever.' This argument had been on the cards for a while, so I laid them on the table fairly clearly. 'It's mine as much as it's yours. I'll learn to use the radio just like you will, and I'll learn anything else I fucking well like, so fuck off yourself.'

With that, he punched me right in the eye. It was a proper wallop too. The unexpectedness and the force behind it threw me back on the lounge, and the sharp, intense pain snapped closed my left eye. Oh shit, oh no, the unexpected had happened again. Everything down the drain. This time, instead of staying and trying to understand the action, Les stormed past me, leapt onto the wharf, and fled. I took flight too, escape flight. As I eased the *Jean King* away from the wharf, intuitively Stryder appeared and leapt onto the deck. Quivering in shock, I steamed across the bay and dropped anchor. Then I entered the pain. Not just the blinding pain of the punch or my tender eyeball damage; no, it was the deep and shocking pain of my love being bashed up, of that most tender, trusting depth being violated. Even if the traditional drums of Mer had been calling, I would not have heard as I surrendered to the cold and lonely void. Metres away on Horn Island's shore, alone and untroubled, a simple, wrought-iron shack, its windows cut out by tin snips, watched. All I wanted was to enter the hut forever, to not be seen.

Feeling degraded, helpless and sad, I submerged into humiliation, and spiralled around in it, like a toy boat does when the bath plug has been pulled. The brutish clout quickly turned into a large gangrenous-green coloured bruise, which visually lent a hand to my shame. Every time we argued, and now with being hit again, a raw, agonising sensation grew deeper roots. With one eye bunged up, my mouth snapped shut and my heart closed down. I folded in on myself.

Sadness, a devious disguise for anger, is the mask women tend to select. Men, on the other hand, do not suffer sadness enough and go straight to anger. Chi, energy, the spirit, the soul, call it what you will, but know that it has no colour, creed, gender or attitude, so it is the emotions we adopt that carry and deposit the seeds of karma.

Two days later he came. Ashamed, not teary but deeply mortified, the man, with head bowed, spread his only ace before me. 'Believe me, woman, it's not you, it's me. If this means us splitting up, so be it. Just believe that I can only love you all my life. You are my ocean' – promises, promises, same, same, he went on – 'so help me God, as long as I live I'll never ever do that again.' It's that specific promise that keeps the battered battered. And in this case, I was a battered fish out of my depth.

Unfairly, I was a casualty of his casualties, of the mother and father's casualty, of that mother and father's previous casualties, vastly going backwards in time. This issue, then, was not a love question, this was a behavioural habit, and although one of us was in error, we were both injured by it. Over and above that, I wanted so badly to believe in him, to believe in our love and life, that I used bad mental arithmetic and found enough excuses: of his boyhood, the cruelty, the abandonment, being sent to reformatory – right up to his well-intentioned promises to never do it again – and instead of protecting my body, my soul and mind, I stayed on. You see, when women don't experience childbirth, sometimes a kind of abandoned recklessness manifests, a more blinded quality prevails.

You might even consider that being so captured by the great beauty of the lands we travelled through and the adventurous expectations of my twenties, I could not let go? That has a certain ring of truth to it too, but either way, subconsciously, my trust in Les was wary and so the seed of change had begun growing within.

Oh, and one more thing: not understanding the reason for being hit is no excuse. As I have said before, women have good brains and using them is not a new invention.

CHAPTER 24

Bramble Cay

*B*ecause the shock tactics of tragedy brought peace, the wounding served some purpose. We three lay low and sat on the anchor, just off Horn Island where the clear healthy waters rocked to and fro and the spunky breeze whipped around us. With no word on the 'Paper Tiger' contract, to breathe new life into our adventure we decided to follow the wake of the famous sixteenth-century 'Canoes of Legend' and go further north, up in between the dotted Torres Strait Islands and New Guinea – to the most spectacular, untouched, open ocean Spanish mackerel fishing grounds in Australia.

In preparation, we set up wooden outriggers which, at the release of a rope, swung down from each side into the briny sea, plus ran one line from the centre of the back deck. Each line consisted of strong nylon rope stretched from the rigging to a thick rubber loop which swivelled into Bowden cable, into piano wire, into ganged hooks, onto which we attached good-sized gar: gar Les caught by simply casting a net into the plentiful sea from our back deck. I was so keen to be in the thick of everything, Les even set up a foot tiller which meant that the two of us could be out there pulling fish at the same time. He also re-gased the freezer and serviced the engines, and me, every night. The *Jean King* gang were geared up to do some serious trawling.

The spot we had in mind was called Bramble Cay, and it was

exactly that – no more than a tiny low circle of sand: on a chart, the very smallest dot in the middle of nowhere. Despite such apparent insignificance, officially this spot delineates the specific outer perimeter of the Great Southern Land's northern-most international border, the very tip of the top. And although on a clear day you can actually see New Guinea from Bramble Cay, us finding the tiny spot way out there was not a simple task. Satellite navigation would never find its expensive way to the *Jean King*, so the only course-plotting tools at our command were a compass, sea charts, tide logarithms, a sharp pencil, half-smart minds and superficial mental calculation. Therefore the only safe way for us to be sure to reach our destination was to use night darkness as a device to pick up on the Cay's flashing light beacon. Risky, even dangerous, but that had never ever stopped us from getting anywhere before. This decision also meant that once again we would have to blindly skim across the unknown for some distance in the night. With that in mind, timing was crucial. Even though the weather was a bit rough, the next morning we departed the Port of Pearls on the right outgoing tide and cut nor'–nor'east up into the Great North East Channel and swept along the famous seaway which still reverberated with the great explorers from the previous five centuries.

Skirting the bommies and reefs, that day the *Jean King* bounced past the swaying mirage of coral-reef encircled palm-freckled islands and sandy cays. Rows of village huts peeped out from behind the curling waves which foamed and bubbled across shallow coral outcrops. Beauty may be in the eye of the beholder, but even blind Freddy could not have missed the dazzling scene that lay before us. Onwards our plucky little vessel pressed through the choppy seas, right up the gizzard between Sue and Moa Islands, then Yam and Coconut, on we wound to the starboard of Yorke and past Darnley. Somewhere thereabouts, our anchor willingly hooked into a solid trunk of reef tree. All we needed now was to borrow some darkness, so with our boat facing into the wind and riding the sea like a bucking bronco, we gobbled a truckies' snack and hit the sack for some open shut-eye.

All sailors swear, and they will also swear that even when fast asleep they can still hear any unusual noises and feel any surreptitious changes instantaneously. For example, if a boat starts wallowing side to side instead of bobbing up and down from front to back, indicating the anchor has pulled loose, the sailor will be startled awake and, while mumbling profanities, leap to the call. Also, there are only two types of people: those who work inside and those who work outside. One cannot do the other. Being the second type, with all the years of living the outside life, our sundial minds had taken away any need of alarm clocks, however in this important instance of definitely needing darkness to see the light, we did set one. Alarm clocks, they're so rude, don't you think? Anyway, its shocking ring made us swing straight into action like wind-up dolls. Stryder was already prowling around, so Les nudged the boat forward over the anchor, and I, at the prow, reefed up the heavy pick like Popeye the Sailorwoman.

Les, I and Stryder knew all about blind steaming – that it was a deadly serious activity, so the first hours of skating over the ocean's unreliable surface went by without any unnecessary words spoken, all the time extending our listening out past the prow, and down below the keel, feeling, sensing every vibe, all the time silently praying that our untrained chart work was on the goods.

Beauty is only skin-deep and somewhere, everywhere, anywhere underneath the vast moving expanse upon which we travelled, just below the sea's thin skin lay a minefield jam-packed with unexposed reefs, jagged, mountainous rocks taller than Mount Everest, and any number of unaccounted-for sunken shipwrecks. The fine line between buoyant life and rapturous death was ever present.

With great relief, Les saw the flashing beacon first, pointing and yelling about it. All those hours, with me at the helm, he had not moved an inch but had stood up the front, scouring the horizon like an eagle on the wing. Just as the three of us gladly dropped our guard, right then, like some exotic bird, a big blue swordfish flew out of the water. 'Quick, drop the outriggers, I'm baitin' up!' my man cried. As he sprang around the boat, I realised that he really was an amazing man, and that I would go on the sea, go anywhere, with this man; that once again, my love for him was back.

Like our beginner's luck at the races, incredibly, before our startled eyes, mackerel started jumping out of the water too! From below the horizon the sun's rays hinted that the fiery sun orb was coming up on high beam, and from the vibrant Ocean of Eden, luscious fish like juice-dripping peaches fell onto our hooks. So, with foot-on-tiller, and consistently pulling decent-sized mackerel, we lit out for Bramble Cay.

All the creatures out there were as busy as the pre-Christmas crowds at Sydney's fresh fish market. Not to mention the airways. Winged silhouettes waved overhead, booby birds landed and took off from the bottle-green sea, fat shags and more, all fervently worked amongst the big fish schools. Everyone should be so lucky! The scene was so sensual that the stunning, shimmering sun looked like it was going down instead of rolling our way. Coming up on the cay, I experienced my own smallness in the grand scheme of nature's earth. We were such miniscule beings amongst the ocean of wanderers, slicing across a drop of water on a tiny, tiny planet of just one immeasurable galaxy; not even a dot on a spinning globe.

'Fuck me forever!' Les nattered on enthusiastically. Neither of us had ever seen anything like this before, and better still my man was more alive in spirit than he'd been since the Jeannie River. 'What kind of incredible country is this?'

The glistening, iridescent coats of the twenty or so landed mackerel had started to dim by the time we swaggered tipsily into Bramble Cay's sheltered anchorage. While my heart once again welcomed back the man I knew lived inside of Les, busily I slit throats, bleeding the fish to keep them as fresh as. Intuitively I also knew that this ceased the fish's death pain, an understanding which came from the deeply embedded compassion Mum and Dad gave us as young kids.

In testament to the romantic long-gone days of explorers and pirates, our entry was marked by a fabulous shipwreck relic: like the rib of an ancient mariner, and taller than the *Jean King* herself, a massive age-old anchor stood plunged into the eastern-most shoulder of Bramble Cay. It had been on first watch since the fifteenth or sixteenth century, and stood as an unmistakable warning sign for those who were yet to come – including us some 500 years later.

'Break out the cigars,' my spunky bloke insisted. 'Let's suck in some fumes and have a few laughs. Nothing like a gut-wrenchin' cough to get ya going. Look, even Strydy's grinnin'.' Rare are dogs who deliberately lift both ends of their mouth and smile – this is not about one breed or another; this is purely the karmic makeup of certain dogs. In Stryder's case, she usually grinned at little people, at those she hadn't seen for a while, and always at people she particularly liked.

Flabbergasted with delight and wonder, neither of us gave a fish tit whether this was beginner's luck or a rite of passage – life as we wanted it had begun to flower again. To make completely sure that we wallowed deeply in the luxurious moment, we tore off our clothes, lit up a couple of thickish cheroots, ripped the lids off a couple of beers and talked like we knew something about the place.

I love words and yet there are none to do true justice to the waters of Bramble Cay, which were so crystal clean, so so exquisitely pristine, so royal blue, and in such extraordinary environmental balance. And the Spanish mackerel, with its lovely long body and pure white flesh, was one sweet succulent fish. Infamously known as the head of the razor gang, this species has a very pointy snout splayed with sharp teeth more vicious than a dozen virgin Gillette razors in the hands of your average punk bully. This was a different kind of fishing, and there was a first-hand lesson flying our way about being careless: indeed, airborne mackerel had been known to slice off a few noses, slash a cheek or two and, in one case, had even blinded a fisherman. Averaging no less than 9 to 12 kilos per fish, a normal session hauled in 25 to 35. Mackerel ran on certain tides and specific quarters of the magnetic moon. Sometimes there were none: believe me, fishermen have droughts too.

Bramble Cay dwelled in a pond built in heaven, but her abundance was only good from mid-year until the northerlies started blowing around November–December. Then the mackerel went on annual leave. Les reckoned they 'fucked off', which was probably more technically accurate.

At about the same time, from the southern waters, crayfish do the most extraordinary walkabout. In a line miles long from head to tail, crusted crayfish hit the sea bed and claw hypnotically all the way up the Great North East Channel, right on past Bramble Cay and into the Gulf of Papua. There they make multitudes of baby eggs which the female carries protectively on her soft underbelly, whereupon the whole cray fraternity turns around, and, in the warm current, walks back south.

For mackerel, being caught is dramatic indeed: the gang-hooked gar 'swims' just under the surface, acting as though it's still alive. At a distance further below and yet not too far away, a lurking shark's beady eyes follow the play. When the mackerel surges past the stalking shark and takes the gammon gar, and thereby gets snared by the big gang hook, the loitering shark rushes in for his own kill by clamping onto the mackerel's tail, juddering up its torso, tearing it in half, and is gone. That is, if the fisherman who's pulling in the mackerel doesn't reef in the fish faster than what's coming in from behind. All of this takes place within about 60 snazzy seconds. From the pretend gar, to the hunter shark to the hunted mackerel, the life of a fish ain't that good.

Thinking we knew it all, in the beginning both of us fished as naked as the day we were born – each with a smouldering cigar clenched to one side of the mouth and one or the other's foot on the tiller directing the boat's pathway. Birthday suits and cigars only! Sounds spunky but five-minute wonders are like that. Didn't take long for us to get the message when, at one session, suddenly the central rubber ring twanged and snapped taut. A fish was hooked. Team talk being vital, I yelled, 'I'm on!' reached out, and pulled the loaded line over. Puffing away on that side-saddle cigar, I double-wrapped the nicely tensioned line and was in general enjoying the scene when from somewhere up front my mackerel burst out of the water at about my head height – the full-size fish was sky high and heading our way. It was a bit like me flying to escape the croc in the Normanby – the mackerel was flying to escape death by shark. He had big problems, and so did I! With the fish now in the sky, the well-tensioned fishing line went loose and haywire, giving me sweet bugger-all leverage to keep the whole motion under control.

From busily baiting up his line, Les glanced up to see one of the razor gang barrelling toward me at a great rate of knots. 'Work with what you've got,' he roared, footing the tiller to make the boat work in with the strategy, 'and watch yer fuckin' face!' With all 12 kilograms of pointy fish unpredictably spiralling my way, did he think I was bloody blind or that I was just a woman?

I spat the clenched cigar out and kept reaching into the sky, double-wrapping, catching and throwing chunks of flaky, squibbled line on the deck. Just as the fish flew in on the off side, from thin air I pulled the piano wire in short, ducked, twisted backwards and threw the fish down onto the deck, released the hook, tossed the line overboard and slit the fish's throat.

'Woman of the sea that was beautiful to watch!' Les speared his cigar into the briny, stepped across the fish carcasses between us and got into some nice kissing – and who doesn't love a good pash?

'Wait, what's this?' His concerned scowl was directed at my elbow, from which bright red blood was flowing faster than an automatic bilge pump would in an emergency. The razor gang had sliced my elbow apart and I hadn't felt a thing. That pashing's got a lot going for it! In a parody of an AC/DC song, we used to joke that it was 'a long way to the shop if you wanna sausage roll'. The hospital was a long way away too, and with the three jagged down-to-the-bone gashes and a few slashed bloodlines, my elbow could have done with some professional attention. Instead, Les washed my arm thoroughly in beer, stuck the slashes up in butterfly bandaid style, we had a laugh and went back to work. I do like very obvious lessons in life, and there was no mistaking this one – particularly imagining other possible places on our naked bodies that the fish teeth could rip into, so donning clothes again didn't warrant a second's hesitation.

Occasionally Pedro and Conj came through and took a load of fish back to Thursday Island for us. With the two boats tied side by side, we'd chain-gang 150 or so frozen-solid fish packs over into their freezer so we could keep reefing fish in and earn more money. As always, Conj seemed to bring a touch of Midas our way.

When the topic of Richard's progress on the 'Paper Tiger' contract was raised, Pedro cranked up straight away. 'Yellow bludgers oughta be shot. The only kind of mandarin in bloody Australia should be the fucking fruit.'

The tedious ranting never led anywhere so I turned to mimicking again. 'Honourable Canberra says, White Australia Policy means no yellow bellies.' If you think we haven't progressed, just imagine having an official government policy today with a name like that – and believe me, the White Australia Policy meant exactly what it said: part of the legal criteria for permanent residency was that only white-skinned humans could apply.

Fishing was my world too, so I did walk the walk and talk the talk, but the men, being more single-minded than painted crays on their annual underwater walkfest, always talked to each other, and managed to blatantly ignore the woman in their midst. And the standard chat drill went drinking, fishing, fish, boats, engines, who got drunk and hit who at the bar, engines, boats, fish, fishing, drinking: so while it looked like I was dreaming to hope for anything different, sticking up for what you know to be true also starts with yourself.

Like most men of the day, Les did not encourage my entertainment either – this included reading two or three fiction/non-fiction books at once, trying to teach myself cryptic crosswords (something I'm still trying to accomplish), and penning poems and short stories. In idle moments I even created my own political party, wrote up the policies and called it 'The Guy Fawkes Party': a name which came from one Guy Fawkes, an English radical who had famously been called 'the only man to enter parliament with honest intent', because he had tried to blow it up. Now that's a policy that would get a few marginal votes.

I was tired of the one-track minds and privately craved intelligent conversation, stimulation, a chance to share, to debate my own independent ideas about the world, the universe and everything. And actions like phoning interstate were still considered a very big deal, something only to be done on birthdays, or in the case of grave illness, birth or death. So besides having the same fish rave to the same fishermen every day, our only other connection to the outside was via ABC radio, and with the freezer engine gunning it 24 hours a day, hearing that was difficult too – all of which made connection with the outside world rare indeed. You see what was going on 'outside' barely affected us at all, so it was only me who actually missed the mental stimulation.

Still, it was fun to have people around at all, and there the strapping, sun-blasted men were, hunched over a chart, gulping buckets of nasty instant coffee, sketching engine repair pictures, and imparting important nautical information. Then Les's bare arm, with its 'Faith, Hope and Charity' tattoo, moved around the smoky scrum pointing out the exact location of gigantic black rocks, rocks that were the apex of ocean mountains, rocks which, being uncharted, posed a life-and-death threat to ships and those living on them.

The fresh young mackerel cutlets sizzling in the cast-iron pan were ready so I tossed diced raw onion into the creamy mashed spuds and opened the last of the tinned beetroot, asparagus and sweet corn. After the blokes had demolished enough to feed the entire Thursday Island population, Conj winked at me. 'Woman, this food's not fit for the King, he's not good enough.' Someone recognising the effort and giving it acknowledgement felt good.

I handed over a list of much-needed stores, enough cash to buy themselves a drink or two and begged them not to forget to bring out any old *Financial Review*s and *Bulletin*s Paddy always saved for me. Seeing the men's eyes roll upwards quizzically at the strange request was not unusual – in this respect a lot of the time I felt like a stranger in a strange land. Les, thinking he was kidding around with me, couldn't have explained the way men thought much better when he said, 'What do you want all those high-falutin' books for anyway? Ya can't read about what we've got out here, no way.' He never really understood why constant information about what was happening on the big world's stage was essential to keep my private world alert any more than I could imagine a world without books.

Before they left, the lads pumped a welcome 100 gallons of fresh water into our tanks. 'That will give us a bit more ballast, so she'll sit back down in the water better,' I commented, hoping that if I kept on talking this way, maybe one day one of them would include me in such conversations.

Left with replenished water supplies and a freezer to fill, Les and I would stay out in the wild. This part I loved – both being so tough and untamed, standing side by side on the back deck of our saucy little boat, sliding up and down five-metre ocean swells, reading the seabird activity, checking the cloud movement and revelling in the taste of the salty, buffeting wind. While we pulled fish, passionate currents of love, desire and strong personality individually pulled us this way and that too. Occasionally, overawed by it all, momentarily we'd reach out and hesitantly touch each other. It seemed that we and the bank account were on the mend.

CHAPTER 25

Last Days at the Cay

*T*he grand curves of the huge fifteenth-century anchor reflected the nickname we gave it: the Cutlass. Working over the constant swirls of bait, often mackerel schooled up on the Cutlass's inside shoulder. Birds knew it too and came in over the top and successfully dive-bombed for their bit, filling the sky with different tones of chatter like an avant-garde piece of music that Phillip Glass might write.

And when the monsoons started, the storm deluge that rushed down the Fly River from the central New Guinean highlands spewed gigantic volumes of barrelling rain out to sea, along with massive chunks of flotsam and jetsam which steamrolled straight past Bramble Cay. Being directly north of us, the Fly, with a mouth that sprawled out over 25 kilometres wide, made its own distinctive sea channel which was easily visible.

Not 20 minutes from the cay was our favourite patch – Black Rocks. This was a perfect name for the massive chunky shards of undersea mountain tops jutting out of nowhere. The place always beckoned us, and sometimes we dreamed of building a glass castle above it.

Chugging around the Rocks in circles, I was head down baiting up when Les yelled for me to turn the boat to the starboard. Without looking up, I yelled back for him to do it himself.

'Don't argue, woman, turn the fuckin' boat!' he roared.

'Yeah, righto. Don't get ya nightie in a knot!' I hollered.

His next scream almost blasted me off the deck: 'Turn it starboard *right now*!'

I leaned heavily on the tiller, the boat heaved sharply, and merely inches away – actually within touching distance, like a fully loaded 30-tonne gas tanker hammering down a superhighway, a humongous, unstoppable tree trunk from the Fly River speared right on past. We both gasped with shock, and I for one, turned white. It was least 20 metres long and 10 metres wide at the base – the tree trunk was *bigger* than the *Jean King,* and just the thought of the near-miss collision made me shudder with death-fear.

Silently, Les pulled in the lines, spun the boat north and broodily headed back to the cay. 'Robyn, you have to obey.' His looming intent was fierce. 'There can only be one skipper on the boat. Do ya get it?' He was madder than the furious Cooktown storm, and finally yelled so loudly that even the dead fish on deck could hear. He had every right. 'If you don't get this into your thick skull, we can't be on the sea!' Wrong, wrong, wrong he went on, and I knew he was right, right, right. 'Otherwise woman, we'll be sunk. I'm deadly serious here. We'll go down, and there ain't no fuckin' taxies out here.'

Instinctively, I knew that this was safe anger, that I would not be hit for this. And anyway, that was never going to happen again, right?

Just in case anyone needed help or was lost at sea, the single-side band radio stayed switched on 24/7 – it was the lifebuoy line.

The radio didn't sound too switched on when we heard 'Calling the Shceean King, cuminyabastards, come in.' It sounded drunk. 'This'z the Oyzter fuckin' shucker, calling the-never-a-dull-dayers.'

The fits of manic laughter that followed must have made the entire eastern seaboard grin.

That was followed by the Conj confession: 'Geezzz, I love youse two, mate.' When Aussie men's minds get drunk, their hearts and mouths get balls, poor things. As we listened to Conj and Pedro wrestle for the mike, the only light in our boat was coming from the moon's full exuberance and the Milky Way – it was like being able to pinch yourself in a lucid dream.

'Mate, we've got a shitload, I mean a shipload of stuff, and, Les, mate, Richo wantz an answer.' There was a silly joke only he and Conj got, before Pedro managed another coherent moment. 'Heseez Canberra wans the job done asssoonas.'

In between their drunken waffle, Les managed to remind them not to fall overboard that night and to tell Richard we were on our way.

Before leaving the cay, I unhooked the dinghy off the separate anchorage, whistled up Stryder and went on-shore. It was time to say goodbye to the turtles. For who knows how long, each winter, hundreds of gentle greenback turtle mums laboured up onto the sand cay, then laid and buried their eggs just below the sand, near the spruce grass – right in amongst the booby birds' nests who were conveniently nursing freshly laid eggs too. Obviously after a long swim, the living fossils cleverly sought out just the right place to lay the family jewels and evidently the cay had been both creatures' local habitat for an eon or two.

When you think about it, the greenback turtle came from the Mei-olania Platyceps group of the Pleistocene era, that is, 60 million years ago, so Aboriginals are mere newcomers, and whitefellas, while certainly much younger again, on the whole, appear to have less wisdom than any other of the Earth's species around them. And this was where the interfering began. Unfortunately for the wondrous four-legged shell creatures, two or three Australian scientists had, for a few years, been coming to stay at the cay imagining they could help humanity by learning the hows, whys and wherefores of turtle etiquette. However, that year they could not determine just why it was that the turtle numbers had suddenly dropped off, or why those laying eggs were laying fewer. Funny that. What the scientists called 'study', we fishermen called inter-fucking-fering. Alright, alright, fishermen were cantankerous and loved disagreeing with authority – it was part of our job description. However, in this specific case, we were right. To me they were just more 'white coats' who should have been in straitjackets. 'G'day, Harold. What are you doin' to my girls this morning?' The scientist rolled his eyes like the men had at my request for books but this one saw me as that menace of a woman, that uneducated, fisherwoman going on about the same-old again. The half-baked squirt looked

bloody ridiculous and I contemplated tearing the daffodil-yellow plastic hardhat helmet with its inbuilt torch off his silly, smirking head.
Looking through the predawn greyness toward the centre of the sand
cay, Derrick, the other white coat, also in the complete boffin ensemble, was plunking a big mother turtle upside-down on the steel slab of
a weighing machine. Upside-down! I mean, the turtle was in labour! I
began thinking about how to get Derrick by the balls, turn him upside-
down and shake the shit out of him.

'Clearly you've never given birth,' I growled at Harold, 'otherwise it would be screamingly obvious to just leave these extraordinary
beings well alone, you know, untouched, at least until they've laid
their babies.' Angry at their meddling, I came at him and his mate
like a knuckle-duster, challenging like a man, ready for a blue. It
must have scared them a bit.

'Why would they ever wanna leave their eggs near the likes of
you two who haven't got a shit show in hell of ever understanding
them?' Talk about an unattractive gorilla wielding a blunt axe, I
squatted close to the turtle he was attempting to pick up, and said,
'Sorry beautiful creature, we just don't understand. When you get
the chance, run for it, and tell the rest of 'em out there not to bother
coming back here for a while.'

Meanwhile, Derrick was stonily measuring the mother in labour
every which way – pulling, scratching and peering at her for any
imperfections or diseases. 'Dear oh dear, there ought to be a law
against it,' I muttered despairingly.

As I approached, he squinted nervously and semi-prepared to
scarper. 'I'd like to be doin' that to you, Derrick. Be gentle. Please,
think of her as your mother.'

He sneered quietly, turned away and continued the prodding
examination. Besides king-hitting the pretentious man to kingdom
come, the impotency of the situation hurt physically.

At the side of the nervous scientists, Stryder and I sat until
daylight, until the turtles came no more. Having no religion other
than the sea, and feeling moved to pray, an old ubiquitous Christian
imprint came in handy. It went something like: 'Please forgive us, for
we know not what we do, oh you who come from the inner peace of
the universe.'

Suddenly, like an illustrious peacock's tail in full display, dawn glistened across the ocean. It was time to be gone, it was time to re-enter the land of people. With hot coffee on the dash, a freezer-load of fish and a playful, following sea, that day we weighed anchor.

We were flourishing, and as pleased as punch about it. As the trusty little Bedford chugged us slowly back to port, Les came from behind and rubbed against me. 'Keep that bearing, my wife of the sea.' He nuzzled my ear and tore off the loose sarong I was wearing. I felt his bite, his tongue lapping and his shaft slide tightly into my velvetness. The fit was still exceptional. While I stood at the helm and kept us right on course, Les swam in the sea of pleasure.

Best to say, we fought, fucked, fished and felt fulfilled. Every-thing else around us did the same. It is easy for descriptions about life and nature to fall short on the job. A photo is still and can only tell of a brief moment in time, so usually we stumble around penning a few words or attempt to write a dinky poem, dabbling on lamely in the midst of Earth's astounding gallery. Our life at Bramble Cay held a real oneness that I don't think we ever experienced again or can be expressed fully.

We would never see the Cay again.

CHAPTER 26

Richard's Joss Stick

*F*or what it's worth, the splendid Spanish mackerel brought no money to speak off. Sure, $1 a kilo felt like a good price; that's because it was a chunk of real cash slapped in the hand. And we did kick back and savour our accomplishment once the fish had been off-loaded, the money banked, and the four-stroke freezer engine had stopped droning away in our ear day after day. But the short and curlies of it all was that fishermen were at the arse-end of the business scale, the middlemen laughed all the way to the bank, and the customer always hoped that the fish they were eating really was the species they had just paid a motza for. So the truth of it lay much nearer to the bone.

After months of frolicking on the high seas, being back amongst the people dipped in black ink was a bit like asking Salvador Dali to think straight. When I was a little tacker, Dad used to entertain us with hand-projected bird silhouettes. When his hands flapped like wings, the black birds would come alive on the white wall. Thursday Island felt like that, like an illusory land.

Perched on the Grand's balcony, sipping, puffing cigars and chatting the afternoon sun away, four of us sat around the lunch table which, in a comical gesture compliments of Richard, was graced with vase of pink tiger lilies. Wrapped in satisfied grins, Havana cheroots and blasts of Hennessy, we were exchanging opinions on the ill-fated, government-assisted, $5 million turtle project.

'Anyway,' Les explained, 'the turtle boat keeps sinkin' because the bilge outlets are too low, so we did 'em a favour t'other night and borrowed the steering wheel. It'll save them leavin' port and drownin' out at sea, and save a few turtles to boot.'

Generous laughter rippled around us as I tipped another decent glug of the top-shelf liquor into each wine glass. 'That mackerel we just ate, I caught, gut and gilled it myself, Paddy. And there's one in the pub freezer for you too, Richie, so keep your eye on it.' Feeling so lucky to be surrounded by friends, I leant over and planted a kiss on the bachelor's cheek.

'Talking of keeping your eye on things,' cut in Richard, gazing out at the Taiwanese long-liner sitting to the lea of the most unin-habited part of the island, 'Canberra's getting jittery about the job. When can you deliver?'

Strangely, our friend never spoke about his past nor his fam-ily, but the private school accent and the diamond-splattered Rolex were a giveaway: by no means ostentatious, he just had that certain air, that throwaway panache, particularly in the money department. I wanted to sink my teeth into his thick, solid-gold signet ring just to check it out. The family emblem inscribed on the band reflected a specific lifestyle, something like a son of a wealthy British indus-trialist, like a black sheep who'd been shipped off to the colonies for being naughty.

Fortunately, we had checked out the long-liner earlier that morning. 'Yep, it'll all be over in a couple of days,' Les confidently predicted. 'The lot'll be dumped out at sea, so expect to see us gone until Friday. There's just one small problem, mate—'

'Spare me the fine detail,' Richard interrupted, his eyes still on the boat in question. 'It's your baby. Just fix it. Do the job, take the photos, put it all on the bill, and I'll draft up a wordy report on your behalf to keep the southern chaps quiet.'

The 'small problem' Les had tried to raise was an important one: instead of the long-liner carrying 300 or 400 sacks of grain, we'd only found 10 half-empty hessian bags all up – basically there was noth-ing to remove. Still, for all Les and I knew, Richard's dad could have been the bloody prime minister of England, the Queen's right-hand man, for God's sake, because what he had just said sounded like a right royal blessing to us.

While Les and I did some raised eyebrow talking which said 'bloody beauty', Richard went on: 'Canberra, like Bjelke-Petersen, does not wish to draw any attention whatsoever to this area. If you had any idea how rich it is you'd be shocked.' None of us had heard him talk like this before, and as his handsome face flushed with cognac, bitterness crept into his delivery. 'The pricks think that by throwing a bit of petty cash around, that by keeping the local blacks drunk and on the dole, and by having the major corporations in their hip pockets, the big, big bucks will just keep on rollin' in.' His face swung back to the long-liner. 'So just go the gutser, my dears. Trust me, there'll be no questions and your bill will be paid poste haste.'

Pouring more lush liquor for one and all, he turned back to us. 'Now, where were we? Oh yes, out at some amazing sand cay, ducking a flying fish, I believe.'

With that, my man raised his glass and said, 'So here's to the girl who lives on the hill, if she don't, her sister will. Here's to her sister!' then turned to the waitress. 'Love, ask Paddy to show you where he hides the Grange and put it on our tab, will ya?'

The thing was I actually did know that there were untold barrels of crude oil sitting under the Barrier Reef – that gold was being quietly mined – and that along with an abundant prawn and cray industry, the region was worth billions. That was not to mention the hundreds of square miles around Weipa filled with the largest, payable bauxite ever found in Australia – enough, in fact, to constitute about one-quarter of all the known resources of bauxite in the world!

CHAPTER 27

Our Pot of Gold

*B*y the time 'Paper Tiger' day came around, we had a plan. Unlike previous escapades, this was not a foolish plot, this was a roguishly simple plan. Given that the contract was paying $100 per discarded sack, and given that there were in reality only ten such sacks, and given that it was our turn to laugh all the way to the bank – why not, we thought, why not photograph the ten sacks 30 or 40 times each? Why not have a lovely day out and make a quick quid on the side, we thought. Genius, no?

Our bed, at about three metres long and about the same at its broadest, filled the entire bow. On 'Paper Tiger' day, Les looked up fuzzily from bed and added alcohol to my shopping list, which already included quite a few rolls of camera film. By the time I returned, Wednesday was already burbling over nicely. 'Where's the grog?' he demanded.

When I pointed out that we were still getting over the previous night's escapade, he insisted, 'No way – we're on holiday. I want a beer when I want a beer.'

I wished he could see himself. 'We're out there for months on end and drink just doesn't matter, but when we're in port, it's like you're a sponge to the stuff.'

Just before the boat pulled away from the wharf, Conj jogged down with a carton of beer on his shoulder. Les beamed. 'Forgot I'd invited him.' He left the wheel and helped the beer, then our friend, onboard. Outsmarted, I went with the flow and steamed slowly toward the long-liner. As Les outlined our predicament to Conj he also didn't fail to remind me, 'Keep on the outside, we don't want them seein' us from the shore.'

As if I didn't know that anyone seeing our shonky operation might have twigged to what was up: they might even have been doing something shonky themselves – everyone up there was doing a bit of duck and weave, even if just for the practice. I dropped back the revs and nudged up on the blind side of the big junk.

There was no denying that Queenslanders had the 'them versus the rest of the world' complex down pat as Conj waffled on: 'Fuck the low-down yellow mothers, I reckon.'

'OK, Conj, enough drivel, make sure all the buffers are down and you, Les, grab the ropes, scale up the side and secure the boat, mate.'

The colder the beer got, the more amicable Les became. 'Yes, sireee.' He mimicked a salute, and did the job easily.

By law, all commercial vessels carried a huge, bright orange, thick canvas tarp ready to strap onto their roofs in case they got lost or hit trouble at sea. It made the boat easier to spot by other boats or from the air. The men niftily rigged up the safety blanket, filled it with the ten sacks and downloaded the lot onto the *Jean King*, and off we headed for a deserted bay a mere bat's blink away to the east.

The barbie spizzled and spat with lamb chops, the beer sank into our funny bones, and the dinghy, at knee-deep to the shore, swayed along to our silly rhythm. Cleverly, Stryder disappeared into the bush and cannily reappeared only as the dusk light began to turn the world into a multi-hued visual.

In the 1970s photos never told a lie, but still it should've been a short comedy flick as the men pretended to swing the same hessian sacks 30 or so times and I shot photos on the Canon camera: there were no faces in the shots, just the sacks, belly buttons, hairy, knobbly legs, and crabby stubby shorts inside of which, unrevealed, sat the men's magic wands, their happy thrusters.

'Make sure the different Taiwanese scribble on the bag is facing the camera in each shot,' I warned as clickety click, clickety click the truth-taker went, and many times we gaily sang a well-known, bawdy song:

Rule Britannia marmalade jam,
three crackers up a Chinaman's arse,
bang, bang, bang, bang, bang.

Personally, I felt the crackers would be much better up a politician's arse than any scapegoat Chinese. I mean really, as founding and only member of the Guy Fawkes Party, what else would you expect me to say?

Later, the pot of gold did rain down on us – especially after a bit of creative persuasion made the final account weigh in at just under five grand. Saying grand is so much more satisfying than saying dollars, don't you think? Richard put it like this: 'That's none for the scoundrels and five for you two,' then whipped out a chequebook and signed on the dotted line.

Conj was also quite succinct: 'We've given it to 'em right where it hurts the most, in the fuckin' pocket.' He wouldn't accept any of the money for jam either. Waving it away, he added, 'Nah, it was a treat to give the bastards a serve and, besides, I just love how yas both operate.'

CHAPTER 28

A Night Intruder

Once in a blue moon Thursday Island held a movie night, but it wasn't the movie I went to see one particularly luminous night – no, I went to be part of the only movie theatre I've ever heard of that had four walls and an entrance door but no roof! Inside was row upon row of canvas picnic chairs all swollen to capacity with a sea of bobbing, nuggetty, curly-haired people laughing chaotically and carrying on like naughty kids. Tucked into the middle of them was me, the only white face amongst them. Finally the lights went low, the buzz settled down, the movie rolled, and every eye in the place lit up in the dark. Only I threw my head upwards and looked beyond the roofless theatre into the tinsel-strewn galaxy: owned by none, free for all, and so stunning it made my heart burst with light. Way, way up I went into the spacious Milky Way whose own unbeatable stage lights were putting on an Oscar-winning show; an infinity of the glittering cosmos which even Hollywood's best could not compete with.

When wolf whistles, cooees and applause indicated the film's conclusion, I came back to earth and skipped light-heartedly down the dimly lit dirt track with Stryder. Surely, I thought, surely there must be a drop of drink in the air, somewhere.

Well, fuck – if you'll excuse the sharpness – while I'd been mentally blown away by the stars in the sky, an explosion of another kind was on its way. With the ferocious tide resting in the neaps (that is, when high and low tide barely moves either way) for once the sea was like fresh-laid, smooth cement. 'Ahoy, ahoy!' Les's voice travelled easily across the water, calling me to a trawler full of partying blokes. The night, the drinks and the gathering of deckies and skippers with never-ending high-sea tales all flowed into one. Behind us, unobtrusively moving around the back deck, a sure-footed Thursday Island man concentrated on spearing fish. Acknowledged silently, unspoken to, quietly, lightly, slightly, the black body was hardly even a shadow.

An hour or two drifted by before I sweet-talked my man home on a promise. This time he came. We danced across the trawler ropes, the wharf, and threw our own ropes, in past the sleeping freezer, simultaneously laughing, chatting and stripping naked, and dived right onto the thick foam mattress. By then any naughtiness was past our collective reach, so we snuggled into the spoon position and let slumber fall upon us.

Wandering through the land of dreams it took a minute before registering that my clitoris was being caressed. Mmm, nice, I thought, but I was in too deeply to come back from sleep's visions, and shrugged Les away with an implicit hug signal. Oh, my my my, I remember thinking, the next couple of strokes felt nearly good enough to awaken the sleeping dragon, but no no, I shrugged another very definite 'no' and rolled apart from him. The caressing persisted – that was very unusual in itself, but then I began to realise that the strokes felt different somehow, not the familiar Les touch. Abruptly I realised that this was *not* Les's touch, that he was *not* the one touching me and with that my eyes jolted open.

Poised above my splayed-out naked body was a huge, dank mud crab shape whose bloodshot, mud-pool eyes were staring right at me. I saw a big back wild thing and knew straight up it was an intruder, a man, it was black – oh it was the stealthy back-deck spear fisherman. Having masked his identity using the white handkerchief-tied-across-the-nose trick, he was waggling his long spindly fingers at his mouth. Emerging from sleep, initially his strange action puzzled me. *Shh*, his fingers were saying, *hush, don't wake your fella up!* The big crab was intimating that I not raise the alarm! Did I have news for him and, as it happened, the man sleeping beside me.

Les had had it coming to him for a long, long time, so had my brothers, the big, loud-mouthed Adelaide doctor, the Cairns gynaecologist, the two turtle scientists – in fact, men in general – all had it coming, so my furious punch, the one that had been edgily waiting for a good reason, just let fly and I socked the long skinny streak's face, crunching his large nose and lazy jaw sideways. What's more, I let the punch continue on until it landed with a resounding blow on to Les's napping face. It felt soooo good. I must confess, it was far more gratifying punching Les than it was crunching the spear fisherman, who'd obviously stalked us back from the party. Double standards, I hear you cry – and fair enough too, but . . . but . . . there was an opening I could not resist so I would be lying if I said there was not a whisker of premeditation mixed into the action. I wonder who would not have done the same.

'Wake up, Les!' I packed the words with the same urgent force as the punches.

'Fuck me drunk!' He'd never needed an invitation from the Queen to throw a punch, and automatically followed through with a quick closed-fisted left and right jab. Expecting this, as he threw the punches, I ducked and flooded out as much dramatic detail as possible. By the time Les's befuddled mind got the story, the skinny arse-end of the spear fisherman had flown from the fo'c'sle, crash-scrambled through the unfamiliar cabin, torn the wheelhouse door open and dissolved altogether by diving over the side – and to camouflage his dastardly trail, the fellow hid under the night sea and only surfaced further down the shoreline.

Meanwhile back at the ranch, Les pitched into the galley, pulled out the cranky old .303 blunderbuss, bunged a few bullets up its throat and careered off into the abandoned turtle boat tied up next door. It was showdown time again at OK Corral with Les blasting bullets into the blameless boat's roof. Just like the Old Man's performance at the Normanby, this was not okay with me. In some sort of inane protest, he then kept firing down into the ocean's clever cover. We've been shooting the shit out of anything that moves for centuries now – when are men ever going to get that this is not working?

I reefed Les back inside our boat with an arm-strength more

mystical than existent. And in a powerful example of when the word 'fuck' really does the job, my low, harsh tone was intensely black and the words very slow. 'Put the fucking gun down, now!'

'But fuck me dead, woman,' he protested in dismal despair. 'I'm s'posed ta be lookin' after you! How could I let that happen when you're right alongside me? I've failed to protect you.'

That was a laugh. Brutally I sliced across his self-indulgent dirge and bailed the man up hard. 'Now let's get this right. It's me who has nearly been raped, remember, me who ought to be bloody upset.' Eyeballing him through the darkness of the cabin, I kept on. 'But first, get the bullets out of that gun and put it out of harm's way.' The nervous .303 relaxed back into the overhead sling. 'Good. Now, Leslie George Coles,' I said, nice and slow, 'get a grip! Wanna get stuck in *all-black* Thursday Island, fronting a black versus whitefella murder trial?' Clenching his shoulders till my fingers ached, I rocked him softly. 'Remember us, mate? We want to be out there in the big blue yonder, suiting ourselves at every second of the bloody clock, not getting screwed at our expense in the establishment's game. Stop trying to kill him! He's gone and I'm safe, now let him go.'

Put like this, Les saw the wisdom of it pretty much immediately. He also found the native's business card lying on the side deck: a two and a half metre-long handcrafted fishing spear with three, reverse-barbed fish spikes leather-bound to one end. No amount of looking around Thursday Island would find us a tall black bloke without his spear and I was not hurt in any way, so why make any trouble? Back in bed, Les grizzled about not being good enough, so I held him tight and smoothed him down.

For me, this was not a horrifying experience, just another crazy page in the chapter. Instead, what completely shattered me was that the man I loved had begun to argue again – so angrily that his attacking language had a terrible edge to it. I seemed unable to shut up either, and vigorously defended myself. Verbal abuse is equally as violent as physical abuse, and easily blinds the reasoning spirit, and because such actions are veiled behind 'love', any one of us can be baffled by it.

Then the turtle necklace went missing from Les's neck,

apparently given to a black man 'down the pub' whose name he could not even remember. He reasoned that once the gift had been given, it was no longer any business of mine what happened to it. In the strict sense that was true too, but I resented that the special gift was gone, and was hurt and saddened that the significance of it had been lost on him.

CHAPTER 29

The Pearl Diver and the Decathlon Champion

*F*ollowing the blunderbuss affair, we gave the wharf a miss and anchored again in the bay off Horn Island, opposite the little hut. All was at peace until the middle of one night when Stryder barked into the fo'c'sle, ran back out and from the top of the freezer stared out in a specific direction.

'Help, help, help, help,' we heard a weak voice floating over the night air. 'Save us. Help, help, help.'

Using the spotlight we quickly located an upturned dinghy surrounded by bobbing heads.

'Holy fuck! Quick, get the kettle on. Get out all the blankets. I'll go and get them.'

Les came back with a load of frightened adult Thursday Islanders plus one shivering little girl: she whom they had propped up and held on top of the overturned boat. Blankets, hot sugary tea, heated-up stew, brandy and listening ears eventually made the saved ones relatively coherent.

'Wow, man, we've been drifting in and out with the tide since night before yesterday,' said the breathless spokeswoman, Maggie. A very big girl with a life-size, infectious grin and eyes bigger than her tummy, Maggie was also built like a male discus-thrower from

Russia's deepest interior. 'I just kept tellin' the others that Jesus Christ would save us. Told them to keep prayin' 'nd the whole time I held this golden cross like bloody hell.' She'd said it a few times already and pointed to her necklace once again. They'd all blathered on, as you would, but Maggie had been the stronghold, the survival force, and still was.

'Wow man, thank God you heard us, but I wasn't givin' up. I've got me grandson and me old man – they still need me, too right they need me. Used to be a pearl diver till he got the bends. Man, he'd be lost without me. Like Jesus saved us man, but youse two pulled us outta the bloody water. Wow man, thanks and praises to you both, and Jesus. Jesus, since I took up Jesus there's no swearin' man. Fuck man, we owe you big-time man.' Eventually daylight snuck up and the grateful mob were delivered in various directions. That's how we met and befriended the people who lived in the solitary hut that sat on the beach at Horn Island, only waving distance from the *Jean King*. Maggie lived there with James, her man, who still stood over six feet tall despite having to bow permanently from the waist up as a result of a pearl-diving accident.

The day they invited us into their home, Maggie promised to spoil us with one of her astounding 10-centimetre high dampers, so calling over from the boat, I begged her not to start making it until I got there. 'I want to learn, and we'll bring a couple of casks over, too.' Maggie nodded, then proudly strutted from the shore back up to where she was preparing a fire.

What a picturesque quadruple we made, all happily ensconced at the front of the absolute beachfront hut partaking of cask chardonnay from vegemite jars, as James the bent diver and Les swapped yarns and Maggie the discus thrower occasionally stoked the dainty fire. Soon the silver-haired old man brightened up and let the long-buried experiences of his early pearling days tumble out – about being deep down below wearing the clumsy, lead-lined traditional brass helmet; about the very thin lifeline of rubber tube that ran oxygen into his mouth on the ocean floor from the boat above; about how that felt, and how much trust was put in the person in the boat above; of how sharks were not the most-feared animal in the ocean but rather the huge manta rays with their broad flapping wings which tangled up and chopped off the life-giving oxygen supply; and about the many men who'd drowned one way or another. 'There were plenty of wharf widows left without a penny to bless 'emselves with. They were beautiful things, them pearls. Sure made us do foolish things,' James grunted resignedly. 'Must be a bit like gold fever Les, big money, but the price we paid was big too.'

Maggie topped up the wine jars again. Les had been a diver at one stage and I could see that he was filled with respect for the twisted-up, toothy old man when he leant forward in sympathy with James. 'If ya don't mind me askin', Jimmy, what's all that scarring from your waist up to your shoulders, and why is it both back and front?'

James stiffened slightly and responded from deep within. 'Son, that was when old man groper tried to take me, he did. The big old fish tried to swallow me head 'nd all. You seen one, son?'

Enthralled, we shook our heads.

'Yeah, they got row on row of long, sharp, needle-type teeth all bent back toward the throat ta get a fair grip on their tucker. Anyway, he had me in up to my waist, squirmin' around in his throat. I was strugglin' real hard and reckoned I was a goner m'boy.' James's eyes became unfathomable.' Then one of the other divers started stabbin' the big fella in the eyes.' Both men squatted on the sandy earth facing the emerald-green ocean, diver bound to diver. 'Must've been in pain hisself, cos his jaws unclamped and suddenly I was free and trying not to swim up the airline to the surface too quick. Yeah, his blood and mine blindin' me, red everywhere, sharks comin' at me from all over the place. That's when I got the bends. Stayed in the bell for nigh on a week before I could breathe proper again. Lost me livin' but kept me life.' The tall, gentle native returned from the deep and squirted more wine into his jar. 'It's the only recorded attack in history,' he chuckled more to himself than us. 'Old man groper's one eye blind now, old man James, him all bent up now. I still swim, hope he can still see.' Old Man and the Old Fish – same: same, I thought in reverence to both.

Maggie filled her jar and decided the time was right to transmit age-old damper techniques to me, so we slipped up to the hut. Although tennis wire was stapled across the cut-out window holes and the floors were dirt throughout, the small wrought-iron shack was spick and span. The beds were veiled in mozzie nets and covered in clean, white sheets. On top of the old-fashioned refrigerator, reigning supreme, stood a framed young Jesus Christ complete with halo and a pious white full-length frock, next to which was perched a black transistor radio. On the pure white lace kitchen tablecloth sat a bowl full of ripened pawpaw and a big silver Tilley lantern.

Out the back behind the hut, on a table under a bit of tin roofing where washing was done by hand in plastic buckets, the amazing Thursday Island woman went into full demo mode. 'Three secrets, man.' Her entire, beautifully ugly beaming countenance was ecstatic that someone in the world was interested enough to listen and learn the old ways. 'Never use all wheat flour, use half cycad palm and half normal. Sift that together, then,' her eyes glanced up to make sure I was following, 'never use vinegar, just add a dash of corned beef stock.' Maggie puffed up a bit, then let the last secret out: 'Then man, it's all in the marble table. It keeps the rising dough cool, just workin' it not too much and not too little, just steady like.' As her large hands softly kneaded the white dough, down vanished another entire glass jar of white.

After smearing the insides of the camp oven with butter and a sprinkling of flour, she tossed in the dough and clamped the lid on top. Like a Greek weightlifter, the big mama effortlessly snatched it up and stomped out to the men. Next to the fire of glowing coals was a shallow hole in the ground into which Maggie shovelled glowing coals, positioned the camp oven on top and covered the lot with more white-red coals and sand. She smacked her hands together making the residue flour fly off in a huff, and wiped them on her apron. Satisfied, Maggie marched back inside and returned in the blink of an eye, another full glass jar leading the way.

'That's it man,' she announced, cheerily clinking the other three jars. 'Give it about thirty, forty minutes 'nd we'll brush the coals off and give her a tap. If the damper sounds hollow, she's done and we'll scoff her. Bottoms up, man,' and down another jar dashed.

'Two, four, six, eight, bog in, don't wait,' we chanted when the melting butter oozed onto the crunchy crust of the warm damper sponge and into our bellies. There we were, the two Aussie fishermen and the two extraordinary Thursday Islanders, overlooking the too, too divine harbour, gaily tossing the afternoon away.

When the faithful sun started punching the clock for the day and the late afternoon cooled its heels, Les and I, just drifting along with the tide of things, were nicely in our cups. Suddenly, a tremulous explosion of ABC chamber music let forth at deafening decibels. Could have been Beethoven's Fifth or Bach's Ninth or even one of Mozart's wizardry Eleventy-levens! Certainly, the orchestral blast startled the shit out of everything. Passing birds bolted, lazy lizards lunged backwards off logs and scurried into the scrub, even the *Jean King* seemed to lurch sideways for a quick look.

I knocked over the last drop of wine, swore and staggered like a newborn brumby to my feet. 'What the bloody hell's goin' on? Where are those two?'

'James went bush for a quick piss.' Les lurched drunkenly and peered hopefully in that direction. 'And the last I saw, Maggie was headin' for the shack huggin' the bejesus out of the unopened wine cask.'

As we attempted to fathom what was going on, the once-peaceful hut walls began to moan and shudder like someone was trying to demolish it by hand. Inside the hut, the radio orchestra got whammed up to the highest almighty level. Then we heard James's well-polished blasphemy erupt volcanically from behind one of the wailing walls. 'You fuck-king bush nigger, unlock the fuck-king door, you fuck-king woman!'

Swaying like champions of the Shaolin drunk tai-chi style, we snuck up to the caged window and peeked inside the kitchen. There was Maggie sitting in the lotus position on top of the kitchen table of white lace. One hand clutched the two-litre cask of cardboard chardonnay and the other tilted the now lit lantern to and fro just like a religious devotee cleansing sinners with incense would. Under one hairy armpit, Maggie the Minstrel cradled the transistor radio which was blasting out chamber music in tune with the woman's maniacal laughter. Securely entrenched, our girl wasted no time telling James that he'd been outwitted, and that the valuable nectar was all hers. In response, James shook the scared shack as though it were a cot in the manger, and roared against the unfairness of it all. 'Give me the fuck-king wine, you dirty bush nigger! Give me the wine or I will tear the fuck-king house down!'

'Mate,' Les ventured, 'I reckon this looks like a bit of a family affair.'

So much for a silent meditation retreat hut, I thought, and nodded. 'They should give away the demon drink and take up smoking green, and we should go back to our joint and have one right now.'

James stalked from around the corner, then slumped, worse the wear, onto his knees underneath the kitchen window. Slowly he pulled himself up until he was looking through the same kitchen window we were by now stealthily retreating from. Not that he noticed, as his spizzle splattered and splashed upon Maggie the Wine Merchant: 'Let me in or I will tear this place down with my blood-deedy bare hands! That is my fuck-king wine!' and so forth.

Carefully, we receded toward the languishing dinghy, feeling the warm, fine sand squelch between our drunk-ass, naked toes, and I laughed and called out, 'Bye and thanks for a lovely day.'

With the mackerel season over, the timing could not have been cannier than when the Old Man's voice crackled through the wheelhouse with the next crafty plot: 'Les mate, the Boof's down Weipa way makin' a killin', the young fella's down there killin' the pig too and me, Rae an' the littlies are on the make, mate. Youse've gotta get down there chop, chop, over and out.' [Direct translation: Trusted friend, my oldest son is catching many, many fish around Weipa, as is my second son. I, my wife and our two youngest children are all journeying toward my sons, to do the same, and you two must join us too, immediately, if not sooner.]

'Roger, roger, mate. I'm all ears mate. Give me the grass.' [Direct translation: Got that, got that friend. I am listening very closely, friend. Tell me everything.]

'I'm givin' ya the real drum mate. There's more barra down south than ya can poke at with a pointy stick on a moonless night. How's things with youse two? Mate do you copy, mate?' [Direct translation: Honestly, I am telling you everything friend, and reiterate again that there are many uncountable amounts of barramundi living in the Gulf of Carpentaria, waiting to be caught, even when one has no idea and/or is blind. How is life for you both? Friend, do you hear me and comprehend, friend?]

As sure as the view through our kitchen window altered with every ripple, a new adventure tickled our fancy; and besides, if the Old Man was game, it was bound to be unpredictable fun. And so, almost as quickly as the call had been made, we were up and gone. From the back deck, I waved to the two men on the Grand's balcony. 'Bye,' I called back, 'nice knowin' you, and thanks for all the fun!'

CHAPTER 30

Snake God

Softly, softly, a little touch of northerlies patted the *Jean King*'s bum down to Weipa, and again we were humbled by the greatest living being in the world: the ocean. The sun now came up over land instead of water, and set over water instead of land. All gone, the iridescent seas of the Torres Strait; no more tear-up tides ripping in and out, this sea was less brazen and reflected the more serene colours of Australia. The land boomeranged into our spirits and in returning we felt renewed. Although 'white', as born Australians we too felt an inherent oneness with our country, our own private bond with 'Tribus Terra Australis'; we too were alert to the ancient echoes that reverberated through the land, to the pure vibrations of our astounding country as it sang out in traditional welcome: all of this had been recorded in our souls also. I think it was Karl Jung who said of that: no matter what country you are born into, the native of that country is an aspect of your soul. Not being rude to Jung, but he forgot to mention that the country itself is also an aspect of your soul.

Happy to be turning south from north, I joked, 'It feels like we're going downhill.' This may well have been an unconscious divination.

The nautical chart Les pored over crackled as it spilt down each side of the table. 'The Gulf is more delta-like, all mudflat, and shallower for further out off the coast, before it drops off the continental shelf, so we're goin' out deeper, and then cuttin' across the bay.'

Driving with binoculars glued to my eyes, methodically I scrutinised the coastline. Pointing in to the shore, Les nodded, mentally timed the sun's distance in the sky to its setting, and suggested, 'There's still enough light for us go on-shore, give Stryd a run, and get a bit of leg stretch, too.'

The perky dinghy surfed into the beach and, trusting the anchor to do the right thing, we left it in the shallows. The dog sped around trying to get enough lift-off to freak out the shore birds and we hot-footed it across the short stretch of sand, skidding to a halt under the shade of the tree-rim. Propped against one of the she-oaks lay a wizened silver-barked canoe.

Caressing the weather-smoothed curves, we named our find 'The Canoess' and wondered about her age and the journeys she'd travelled. Such finds were quite rare, and normally carved from ti-tree; yet this one, still in fair condition, appeared to have been sculpted out of the buoyant softwood of white beech. There was even an intact baler shell nestled inside, no doubt used for bailing sea water out, drinking fresh water from and for digging. He and I sat for a long while in the slim, five-metre long craft, letting her vibes relax us.

'Didn't think the Aboriginals ever built canoes,' Les pondered. 'Anyway, she's definitely been restin' up here for a few decades.'

'Just because some white so-called historians didn't record it, doesn't mean a thing. Bastards probably got around in white coats, even up here.' Both of us were always sticking it to 'the establishment', using our mocking know-it-all way to blame bureaucrats/authorities for what we deemed to be wrong. Feeling untouchable and invincible was smugly comfortable – but there would come a day when the powers-that-be would be 'sticking it' back to us big-time.

The afternoon breeze dropped and the tide started going out, which left the dinghy sitting on the sand. Les flicked a glance between the departing tide and the sage canoe. 'Remember, woman of the sea, when I snatch it,' [he meant die] 'you're gunna give me body back to the ocean like you promised, aren't you?' I saw into his eyes, the sky-blueness, I saw the importance of this question in his soul.

Stepping out of the canoe's belly I touched his heart. 'Yes. Why?' We had, still have this same pact: till death do us part, no matter what.

He cupped one end of the hollowed shell and helped the Canoess to her feet. 'Come on, we're taking her off the slip and lettin' her drift home.'

As the legendary wanderer took up her old rhythm and rocked back out with the newly receding tide, I waved and said softly, 'See ya later. Safe sailing.' Les shook his head in a resigned 'I-don't-get-it' kind of way. How could he, when I could not myself explain how the Canoess was more than just a historical piece of timber, that somehow she felt like a living connection, that intuitively I was interpreting the Canoess as a sacred initiation of my own by recognising that she was welcoming me into the lands which I would later describe much like Aboriginals do, as my home country.

Maybe the Canoess leading the way was what gave us the courage to travel for the third time, sight unseen, across the ocean at night. That is, after both of us avidly reread the chart one more time to make sure there were no reefs or rocks to stuff us up. 'The bay's about a million bloody times deeper than Black Rocks. Nothing's a problem.' Les's precise prognosis had a definite logic to it, so I agreed. But as he set the *Jean King*'s course, what Les proposed next was something I was never going to agree to. 'Let's tie the knot.' It was so unexpected, and he said it so casually that at first I thought he was using the term 'knot' as in marine terminology for speed – but no, Les meant we take the plunge and get legally married. You see, the Cooktown wedding had not been legal because Big Ed didn't hold an international skipper's ticket – a significant piece of knowledge which I was fully aware of at the time of the fun nuptials.

Trying to deflect Les I countered shrewdly, 'Don't be silly, we already are. I mean, our spirits, Lesy, are joined forever. You know I love you rotten.' It was a mouthy cover job, and if he had picked up on my skittish tone like I did, he would have known that I felt cornered alright.

He kept on pitching marriage until finally, just before going below, he dropped an ultimatum that had a bit of sting to it: 'Well, if you don't marry me,' he declared, 'I'll leave you,' and huffed off. What classic bloke sense – still, it offered up my defence on a platter.

Laughing a bit too hard, I slapped my sides loudly and said sarcastically, 'Jesus love, sure you're not going all religious?'

At least I'd gotten the last word in, but what a revelation! No, not the proposal, but the speed of my denial. Even though my bloke's snores could have kept heathens awake, being alone gave me time for a bit of thinking: at one level I lent an ear to the soft swish of the water under the speeding hull, and the gravel purr of the Bedford, while constantly checking the dinghy at heel out the back, and regularly looking even further out into the darkness past the stern. On another level, he and I on the ocean felt unbeatable and I had no plan to up and leave Les, but traipsing down the real aisle? The thought of marriage, of being *legally* entangled with any man, held even less attraction than it had the first time. For me, marriage meant ownership in an uncomfortable kind of way.

Stryder lay on the lounge, dream-shaking every now and then, the *Jean King* was flying along beautifully, and there wasn't even much real steering to be done – just an occasional turning the wheel five degrees either way to bring us back on course. At this rate we were home and hosed, and should be turning left at Duyfken Point, steaming up Roberts Creek and be at the Weipa wharf by the next afternoon, which meant in excellent timing, by Friday night we'd be at the infamous stubby shop – or, as it was more satirically named, the Palace – having a sip. Wanting to look my best, using seaman ironing, I carefully placed my slinkiest shirt and best jeans combo along the lounge frame, brushed out any wrinkles and laid the heavy cushions on top of the clothes.

It looked like the only way we were ever going to comprehend that night-time travel was not the 'go' was telepathically, because when I stepped back to the compass and attempted to bring us on course, the wheel would not turn. Please don't do this, I prayed to the wheel, and tugged harder, but it was stuck fast. Bloody hell, in a black night, above a very very deep bay in the middle of nowhere, our boat was steering us in the wrong direction. Then, an awful, grumbling shudder came from the stern and a juddering noise rippled through the boat, followed by a dull, heavy clunk. There's no describing that first instant of clutching terror – I just hope you never feel it.

By the time I knocked the engine out of gear, Les was in the cabin and checking down in the keel for incoming sea water, checking to see if we'd hit something and were sinking. 'S'no water comin' in, quick, kill the engine, shine the torchlight down here, put the big toolbox over, get Stryder below. What the fuck did ya do?' He jumped in beside the burning hot engine. 'Get the coffee goin', don't speak, I'm thinkin', come here.' All of which I immediately did.

His instructions kept spewing up from the sweltering engine, 'There's no use dropping the anchor, it's deeper out here than the black pits of hell. We just have to drift.' Probably wasn't enough rope in Queensland to reach the bottom of that bay, and in the sudden silence, the Bedford's heat made Les's perspiration pump and sizzle as it dripped onto the rocker cover, hissing almost too loudly. 'Fuck me blind, can't see what I'm up to down here, get me a towel.' The black night slipped eerily into the cabin and the water slapped impatiently on the hull. This was the wide open sea and we were out of control and at its mercy.

Les seemed to pick the problem quickly, asked for more coffee, and said, 'I love you woman.'

As he reconnected the propeller shaft to the engine, I did the operating theatre nurse routine, slapping tools into his palm on request and moving the torchlight to wherever his hands were working. The man could have said, 'Get me a scalpel,' and I would've come up with one. Hats off to the astounding jacks-of-all-trades, him being one of them.

'Fuck me lucky. Kick her in the guts.' That was his way of saying a short prayer followed by an instruction for me to start up the engine.

The steering still would not move. Bloody hell – we were up to our necks in drama.

Les's eyes lit up with a brainwave. 'Kill the engine, get my knife and goggles, I'm goin' over the side.'

What? He was going to leave me up there and go down into the totally dark underworld, sightless in the unknown, knowing nothing. But, but hang on, what about me, what if he drowned and I got stuck in the middle of the ocean with a fucked engine? Was my rave on Thursday Island about learning how to use the radio unluckily coming true? Thank God I had forced that issue. Feeling hopelessly helpless and nakedly exposed like that made my belly stir and twirl up in my spine like a graveyard cobra.

While I spiralled into selfish survival mode, Les tied a safety rope around his waist, kissed me like he was going down the pub for a beer, flipped backwards over the side, surfaced, washed out the goggles, sucked them onto his face, waved, and was gone. Slowly the rope, doing laps through my hand, went down, down, down. It was midnight quiet and the century of time was locking my ever-tightening fear into a fixed coil as I watched the lustred bubbles of my man's breath appear on the surface: so fragile, each perfectly round one rose to the top and then burst, telling the story of breath and death.

Suddenly, like a footy cheerleader bouncing through the club victory banner, Les, with buckets of ocean slushing off him, sprang from the depths below onto the deck in one unaided motion. Who gasped the loudest, I don't know, but the four or five metres of writhing, poisonous sea snake he was waving around like a snake God from kundalini-land shocked me enough to drop the lifeline and try to flee – I mean, it wasn't just long, it was about a metre thick! Bringing the snake spirit alive, Les's boggled eyes darted everywhere as he splurted out, 'Fuck me scared, that was heart attack mate-rial! Should've seen the size of this monster, all wrapped around and tangled up in the prop. Sliced into three, he was. Reckon I left at least another six or seven metres down there.' Using both hands he raised the sacrificial snake to the heavens and defiantly roared, 'AAAAAAHHHH!' Aside from no longer feeling abandoned to a bloody scary fate, there was Les the brave and fearless one saving us again. Can you have such a one and expect him to be passive and considerate too?

Quickly we squared away the engine, sorted out our bearings, got back on course and while I rested below Les took the second watch.

Scarlet liquid, spiralling cherry-red blood splurged through my dream, then one supple, ruby-red snaking, quivering vein stretching – snap! Even as I gasped awake it felt like a physical cord was shrinking back, and in the cabin's darkness I was only stabilised by catching sight of the semi-lit compass, of Les, yes this life, yes I was here.

Still completely hyped up, Les hauled me off the floor in a boa constrictor squeeze and announced, 'I'm up on the roof, gettin' some star fuel.'

I took over the watch and as the steaming coffee helped clarify my mind, I was relieved to think that in amongst all the excitement, Les's wedding proposal had gone unanswered. He was only ever to ask for my hand one more time.

While the *Jean King* skipped like a hydrofoil through linear time and space, I listened to one of my favourite singer's gravelly undertones as he grappled with a question about the problem angels have getting to sleep when devils leave the porch light on, which was more insightful than I knew, especially since where we were going all the angels looked like devils and vice versa.

CHAPTER 31

Weipa

*I*t should be mentioned that while our debut into the society of Weipa worked out quite well in the end, it certainly could have been a bit more stylish. There was no denying that my man turned the event from an icebreaker into a ball-tearer, alright, or that he became an overnight sensation, nor was it purely coincidence that we whisked into the safety of the Weipa wharf just as the stubby shop was slipping into the Friday night groove. And even better still, we would find friends that same night who would last a lifetime. And honestly, with friends like these you didn't need many others.

Keen to get with the crowd, we parked the *Jean King,* headed up the copper-coloured road, and stepped into the stubby shop. This was in no way a conventional hotel, but rather a very crude drinking hall which, other than Sundays, opened in the late afternoons only. It, along with an equally unattractive 'food mess', had been specifically built to accommodate the workers living in the 'single men's' quarters; that is, in the 100 or so demountable wrought-iron huts which were bunched together like an old-fashioned refugee camp. All of this was set well away from the township and the actual mining fields – and there was good reason that the stubby house was ironically referred to as the 'Palace'. The drinking hole had been built so cheaply that it consisted of one big slab of cement with three walls, two of which elbowed-out each side, and a wrought-iron roof which covered the 30-metre long bar below it and not much else. Comalco, the mining corporation, were running a huge, very profitable bauxite operation there, and as you will learn, they were not known for their compassion. Anyway, at least from the Palace all the boats were within sight, so it was perfect for seamen to check the wharf, the weather, the boats, the river, and out to sea.

The Palace was a straightforward design for thirsty men, a place where you could lean on the bar, have a firm grip on your beer, abuse bastards and chat casually with buddies – just the type of crowd that loves a fight, as long as they're not in it. Inside, it was packed to the eyeballs with brawny mining men and backwater fishermen, the result of which prompted me to shout above the din, 'Looks like the inmates have just escaped from the local loony bin!' The only thing missing was women – other than myself that was, and Colin, the gay manager of the seedy hall and of marginal men.

In a place like that, us being new and me being a woman should have meant keeping a really low profile, not short, nuggetty Les having a bare-fisted fight with a tall, muscle-bound Norwegian big-mouth. Still, it wasn't long before some provocative statements gave the night a ring of bad tidings. When my man kicked his chair away and muttered darkly, 'A man's gotta do what a man's gotta do,' I whistled up Stryder and we both went to the light's edge, just between the inside and the outside of the pub, so we'd be ready for whatever way the dice rolled. For Les, having a blue every now and then was a healthy way to let off steam. Having seen it all before, already I felt sorry for the Norwegian.

The crowd gathered around so I stood lone sentry from the sideline, ready to sink a boot into any bloke who didn't have the right but might be trying to get a devious thump in anyway. Through eye contact, a man in the crowd singled me out and nodded thoughtfully. I nodded back, knowing that should any unexpected trouble erupt there was at least one ally.

After giving the big bloke a three-hit start, and not flinching from the impact of the first two, I could see that Les was ready to fight from the black and white side of his orphan days. The Norwegian must have seen something too because he spun heel and fled out into the far less intimidating darkness. To say I was mightily relieved is an understatement.

Anyway, the crowd went mad with the decision and scrambled hastily back to the bar. While the joint's tills rang their tits off, the bar manager noticed in Les good bouncer material. Col was clever like that and, later, would only have to outlaw Les, and by implication me, from the Palace once. So from then on, like father like son, Les's reputation preceded him. And Mudgee, the knuckly bloke who had indicated his loyalty in the brewing dust-up, introduced us to his band of buddies, all of whom turned out to be honourably untamed in their own right. We liked the men immediately and took allegiance with them on the night.

There was: Frank, an ageing croc hunter, ex-French foreign legionnaire and, post-war in Europe, a croupier; handsome, witty Bobby Giles, possessed with the same kind of intense nature as Les; racist Riley, a generous man with radical, sometimes bitter views; Russ, an ugly, smooth-talking South African whose broad knowledge led me into the wee hours of intellectual tete-a-tetes; and up from Cooktown, our old friend German Jack, the legendary croc-shootin' jungle jaunter; and my favourite, the wild but wonderful Mudgee Mailler.

How had I stepped from the loving, intelligent arms of Mum and Dad into a bunch of such anarchistic nomads who were almost lawless and certainly unafraid of just about anything? If you aren't living on the edge of your capacity – that is, if everything around you is neat, tidy and predictable – how will you ever know who you really are, and isn't life meant to be an adventure anyway?

With still a couple of months' wait for the actual barramundi season to officially begin, we settled down into the lagoon of plenty, bought a rustbucket ute, built mateships and drank willingly. Hardly from the cute side of town, our newfound friends manhandled the C-word badly and constantly. My dad reckoned that people who swore just lacked vocabulary, and I was conscious of all the swearing. True, I swore myself too, but I always tried to keep it in check. Late one evening, while a particularly wilful wind and strong tide whisked around us, the gang sat on the *Jean King* drinking. German Jack's use of the word 'cunt' became increasingly insulting, so profuse in fact that finally I cracked up. 'Listen, Jack,' I demanded, 'I happen to own one of those and it's a beautiful thing. If you don't stop saying it, I'll kick you off the boat!'

He was so intoxicated he could barely walk let alone negotiate the wicked tide, but when the profanities continued I ordered that he be gone. Jack was never scared about anything, including his own death, and when drunk, if it's possible he was even less scared. 'Good riddance to bad rubbish,' one of us snarled as we angrily bailed Jack into his tinny and let the man loose into conditions he should have been scared shitless about.

As the winds buffeted him around and the cantankerous tide impatiently whisked his dinghy backwards into the curtain of darkness, like a scene from a B-grade movie we watched Jack sway uncertainly and raise a defiant fist to the sky. Grinning at us and the feral, uncontrollable elements that were about to consign him to a fate of 'lost at sea, gone missing by drowning', fearlessly he roared back, 'Never ever give up, you cunts, never!' and let his lunatic laughter spread over the wharf. Although disappearing into the ruthless void, I knew his statement about life was profoundly true, and that even his abandoned bravery was a part of that too. I think it is important to realise that wise words don't only come from famous leaders or celebrated religious personages, that often it's the everyday experiences and the people around us who teach us the most profound lessons. In this case, I leaped into our dinghy and sped out into the black fray to save Jack – after all, aside from one explicit noun, the drunken, babbling man had just given me a very important message.

So while 'fuck' got abused somewhat, the C-word ban stood in place for years. And our motley friends' hearts held more wealth than all the bauxite Comalco thought it owned, so with no questions asked, we splashed all the money we had at each other all the time, living the philosophy that money was like manure – there was plenty of it and it was meant to be spread around.

We were on the west coast of Queensland, but certain rites are probably the same the world over. At first light, each skipper appeared on his back deck and nodded at likewise other back-deck fellows, then they'd all do a 180-degree head scroll from across the sky to the sea horizon, downloading the latest on their constant main study – the weather. It ran through their blood; they could smell it, feel it, just know it uncannily; it clothed their view of every day and every night; it created their living; it took or saved their lives so it wasn't news that they understood it better than the weather bureau. The weather was their master and had to be obeyed.

Whilst assessing the weather, the first deep drag on a chunky fag assisted the first hacking cough to help force the lungs into submission, which went with the first phlegm spit and the first harsh-tasting instant coffee. Then the fag would lip-dangle while everyone cranked their freezer engines over by hand and a further three or so scalding double-dip coffees had been poured down their jaded throats. Even though the men's wizened hearts were still in rehab from the previous evening's soirée, this routine helped kick-start them into the new day. The only duty left to perform was the quick check of the boat's ropes and up onto the wharf they'd spring, to join the rest in the unceasing daily weather debate.

As the dock came alive, the gathering would grow until off the merry men tore, to the rubbish dump, to the tip – or, as Les aptly named it, the Lucky Dip, because it was. Weipa was a company town so other than a Woolworths supermarket, a newsagent and an unfashionable boutique or two, there were no retail shops at all, and Comalco threw only the best stuff away – so for fishermen, that made the dump a very necessary, very healthy hardware shop. Yes, bargain-lovers, it was a gold mine of engines, wire, pumps, pipes, tubing, nuts, bolts – you name it. The pickings were so good, the back of our ute became a self-service source of practical spare parts for many a desperate skipper. Indeed, given the amount of good stuff that was so disrespectfully discarded, everyone reckoned Comalco had a screw loose.

Maybe the steering problem we'd experienced on the way down was an omen because before too long Les and I started heading in the wrong direction again, and had dropped back into petty arguments. And with the government's annual fish netting ban still on, there was another month or so with nothing to do but hang around in port, niggling away at each other. Given that the Palace opened in the evenings only and for two hours on Sundays, there we were as usual propped up in the township's only hotel, the Albatross: a bird's name, which was a mocking insult, considering that in the legendary Ancient Mariner's tale the lone albatross actually led becalmed and lost souls back onto the right course.

Scanning my mind for a way to break both my drinking and our bickering patterns, suddenly the answer was right there in front of me. Promising to return, I slid off the bar stool, stepped through the public bar's entrance doors and out into the back car-park. Even if the absentee landlords who owned the hotel cared little for its patrons, still, there was no excuse for what lay before me. Too drunk to help themselves even get up, ragged and torn, snot-splattered semiconscious Aboriginals lay slumped over the pub's back entrance: at the gates of oblivion, every day it was the same. Those with money had already gone inside and were getting drunker. Although critically hungry, there was no time for food until the money was gone. Money wasn't gone until just after the pub had stopped serving lunch, so bags of potato crisps and peanuts sufficed, which bought a second wind of desire. Although now strewn about and defeated, later some even scrounged up more money and whisked themselves back into the bar, and deeper into self-annihilation. With a diet as shabby as the rest of their hazy existence, it was obvious that the Gulf Aboriginals were not only a race apart from the Thursday Islanders, but they wore the signs of deep molestation on their sleeves, in their hearts; in fact, wore it painfully through every fibre of their lives. You see, for them, in more ways than one, it was all over; for them, there were infinite catch-22s, as will be explained soon enough.

So when I walked into the tropical temper of the day, I entered the suppressed anger of neglect. It was about mid-afternoon, and the sweltering tempest of the Wet was making everyone even more crotchety.

'Yeah, come on, pretty white gel. Give us some money there, sis.' Skinny, black skeletal arms stretched out toward me, pus-filled eyes sought mine, empty souls begging for relief. 'You got good fella. Money, plenty money. Give us some there, sis, eh sis?'

'Sorry girls, not today.' Although the whole scene was physically painful and I couldn't escape my 'white' complicity in why it was like it was, I was still in no mood for being held up.

Wild and cunning, two women lifted their fists and came at me. 'Fuck you, bitch. Ask you whitefella. He got money.' Lit up and prancing around in my face, they urged me to step up: they wanted white blood, they wanted mine.

I snapped. Women have plenty of fight in them, a swag of pent-up anger, much more than men – we have every reason – and I was no different. A dark circle quickly gathered as the three of us shuffled a bit, and for an instant, both worlds stepped into a time gone by. This was ancient and, yes, the primitive fighting urge felt exhilarating. Spoiling for battle, the black figures took on animal dimensions, craning and strutting like bad-tempered jabiru. They blocked my pathway and sparred into my face. It was strong, exciting, and my belly-fire came alive. Spontaneously I was part of the game at hand. In that moment, I saw the women's warrior beauty, felt my own and stepped into the space. Those still standing closed in excitedly, and huge, glossy black crows propped like ghouls on the pub roof.

Even though those two were in no shape to win, at least they still had some courage, so as the women shuffled and swung, I ducked and weaved. It was damn fine to tread the warpath. I could have, wanted to, jettison the spindly fighter women into next year, to feel the gratifying pleasure it would give. Still, my conscience had a punch of its own and leapt into the fight, reminding me that this was a no-merit match, a no-goer; this was the whitefella doing it all over again. It was time to return to reality.

Deftly stepping sideways to avoid a punch, I tripped the snarling woman backward, gently broke her fall and held her easily on the ground. 'Stay there, sister. I won't fight you. We are all sisters.' I spun around and ducked under my next opponent's guard, hugged the perspiring, pongy, emaciated little bag of bones into stillness, then spoke firmly into her ear, 'Go back to the mission, my friend. Go home and rest.' In some clumsy private way, I prayed then and there that the next generation would be capable of forgiving the rape, be able to move on.

Please understand that under Bjelke-Petersen's rule, Queensland catered to corporations and for the big business that lived in the underworld. In the Weipa region, on Aboriginal-owned land, it was the global corporation Comalco that legally owned the mining rights to a bauxite reserve estimated at 2000 million tonnes. With criminally elitist legislative protection, Comalco's immeasurable profits were safely tucked into the offshore pockets of international robber barons. Plus there were a few perks in it for Bjelke-Petersen and his cronies too. All of this while the true landowners, the shanty-town people, wallowed in poverty, grief and despair: ignored and forgotten, it was a bittersweet genocide the outside world knew nothing of, a genocide I was about to experience first-hand – that is, after I had conducted some business of my own.

Brushing past the receding mob, I strode up to the Albatross Hotel's front entrance, through the carpeted foyer and into the toilet. After splashing some fresh water on my face, I pulled the crimson lippy from my bra and dabbed some onto my grim grin. Coming, ready or not, I thought, and I stepped up to the manager's office and knocked.

'It had better be quick, it's pay day.' The eyebrow-furrowed balding fellow did not smile at me, instead he attempted to cover up the towering piles of cash with accounts ledgers.

'Robyn, and don't worry, I'm not here to rob you. I've just come from the front bar and it looks to me like you could do with a reliable barmaid.' The strategy had worked for me before so why not give it another shot? As my dad used to say, never change a winning move.

Probably way too far through a stony marriage, the sad man pulled the half-inch wide tress of hair from behind one ear across his bald patch to the other ear. 'Glen,' he muttered, 'and matter of fact, yeah, you any good at puttin' a decent head on a beer?'

'Born with a tap in my hand, and I can give you references.'

He didn't care, as long as I was warm and breathing. 'Goodo eh but.' Glen glanced over me hastily. 'But the public bar gets pretty tricky at times, what with the blacks and the fishermen. Might be too rough for you, you know, with all the swearin' . . .' He was easy to read, and suddenly scoring the job was important.

The kafuffled manager had gone just the right wicket so softly softly I went to it. 'Glen, just give me the fuckin' job. Glen, I've handled worse you know, and I'll do the right thing by you, Glen.' I knew the pitch and he was out for a duck: the job was mine.

Returning to the public bar, back-to-back bums packed the bar stools and drinking arms still rested on the elbow-level bashed-up tables supporting the drinkers' habits. From the fishermen who had just swept in off the ocean to Aboriginals unfortunate enough to still have money after non-lunch, to the rare, well-combed, smug on-shore locals, the listening room was filled with waffling talk, quiet chuckles and the standard smudgy cigarette haze: a predictable scene, stale with familiarity.

I fluttered the ute keys at Les saying, 'Just off for a quick spin, I'll be back later.' He nodded without thinking, and I vanished out the back again, to the broken-backed people.

The carpark was blessed with an enormous strangler fig tree whose shock of aerial roots looked appropriately like a bunch of frayed nerves spilling from its heart. There was Stryder, wide awake, sitting expectantly below the big shady tree. Quite apart from her, the cringing Aboriginal dogs hung around in a pack, a bit like the politicians who had cleverly, indeed deliberately, wiped their irresponsible hands of that which no one should experience. Beside Stryder, like one of the tree's broken boughs, lay one of my sparring partners. The other was nowhere in sight.

'Okey-dokey there girlfriend, come on, get up and get in the ute. Come on.' My tenderness was no wily trick – I'm sure anyone would have felt the same. 'Get up, we're goin' on a journey. No, no, not in the back. In the front you get, with me.'

She was frail and so young and lovely underneath the agony, and she cried softly as we cruised slowly through the paved avenues of Weipa town. Friendly geraniums waved innocently through the white-picket fences and newly mown green lawns, which led up to tidy verandas of neat redbrick three-bedroom homes of Comalco 'staff' members and their families. Not that the tribal people would ever want to live like that, thank you very much. But when the smooth ride of the tree-lined black bitumen gave way to the deeply rutted, copper dirt road of dust and potholes, fair sense gave away to speechlessness – did prejudice towards these people stretch even as far as the Main Roads Department too, I wondered?

Weipa South, the Aboriginal mission village, resembled a discarded, dirty rag; a refuge camp without guards. Inside it a disaster of aimless, disinherited humans with shattered hearts walked around in a daze, as though there was no strength to rage against the terrible life being dealt them. Only the spotty inbred dogs and the kids had any spirit: the shoeless little people who kicked flat footies, laughed through their phlegm, and remembered to forget.

I dropped off my passenger at a battered, bland pole home whose window-lights had been punched out long ago and whose smashed-in wall holes seemed to emit the feeling of hopeless frustration. The squabbling mob milling around the house came toward us like praying mantis ghouls. It was a crap place to leave a fellow woman yet she was unfailingly grateful.

'Hey, thanks sis.' The young warrioress's toothless grin, her bravado, struck me in the heart. In thanks she stretched down to scoop up the few ripe, pockmarked pawpaws fallen from the only tree still standing in the front yard and one of her milkless breasts fell through the arm of her ill-fitting dress. 'Here, take some mummy apples. You've been real kind. Us Abos don't forget.'

'Keep your guard up, girl,' I offered pathetically, mustering up a weak, guilty kind of smile before driving off. What use were those words? Feeling a deep humiliation and, aching for the wrong of it all, I caught Stryder's eye in the rear-vision mirror. 'Them and us, eh Strydy, we're all in the same country, but us whitefellas are the only ones in the lucky country!'

The sun was still up but the moody village felt dark, dank and down. It was a victim, no two ways about it. The car moseyed its way back through the mission, where sheltered under a wise old Morton Bay fig was the kids' playground – and even that looked all skew-whiff, broken and discarded like a fractured toy. The whole township was a wreck, just like the minds of its unlucky residents. Selfishly, I felt relieved to be leaving the stark, unfixable nightmare.

Slowly, slowly, down the street, past all the junk-strewn front yards which led to bombed-out shelters I went, until up front, something caught my eye. Why were all those Aboriginals coming out from under their houses and lining the street? Shit! It hit me like a tonne of bricks: maybe being way out here all on my lonesome wasn't such a brilliant move. Instead of doing the clever thing and hoofing it, inquisitively I poked my head out the window and craned around for a closer appraisal. Stirring up a dust-storm of dissent, the mob of clench-fisted blackfellas, scruffy kids and mangy dogs were quickening their pace and above the noise I heard, in a crooning singsong kind of voice, 'Nigger, nigger,' wafting down the cruddy street. I could tell by the unmistakable tone that it was someone kindly calling their pet dog, a dog with an inappropriate name like Nigger, especially in a place like Weipa South Mission. Then, out in front, bobbing up and down just above the swelling mob's anger, I saw a person riding a bike.

Trouble was brewing. As I stalked the ute behind the excitable groundswell of protesters, the person riding a bike turned and his face registered the danger heading his way. It was a bloody whitefella and the bloody blackfellas were after his scalp. Shit, shit, shit – it was Conj, and there he was cycling up front, definitely singing the wrong tune. With one long blast of the ute's horn, the het-up mob divided, allowing just enough room for the car to nudge through and run alongside him. 'Quick,' I yelled, 'chuck the bike in the back and jump in!'

Once, maybe twice in a lifetime, you get to see a 'saved-from-a-fate-worse-than-death' smile – it is reward aplenty, believe me. Conj chucked the bike in the back like it was a toy, yelled, 'Job's right,' leapt in like a pro motorbike sidecar king and we sprinted away, leaving behind a wall of dust.

'Mate,' he blubbered, 'you're a sight for sore eyes, thank Christ you came from nowhere, just in the nick of time. Thought I was a goner for sure,' he jabbered on. 'Jesus H, I just went for an innocent ride with me dog, me black dog.' Out came the Tally Ho papers onto which he shakily spread a few strands of tobacco and a very small crumble of sticky hash. *Skpsizzle, skpsizzle* went the lit-up end as he took a drag. Sounding like he'd sucked air from a blown-up balloon, he went on, 'Me black dog, Nigger, got lost down this way, so I just kept callin' him, and got lost meself.'

Finding hash in Weipa was like finding the Holy Grail in Queensland so I pulled over, readily drew in the smoke of kindness, and commiserated. 'A dog-day afternoon, Conj.'

As the bottled-up fear turned to hilarity, we laughed until we cried, and both let the tears pour out for as long as possible. With him, it was a rare chance, especially being an Australian male which automatically implied that any crying, public or private, was just not done. For me, so what if I let a fair bit of sadness, guilt, futility and shame creep into the flow? It's always better out than in.

Stryder's bark brought us back as the tail-wagging Nigger exited from the scrub and jauntily swaggered toward us. 'Good on ya, Nigger,' Conj said, and we laughed again.

'Reckon Nigger'd like it better if you walked the other way, Conj, out toward the tip – you know, the Lucky Dip.'

'Jeez, Les sure won the lucky dip when he won you, Robbie. You're amazing. You know I . . .' Sensing a confession, I tried to stop him with a friendly peck on the cheek, yet somehow the movement turned into a kiss, a fair dinkum pash on the lips. 'You're amazing too, Steve. I know life's all smoke and mirrors but Les, he's my man.' I eased back, held his gaze, and suggested we go pick up Les. 'Oh, and by the way, you're a good kisser too.' That last bit helped us both.

He wasn't the first of Les's friends to go behind his back and put the acid on me. Flattered, I always took it as a compliment and never mentioned it again, to anyone.

In the back of the ute, Nigger and Stryder looked like flying sky horses as we raced along. Halfway down the stretch a plump, tall black woman pacing toward town intrigued us enough to pull up. In the flurry of red dust, the door creaked open, and Conj motioned for her to sidle into the middle. We were all scrunched so close together, Conj looked like he was wearing kneecap earrings. As we snaked away, he heaved the old ute's door closed.

'Conj, stop slammin' the door, you'll give my car arthritis.'

The woman beside me smiled easily. 'Training, girl, it's all in the training.'

'Yeah, but how many lifetimes does it take 'em?' I countered.

'Till they liberate themselves.'

I liked that a lot and turned to her and stuck out my hand and introduced us both.

'Pequitta, and I've seen you before, Robyn, you're with Les.'

'Yeah, but don't hold it against me.'

Nestled back into the arms of the ute, we girls laughed harder than the repartee deserved, but for both of us I think it was more about finding like minds in amongst the swell of no-brainers.

Pequitta explained that her husband, Barry, was picking the girls up from school, then coming to get her. 'It's a nice piece of country out here so I thought I'd walk for a while, you know.' She was about as tall as your average bloke, and like our Thursday Island Maggie, Pequitta's beauty was unusual. She was thickset, had body-builder muscles and her two surfboard feet were planted securely on terra firma. Recognising a friend from the first second helped me to rebalance the terrible things I had just seen.

'You meet some of the best people along life's dusty trail, don't you think? Help yourself to the tobacco. How many daughters?' I asked.

As the big woman spoke, love for her three kids expanded out from her heart and into us. She rolled a smoke for me and one for her, lit them both and passed one over. 'Bin workin' at the Abo community centre a coupla days a week for a while. It's time they started pullin' up their socks.'

Conj and I lifted our eyebrows in surprise.

'Look, I'm a Thursday Islander and my people have copped a rough deal for a century or more now, so I know. Some reckon the missionary people up here in Weipa were too cruel but at least back then everyone had manners and pride. I reckon this mob were better off then, being clean 'nd sober and doin' a fair day's work.'

This was a rare voice of discriminating awareness in the debate, let alone one of their own speaking out. Liking this unruffled, expansive black woman and her different, fresh way of seeing things, I urged her to continue.

Pequitta must have felt comfortable too because she didn't mince her words. 'It's easy to pick the mission-raised Abos from those on the dole. They stand taller, carry themselves good. Nowadays, what with all the government money coming, the others have gone cunnin'. They just abuse the old lore.'

From the radio came the beginnings of the news, but something more important was happening and I hurriedly turned if off. 'Er, you mean the Aboriginal sharing thing? The "if I'm in your tribe and you've got food and I haven't, you must share it with me and the rest of the tribe" lore?'

She nodded yes while her hands waved vigorously, like a cricket umpire calling a no ball.

'Yeah, but that's a terrific tradition,' came my white protest.

Without hesitating, Pequitta kept on batting. 'It's true and that's the way the world *should* be, but up here they abuse a person's hospitality. It's like an illness, where they won't stand on their own two feet. I got sick of them comin' over to my place with nothing, tellin' me I had to share. Then eatin' and drinkin' till there was nothin' left, then up and leavin' till the next time they ran out of other places to go.' Her tone was not angry, just honest. 'Then when their dole money was all gone, they come knockin' on my door again.'

We drove for a while before she next spoke. 'In the end, I kicked 'em all out. Told 'em to go bush and get some respect.' Pequitta puffed her cigarette a bit. 'My husband, he works hard every day, eh. Them fellas've gotta get the smarts too. They're just too bloody lazy for their own good these days.'

Her rave was good food for thought and as it ran across our outsider minds, the brick veneers appeared in the distance. As we left the last of the bush I made a point of remembering those left behind.

On the edge of the dirt-bitumen road seam, Pequitta saw her husband and kids coming the other way, so we pulled to halt. I gave her the best-looking mummy apples and reached into their car window, ruffling the hair of the bright, irrepressible little girls. 'It's just like shaking hands with an old friend,' I said to Pequitta as we parted.

'Me too Robyn. Les knows where we live. Come over anytime. We'll have a real feed then.'

That evening our vibes came courtesy of the hash. The black chunk was sweet and earthy, and as the crumble and the texture clogged in my fingernails, I was reminded of the Normanby River soil. And for once, different kinds of stories wended their way through the chatty night; for once, interesting stores replaced the normally alcohol-fuelled raves.

CHAPTER 32

In the Swill

While I got out of his hair and went barmaiding, Les knuck-led down, put the boat into dry dock and installed a 2000-kilo freezer compliments of the slippery 'Paper Tiger' money. Of course we still slept on board, just instead of floating on water, the *Jean King* was suspended in a cradle on the land. On the waterfront there was no telling who was sniffing around minding other people's business, so Les made it a habit to sleep with the .22 pistol under the pillow, just for safety.

Lying back in bed one night, both reading, I turned to him and said, 'Wish we'd brought Stryd up the ladder tonight.'

He nodded snoozily, and hooked me down beside him. Purling through our 'Paper Tiger' porthole came the night's moonbeams, so, using my feet, I juggled the hatch off onto the deck above, letting the brilliant energy of the Milky Way fill our bedroom. Abruptly there was a noise, then from the wheelhouse came scuttle, slip, cough, cough, spongy cough, grizzle short breath, stumble.

'Don't move or I'll shoot! I'm warnin' ya, I've got a gun, and it's aimed at ya.' Silently I rolled sideways as, with the pistol cocked and pointed into the invisible wheelhouse space, Les began crawling silently toward the trouble.

'Sssmemate,' came a wheezy whisper.

Clatter, trip, out of control, in through the fo'c'sle opening crashed a loose, skinny body which rolled effortlessly onto the bed's end. Beelining for the unknown's temple, Les swung the barrel toward the screwed up, brown paper-bag body. 'Ssssmemate, don-shoot, mate iluvsyas.' As pissed as a pirate, the ethereal man who had christened our boat, Boydie Lee, grinned as his crinkle-cut eyes blinked up at us.

Following a plate of curry and a brief chinwag, I tucked his frail, beloved frame into the lounge bed. Since he and the dog had often shared lodgings before in the Big Shed, Boyd easily managed to slip past Stryder's guard. The next day, so as not to dent his pride, Les asked him to consider guarding the *Jean King* anytime we were both away from it. In turn, we agreed to feed and water the dear being. Impishly, he saluted then wandered off in the direction of the Palace, where he put his life's main purpose into practice: the art of swaying around bars borrowing money, then reeling off to find someone who needed it and giving it to them with no strings attached. Boydman was a middleman without the paperwork, an impeccable money launderer. At the end of each day's work, Boydie, always without a cent, quietly lurched down the way of the slips, bless him.

By then it must have been close to the late 1970s. And sorry for not being able to pinpoint the years exactly, but the outside world and its events simply did not define or affect ours. However, I do remember Christmas manifesting in the mining town as a fountain of endless beer elixir. There must've been a brewery strike somewhere because everyone seemed to be drinking twice as fast and twice as much, as though making sure they got their full quota before it all ran out. The instant the pub door unclicked at 10am, desperate Aboriginals exploded into the back bar. The way they stomped to the counter and begged for more, it was like Bjelke-Petersen had put a Christmas bonus in that fortnight's social security payment. Less outlandishly, but also from that early in the day, local white chappies, stragglers, outsiders and fishermen streamed forth: all of them stayed all day. And my my my, how those cash registers sang out, and how quickly they filled with holy cash-eluliah.

With no break for the workers, I and fellow barmaid Cheryl

kept those drinks happening, no worries. It was like having the taps turned on to flow and doing the beer glass conga line beneath them: and at regular intervals, we two also shouted ourselves to heavily laced short black coffees. Cheryl had just fought a few pirates on her Asia-to-Australia yacht run so this little shindig was a snack.

Each day, having missed the lunch gong, the ravenous natives got restless and started brawling, so we two beer bunnies reasoned that the crowd might settle if we played some tasty music every afternoon. Using Cheryl's portable tape deck, we switched the boozy crowd onto a kind of 'down-on-the-range' mix. I think everyone was totally surprised at the success of our innovative move because all the head-butting, sad and hurtful battles that normally occurred ceased. Music speaks all languages, especially to the heart.

The true surprise was the best one too, because the Aboriginals got original. Being so perked up by the music, the next thing we realised the black end of the bar was singing and canoeing away into karaoke dreamtime. It was such a win-win, *everyone* in the bar loved the harmony it brought and with old tensions gone, a new mood blossomed. 'Happy Christmas Jesus H!' Cheryl and I chimed as we downed another Drambuie laced with coffee, and kept the liquid–cash conversion pouring steadily into the till of good tidings.

Of course it's important to keep in mind that just like laughing till you cry, the good vibes of happiness can flip the other way and burst into a fight, all in the spirit of things. At any rate, by the week before Christmas, the floodgates of brewery heaven must have been swinging off its hinges as the throng flocked through the place. For us barmaids there were no more coffees in camouflage, it was heads down and brains in gear as we waded from end to end through the soggy alcohol swill. With the demanding crowd four deep, all I could see was a thick band of beseeching arms and thirsty men bleating for more drinks.

Cheryl squelched past from the other end saying she should have worn a Dryzabone (the farmer's favourite full-length wet-weather coat). I agreed and jokingly countered with a suggestion that we toss a carpet snake in amongst them or pump a few shots into the roof, then moved to the next customer, a white bloke waving paper money at me.

'Gimme one pint, two quarts, one shandy, and one gin and tonic without ice thanks, love.'

Cheryl and I were so busy that there was no time for finicky orders. So I said, 'Mate, we got pints, pints or pints, OK!' and shoved five pint glasses under the never-ending tap of frothy brown liquid. Slip, slop, slap, I scooped the foaming pints up onto the drowning bar, plucked the 'near enough' sheets of money and while cramming the stuff into the till's pocket heard the next voice call out, 'Hey missus, serve me. I bin waitin' a real long time. Give us four beers there, missus.'

At least the Aboriginals knew how to order, I thought, and shoved the beers onto the bar, took the right money and moved on into the pandemonium as the next order spewed forth.

'Hey you there, you gunna hand 'em to me?' the black brother I had just served demanded in a narky tone.

As if he couldn't see that I was busy beyond control, and the four beers were no more than an arm's length from both of us. 'Reach out and pick 'em up yourself, you lazy bastard.' Next thing they'll be wanting blood, I thought, and swam on to the next eager patron.

Hours later, as closing time nudged nearer, the din dropped, Cheryl punched the clock and the tills were balanced – well, near enough – so I scanned the room to see if there was anyone still standing, noting only six or seven gawky black blokes skulking around in the semi-lit corner, nearest to the back doors. All afternoon Charlie Pride, the Aboriginals' favourite country and western singer, had been whanging out simple lovesick ballads. Now with just myself and those few stragglers left, I put on a favourite and gave it some volume, letting Mr Bojangles from the jail of wise regret sing his story of unfair imprisonment by those more powerful than him. There was only a quick floor mop and it would be home time.

'Hey you there!'

Looking up from the mop to the voice, I saw the bloke who had given me a bit of lip earlier in the day, the black man, and he now stood much too close and there was no doubt that his edgy, scornful tone was a standover tactic.

'Yeah you, you white girl, you call me black bastard back there a while ago!' No matter what colour he was on about, straight away I picked him as a drunken menace.

'No, no,' I said apologetically, 'I didn't say black, I said *lazy*.'

Before there was time to sweeten up my assertion, the dark fellow skittled back to the other black bone shadows. Lazy bastard, black bastard, he was definitely a big bastard, and as I watched, he kept squawking my way every few seconds. The scrummed-up, brooding mob around him were muttering discontentedly too. They were shitty, inebriated, and giving lip service to their own deluded visions. The air bristled and my neck hair stood up like vulnerable echidna quills. It wasn't hard to feel that something serious was on the brew and that I needed to do more than the Mr Bojangles shuffle to save myself from harm.

Quick-smart I pussyfooted the sudsy mop bucket to sit directly under the flip-up counter entrance making a slippery, shin-cracking trap-shot if ever there was one, then opened up the doors that led more deeply into the office part of the hotel. No way was I protecting the pub's money so the instant plan was to call their bluff, and if that didn't work, run for it all the while screaming like a woman possessed (which I would have been).

The trouble corner stirred agitatedly then, shadow on dark, they rose and started pacing my way. Shit! The mop was close to hand and stood ready for action too, so 'up 'em' I thought, and started smashing the two double-stacked empty glasses trays up and down, up and down, up and down on the top of bar – clashing, jangling, clattering and smashing the glasses.

Adding to the tremendous noise, I screamed, 'Fuck off, fuck off, fuck off!' hard and long and on and on for dear life, until the noise was deafening. The violent din and my madness spooked the bejesus out of them, and nor did I stop until the scruff-bags oozed outside and the exit doors had stopped swinging.

Stumbling over the bucket of slop, with the trusty mop in samurai position, I stepped cautiously to the glass entrance and snapped the lock closed. There, that fixed the bastards, colour or no colour, and broken glass was better than broken bones. With a hammering heart, I reflected that the dollars in the job were a joke, but where could you get excitement like that? Whatever, I had jumped those pack-bullies and foiled their cowardly plan. Down went one, two, three shots of top-shelf cognac, which licked my already frisky button of desire, and so with specific intention, I sped homeward.

And then the silly season was over and the fishing season was upon us. Thank Christ for that, the entire fishing fleet murmured. Our boat slipped off the dry dock, returned to the wharf and was ready to rock. Storing up for two or three months at sea meant filling 30 foot of boat with all the necessary crap. Even though we now had a 2000-kilo freezer, there was still no indoor fridge, so provisions were either a frozen solid brick or, in the case of vegetables, lived outside in the weather, stored in the fishnets strapped underneath the canopy of the back deck. There they could roll around without bruising, could breathe, never went mouldy and, in the case of chokos and potatoes, keep growing. Then came the outboard fuel in bulky 44-gallon drums, gas bottles, fishnets, coils of ropes and string, needles, anchors, buoys, engines, outboards, and parts for all the different engines. To be specific, a ship-load of crap. Plus the beer and the tobacco, of course.

Winslet, one of the devious long-time barra skippers, slipped some cunning advice to Les: 'Son, if I was you, son, I'd head north.'

What was it with blokes? Was I invisible or were they blind? Still, with a name like that what could you expect? Wince the Mince, I thought, and shovelled way too much coffee in his coffee, knowing it would leave a bad taste in his mouth. Les nodded eagerly at him and kept tossing the cartons of supplies down below where the ABC news was rattling on:

> *... the public outcry surrounding the Belview Hotel has forced the state government to fully assess its decision before any demolition orders can be issued ...*

This drawn-out political story of manipulation was affecting people like the silly season did: everyone was getting het-up, intense and frustrated, and Les's comment was as arrogant as Bjelke-Petersen's handling of the issue ... 'Fuckin' greenies,' he mumbled, 'they're nothin' but trouble.' He flicked the news off and I said nothing – getting out of port was exciting enough. At least then there'd be much less drinking and plenty of swooning – where we were heading, the scenery was enough to make anyone faint. It was the ripest, most virginal wetlands of the whole continent.

The *Jean King* ploughed through a squabble of seagulls who squawked resignedly before lifting off the sea pathway, allowing our dinky boat to steam past the wharf. From the back deck I saw tiny mudskippers busybodying up and down their own silty patch of turf on the river's edge. Just for a lark I opened the front of my sarong and did a couple of quick nude flashes toward Weipa for those who might, or might not, be watching. Who cared?! When a couple of working johnnies' jaws dropped in appreciative surprise, we laughed merrily, swept out on the tide, turned left and went south, down into the Gulf. In the wake of Wince's advice, I questioned our direction. Les grinned and looked out into the open horizons. 'Yeah, woman of sea, that's why we're goin' south.'

CHAPTER 33

Reunion with the Mulligans

*I*n the brand-new world of the Gulf, the stark contrast of the ochre-red cliffs of Pera Heads gave an incredible blueness to the sky and the glittering white sand double-shuffling below, as above we dipped along on the incredible substance that the whole world floated on – or was it in? The ocean was a constant source of magnetism; it defied knowing, and just like a little kid's intrigue at touching bubbles, the liquid experience of it held me tirelessly enthralled. And the luscious bush country just kept on coming.

Les decided we'd head for Cape Keer Weer and anchor out the front of the Kirke River, then go in on the morning tide. From a local history book I explained that 'Keer Weer' was Dutch for 'turning around', and that it was where the natives had repelled the European intruders in the 1600s; and how the Dutch logbooks had mentioned that there was nothing worth staying for. 'Bloody idiots! Imagine how the barra would have been jumping then, not to mention the bauxite.'

Just on nightfall we heaved-to at the river's mouth and prepared to sit outside until first light the following morning. As the boat jazzed to and fro from the outgoing tide, I decided it was time to take the shears to Les's hair. Commenting that I looked no better, he raked through one of the toolboxes and handed me a gummed-up pair of fibreglass scissors. Hardly a craftsman's tool, so I suggested we both go bald.

Les was quick. 'Yeah, you'll do mine, and then won't let me do yours.'

I randomly hacked through a coiled chunk of my locks and let the strands flitter off on the breeze. 'There, now who's first?'

It was before dawn when the *Jean King* romped in over the sandbar, slipped up the broad, strong-flowing river and prepared to set up camp. We were both were wearing No. 1 crew-cuts and a few throbbing lovebites. It was a brand-new look, a brand-new feeling, and brand-new country; it was the river of promises, the lovebite lagoon. The plucky dog swam ashore immediately, chased away a couple of pigs, scared a bunch of unsuspecting baby crabs back into the water, dug half-a-dozen sand holes, marked out her territory and strolled off into the wilderness. You didn't have to be 'a greenie' to see that this was splendid country. Immediately it felt good and abundant and absorbing, just like home should.

Fuel for the outboard and the freezer engine were absolutely crucial to our operation so first off we hurled the big drums of petrol into the water, towed them over to the shore, rolled them up the sandy spit, and stood them under a family of robust she-oaks. 'Ow, ouch, ah ah, haaa,' I moaned, shuffling away from a prickle patch, 'that should keep thieves away.' Being a long way from 'civilisation' didn't mean we were on our own out there, it's just that we didn't necessarily know who else might or might not be lurking around.

Then went the tools of trade – nets, anchors, rope coils, buoys, gas bottles, etc – and then a protective tarp went over the lot. Stryder sniffed around, picked a cool, comfortable position and settled in to keep guard on the arrangements.

Later, racing upstream along the broad, tree-lined waterway our dinghy made the ibis, egrets, wedge-tailed eagles and black-breasted kites all screech discontentedly. Well, it was their bad luck, because we were staying. And sure enough the river's foreshore lagoons were like the Babylonian Pure Lands. It was so luscious, I half-expected to spot a herd of snacking rhinos. The Kirke was over 25 metres wide and stretched inland for miles and miles, harbouring at its headland a vast lagoon that spread out like an ocean in all directions. Inspired, I stood on the bow of the dinghy, tore off my shirt and held it up like a flag. The other hand I raised, and declared: 'Let it be known from whatever day it is today, that from this day forward, the great Australian inland sea has been discovered, and I do now declare it officially owned by every bloody body.'

Work, that other four-letter word, could now commence. Yep, watching, waiting, guessing, plotting – for the weather to drop; for the tide to go in and out; the fish to move, run or arrive; the half-moon to fill; the still of the neaps to start going up and down; the wind to drop; the sea to turn. Every day and every night, side by side we ran the nets, filleted, skinned, scrubbed, weighed and packed fish down. It was quite a game.

Naturally only the best fish from the morning haul went into the cast-iron pan with just a lick of butter – the smaller, the sweeter: jumping cod fillets, barra wings, white salty rolls of flathead or seasonally sweet glistening fish roe together with peas, honeyed carrots and eggs. While I cooked, Les would get on the radio every morning and start straight into the essential lying caper. Although we said it every day in every way, the fibs all boiled down to, 'Nah, she's pretty quiet down here. Thinkin' of movin'. Not worth stayin' really. Reckon they must be north of here . . . over and over and over and out.'

Honest, lying was necessary. Then whoever was on the other end of the line would lie right back, with everyone listening in and taking their turn, until finally the whole coast would be content and everyone could take a quick nap in peace.

After the morning lie-down it was scrub and scour time – of the dinghy, the wet weather gear, of the back deck, of clothes soaking in the plastic bucket, everything got scrubbed clean. Then we'd scrub and scour ourselves with bucket upon bucket of bailed-up sea water, using Teapole, the sea-friendly disinfectant detergent. We'd dip into all the body's folds and marshes, then follow with more chilling lashings of cold ocean water once, twice, three times over the body, and quickly sprint into the wheelhouse. That we would do daily – well, almost daily . . . well, weekly kinda, depending on what was happening. Precious fresh water was used with conscious discipline and sparingly, intelligently, for cooking, drinking and washing of hair only. Later in the day, after another snooze, it was back to working, watching, waiting, guessing and lying to any opportunistic other-river outsiders trying to come inside.

It was pre-Buddha, a paradise from ancient times, a David Attenborough spectacular. The plentiful water kingdom was ripe with sharks: grey nurses, tigers, saws, shovel-noses, hammerheads plus mud crabs, dolphins, pygmy whales, barramundi, prawns, oysters, dugong, rays, king and blue salmon, queen fish and mangrove jacks, to name just a few. In the middle earth, the roaming population teemed with kangaroos, wallabies, brumbies, cattle, pigs, snakes and dingoes (probably a few giraffe melded in with the dabbled trees too). As below, so above: the skies were a potpourri of jabirus, brolgas, Torres Strait pigeons, ducks, swans, geese, bats, sea eagles, shags, and flocks of bitchy pelican to cite just a few. What one species calls poisonous another species uses to heal with, so everything has its reason for being on the planet, including the less desirable characters from the poisonous realm also trying to complete their life purpose: box jellyfish, log-pretending crocs, killer sea snakes, deadly taipan and fatal stonefish, to mention but a few.

We new kids on the block wandered between the three realms like the Aboriginals must always have done: by day we walked the earth, and by night we surfed across the ocean letting the southern hemisphere rain her sparkling diamond galaxy down on us. As the speeding dinghy's wake dashed through iridescent polyps cutting the cross of Christ behind us, all the time our backyard ocean kindly provided us with a healthy living. Nice work if you can get it!

Australia's only stork, the big-beaked jabiru, is black and white, stands about one to two metres high, is yellow-eyed and red-legged. However, getting more than a peek at the intensely private jabiru is considered very lucky. Why then did this particular big bird establish her three gangly babies so close to the *Jean King*? It's a mystery you wouldn't want to be asking a white coat. She just did. Certainly, the splendid wetland was prolific with baby bird tucker, but allowing us to be privy to the babies' training episode? Suffice to say, she was on a tricky mission as, like a trained ballerina, repeatedly she'd pace a few steps down the sand, lift off, and be up, up and away. With wings wide enough to cast shadows over the little winged folk watching from below, she would land again like a falling silk scarf.

Keen as mustard those little bird babies, like newborn wildebeests, stumbled gawkily down the sandy runway, their awkward stick-legs trying desperately to keep pace with their plumy, fresh-feathered body and oversized flapping wings. The laws of bird ballast, not! Which part was actually in charge of lifting the out-of-sync fluffy white bags on pink sticks off the earth was up for discussion. Their landing gear had problems too, as clacking loudly to their mum, time and again they crashed nose first, arse up, flapping and flailing about, trying to avoid the very stationary she-oak tree trunks at the end of the runway. Certainly, it was an anxious time for all concerned. When lift-off finally happened, the shock on their downy faces was priceless. Privileged with the best view, we sat in the back-deck members' stand and watched the committed bird mother persist until all three made Chinese calligraphy strokes on the horizon, and flew away together for places unknown. If you want it enough, do the practice.

'Rae, Rae, investigate the fire, Rae. Where the blazes are the boys? Get 'em inside! Rae, pump the bilge. Extinguish the fuckin' fire, Rae!' With the minimum amount of drama, the Old Man, Rae and the two little people snuck into the Kirke one mid-May afternoon. It was a good reunion between compadres, and some well-timed intervention too. Things on the *Jean King* had been getting squabbly – stormy, in fact. Thirty foot of boat, two lovers and a switched-on dog every day: why be happy in paradise?

The Mulligan mob's boat – a cluttered, old-aged crate that by rights should've been laid up and resting on the bottom of the ocean – brought with it everything, and the kitchen sink. 'A clothesline out the back, a veranda up the front, and an old rocking chair,' I happily sang and kissed the Old Man right on the lips. Without resisting, he spluttered demonstrably, herded the littlies from under everyone's feet, issued instructions and started preparing a major food fest. The now taller little people were still tender, beaut kids who excitedly tore round and round the boat, hanging lovingly off any available leg.

'Rae, you work harder than any bloke I've ever come across.' I hugged my dear friend closely. A dry hacking cough doubled her over, but when I suggested she go straight to bed, she grinned toothlessly, shrugged and said, 'Yeah, the flu's getting me down, so I figure fixin' this outboard leg is the best way to kill it.' Try telling that to a western doctor!

With Rae outside poring over the outboard gizzards, inside, Davey, Les and I hit the room temperature beer with a heavy hand and got stuck into theorising on the actual whereabouts of fish. There was the 'just before full moon', the 'on the full moon' and the 'just after the full moon' theory, the incomings and the outgoings tide theory, the monthly theory, one of us even suggested that maybe the fish just got their periods and laid low. Since no one really knew anything, and the fish weren't telling, it was a ceaseless guessing game.

'The best part is that no one knows. It gives the fish a bit of a breather.' Old Man wisdom. He kept peeling spuds and intermittently patting the little boys' heads.

My theory worked every time – if we got on the drink then checked the nets, there'd be no fish, but if we got on the drink and didn't check the nets, there'd be more fish than an illegal long-liner could haul up in one day. And unlike some, except for catfish and shark, Les and I processed every fish caught and made it our duty to ensure that no fish was left long enough to go rotten and therefore die meaninglessly. As a good reminder, fishermen used to say that you could only catch a fish once. On that day, my fish theory proved correct so although there weren't many fish, with a few drinks running through our bodies, clearing the nets must have been like watching circus clowns rehearsing a new routine: unrefined but very very funny.

Following the performance, we dined at the Restaurant at the Edge of the Gulp, when Old Man Mulligan fed us thick roasted slabs of a just-caught bush turkey, shiny gravy, spuds, and plenty of parboiled fresh greens. It was so delicious Les proposed marriage to Davey, who snorted, 'Get it right, son, your girl's me best girl, eh but.' He then turned his attention to scheming.

'We gotta outsmart the Boof and the young fella [his two older sons]. They're killin' it [catching plenty] down Holroyde way [a particular river] so let's throw a cat in amongst the pigeons.' All mischievous fun remember, for although the Old Man might be going against his own, it didn't pay to mess in his family's affairs; their blood was thicker than the walls of an igloo. 'The next few months've got fuckin' good tide movements and I know a couple of tributaries runnin' into the Holroyde that they're not fishin'. This way, we'll cut 'em off at the Khyber Pass [outfox them].'

Karma had thrown us back into cahoots with the Mulligans so within a few days the entire shebang put out to sea once more.

Trotting south with no time agenda, Les called up Warwick who had a camp set up on the Kendall River. He was a good man whom we had become close buddies with while marking time for the barramundi season to open. Warwick had also told us about Peggy, his Wollomby tribe woman, and I was very keen to meet her. 'Ask him if Peggy's back yet.'

Ignoring me, Les waffled on. 'Put on the kettle, we'll be down your way in about two hours, mate.'

'Ask him, ask him!' Frustrated by Les's control techniques, I tried unsuccessfully to swipe the mike from him. It was that kind of aggravating, deliberate manipulation that easily became a battle of wills and turned into nasty words, threats or sometimes worse.

'No worries, Les,' Warwick replied. 'And Peggy says she'll make us turtle omelette for lunch.'

When we pulled up beside the hand-built, weather-strong pier, Warwick and Peg were there waiting to welcome us. The middle-aged lovers had a great thing going on in the Kendall River, what with their houseboat tied to the jetty, a proper shack sitting on the shore with a few chocked-up 44s beside it collecting fresh water, and a small farm tractor parked comfortably under the string of she-oaks.

The blokes fell into talking straight away so we girls didn't wait for introductions, we just touched hands, hugged and that was that.

In the shack, the kitchen table was filled with precious things like chocolate biscuits and butter for the fresh scones. Pouring the tea I asked about the sprig of purple-backed leaves, a native cutting, in an empty coffee jar vase and Peggy explained that it was native ginger, used for cooking and easy to find if you knew where to look.

'You know, the Dutch came down this far in the seventeenth century,' I, the apprentice, said to the master. 'They reckoned there was nothing of value here. Must have been blind as bats!'

Taken aback by my keen interest, Peggy hooked her arm into mine and walked us out of the houseboat, our cups of tea in hand. 'Nice to hear you've read a bit about us,' she commented kindly. 'Wollomby history always got passed down verbally through the centuries so Mum and Dad told us kids all about the Dutch when I was young.'

The country hummed like a well-stocked menagerie, a collector's dream of birds, fish, animals, flowers, plants and trees. Just a glance away, pristine lagoons ran up and down the whole coastline.

'I know you and Les bin fishing the Kirke. Our country goes way up beyond that.' Asking Aboriginal tribes' permission for anything was not even a token concept then, but just knowing Les and I hadn't asked if we could live there, let alone hunt and fish, made me feel bad mannered and uncomfortable, so I blushed and said something insipid like, 'Is it ok if we . . . ?' In no way was it the proper, honourable request it should have been, but she patted my hand, chuckled good-heartedly and nodded.

We stepped away from the water's edge. 'See these marks here on the sand? This here's where turtle eggs are buried; and see under this pandanus 'ere, see the baler shells, they're sign shells.' Using one of the shells, the black woman dug some water up. 'We leave the shells bunched together so anyone goin' past knows exactly where the water is, and can dig and drink with the shell too.' Peggy dug again, skilfully extracted six turtle eggs, re-covered the rest with sand and calmly handed the eggs to me. 'Feel 'em. Turtle shell is soft, eh! No use boiling 'em, they won't set. I'll scramble these fellas when we get back.'

The two of us walked on toward the mouth of the creek. As Peggy taught me, I sensed a certain elegance, an air of graciousness, a style one could only be born to, not acquired. She was a kin sister and already I cherished her unique company. Quietly she pointed into the clump of sculpture-like pandanus and young saplings. Dappled into the terrain were lizards — three big ones easily four metres long from head to end of tail, and their littlies, all with glistening tongues darting in and out; a local family out on the food trail. The prehistoric reptiles looked up, acknowledged the two-footed creatures in their presence yet remained unbothered: Gondwana goannas, unchanged, grazing in the time-warp loop.

At a certain spot along the creek edge Peggy extracted half a dozen fresh barra skins from her handwoven pandanus bag and handed them to me. 'Just walk real slow into the creek up to your ankles and splash one of them skins around a bit.'

As I did this, a wild stingray about three to four metres in circumference flopped over the top of my wrist and slid slowly down across my hand. In a place that felt as harmonious as Bramble Cay, in a day of marvels, the trusting, living being's tiny mouth nibbled my palm skin, found the barra skin, sucked it from my fingers and fell back into the shallows. In a privilege the rays allowed, three or four of them did the same — it was an indescribable honour.

Peggy's soft laugh lifted in the breeze. 'Some blackfellas come up from the Holroyde last week and tried spearin' our rays so Warwick let off a few shotgun rounds in their direction. They scattered like panicky crocs.'

Both laughing, one arm slung comfortably across the other's shoulders, we wended our way back to camp. Like Pequitta and Maggie, again I had been blessed with a knowledge-swapping woman.

Peggy told me that although all the Aboriginals in the area were known as the Wik or the Wik Munkan people, there were different tribes all with different dialects — she spoke about six of the dialects, and English. 'Don't forget the Australian dialect too,' I added. She laughed softly again, saying, 'Me dad loved the word *tickety-boo*, reckoned it was the only word in the English language worth saying.' We stopped walking, held hands and momentarily visited each other's soul. 'I know you understand when I say that love's not the right word to describe how I feel about this country,' Peggy said to me. 'It's deeper than that, it is me, I am it.' I did understand and felt the same about that country too and still do.

The dusk horizon began filling with a smouldering, vibrant

golden orb that was sinking into a sheer-silk powder-blue sea. The dipping, unspeakably brilliant sun was almost too much. Pointing to it, the black woman commented, 'Now that's tickety-boo.' For a while, nothing was or needed to be said. And it's not necessary to be in the pristine wilderness to appreciate the sun going down through the office window, or the living trees in the street where you live, or the little lizards in your own backyard – we are in all of it, all the time.

Before long it was time to go in different directions. Peggy and Warwick had nets to check, and we wanted to reach the Holroyde before dark. She and I hugged mutual goodness into each other. 'You're a good woman, Peggy, and I'm indebted to you.' This was true, and that I loved her.

As we sped away, I was filled with a flush of pride for our friends and the ripping adventure Les, Stryder and I were in. 'What an incredible place. How lucky are we?'

'Well, Peggy's what we'd call a princess,' Les explained. 'You remember Wesley and Solomon? They are elders of the mob, and Peggy's brothers, but she still had to get special permission to build the permanent on-shore set-up. The Wollomby tribe owns all this area right the way up past the Kirke.'

The place was like accidentally stumbling across an award-winning doco from an earlier, undisrupted century with a soundtrack that had only one voice, that of the landscape. Just how anyone can say they have an abiding, grateful love of nature yet kill fish for a living, I'm not sure, but that is what I'm saying here.

CHAPTER 34

Lost at Sea

Skallywagging the Mulligan boys out of fish gave the Old Man and us some glee, and paid immediate dividends. By July, the Old Man, Rae and the two little people were upstream and firmly ensconced on-shore in a very liveable camp set-up. However, all the spawning barra had well and truly abandoned the river system and gone walkabout in the Gulf by then.

With the fish being sporadic and unpredictable, we weren't content to stay in the river and decided to chase sea fish along the shorefront. So Les and I went solo again, moved down to the beachfront 'suburb' and got closer to the outside action where the oldest Mulligan sons were fishing too. By eyeballing the constantly shifting sandbars, picking the right channels in between, then netting the underwater gullies which the shallow foreshore fish drove around in, we hit upon the secret of success. Oh, and add a dash of canny.

Come hail, rain or shine, two or three times every day we charged into the fishing vortex – naturally, running more and longer nets than was legal. Anchored from shoreline out, one would feed out the net while the other reversed the dinghy into the sloppy incoming waves. Out, out, out, then at the other net end, a sand anchor was dropped and a big white buoy clipped on: all the better to spot the unseeable net at night, especially if the net had dragged. Choppy white-cap waves slapped our dinghy up the rear as the tide went in, the current went across and up the coast, and the changing wind cut across both, all going elsewhere. With anywhere between 10 to 15 nets to deal with, to pluck fish from, to wrestle straight, detangle, pull tight, anything could happen – and usually did. The fish were good to us, that year, the Gods were kind.

Whether the night galaxy shone down or overshadowed us with a shifty school of clouds, still, everything ran like clockwork. Looking back at the dinghy's Christ-cross wake one midnight, Les yelled over the outboard noise, 'Looks like Jesus is with us!' as we cut out of the heads and shot down the shoreline to the last net. Decked head to toe in yellow wet-weather gear, we romped around in the black open sea searching for net buoys. Once found, I'd snatch up the net rope as he lifted the engine. 'It's a good haul. Jesus H, hope they're all like this.' What the hell is it with the H anyway? Jesus Hiram, Jesus Hymie, Jesus Harry? Using the net to pull us along, I worked the dinghy up and down into the waves, focused the torch on the fish being extracted, and kept the whole thing moving along the net to the end. Concentrating, perspiring, the fag in his mouth on beacon duty, Les reefed the fish free of the net, sliced throats and dropped them on the dinghy floor. 'Keep the torch steady, lift the net, higher, lower, don't flick it, pull it, push it, get a move on, look out for the crab, drop it, let's go, mate.'

Even though we stood ankle-deep in bloodied water, dead silver scaled fish, live crabs, clingy weed and poisonous jelly blubber, each net demanded our full attention. Hours flew by before we started eye-fumbling through the pitch black trying to sight the river mouth. This usually worked better after requesting some mouthy divine intervention.

'Jesus, why do the stars always reshuffle themselves? This astral navigation's hell. God help me, where's the bloody entrance?' Les would grizzle.

As the day's first light rose, the hint of predawn led us back in through the heads and up to the *Jean King*, where we'd spit out drenched fags, chuck Stryder up onto the boat, then slap the night's catch onto the back deck. I'd flush sea water over the blood-matted dinghy, then bail the water out with a bucket. On board, we'd give the already razor-sharp filleting knives a good lick of the steel, sniff the curling coffee aroma, and let its hot essence gratefully slip down, then the filleting would commence. From each run there'd be up to 15 ten-kilo trays to process, and fish are highly perishable, so there wasn't much time to muck about.

After the back was washed down and the dinghy refuelled, we'd go back out right away and do the same again. Later, the fish trays were knocked out, bagged up and restacked inside the freezer. Following shovel-loads of tucker, we'd grab some sleep then do the final day's sea rerun-check. From the midnight hour on, it ticked. We must have looked like Mr and Miss Universe as we ripped across the country, day and night, casually trusting survival. And drinking alcohol didn't seem to matter – life was so engrossing that we barely argued at all.

Those were good times, and there were many others like that. Les loved me exclusively, and I always supported and obeyed his decisions at sea like a proper first mate should. So far, he'd known exactly how to get us everywhere. But who can stop an enquiring mind? Right or wrong, every so often my ideas met a foul-mouthed, boxing stranger filled with smouldering resentment. As though I'd shifted the tectonic plates of his private lava bank, perplexingly he always erupted at a volcano's notice. Knowing from a young age that everyone has the right to think for themselves, the heated words between us jumbled up the contents of my head every time. One thing's for sure, arguing is enough to make anyone sick, especially if it becomes contagious.

How full or not was that ethereal spotlight in the night sky? Was it waxing or waning, was the tide at its top or its bottom, which way and how hard was the wind blowing? These things we both knew, and the fact was that we were meant to be together – but how does one marry fierce independence with passionate love?

A few weeks later, the Old Man pulled up alongside our boat. Never one to pull a punch, he launched right in. 'One of youse people is gunna go missing, I'm here to tell ya. All up yourselves, thinkin' ya fuckin' heroes! Gettin' too greedy, using all your anchors on nets instead of carrying one in ya dinghy in case of trouble. Stuff me dead, you two got an anchor in the dinghy?'

Embarrassed, we shook our heads. The two of us might have been

Conquerors of the World but, stupidly, we were breaking a very serious safety rule. The Old Man's skipper's hat sagged and shook sternly. 'Now listen here you kids, I'm warning ya both, stop going outside with no dinghy anchor. There's some over on the shore. And take some fresh water too. Stop being lamebrains.' His crusty stubbies stood off his legs like umbrella shades. 'What use are the fish if ya dead?'

I tried to wave the Old Man inside for a cup of tea, but he shook his head, 'No thanks. I'm off to give me boys the same serve.' Wagging his finger in earnest, Davey glanced out to sea. 'I've got a feeling, girl. Trust me and do as I say.' Later we heard his outboard steadily motoring back upstream.

The night train came. Before spearing up the middle of the river and out into the open sea, Les pulled into the riverbank, stepped onto a pile of Davey's good junk and grabbed the only remaining anchor. Working hard, the night hours quickly slipped away. Finally, with Stryder on my lap, collared raincoats buttoned up to the neck and bare legs sunken into the fishy brew, we left the office and headed for home. Satisfied with the catch, mentally we dreamed on about fish fillets multiplied by dollar signs, hot coffees, cleaning guns and suchlike. Racing along the coast, just as the river mouth came into sight, our daydreaming stopped short because the outboard engine cut out completely.

'Shit,' we chorused. I lunged for the torch and Les started feeling the outboard leg in the dark. One shine onto the prop confirmed what he already knew.

'Easy-peasy. It's just a shear pin. Get the spare in the plastic bag.' Without a shear pin, the propeller would not turn and therefore, the dinghy could not propel us anywhere.

I fish-walked over the catch to the under shelf at the front, but there was no sign of shear pins at all.

He shone the spotlight at me. 'Bring the bloody bag up here, mate.'

As I avoided a cranky crab and handed him the sealed plastic bag, an unusually early land breeze gently started pushing the boat sideways out to sea and I shivered like someone had walked over my grave.

Right then, the torchlight dimmed, flickered and went out. 'Shit, I gave Brucey [one of the Mulligans' deckhands] our last torch battery this morning. What a dick . . .' Just as his hand went to reach for the important spare parts bag, it diverted and slapped the middle of his forehead. 'Oh Jesus H, I gave him our spare fucking shear pin too!' Although it was night, I'm sure the colour drained from his ruddy face. 'Said he was having outboard trouble. Fucking fuck!'

See, smartarse, I thought, and looked at the shore for bearings. We were a fair distance out and drifting, so I raced back up the front, chucked a few dead fish into the centre, hauled Davey's borrowed anchor out from the gizzardy bilge, sunk the pointed anchor over-board, threaded the rope through the bowsprit and felt it unravel. 'Better start prayin' we're in shallow enough water for the pick to hit bottom,' I said gravely.

The rope slid through my palm and spiralled its way down, down, down, shit, down, down. This time my body shiver did that tomb-tingle spine-shudder – you know, the shiver that scares you. A fathomless chain-length second later, the pick touched bottom, the rope slackened in my hand, and the tomb-walker trotted off. I leapt up onto the front skirt of the dinghy. 'Now all we have to do to pre-vent us drifting into our next lifetime is make the bloody anchor hook in.'

'Just fucking jerk it up and down a bit.'

'I'll give you fucking jerk,' I muttered, and yanked the anchor so it arched up, gouged into the sand and pulled the dinghy to a halt. The relief injected some humour into the situation, and Les, lifting his cap, bowed like a gallant knight. 'Which bed would one prefer, madam?'

Sleeping – well, resting – above 25 or so slaughtered barramundi and a few scuffling, nippy crabs on a cold, blood-wet, skinny slab of aluminium looked mighty fine from where I stood. Grinning, my arms went out: 'One insists on a hug first.'

All decked out in fish-splattered yellow raincoats, we cuddled for a while, keeping a discerning eye on the shore just to make sure the dinghy wasn't drifting. Then, with arms tucked under head, he and I stretched along each plank and drifted off while the clouds played tag with the crescent moon. Like a dogfish God from Egypt, Stryder rested on all fours across the front lip of the dinghy, watching over us. She knew, as we did, that the Old Man would be out in a jiffy.

About an hour after dawn, Davey's big punt burst out of the river mouth and tore like an ambulance toward us. 'Glad ya took me advice, eh?' Leaving it at that, he grunted and shoved a flask toward us. 'Get this into ya. I put a bit'a brandy in with the tea.'

More like the other way round, I thought, and gladly gulped down the hot, rich drink then handed the 'medicine' over to Les who opened his throat and tipped in the fluid as though he had just crawled into an oasis on the edge of a desert. 'What took you so bloody long?'

'That's the trouble, fellas,' the Old Man told us grimly, 'Brucey's gone missing!' His eyes were filled with worried anger. 'No fuckin' anchor!'

Using binoculars at first light, they'd seen that we were alright, but the missing deckhand had been out at sea since noon the day before. While our dinghy was being towed back into the river, the three of us tried plotting how far out the lost one might have drifted. Such machinations leant more heavily on hope than actuality since there was none. Tides, currents and winds owned the sea and cared not which way the flow went, all working successfully on the unequivocal non-equilibrium theory. Our little plight didn't rate a mention, and never did either of us ever mention it to anyone: shame on us, the lack of water, of shear pins, of torch batteries and therefore of light.

Instantly, all the usual chatter and compulsory lying that normally waffled right across the western Gulf stopped. The only business the radio did was spread the word. And the word was Bruce. All the trawlers in the near vicinity stopped prawning and began combing the ocean. Pedro was out there, so Les told him that by our reckoning Bruce should be somewhere off the Love River, and asked if Canberra had put any spotter planes into the sky.

Pedro radioed back, 'Yeah, for once they're doin' the right thing. Tell everyone that the whole prawn fleet's lookin' like fuck.' His way of saying 'in dire earnest'.

One of the saltwater tribe was out there walking the plank, so all river fishermen pulled their nets and went looking too. It was us out there. The entire clan, binoculars stuck on like eyeglasses, scoured the Gulf with a fine toothcomb. While everyone crawled all over it, the lost one, without a skerrick of control, sat in a miniscule dot of a dinghy wallowing helplessly in the middle of the immense ocean of water. Get on ya knees and pray, Brucey, I thought.

When the third day drew to an end, everyone in the vicinity gathered on the *Jean King*. There was the Old Man's older sons, Baz and young Davey, and their tribes, and the Old Man's younger tribe of the two little ones and Rae, and us, all permanently glued to the crackling static of the radio. This was most grave.

'By the livin' Christ, bloody Canberra better keep them planes up there tomorrow.' The Old Man echoed everyone's main fear, that the search would be called off.

Suddenly the wireless burst into life. For a moment, I swear, you could have heard an anchor drop in Anchorage, when a spotter plane came over the air giving chart coordinates of the drifting seaman. Get off ya knees and start wavin', Brucey, I thought.

The split second broke and everyone started breathing again, but with dusk approaching, the game was far from over, and our silent barracking was never more urgent.

'We've got him, Canberra. He is now in sight and wavin',' Pedro broadcast. 'It'll take us ten minutes to reach the lucky bastard, but he is alive, Canberra, is that clear?'

Pandemonium let loose, and I heard the Old Man grizzle in relief: 'I'll tan his fuckin' hide!'

Seconds take time, just some take a little longer – like the time-lapse between the moment the trawler salvaged the fluky drifter and his rogue dinghy, heaved him safely on board, and Pedro hitting the radio waves with the tale. As the entire ocean nation hung on a thin thread, not a voice interrupted, nor was a listener unaffected, when the Queensland redneck cried over the airwaves. 'Fuck folks, I've just seen the most incredible smile I will ever see in my life.' His sobs of joy reached into everyone's hearts; even a few of the hardened, never-cried-in-me-lifers couldn't prevent a drop of compassion from escaping the tear ducts' gates.

'It was unreal pullin' alongside, and there was Brucey grinning like a Cheshire cat. Man, that smile, it touched me. I had a joint in one hand and a beer in the other, and when I asked Brucey what he wanted first, he said, "I really wanna enjoy this," took the hooch, sucked it in like the eye of a cyclone, then grabbed the beer and downed it in one guzzle.' The story touched us even more because Bruce was a 100 per cent committed hippie, which amongst other things meant that he never drank alcohol (in the vernacular, he was a pothead not a juice freak). And his chances of being saved like that were so infinitesimal that Brucey had been a very, very lucky young man and, we all reckoned, had used up one of his nine lives. Get back on ya knees Brucey, and thank your God many times, I thought. Never, ever give up, and always keep your sense of humour.

Pedro delivered him back at the Holroyde the next day. By then, three extra trawlers lay anchored outside and a rippling of barra fishermen also trickled in from the surrounding rivers. The lot were hell-bent on raging and didn't give a bugger, so we lit up a huge, blazing fire and held the Brucey Barbie Bash. While all and sundry rocked on and burnt beefsteaks bigger than whale ribs to a delicate crisp, the fire performed massive Aboriginal leaping shadows, and the untameable mob drank as much of anything as there was. On the premise that it could just as easily have been any one of us out there, everyone partied as though it was them who'd been saved – therefore despite reeling from the elation of having been rescued from the jaws of death, the fishing fraternity was still stable enough to manhandle the big ribs in one fist and keep their drink upright in the other.

Resembling charcoal-stained neanderthals hovering around on the edge of the universe, everyone but everyone listened as the saved man told his story. 'Yeah man, like firstly the shear pin snapped off man, and then it was too deep for the anchor chain to reach the bottom. Like freak out man.' Brucey's grin was a radiating sun.

Les scratched his head. 'But mate, I gave you a brand new shear pin on the mornin' you went missing.' Everyone was listening like tigers in the rustling grass.

Bruce took such a deep drag on a fag that his lip blistered. 'Ouch, man, I've dropped the butt, eh but.'

'Fuck the butt, mate. What about the pin?'

The lucky hippie grinned, 'Oh yeah, the shear pin . . . it was like the wrong size for my outboard man. Unreal, eh but.'

Like some coming together of long-lost tribes, lit up by the gigantic bonfire, the mad bunch leapt about merrily and celebrated life. The missing-at-sea saga brought life and death to the surface for a few people. Certainly for us, it pulled the bickering back into line and wetted our love for each other once more.

CHAPTER 35

Waiting for Barra

'*W*e've got enough and done enough and I've had enough so, Lesy, I vote we get outta here and head for town.' As Christmas closed in, I was yearning for change, and because he agreed instantly, the notion had obviously been swimming around in his mind too. Just then, Warwick called up and invited us over for a barbie, saying a special surprise awaited. Peggy was one of the few women whose company I looked forward to and joining up with our friends would be fun.

Early the next morning, with the four saved-up bottles of beer and the plastic-bagged last two remaining cigars secured in the dinghy, as the sun buzzed a soft warmth into the day, the three of us zipped up the Gulf. It was a three-hour journey so both constantly telling the time from the sun and keeping watch on the shore landmarks, I rode side-saddle and Les drove. Stryder, without being held, travelled on my lap, probably reading the signs too. Feeling like we were the only people in the universe, being out there in the elements alone like that was so extraordinary.

Over the first cup of tea, Warwick sprang his surprise on us – that we four have a *heated freshwater bath* below the she-oaks, under the full moon that night. The rationale was good too. 'It's near the end of the year, we got plenty of fresh water, and Peggy's predicting that there's gunna be a huge Wet next February.' Peggy probably could have taught the weather bureau a few tricks – let's face it, if anyone was going to know, it was her.

What a bucket of fun it was as the tractor-scoop plopped a fully sealed two-metre deep by four-metre long air-conditioner duct joint under the tree stand and then hooked the big drums of water up and into the tub. The S-bend looked like it had come from the dreamtime, like a spice worm from under the sands of *Dune*. 'Fair dinkum,' Warwick shrugged as he lit a fire below the tub, 'the air duct just washed up on the shore after the last storm. All I did was chop the top off.' While the open-air bath heated up, Peg and I caught and cooked some sand prawns and baked a damper.

Our beer went with the barbie, stories became jokes became yarns became history became the world became peace in our world. Like favourite background music, the ocean sang softly, steam from the bathwater rose to the sky, and the filtered afternoon's sunrays slipped into the river. Birds flew to their rookeries, cocooned bats started unwrapping themselves, frogs garoocked and the bush crackled and crunched. The sauna baths in the Gulf Pond were waiting so the four of us stripped off and dropped into the bath of baths, stoked up our half-cigar each and let the endless galaxies around the sensational Southern Cross family watch on as the full moon bathed us in its silken beams. Stryder lay with her back just between the fire's mellowing halo and the fallen darkness, watching for any new movements, and listening to our quiet chatter as the cigar smoke disappeared up into the night.

The journey back to civilisation always felt like returning home after a long overseas holiday, so packing all the acquired crap back on board was a pain in the proverbial, only lightened by the dreams of the well-earned break. With the *Jean King*'s butt sitting very low in the water – meaning that our pockets would be fuller with lovely money because her belly was swollen with fish – we weighed anchor, took off our clothes, and chugged lazily out into the Arafura Sea and headed back into society. I waved to the Holroyde. 'Thanks very much. Catch ya round the ridges.'

Not far behind, the rest of the barra skippers started winding up their operations. Everyone was tonguing for the three months of freshwater showers, sleeping through each night and chinwagging. For me, at least and at last, there would be conversations with people from outside the fraternity.

Experiencing unlimited fresh water was always a celebration. Pulling into a cove, finding a spot to wash the dog, our bodies and the clothes we wore felt more extravagant than having a ginseng bath at Kings Cross. Afterwards, we'd lie naked on the grassy banks and let the place talk. On this occasion, the untouched lagoon reflected early summer: trusting water fowls paddled past for a quick look and kept going, no doubt off to visit some relatives up Kakadu way, black swans, peckers, crowds of pigeons, and a few unnamed things all skirted the listening waterway. There was even a family of rare black orchid blooms – black, I tell you. This country was from another realm, and so were we.

Sometimes as the *Jean King* wended its way along the coast, heavy grey clouds would appear. In edgy excitement, we'd both get the soap and shampoo, get naked, then wait until the gusty messenger winds let the rain come splashing down by the truckload. Totally naked on the restless ocean, up on the front deck covered in white frothy soap foam, defiantly Les and I would laugh, reach out and rub against each other. As the drops pelted our taut frames, physical and raunchy, we would slide into pleasure, right there on the roof. Even then, I think we knew that every good second together was precious.

In light of the above, from the moment we arrived back at Weipa the first destination was the greatly appreciated ablutions block where, with just the turn of a knob, water, glorious water, glorious hot water, streamed down on us! Standing under the first real shower in many months was an indescribable delight. It was hands free, and ran right over the head and down the body – *continually*! With just a thin partition between the men's and ladies', Les and I yelled out to each other as we scrubbed till we shone like our Thursday Island cousins. Next door, all the previously saltwater-washed clothes, the sheets, towels, everything, would be churning away in fresh water in a real washing machine. At my feet, Stryder let the downpouring suds clean her, then streaked outside, shook like mad and rolled in the tiny copper-earth dust balls until her coat gave off a respectable matt finish.

Back in town, safe and relaxed, each evening we joined another session at the Palace. Our cash flowed hot and readily like the water from the shower, and there were plenty of buddies to babble to. Les was happy to repeat the infernal fishing diatribe but I was keen to get news from the outside world and listen to a bit of original thinking, so I sought out the others, the few and far betweeners, the travelled ones with bright enquiring minds, those who could wet my keen appetite and help me catch up with the latest. With them I gratefully sank into eclectic topics about global events, particularly of politics, of everything music, and philosophy, and writers, and shared my own take on how it should be.

Still, sooner or later, the *Jean King* would have been in port too long. It was like that: couldn't wait to get into port, couldn't wait to get back out into the wild. Catching me deeply immersed in a book, Les sighed, 'Why waste your time readin' that stuff?' He never understood. 'It's Sunday and the lunch session's on. Let's go sink a few. We'll be gone soon enough.'

As my inner voice promised that my whole life would not be made of this, the need for others won the day. So after a quick tizz in the mirror and a slash of lippy, we took the three-minute stroll to the Palace.

Being the only drinking session on God's day, and lasting from the dot of noon for two hours only, this was *the* session to which everyone at the landing devotedly flocked. Those present also made sure that the rest of the holy day was spent in a semi-rapturous state, so *fzzzzt* went multiple beer-tabs and crash, crash, smash went the hymn of empty stubbies being chucked into the dozen or so aluminium garbage bins that stood toe to toe at the bar with the drinkers.

At two o'clock sharp the final bell pealed and the tills ceased to toll. As usual, the miners and the fishing crowd sprawled out over the outside wooden picnic tables and kept cracking open six-packs. Close beside us, fishermen's kids biffed and brawled, laughed and played and chucked rocks into the deep green, flowing river. Jamey, one of the Boof's (also known as Barry) offspring, rode around on his new bells and whistles bike. Already as strong as most men, certainly as tough as some, Jamey was an independent little kid who at the ripe age of nine or ten had already been fishing for a year or so using his own nets and dinghy. His dad, although not a big man, was wiry, wilful, thin-lipped, as strong as an ox, and very unafraid – tough like his dad, the Old Man. Just how tough? Earlier in the year, out on a cattle shoot, I'd watched the Boof single-handedly heave a small, freshly shot cow across his shoulders then sprint the kilometre to his dinghy, humping the unbelievable dead weight through a wetland of snappy crocodiles!

Being a warm day, the drinks hit the right spot and fermented quickly. By tossing down more than his fair share of drinks, Les had managed to attain the 'three-quarter drunk' status. He was a happy drunk that day, and as we strolled amicably down the slope to the wharf, Jamey, straddled on his new bike, rode with us. Les, half silly and flushed with beer, took a childlike shine to the bike. Lollygagging around, he playfully grabbed the kid's bike, jumped on and careered off down the rutted dusty road, at which Jamey turned tail and disappeared. Seconds later Barry, having also quaffed quite a few Sunday beers, materialised on the scene. 'Fuck you, Les. Me kid says you've stolen his bike.'

Les just laughed and kept careering around on the vehicle, whereupon Baz reefed the bike to a standstill, grabbed my man, tore him from the seat and hurled him full force to the ground. This feat made him look every inch like a God from on high, and that should have been enough to satisfy the kid and his dad. Instead, Baz started kicking Les while he was just lying there. It was a Sunday, and as unchristian as this was, the inevitable crowd of loners gleefully gathered around. 'Ooooh, on ya. Garn, git 'im, mate. Kick the bastard.' Barry was already 'known' to have a temper, so to the watchers this was a chance to get on his good side. No way would any of them be silly enough to get in his pig-headed way, so the gutless tossers urged him on. 'Don't let the mug get away with it. Have another go!'

My man, caring less than a bent pin, just lay on the dirt, rolling with the kicks. Pity he didn't do that on the home front, I thought, and with both fists up deftly stepped in. 'Hey, Barry, Les didn't steal the kid's bike and you know you never kick a man when he's down! If ya wanna have a blue, have a go at me.'

Like a rehearsed choir note, a gasp arose from the growing crowd as they contemplated whether any one of them would be game enough to fight this scrawny, power-packed man.

Shaping up for action, Barry and I skipped around each other. Abruptly, I threw a clean left which connected with his skinny jaw. Then, as his return right punch came through, I ducked and threw a straight right which also connected. Wow, I thought, what an excellent surprise. This was my first real stand-up fight and both punches had worked! Of course they hadn't done an ounce of harm but the man's pride had copped a hiding so he swung out at me. Along with some nervous laughter, next thing I was calling him out: 'Ya missed, Big Baz. Carn, carn, have another go then!' What the bloody hell was I thinking? Of course I had been drinking too and didn't like what was happening one little bit, but my impetuous actions came from way back. Even as a kid I'd always been a protector of the under-dog – defending other kids from school bullies, bringing home the stray cats and dogs, and let's not forget, I'd been an underdog myself.

With fists braced to crunch at impact and a face marked with infuriated determination, the man was madder than a wild bull. Not only had my big mouth gotten big-headed, but up until then I had quite a pretty face, and didn't have to be Mike Tyson to know that Baz badly wanted to rearrange it. The crowd drew more half-baked onlookers, all hooting and jeering like it was the inter-county boxing final.

'Look, she loves me, she loves me!' I heard Les crowing in the background, geeing up the ringsiders, inciting a bit more riot.

Bloody men, I thought. I was about to be ripped apart and Les was going on about love! I was in deep shit. While this terrible truth ran amok in my belly, one lone voice of reason rose above the skirmish. 'Barry – you can't hit her, Barry!' His wife, Mary, was an acquaintance kind of friend, not even an ally of mine. 'Barry, don't hit her. Barry, you can't.'

With his bloke thing being whacked right out of joint, Barry's shifty eyes almost punched Mary out as he glanced back sharply at her, pleading, 'Yeah, but . . . but why, Mary, why can't I?' He wanted to knock my block off, tear me in two, and laugh victoriously as I floated down the gurgling river of no return.

'Barry, you can't!'

'But she hit me first, Mary!' he whined.

Mary, Mary, Mary tell him, Jesus H, Mary get lucid, I prayed as we shuffled about.

His wife's nasally back-country twang delivered the cruncher: 'She's a woman, Barry. You can't hit a woman!'

This made all too much sense for the Boof. The fact was that he had been left exposed and naked, especially before the titillated, baying mob. With his back against the wall, the man flared up, tore me off the earth and shoved me up into the sky above him. I bet it was the best snatch and jerk seen in those parts in quite a while. Looking down I saw Baz's steely eyes almost pop onto his cheeks and the sweat pour over his bony, twitching face as he shook my skeleton into a bag of rag-doll bones. Barry was filled with indignant anger and his roaring words said the same: 'Aaahhh! You – I could snap you in fucking half . . . You, you, you . . . I could rip you to fuckin' shreds and, and . . . Aaaaaahh!'

He let go of me in midair and let me fall from the sky, and thundered away like a storm threatening to become an epic cyclone. Ever appreciative that Baz had succumbed to the politics of the matter, I still put maximum effort into crashing to the earth and lay there cagily, like any repentant sinner would do, hoping it might help him feel better, and thankful too, in fact terminally grateful, that my now-shredded T-shirt had taken the brunt of his super-normal aggression.

Just like when you first fall in love and your perception is heightened, the Sunday battle between right and wrong, between male and female, made me feel so damned good, I got up, started whistling Dixie, bounced into our dinghy and ripped upstream, feeling the fast lane in slow motion. Let me assure you that I did so only after Barry was out of sight.

Naturally, for the remaining months of the fishing closure, Barry would not look me in the eye, let alone talk to me. Still, there's more in the blink of an eye than one sees because on the positive side, the Boof's wild fury meant that none of the onlooking wankers ever bothered messing with him again. They left me alone too, and the distance this afforded was welcomed. While Les adored me even more, no doubt the Boof vowed to lend a closer ear to his dad's oral lore of 'never deal with women or cripples because they come out on top every time'.

As sure as eggs, at the beginning of each rainy season, the barramundi swam upstream and threw their babies: then when the rain was over the up-going ocean water met with the down-coming flood water, and it was in that specific matt of fish fabric, that fine line of fresh-mingled salt solution, that the barramundi reacclimatised and surfed back down out into the ocean. It was a saline/temperature thing, and it was in that particular brine of water that the fishermen made their first and best season's killing of barramundi. After that, in mid-season, the fish roamed out in the Gulf, staying put till the new oncoming Wet wound up their baby clocks. Waiting, waiting, waiting, the pesky fishermen were busting their gut to get off the wharf and back into their beloved ocean country.

And just as Peggy had predicted, that next year the Wet was unusually wet. So big in fact that the barra boats pointed upstream day and night because even the incoming tide held less power than the volume of fresh headland water gushing back downstream. That year the rains even spilt up over the riverbanks and flooded the headlands. All the signs indicated that a big, big killing was in the wind. Thankfully, the first expedition was upon us and being primary producers we were badly in need of a decent start to the yearly season. So the edgy barra fleet loaded up, screwed new outboards onto new dinghies, tinkered with main engines, conducted sea trials and with dick-gripping excitement kept the local beer-taps flowing.

Having done the final, big grocery shop before steaming out, I was fuelling up at the town's only petrol station when a crowd of inquisitive four-wheel-drive tourists gathered around and gingerly asked if they could take a picture.

'Sure, why not!' While the bunch of camera-toting southerners peered into their view-finders and focused up, I, flushed with flattery, peeked in the car's side-mirror, flicked my fingers through the springy sun curls and adjusted the mini-skirt.

'No, love, not you. It's just that we've never seen a ute riddled with so much rust and still bein' driven legally, still on the road even.'

Our rusty-red, sea-salt-cancered car with the sturdy outboard fuel tank oxy-strapped on top of the roof certainly was a town character. There'd been a small fuel-blockage problem with the one-tonner, so devious Les simply fed the fuel-tank hose in through the driver's side window, down through the dash and on into the car's fuel pump. All it took was a couple of quick squeezes of the outboard fuel bulb, which hung conveniently at window level, to get the flow of petrol to run down the line into the engine.

Smiling like a new pearly button, and with Stryder next to me, I stood beside the big rust patches, insisting as they shot away, 'No me and the dog in the shot, no picture!'

Afterwards, with the best part of the day rapidly slipping away, I rumbled swiftly down the road, pumping the fuel bulb along the way and waving to others heading in the opposite direction as Les's favourite country singer, Frankie Lane, crooned a cowboy song from the car's tape-deck.

Our pock-holed ute overflowed with necessities and the daylight was getting thin so I'd be needing help to offload all the guff from car to dinghy, from dinghy to back deck, from back deck to stowaway stage, the pain-in-the-butt stage. Finally back at the wharf I noticed Les sitting in a fisherman's car with a couple of other blokes either side. He was trying to hide between them because obviously they were all off to the pub for a few drinks. This was one of my pet hates, and a common trait of his – leaving me to do all the laborious work. Skidding the ute to a halt, I sprang out through the red dust and stuck my head into the getaway car's passenger-side window, demanding to know where the hell he was going. With masks of virtue looking too good to be true, and with Les tucked in the middle, they nodded compliantly as the lie tripped off his tongue. 'Oh, just goin' up to get some rope in town.'

'And that takes three of you? Please, please help me offload.'

Just to stir up an already heated scene, Frank, the driver, deliberately revved the engine heavily. Les, thinking he had the upper hand, snuggled in and promised to be back soon.

Quicker than a gloved-up Muhammad Ali, I stretched through the window and threw four or five short jabs his way. I missed, but the action made their heads all bob this way and that, like a row of big-mouthed clowns in sideshow alley. The car filled with mirth and Frank gaped admiringly at Les. 'Man, wish I had a fierce woman like you, you lucky bastard. Why isn't your f'ing missus fuckin' my missus?'

A trick question maybe; still, I reached through and attempted to swing a wide one his way. 'Fuck you too, Frank. And fuck your fucking missus yourself, so here's one for her too,' I mimicked, as the laughing car eased away.

That was the funny side, but always being left with the nitty-gritty stuff annoyed the hell out of me and just added more to my deeply held resentment. Les didn't mind me doing a lot of the 'men's' work, but like 99.999 per cent of the men surrounding me at that time, he just assumed that 'women's' work was beneath him. What was so feminine about scrubbing the dirty clothes in a bucket, cleaning the scungy dinghy, or scouring the back deck down after hours of filleting fish, I ask you? And trying to get through to him on such issues was like talking to a brick wall. So yes, sometimes words failed me too, and as much as I want to justify striking out, I cannot. Born without an ounce of strategic guile, another mistake I made back then was to fight for my 'rights' instead of softening up a bit and letting some things go.

Obviously money was not our God and to ensure it never stuck to our fingers for long we spread the rich manure of life around carelessly with family and friends, fools, hobos – in fact, anyone with the karma to be standing with us at the same time, at the same bar. Similarly, being on the bones of one's bum didn't mean anything either – there was always an exhaustible supply of mud crabs, fresh Morton Bay bugs, prawns, you name it, to eat, and always buddies whose open hands sprouted folding money upon request. All of us knew that what goes around comes around. Nice philosophy that, but *exactly* when it comes around is another matter – with fish thumbs like ours, supposedly right after the annual three months' closure.

But wait, Father Fate was about to deal the single-minded convoy a potentially devastating blow, a real curve ball. Literally days before the official season was due to begin, word came from the

Wollomby clan that a tribesman, let's call him Remus, had up and died. By traditional rite of passage, the dead man's spirit needed time to figure out exactly where he was going to settle. As such, no fishing was to take place in Remus's country – that is, from Weipa to way down south past the Kirke, for the following six weeks. All the fishermen got this news and, being whitefellas, it was a call of conscience, a question of how they really felt about the sacredness of this abundant land and the born owners of it.

'That's fucked that then. We're not fishin' anywhere till it's right. Case closed.' Mouth puckered, arms folded, stubborn and solid, Les stated the case outright. 'We don't fish there, and that's that. We'll just figure something else out.'

Because of our many battles, I had learned when to shut up the hard way, and anyway I agreed wholeheartedly, so in this case there was nothing more to say. While the 'for' and 'against' arguments raged back and forth amongst the others, we were very clear-cut about the issue. The rest didn't have the faintest idea, and to suggest to them that the Aboriginals had a deeply rooted, profound culture, or mention the word 'permission', would have been like asking them to think so far outside of the square it was impossible. Blind to local culture, and thinking they had the right to do whatever they wanted, everyone else, wearing white blinkers and driven by the almighty dollar, went fishing as per usual. I wondered what would have happened if the Aboriginals started pulling hundreds of thousands of fish and dollars from the white blokes' backyards – even if they did ask for permission first!

Although we were clear on our decision, it was incredibly difficult sitting in port watching the boats troop off. 'Work's costing us a fortune and life's a full-time occupation, so it's no big deal, Robbie. Anyway, we're gettin' outta here too.' He just cranked up Wednesday, popped a cassette on and sang along with Frankie Laine, one of Memphis's favourite sons and we chugged up the heads. But instead of turning south, we were the only ones to go north, back toward the Canoess's neck of the woods. *'Bullet in ma' shoulder, Blood, runnin' down ma' vest,'* Les and Frankie sang. When my man was like that, I loved him more than I can tell.

CHAPTER 36

The Deep Pain Within

*T*he northern country seemed sparser, a bit like the fish, which were few and far between. Still, flocks of Torres Strait pigeons were preparing to return to New Guinea, the grey brolgas danced in the resplendent, moist wetlands, exquisite pandanus stood like exotic living sculptures in a land scattered with fabulous anthills shaped like gothic castles. Our skin may well have been white yet our hearts were the same colour as the Aboriginals', and there was no doubt our spirits were connected to the Gulf Country. Today, I feel no differently and no matter where I am living in the world, the vibration of the Gulf comes to me. Although I was born in Adelaide, the Gulf Country we lived in will always be my heart home – until way after I die.

Sometimes we'd lie on the bed with Stryder and through the porthole watch the splendid, gigantic weather: tropical rain would pour from bulbous basin lakes in the sky, crashing all over the *Jean King*, the baritone chorus of belly thunder would join in and the intense deluge would turn the river, which was earth to our boat, into a constant roll of rippling waves – and as Harley Davidson thunder rode from horizon to horizon on startled lightning bolts, every bush creature, twig, plant, tree, the river and the ocean – everything took a huge swig.

Les was restless, the early morning work done, and meat was

needed, so we dinghied up the shoreline a couple of miles, and slid in. Stryder, like a theatre usher, immediately went to the edge of the bush, looked back, wagged her tail and waited. Les, carrying the .303 broken-barrelled over his arm, I with my Winchester pump action, and the savvy dog melded into the lagoon country each thinking like everything else there, like the sky of birds, the land of beasts and the sea of fish – all of us being aware and feeling the ways of nature. A few steps in from the shore, through ti-trees and native gums, the meandering clear water lagoon eased on peacefully, abundant with orchids, wasp nests, bees and bats. Above the smooth blue lagoons brimmed flowering lily pads and grazing flocks of water hens, coots, reed warblers; animals native and feral. It was always breathtaking, and something we never took for granted.

'Shh.'

In half-stride, the dog stopped moving, her pricked ears already on sonar alert, glistening nose sniffing, eyes and mind keenly reading the scene. Across the way, a fully grown cow, innocent of its fate, grazed by the billabong's edge. With beef-on-the-hoof, out in the wild, the first one sighted was the one that got shot; that is, the one closest to the dinghy.

'Well, it's gunna be tough meat this time,' Les whispered as he raised the rifle and sighted up the big animal.

Boom – just the one shot rang out and the beast staggered, then dropped dead.

Momentarily Eden was no more, the harmonious lagoon turning to chaos. Peaceful waterbirds squawked and splashed out for the open sky, wallabies and kangaroos spun around, then scarpered swiftly for anywhere away from the resounding bullet echo, while we three gazed intently over the tiny stretch of lagoon, studying the cow, making sure she was down for good and not wounded and stumbling off into the scrub.

Like a shock of scared-witless wild horses, thundering sounds coming at us from one side echoed through the bush. Suddenly a herd of wild pigs burst onto the scene, at least 35 of them, with a mass of piglets streaming out behind. Mindlessly bolting for their lives, the frenzied, wild-eyed, huge sows charged straight for us. In amongst them, the littlies' legs scuttled, and their squealing panic filled the air. As Les roared, 'Quick, get behind a bloody tree everyone!' Stryder and I were already doing exactly that. Standing silhouette-like, hugging up against the closest tree trunk, Les and I prepared to fire. Leading the pack, charging us with deadly sharp tusks, came eight or nine enormous black boars, each looking fanatically serious about goring the creature responsible for freaking out their backyard. As we both shot away like a couple of Hollywood cowboys, the huge, hairy, feral pigs blindly screamed right past us and crashed off out of sight. The mad mob, including us, were scared shitless, so even with all those bullets we managed to hit nothing. With everyone's rising hackles taking charge, it was a true case of equal fear.

Stryder bounced about while he and I just stared at each other in bewilderment. To relax the atmosphere, Les cracked a joke: 'I've been harassed by pigs before, but I've never been able to shoot at the bastards!' Pigs, an Australian nickname for cops: at that time, both types were feral flounderers on the make in the fecund swamp of plenty. With relief bubbling just under the surface, we hugged, swore and laughed out loud at such lousy gunmanship. The neighbourhood also exhaled a whoop of relief and got back to what it was doing beforehand and so the natural noises once again became familiar.

Les refocused. 'Let's carve it up.' We three moved steadily toward the other side of the lagoon. Under a sky of already circling birds, the beast was bled and its underbelly sliced open. Onto the ground sluiced an unborn, fully formed calf.

'Part of the game, Rob. Least it'll get to feed a few.' His survival shorthand made sense but what I felt was different and a great sadness struck my heart remembering my own lost one, and seeing only another innocent new life gone before its time. He hauled the baby off to one side. 'Look, whether it's the jungle in the city or the jungle out here, it's all wilderness. Fuckin' life an' death goes round and round. Happens all the time.' *Boom boom* went my heart as he proceeded to carve the pelt away. 'Just keep your eyes open.' With that, Les checked for disease and deftly began to dissect the animal, reiterating, 'Watch out for crocs, mate.' I knew. It was second nature out there to have all the senses switched on full alert every second, especially one's intuition. Still, it felt like I could almost hear the call of my own lost one somewhere out there in the backwoods.

The dog had good bush sense, so any decent chunk of meat thrown her way was buried and the final layer of dirt guided into place by her memory nose so she could sniff it out later. Into a leather carry bag went the kidneys, heart and the fillet roll from each side of the spine. He honed the knife again, and effortlessly sliced through both hindquarters.

'Ready now woman? Stryder, stay with Robyn.' He snatched up one of the hindquarters and rested it across my shoulders. I grunted at the weight. Grabbing the meat bag and swinging the other quarter onto his own shoulders, away we went, semi-sprinting sure-footedly through the rainforest swamp.

Feeling the musky meat at my neck and the warm blood run down my back I plodded forward. Finally through the last layer of bush, I plunged on down the sand toward the dinghy where the first quarter was already stowed.

Out of the sky came the ominous overhead putter of the fishing inspector's aeroplane heading our way. 'Quick, drop the carcass into the ocean and flop your body over it,' Les warned, 'and pretend you're swimmin'.' He called the dog into the water too, so while we smiling cattleduffers enthusiastically waved upwards, the lovely dog also frolicked about merrily.

The small grey government plane swooped down low and cruised right overhead, and one of the binoculared inspectors stared down intently, probably thinking we were lazy fishermen having a swim while they were up there working their butts off.

'Nosy parkers! Why don't you get a real job?' I yelled, flashing my perky breasts at the plane as they peeled off and out to sea.

'That's right, you tell 'em, Tiger,' Les agreed.

Back onboard, the life-sustaining meat was salt-rubbed and hung. Later, in the evening coolness, each quarter was sectioned off into its different cuts and packed away in the freezer.

I could write ad nauseam about the persistent arguing, the brooding silences and the unhappy times we lived in, yet in the bush or when we needed to be, the two of us were an excellent team, and our power struggle forgotten. This was the baffling dichotomy, the opposite sides of the coin roller-coasting across my mind, this was the thing that held me there for too long – beneath the battles, we seemed to be one. But the harsh reality is that none of the underlying patterns were forgotten, we were just putting them aside. And I was just kidding myself.

Like when, somewhere during the late 1970s, Les smacked me across the skull with an electric drill. It was one of those very old-fashioned, big commercial, heavily cased things, so heavy in fact that to use it, even Les needed to hold it in two hands. His action was absolutely brutal, so unnecessary, and so clearly over absolutely nothing that, confused as my mind might have been, I knew this one was not my fault.

We were reshuffling the boat and I was literally stepping from it onto the wharf to untie the ropes (that is, to do what he had asked me to), when I heard a loud crack like a brittle bone crunch, felt a sharp unexpected pain, and then sensed some kind of soft warm fluid pouring down my face. Cringing away in puzzled shock, too late I swung my arm up ready to defend myself. 'What the hell was that?' Thinking I'd smacked my head on something, I spun around to see Les still holding the drill and there was blood on it.

His reason was even more shocking. 'I told you three times, unhook the fuckin' ropes, you're too slow. Jesus Christ, do I have to do everything myself?' And he meant it!

Seeing the red fluid and realising it was blood flowing down my face and onto my opened palms was shocking. Les let the clumsy, solid metal drill thump noisily to the floor, justifying his action with, 'Too fuckin' slow, outta me way,' and impatiently shoved past, or rather, blustered past in embarrassed panic. Intelligently, Stryder hated our arguments and lit out for the shore. Stemming the gush with a clean work rag, I snatched up the ute keys and stepped onto the wharf.

'Where do ya think you're goin'?' the man bluffed and barrelled over blocking my path.

'To the cops! You don't know what you're doing. Look! Look at this. It's me, the one you love. It's time you understood. Get out of my way.' He reached for me. 'Don't, don't come near me, get away.'

And on it went. My lover blustered around me, muttering

platitudes, promising not to repeat the violence, finishing with, 'Dunno what come over me, *but you never dob in a mate.*'

This fateful sentence, one of Australia's most powerful, unwritten, oral lores has probably been the tool of many an abuser. Between that and the essence of my parents' early, and innocent, 'forgive and forget' teachings, I screwed up again: I took the wrong action and did not go to the law. A pity someone didn't knock some sense into me, and bad luck someone didn't knock down the man I forgave, outwardly anyway. But this time, the changes within me manifested at a much deeper level. Even though I felt up to my eyeballs in a deep, oddly echoing pain, a terrible truth was becoming evident, a truth that was starting to scare me, a truth I had been avoiding – I was going to have to leave, and it would have to be an escape rather than a polite discussion.

With experiences like that, sex stopped being a pleasure and started to become an unfeeling duty of submission. I remember the greyness and of secretly shutting up more and giving in.

Paradoxically, for such an outspoken woman I never sought the counsel of my own wise ones – Mum and Dad. Was their example too luminous? Was it shame, or was it more likely that they had the answer I did not want to hear? A funny girl I may have been, but by then, not funny-good.

CHAPTER 37

A Harbinger of Fortune

*W*hile the silly, twisted white cultural law of never dobbing in a mate remained alive and intact, another in the black culture – about honouring the sacred death rituals – was being broken by the selfish, grasping whitefellas. However did we 'civilised' people become so unattractive?

Over and above Remus's death, everyone had gone south because the northern country had never been famous for big fish hauls – still, the results were enough for us to attend to the important stuff like paying back borrowed money, settling the bills and buying groceries. What we didn't want to hear was what our radio kept telling us. In a first ever, the unbroken code of lying ceased and the big-mouthed fishermen blabbed the truth. All the pre-season predictions of a bumper catch were way below the real result as daily the opening season's catches grew to unprecedented levels. Even the prices being paid by the Fish Board were an all-time record. The fishermen, like all primary producers, milked the fish cow mercilessly. So while we two were still giving the dead man ample opportunity to decide where he would come to rest, everyone else was rolling in dough. Then, for no apparent reason that anyone could fathom, fish in the south dropped off the edge and disappeared. This was so sudden it was a bit spooky.

After the ban lifted, we moseyed down to our old backyard, the Kirke. Most of the Wollomby tribe were around there too, preparing for Remus's spirit's homecoming. They were doing the customary seasonal burning-off at the same time. By using carefully controlled fires, the undergrowth was cleared quickly, thereby regenerating all the plant and grass species, giving the local animals a good feast on fleeing insects, and allowing fresh crisp new growth to sprout immediately in the fire's wake.

Mid-winter was always slow but this time the fish were nowhere. On our own in the river, engine maintenance, repairing torn nets, reading, resting, arguing senselessly and dreaming swirled around us.

One day, on the river's eastern bank, there staring at us was Australia's ancient wolf, a dingo. Fully mature, the dingo's rusty white coat had sucked into her bony frame like the skin on the face of a recently dead person, and her sorrowful, desperate eyes and a swollen, slack tongue protruded out of deep-sunken bones. We were agog. The dingo was starving to death. No way would any animal in their right mind be caught dead standing in the midday furnace heat, yet there she was, fully exposed, staring intently out over the water at the *Jean King*. Hands up who can't understand dingo dialect.

'He needs us, real bad,' Les said, scrambling to attention.

'He's a she, and by the colour of her hide, pretty rare and it looks like she's been without food for a fair time too.'

Instantly, we were at the freezer, pulling out the entire haunch of our latest cattle kill, all up about 25 kilos of frozen hindquarter.

Les told Stryder to stay on the boat and, being smart like that, she did. As the dinghy roared into life, Les said, 'Take it easy, I've heard they're real skittish around people.'

The sun felt like a spotlight from hell, and the stock-still creature's paper-thin, almost porcelain frame silhouetted harshly against the stark brightness. I cut the motor to let the dinghy drift silently the last few metres into shore. The wolf did not budge; she just kept staring at us. The implicit trust holding this fragile scene together felt brittle yet dense. Les, all nugget and strength, snatched up the concrete-heavy hunk of rock-solid beef like it was a feather and stepped carefully across the searing sand to the shade of a she-oak tree and lay the meat iceblock down. Mere paces away, the haunted skin and bones stood frozen to the spot, her eyes locked on the human. He turned away, walked the dinghy out into deeper water, then I started the outboard and drove back to the boat. From there we watched in fascination as the dingo brutally gnawed into the still-frozen flesh, licking, tearing, so desperate to stay alive that blood poured from her gums.

'She's been outcast, abandoned somehow, poor bitch.'

'I know how she feels. It's been happening to women across the world for centuries now. Incredible, being that close, feelin' her trust. Reckon Stryder's got a bit of dingo in her?'

'Yeah, they're both dogs.'

His scepticism was a bait so I bit my tongue, went inside, started cooking tea and watched from there.

Beyond exhausted, the gaunt-eyed she-wolf was still there at dusk, resting beside the half-shredded leg bone. By the next morning there was no sign of her or the remaining haunch. Aboriginal legend says the dingo is a powerful spirit, a restorer of life, so we had restored a restorer. In the following days, occasionally we glimpsed the lone wolf hanging around the jabiru lagoon area, looking healthier and glossier each time. She took to sitting up in the sand dunes, watching Stryder gallop along the shore like some champion Melbourne Cup winner on the home stretch in her game of trying to stay level with our speeding dinghy.

'The dingo wishes she could play too. Wish she could talk.' I was reminiscing thoughtlessly – of course the dingo had clearly communicated to us from the beginning, it was just that I had only recently started listening to myself.

It seemed entirely auspicious that within a couple of weeks, and standing on the same spot as the dingo had, other unexpected ancient visitors appeared. Peering out the window, I saw a fair mob of Aboriginals milling around and looking our way: there were men, women, a straggle of little people running through the tall ones' legs like they were playing amongst trees, and a small contingent of mottled dogs surrounded them.

We grabbed gifts and dropped over for a visit, and soon the gathering was happily ensconced under a cluster of spiralling pandanus shaking hands, hugging, murmuring and chatting. Like all old friends, there was a lot of catching up do.

'Pull up a stump,' Solomon (Peggy's brother) motioned, then sat cross-legged in the shade. The rest followed. While the little people fought over who got what soft drink, the dogs lapped up cool, fresh water and the big people dug into a mega barrel of vanilla ice-cream until there was absolutely none left.

'By gee there man, this cigar's proper good.' He and Les puffed away on the smouldering sticks. Everything on Solomon's face smiled. 'Never smoked one of these fellas before.'

After sharing a tin of ready-rubbed tobacco, the girls lit out in all directions and quickly returned with bundles of dry wood. Soon the decent-sized rollies soothed everyone's souls, and the moody fire brought a universal luminosity to those present.

'Just bin out here burnin' off for the last few days.' A trusted leader, Solomon was sharing with us his mob's private business, saying that they were waiting for Remus to settle too. 'You fellas know him, hey,' said Solomon, using the present tense for the dead man.

Les put his hand on the elder's shoulder and spoke for both of us. 'Sorry he's gone, friend, but looks like the best way, eh?'

Solomon's voice came from true knowledge. 'Don' worry. He gunna be okay now, he's home now. What about youse two? How's the fishin' eh, and the *Jean King*?'

Cigar smoke swirled around the men's faces. 'She's a bit slow, Sol, and God knows we've tried every trick in the bloody book.'

Solomon was a good-looking, healthy bloke for his years and stood over six feet tall, so when he pointed to the southern bank of the river mouth, his gangly, leg-long arm stretched out over the top of everyone. 'See that sandbank there eh, runs off the mouth?' His eyes drilled into Les's. 'You see eh? Yeah, all our tribe turn up there sooner or later after they die. Yeah, our spirits, before they decide which part of the country they're gunna stay in.'

The black people broke into Wik, talking amongst themselves. Listening to them confab in a dialect as old as fire, being amongst these gracious bush people, it felt like family to me. While the camp flame flowed into the nocturnal surrounds, such intimacy allowed us whitefellas to feel very much at home. Stryder sat between us, listening to every movement and voice through the dark. In a while, the mob stopped jabbering.

'Listen here Les, Robyn, us fellas are the main owners of the Wollomby country including down here around the Kirke, okay?' We nodded. 'Our tribe bin talkin' and we all agree that you two fellas can fish and hunt our country, anytime until you die.'

The mob stirred in the flickering light, our dark and light hands reached for each other, and mutually we signed the heart contract with the centuries-old bond of a handshake.

'Thanks very much. We love it here, and always try and look after the land,' one of us spoke for both. The invitation was big-time magic, a huge honour, an unheard-of authorisation given in such an unfettered, genuine way that it felt pretty right, same as the night stars looking down from the infinite heavens.

Solomon gestured toward us. 'Yeah, we bin lookin' out when youse didn't go fishin' that time Remus died. You got respect for our ways.'

As the ocean started singing that the tide was returning, becoming full once again, wings flapped, animals rustled through the scrub and the earth spirits went their way. From outside the unique circle, the night-time creatures who'd taken part in the giving of permission started to go walkabout again. Water lapped in our ears as the she-oaks whispered of the legend they had just witnessed. Everyone there knew that all things belonging to the Kirke River had been a party to the turn of events. For the past hours, the 'civilised' world had not been on the same frequency – that Les and I had been honoured by this tribe from the olden times.

'So listen up there, thanks plenty for everything eh.' Sleeping kids sprawled like baby brolgas in loving arms, hands touched, laughter tinkled softly and whispered caring was breathed all round.

'Jeez, that star fuel is somethin' else,' Les sighed. 'Come over, stay the night on the boat.'

'Nah, still got things to do, you know,' Solomon looked at us implicitly, 'for Remus.'

Back on the boat, lying under our doona on the roof with Stryder, the invisible night hung like velvet. As the significance of what had just taken place dawned on us, it felt quite remarkable. 'Unreal gettin' the rights like that. It's a bloody blessin' all right.' And after more deliberation, we both came to the conclusion that Solomon had also deliberately told us to set nets off the southern sandbar the next morning.

Although by this time sex had become a perfunctory duty, that night was enchanted and Les and I responded in a way we should have done all the time. That night I also dreamed a dream, the potency of which I have never forgotten: of a vast valley, and lava-forged red-molten lakes, telltale smoke corkscrewing skyward and drifting flakes of grey ash fluttering over me. With yeti hands and feet, I and another, taller one, at my side had naked sooty bodies which were matted in tufty hair, and walking beside us were two much shorter similar-looking child beings. Way off to the north, newly chiselled mountains, rare igneous rock just set free, jutted out and cut haphazardly up through thundering clouds. Rivers the colour of mercury scorched down the sides of these massive, smouldering bergs. The brilliance burnt into my mind. We four were part of a surging herd of massive animals, diplodocus-like, gargantuan bird and other pre-glacial creatures – an exodus, striding as far as the eye could stretch, way across the pulsing valley floor.

Following a dream of significance, it's always the first interpretation you have upon waking up which is likely to be the right one. For me it was like a glimpse of man's primary origin, like a look at the original Aboriginal when language, colour, creed, race and the apple all got their primary gig, when the first circus of this epoch had kicked off. And as I saw it, maybe the animals had shrunk a tad, certainly the apple had been bitterly twisted, but same, mostly barbarians still.

Instantaneously life got busy. At first light the next morning, Les and I put in nets directly off the specific sandbar that Solomon had indicated. When the fully buoyed nets sank continuously down below the water's surface with the weight of fish, Neptune's cup overflowed and we recently initiated fellas were up to our gills in a catch unparalleled. Night and day, with every run, the dinghy's arse pushed heavily through the water as laden down we rode back to the big boat.

Despite labouring around the clock, at least once a week we tried to have a bath. On the other days, the work clothes stood up in a corner as our unwashed bodies collapsed into serious sleep. And here's the thing – none of the other fishermen along the coast were catching any fish at all.

After a couple of weeks, and having just stacked down another 12 ten-kilo trays, Les rose from the icy freezer saying, 'We're processin' a good 200 kilos of fillet every day, we're just about full and the fish are still runnin' like it's the beginning of time.' It was around 4.30am in the morning, our back deck lights shone down on the grey sharpening stones, the sword-sized steels, knitted stainless-steel gloves, and the knife tribe of long, thin flexible skinners; short stiff filleters and the broader choppers – all sharper than a Japanese seppuku sword.

Hurling water against the inside of the dinghy, scrubbed furiously, then bailing without losing the rhythm, I crooned, 'Two hundred kilos a day, it's time to go to port and play.'

When we pulled anchor and left on the run out, there at the river mouth was the she-dingo, just sitting and watching us go. I waved Stryder's paw and called out on her behalf. 'Thanks. See ya on the edges, Wolf Woman.'

CHAPTER 38

Outlaws on the Sea

How to Stay Out of Fucking Trouble: The Do-It-Yourself Guide for Pesky Fishermen. Now that would have been just the right guidebook to have on hand as, impatient for the opening season, early each year the mud skipper clan all fossicked around in Weipa looking for trouble. Not that anyone (except me) would've used such a guide, reading not being a favourite pastime of the water tribe. And although there were a few folk who were keen to have the fishermen out of port and gone from sight, nothing made us think that the local constabulary and the king of Comalco were busily dredging up some unexpected, nasty trouble.

To top it all off the state government insisted not only that the barra fishermen take part in a month of nautical lessons, but all of us had to pass official exams to obtain commonwealth government skipper tickets. No ticket, no more fishing. Shit! Now that was a major worry. Not the passing of exams, given that most of the mud skippers had been walking on the sea longer than Jesus – well, at least since their dads had pulled them from school at eight or nine years old and put them to work fishing. In that way, arguably these men knew more about the sea than the blokes writing the exam questions. The major worry was that some of them couldn't read or write.

Contemplating the idea of exams one morning while partaking of an early seagull's breakfast – that is, a sip of water and a quick look around – I noticed our Brisbane friend Pete's unmistakable ex-Second World War PT boat anchored in the channel. Before Les could indulge in his first fag and resultant hawking cough, Pete was pulling up at the back deck. A big man, and a top bloke too, we were glad for Pete's company.

'Just come up for the new season. And I'm rarin' to go to the dump. Quick, get ya act together, let's go.' True friends just step so easily into the 'that's happening next' stream of consciousness, don't they?

The Lucky Dip was a buzz every time. Once our ute got a flat tyre there and by the time we arrived back at the dump with a spare it was propped up on bricks with all four wheels missing! Weipa was a master dump, a shopping paradise – imagine if the pub had been right next door. And pumpkins love dumps too because there were always fruiting vines twisting around the place. As I picked up a couple of ripe ones from the all-pervading vine, Peter's animated holler drew us over to him. 'Get a load of this bloody alternator, will ya!' Swatting flies away, we fiddled and fussed around the engine a bit before declaring it to be in good working condition – or, to be more precise, 'a bloody ripper'. With that prognosis, Big Pete beamed like a satellite dish. 'It's damned near new, and just perfect for the PT boat. Unbelievable.' Aside from being almost impossible to locate, apparently such alternators cost in the order of $3000 each.

Already we had scored rolls of unused flywire, lengths of good quality water hose and an unopened box of metric Phillips head screwdrivers – so it was time to go. 'No use protesting, we're off to celebrate with a few Tooheys newies, and I'm payin',' Pete decided. Using all our strength to hoist the huge alternator into the back of the ute, Stryder emerged from under the vehicle and sproinged up next to it, so off down the narrow dirt track we trundled, happily bouncing into the Albatross carpark just minutes before official opening time.

There, like dying black swans, a swarm of Aboriginals languished outside the still-closed doors. After trying to sleep off hangovers overnight, the desperate loungers needed another drink, right now. One woman, sprawled at odd angles, lay out cold right on the hotel doorsteps. A soiled drunken male lay beside her, slithering and sliding around, trying to have intercourse with her. So sunken and low, the lost soul was incapable of entering the unconscious being. The rest, zonked out and juice-addled, watched, suffering the scene silently.

'If the pub stopped them from drinking, whitefella do-gooder lawyers'd be up here making a legal hullabaloo and lining their pockets.' The scene and my bitter remark caused Les and Pete to fall silent. 'Bloody white people, they've got no values. We've just come from a place where they chuck away good things, things they reckon aren't worth anything. And now look how well we've dumped an entire race of people. And this lot are so buggered they can't even help themselves.' The burning hot bitumen carpark was a terrible hell realm. Wanting to boot the slithering black bloke to kingdom come, purposefully I headed toward them, hearing Les warn me: 'Don't be doing anything silly, girl, we can't afford to lose our bloody licences.' What a joke, I thought angrily, him reminding me not to get out of control!

'Hey there, fella, get off. Just get off. Leave her alone. Can't you see she's bloody sick?' A vacant mind, scud-filled eyes, a comatose face gazed in my direction. Shamefacedly, the scrubby man rolled off to one side, so I slid one foot in under and rolled him further away. 'Go on, git.' With filthy trousers still undone at the zipper, the being lurched off into the trees. Just before stumbling into the undergrowth, the man looked back and showed me from his eyes the pain, the terrible, unfixable pain.

I pulled up the woman's pants, dragged her sorry body out of the sun, rearranged the thin cotton frock around her and propped her limply against the shading strangler fig. That minute the pub doors opened. Feeling profoundly sad, I watched as the empty souls stood up and went inside that bar, on the binge again, the ceaseless binge. Defeated, we three stepped past, knowing from experience that too much interference was not possible or welcome.

'Make that three beers, one tequila chaser and a big jug of water with plenty of ice, thanks.' Tequila, the doorway to illusionary states, was just what the doctor ordered, I decided. Feeling upset and useless, I tossed the beer down, closely followed by the tequila, grabbed the water and went back out. While the sister guzzled some, I used the rest to douse her face with a clean, drenched rag and a squadron of invading flies buzzed around expectantly. 'Go find another face to walk round on. Go on, shoo! Not you momma, not you. Here.' Too young, so gutted, like a timid child the woman guzzled down more of the cool fresh liquid. By the time I got back from the pub with the next jug, the ill woman had vanished.

'Make that the same again thanks, but go double on the tequila.'

One drink led to another led to another, and a few hours later, well and truly primed and intending to head for the landing, we left the bar's false air-conditioned stratosphere. Vampire heat instantly fogged up our sunnies and sucked the cool breath from our lungs: all the better not to see or feel, I decided, as we plunged past the gathered horde of penniless Aboriginals.

'Well fuck me dead! Some enterprising bastard's ripped off the alternator.'

The irony was too much, and when our infectious laughter filled the carpark, it rang in the Aboriginals' hearts, which made them smile too, showing again that they were good-hearted, willing people, living under such a marauding genocide.

I was to drink alcohol for a lot of years after then, but that was the last time I ever got so drunk I threw up – but of course drowning my sorrow didn't help the ones beyond repair.

It was skipper ticket time so we barramundi fishermen and our wetland kids and boat dogs straightened up, tidied up, fronted up and gave structured learning our best shot. The bronzed wild men shaved chins, donned good clothes and even tried to tame their locks. All smartened up like that felt strange, like being with people who reminded you of someone, of unfamiliar friends. All of us even wore shoes for the event – well, thongs for the first day – and sat still for a month listening intently. The technical language was easy to grapple with but the memory banks had been resting who knows where, so it took a minute to hold it all in.

Getting the attention of such people took a special knack. Luckily our teacher, Captain Doug Pattersen, was an insightful, genuine bloke; a gem, really. Doug's history included surviving bombs in the English Channel throughout the Second World War, and since then moving vessels all around the globe. That filled us with admiration. He took one look at us quaint mud ducks, realised the nature of the deal, and loved us all the more. Love? Maybe that's too strong a word. How about man-to-man respect?

One morning, unannounced, he even lobbed onto the wharf and called out to the gathering. 'Today, I'm teaching the Law of Storms and the Laws of Ballast. Believe me, this pivotal information will save your lives one day, so I need every so-called seafarer, yachtie, deckie, cook, every able-bodied seaman here in Weipa up at the class. I've seen good men lose their lives over this, so don't give me any excuses or tell me you can't afford it; this one's on me!' Significant lessons in life usually come at a price, so we were lucky there, and Doug must have had a private laugh that day because the classroom would have been a classic picture of clever misfits.

What I revelled in was that with our focus adjusted, the level of conversation and the quality of life lifted dramatically. When the final exams came along, those who couldn't read or write did the week of exams orally. No one failed: Captain Pattersen was smarter than that. First up he got respect, but by the end he was part of the tribe. Not that the official tickets made much difference to the way we rode the seas. Except, of course, a few weeks hence when the weather blew up into a cyclone.

Around the same time, university white coats requested by mail that all the barra fishermen make a record of every single box jellyfish sighted. Whatever happened to talking? Didn't they know that as far as the eye could cast, as far as the horizons or rivers stretched one way or the other, the multitude of box jellyfish and stingers (another more solid type of jelly), inestimable in number, unkillable and out of control, clogged up the ocean? They even provided one sheet of paper for each sighting, with headings like length of creature, how many tentacles, time of day, specific location, wind direction etc. What land did they come from? Oh I know, Lab Coat La La Land.

Yes, box jellies – those mushroom-shaped, mindless creatures who brought death within three seconds – looked like exquisite codes from the fourth dimension. Every year along with the big rains the deadly blubber jelly swept across the Gulf in a thick blanket, with any current and every tide. The strange transparent things with sticky orange tentacles filled every net by the slimy, glue-gum thousands.

It needs to be said that the wetland fishermen, the same as the Aboriginals, possessed very accurate knowledge about the extraordinary Gulf environment – they knew all the stuff. For example, everyone knew that the box jellyfish had been around since just after the first atom bomb was tested in 1966 on Moruroa Atoll, out in the South Pacific Ocean. Think about that, scientists! Sadly, just like the Aboriginals, the fishing fraternity didn't get recognised as people, so most of us shook our heads unintelligently, said 'fuck that' and gave the paperwork the flick.

Needless to say, all this officialdom made us more restless than ever. 'Next thing, Big Brother'll be telling us when and where to take a shit,' Les grumbled. 'No bullshit, I wish some bastard'd pull their bloody finger out and send this prick of an engine part up so's we can piss off.' While all swearwords are part of the human body, and this was premium Australian dialogue, waiting for engine parts to be flown in from 'the south' was always a diabolical evil from which there was no escape.

Ah Weipa: a bittersweet, far-distant place; a magic hidey-hole for men of all persuasions, known and unknown. For as many reasons as one can mull over, to the isolated mining town came a big dollop of the strange, the mad, the angry, the lonely. Fugitives all, succeeding in the daily attempt to drown their suite of hearts with each gallon of beer or Bundy downed, these men were stuck in their jittery co-dependency with the stubby shop, yet in a strange kind of parallel, beside the iconic drinking hole, a lusty river flowed, ever moving onwards.

On another Friday bloody Friday, in an all-too-familiar state of being impatiently patient, there the *Jean King* was in Weipa marking time again. And there was the entire town, spilt over the front lawn of the stubby shop: miners, fishermen, contractors, Aboriginals, kids, seamen, skippers from the coastal container ships, and most of the local family ensembles: that's right, the night was a very big deal. In a corporate illusion, 'benevolent' Comalco had erected a big picture screen in front of the Palace and the first-ever outdoor film night was about to commence beneath the Milky Way.

Choked to the walls, the Palace crowd of probably 200 hard-working sun-blistered blokes stood in hard yakka clothes and busted work boots. With faces thickly coated in copper bauxite dust, and cracked lips pursed permanently at the rim of endless streams of icy cold beer, the lot were quenching the unquenchable, downing the addictive stuff as though each drink was the last in creation.

Also inside was Les, already with a few under his belt, and laughing his mischievous head off. 'Listen, Bobby, if you stir up a blue with Joe the Slav right now, and get him fightin', I'll give you a thousand bucks cash on the spot.'

Nearly six feet tall, Bobby Giles was a strong, stroppy young buck. He also nurtured a nasty streak and thought nothing of hitting people, especially those not as strong as him. And like most of us in the world today, Bobby was constantly on the lookout for easy money. So my man intended to pay for two punch-drunks to get their rocks off in a one-sided bout. And pray tell, how hard was it going to be to get into a fight with a five-foot-nothing vindictive loner who poured slivovitz instead of milk on his brekky cereal every morning?

Bobby was at Joe's side faster than a pro-boxer could skip a rope. He leant over and whispered something in the shifty misery's ear and right away bottles sprawled, drinkers scattered, and a space busted open in the centre of the place. Whack, doush, crunch went the music as the two Comalco contractors ploughed into each other. A few sharp fisticuffs later, the Slav lay ironed out on the cement floor. Glugging beer, yelling, cursing and laughing gleefully, the block-head ringside miners were all fired up, and in the thick of them, Les-the-hero whipped out the *Jean King* chequebook, called for a pen and said loudly, 'I'll cash it at the bar right now.'

Everyone was loving it – except me. I bounced through the crowd and sprang right up in front of Les. 'No way,' I cried and half-sparring, snatched the chequebook and sped into the startled throng. That money wasn't going anywhere without a fight.

As I weaved, stepped around and ducked through the rowdy mob, abruptly a very well-known nasty, Basher, real name Kevin, deliberately blocked my exit. Although probably kind to his mum, Kevin had earned the name Basher by head-butting other blokes' skulls, just for fun. Had it never come to his attention that he was fucked in the head? Drunken Basher's thick bulk loomed right over me. 'Robyn, wait the fuck on there.'

The man was bigger than a Canadian tree feller and with the mob of men closing ranks, the way out was getting slimmer by the second so as I saw it, there wasn't much choice other than to shove the chequebook in a pocket, take a half-step back, and with every bit of resentment and wild fire, let fly with a sharp right. The big ginger-headed standover merchant hit the deck hard – actually he went down like a Bedford dropping from a great height. About then I think my lifetime supply of glass jaws had probably just run out because my jammy punch landed right on his chin: it was a winner. My hand didn't even hurt, and the thud of his body meeting the floor was a huge relief to hear. I sprang over the laid-out tree trunk and kept hightailing it right out of there, all the time congratulating myself. Maybe sometimes I acted like a bloke, but we had worked harder than anyone in the place for our money, I wanted a say in where such a large amount went, and I definitely didn't like the way the unjust deal had been cooked up – it was just not on.

Outside, under the cover of dark, I padded silently down the shadowy beach side of the track and hid below the wharf. The tide lapped at my thighs and my heart beat nearly loud enough to give the game away as above me Les, Bobby and the silly Slav stropped up and down the wharf in a blither of nonsense. When I saw Stryder in the street shadows, watching fixedly from a distance, a new strength ran through me.

'This is cuttin' into our drinkin' time. Fuck this,' one of them ingeniously pointed out. Just the excuse the hunters needed, so they flabbergasted back to the bright lights of the bar. Alcohol and short attention spans must be incestuous cousins.

One glance at the river told me that soon the dinghy would be stranded high and dry on the mudflats. It was the right time to go, the tide would help and besides, what a beautiful night it was for a drive. I whistled Stryder who manifested immediately – she I could trust – and together we both moved warily toward the dinghy: even though it was the end of the Wet, crocs could be anywhere and they did get snappy if strangers disturbed their peace. While Stryder stood guard I tossed the sand anchor in, spun the dinghy's nose around and dragged it to the river's edge. Then the dog flew into the dinghy, I pushed it off, hurdled in, pulled the starter cord once and reversed us out of the shallows and into the main river.

This was my private playground, the clarity of the night was the torch which guided us, and even though I had done this thousands of times, each instance was more bewitching. The galaxy was like a display of diamonds held in suspension, and the river surface became the sky's mirror, and the two dissolved into the other. When ocean spray kicked up from the side of the dinghy splashing us, somewhere a fallen star wrote in the sky.

Just to set the 'double standard' record straight regarding hitting and being hit, acknowledging that I wasn't perfect either is not so difficult, yet to me, such an action was nothing like a man punching his loved one, wrongly bullying her into submission by force, or belittling someone less strong. My blow probably didn't even register with Basher. It certainly didn't hurt him physically or emotionally – the man was just a thick head full of Friday night beer and I had been fluky to catch him unaware. So all I can do is let you decide if my actions were anywhere near as deliberately hurtful as the kinds of violence that reach into the depths of the heart.

In a man's world, by hook or by crook I had positioned myself in a bloody hornets' nest of them. Reasoning with Basher or Les about the writing of such a cheque would have been less successful than explaining to an old, partially blind groper why James the Bent Diver still cared whether he could see or not. Besides, a scheme to save myself was faintly starting to take shape, and I'd need money.

The following morning, before Les was conscious, I stood under the fresh water shower while next door our dirty clothes sloshed and swirled around. Having a toilet, a shower and a washing machine is something most people take for granted. But we fishermen deeply appreciated these simple things, and just like having lights on the wharf at night, and proper ladders to climb down on board our boats, these standard assumed rights made us feel human.

Churning over my predicament – and not just about the night before, but how arguments, whether alcohol-fuelled or not, always melted into very nasty, accusative verbals, or with me left feeling empty inside. This man, my lover, the life, my boat, knowing in the end he would win me over once again, too trapped, too much to lose, and not enough money to go, it was all too hard. And because I knew how scarred his early childhood had left him, a lot of the time I forgave Les, not in a fawning, sympathetic 'oh you poor thing' way, but by remembering his heavy, unhappy experiences and letting that excuse what was inexcusable. The line between love and hate, happy and sad, right and wrong was finer than a ripple of the sea and by then just about more than I could discern clearly.

Reluctantly returning to the boat, I knew he was up and about because the radio wafted out from the wheelhouse:

> *. . . Following a report tabled today as expected, the major recommendation is that the Belview Hotel building not be demolished . . . The premier also intends to introduce an anti-abortion bill into the current session of parliament. Angry protesters accused the premier of conspiracy, given the timing of such controversial . . .*

It sounded like the foxy premier was creating a double blind to get his way – something I needed to be considering too. And although I had no idea at the time, Bjelke-Petersen's political strategy was going to haunt me.

After pegging up the washed clothes, looking into the cabin, I saw Les and even though I felt anxious, my accusation did not reflect it. 'Looked like you were doing a bit of manipulating yourself last night!'

Les spoke from the main engine bay: 'Yeah well, I've got worse news than that for ya. Comalco are gunna knock down the bloody amenities block, rip all the wharf ladders off, and disconnect the jetty lights, love.' The thought of that was ridiculous and completely dangerous.

I snapped, told him not to call me 'love' and said, 'How are the kids going to get on and off the boats?'

More than a few sailors ended up floating head-down after slipping and smacking their head on crusty pylons and drowning, so having no ladders or lights was too dangerous for any of us. And our eight to ten boat wharf was well away from the modern Comalco wharf, where container ships took on bauxite day and night. By comparison we fishermen were so insignificant, I don't know why 'the man' even bothered.

Then Les reminded me that Comalco hated the fishermen being in Weipa. There was a reason for that – with no private tradesmen or commercial business houses, the only tradesmen were Comalco employees. As a result, a certain unwritten custom came into play when the fishermen called on the tradesmen to help fix engine problems and occasionally, just occasionally, the same men willing plunged their unwelcome hands into the company's pocket: a well-heeled pocket gained by turning its back on the real bauxite owners. You might call it foul play, but sometimes it was necessary. Truly it was a very small-time practice, and such 'arrangements' were paid-in-kind with fish, fishing trips, and/or drinks.

'Comalco fellas give us less than what is tossed in the dump every day and we always pay our side of it,' I protested as my gut churned around like the old washing machine.

Les went on to explain that while I'd been under the shower, one of the head honchos from Comalco 'in a fuckin' safari suit' had been down on the wharf having words with the harbourmaster, accusing the fishermen of stealing; and that he was blaming Les specifically for his own employees' wrongful activities. This was big-gun stuff, and nothing remotely like this had ever happened before, so the whole episode had a strange feel to it.

Apparently, Henry, the harbourmaster, then warned Les that we fishermen were about to be chopped off at the socks. 'Funny how the rich pricks come and buy all the fresh barra they can get their hands on to take down south and impress all their buddy politicians—'

I cut in: 'But why would the spiteful bastards take away something already in place?' It might have been them versus us, plots and plans, bullshit and brains, but with the amenities block gone there would be no toilets, and using boat toilets in port was against the law. It looked very much to me like the 'Brown Shirt' (the common nickname adopted from the beigey-brown uniform shirts Comalco 'staffies' wore daily) knew exactly what he was doing, and had decided to make us his scapegoats.

I was absolutely livid. Then it dawned on me that that must have been why the cops pulled me over the day before asking questions about having the fuel tank strapped to the roof of the one-tonner. What had got into the town? This was the last straw. Something was brewing and nothing would ever change unless someone stood up for our rights. Leading with my chin, I strode off to the one and only public telephone box outside the post office, and rang the spiteful 'Brown Shirt'. Unexpectedly, he answered, so after introducing myself as representing the fishermen, I tried to make an appointment.

In an accent of the same ilk as Richard from Thursday Island, he refused: 'My dear girl, I will never allow an appointment. What's more, I don't care one iota for you . . . you thieving, fisher people.' His distain was palpable.

Putting on the boxing gloves over the phone was all wrong, but with no face-to-face meeting likely, I decided to throw a few punches about his workers illegally netting healthy creeks, then dishonestly selling their amateur catches in town to cover fuel money. 'Trouble is, they've already got good paying jobs. Larrikins we may be, thieves we are not. We're hardworking business people just like yourself and what's more, it's bloody tough out here.'

This highly educated, well-paid, top-notch executive probably enjoyed rudely deflecting every which way I turned. Finally I asked if he had any children and he said yes. 'No doubt you get concerned for their safety, as I am for the safety of the kids who live on boats, so at least please don't take the wharf ladders away.'

'Frankly, dear fisherwoman, safety for your type is none of my business.'

His condescending tone added a match to my fire and inflamed my passion so I cut in rudely, 'I bet you know it's illegal to use boat toilets in the harbour too. Fair dinkum, Mr What's-your-name, I hope your kids grow up to be fishermen.'

As though it was the phone's fault, I slammed it down viciously and sprang from the red booth with tears bolting down my face. 'Why can't we have respect for each other?' I shouted to the tough, indifferent men around me who shrugged uncaringly. All the time I was on the phone, two bobcats had been intently knocking the amenities block down before my eyes.

Walking, no, ploughing back to the boat, I passed Les whistling his way up the road, rolling a fag. 'Off to the toilet for a poo,' he said delicately.

When I told him that the block had already been razed to the ground, 'So what,' he countered, 'I'll outsmart the uppity prick and use the Palace dunny.' That 'kick authority's arse' attitude must've been part of the Eureka Stockade gene.

Skimming upstream minutes later helped purge my thinking. Les's little caper the previous night had lost its wind but he would not get off scot-free. Going flat-chat, with the dog beside me, the wind blew the cobwebs from my mind and the threads of my escape plan really started to come together. First, I needed to get to the bank in town, so I spun back and headed for the *Jean King*.

As I zoomed in, the Palace manager was leaving. 'Hello, Robyn, sorry about all this, but I'm leaving now, and I mean what I said, mister!' Col kissed my cheek, stepped up onto the wharf and was gone. That didn't sound at all like the Colin I knew.

'I've just been banned from the stubby shop. Fuck him. Fuck Comalco. Fuck Weipa! Take these over to Turtle Creek and get Jack to stash 'em.' He handed me a bundle of croc skins and the unregistered .22 pistol. 'The bastards are against us alright.'

Apparently by the time Les reached the Palace that morning there were sturdy locks on all the toilet doors, so my man simply crow-barred one of them off. 'They don't mind takin' our money every night, year after year. We're not second-class citizens.' All fired up and wild like that, I still admired the man, despite everything else.

By the sounds of it, any illicit little bits and pieces on the *Jean King* needed a quick tidy-up too, which meant that the orchid spray hanging off the back deck and the latest kill, a good-sized beef haunch, had to go. By about midnight, out the *Jean King* rolled, and down we went to Pera Heads.

'The only way to be free is by not lettin' them think they control ya. We'll outsmart the bastards. Stick with me, woman, stick with me.'

As Les tried to pull me close, struggling intensely I pushed him away and we wrestled, fiercely pushing, pulling, jerking, pitting will and strength against each other. Knocking who-cared-what away, we battled on, crashing, bashing into things, pushing each other around the wheelhouse. No words, just grunts, groans and moans, foot-scuffling, squeezing, shoving, neck-biting. Finally, he tripped and fell flat over the engine box. Not like a woman, like a man I flung into him. Manic, feeling in it, possessed with the right to battle, on top, my legs locked his down; hands forcing arms, red faces, throat grizzles from the gut of anger – by handling each other that way our spirits freed up, our love loved it. Essential madness set us free. He scooped me off and under him, swiftly tore at my clothes with the other hand, and thrust into my wet, open gateway and on into me until we got to the place of rest and found each other again. Les had tamed me momentarily, and my escape plan would have to wait, but at least I had one now.

By morning, via radio, Baz, he who I had hit, he who had never stopped talking to Les, he who had yet to say a word to me – that Baz – gave us the latest update. 'The word is youse are both banned. The Brown Shirt's pulled some legal stunt making himself an "Authorised Person" which somehow gives the prick jurisdiction over the Port Authority and even over the harbourmaster too. Henry's fumin', but don't worry, I'll support yas.' A breakthrough, I thought, the Boof loves me again.

Officially being banned from ever entering Weipa port again meant that the gulf between us and Comalco was as wide as that between the River Thames and the starving convicts who had been shipped to Australia two centuries earlier. And just like those first convicts, Les and I had been unfairly judged and were paying for crimes far less serious than those committed by the people who sat in judgement.

While one door shuts another opens, and our hearts did just that. With reunified mateship, we stayed out at sea while passing boats took our frozen catches to port and returned with enough mail, supplies, library books and stories for us outcasts to survive on. In those days, the whole movement was a way of life, not a job or a precise money machine, so the clan swapped booze, knuckle sandwiches, precious fuel, tobacco and cash, big wads of it, with no contracts. Our boats were our homes and the rivers our backyards, the Gulf our suburb, or that's what we thought – whose rivers and whose country it truly was shows just how deep the gulf between the tribal people and fishermen, and even Comalco was, back then.

Everyone bent over backwards; they came to our cause without question, including the Boof, who led with a Joe Frazier handshake, and a pursed lip grin. 'Don't you ever go doin' anythin' like that again, girlie.' My loud, ringing laughter only just hid the excruciating pain of him ruthlessly crunching my bony little hand almost to pieces.

Being fugitives Les and I let the sea have its way with us and choofed around in the ocean wilderness for a couple of months, bobbing up and down or wallowing in between sloppy swells, always battling the shove and push of weather. Friendly trawlers bellowing out the latest rock 'n' roll music sometimes tied up alongside, and a party would instantly commence. Oh, and always, at some stage in the merry proceedings, the focus would swing around to 'the trouble with women on the sea', that one about it being bad luck to have a female onboard (unless of course it was in the cot). Such a handy prejudice too: the women could be cooks, they could clear, clean and mend nets, do watches, be the skipper's lover, nurse him through divorces, teach twerpy deckies how to sort prawns and get paid a swag less money than anyone else on board.

The fishing fraternity read boat silhouettes like they read the weather – at a single glance – so it was unusual when overnight three unrecognisable trawlers tied up together in the same small sheltered bay we were resting in. Equally unusual was that Les was laid up with the flu. When one of the trawler's skippers called up and invited us over for a rage, I accepted, and sped off to join the frivolity on my own. Overhead, the clanging voices of white-bellied sea eagles called to me. Magnificent, aggressive hunters and vigorous defenders, the two fully grown with a chick in between used their long, powerful inner-wing rhythm to herd the younger one along the shoreline. The azure sky and the gentle wind whispered across the top of the pea-green sea: the day needed no nudging. All gathered on one trawler, the men looked stronger than Mack trucks, and were already busily gulping beer.

Snapping the top off a stubby and extending a hand, I introduced myself affably enough.

The pointy-faced, sharp-nosed, pencil-lipped one did not offer his hand in return, just a curling smirk. 'Yes. Felix.' More of a sneer than a sentence, he almost clicked his heels. 'Well, well, well, a woman. You know it's bad luck, don't you?' He was South African, a pretentious white Dutch Boer, a tensile coil of intolerance. Standing rigidly straight, with no hat and blond hair parted and combed down, right away he was different.

'Hi, Felix, nice boat you've got here.'

'And how would you know about boats? The right place for all women is at home raising the children.' His semi-grin felt false.

'Not if you don't have any.' I swigged my beer and relaxed a bit. Not wanting to buy into the old repetitive rave, my light joke was meant to soften the prod about these monotonous, common judgements – and who hadn't heard them all before?

One of the others, a braggart too, added fuel to the fire. 'That doesn't give you, or any woman, the right to be out here. The sea is for fuckin' men only.' Men in a pack do to lone women what they would never do to their own and were they so subjective that they'd forgotten that every woman is some man's mother, sister, wife, daughter or lover?

When another repeated, 'All women should be barefoot, fuckin' pregnant and in the kitchen,' I bit the bullet. 'Each to his own, but at least the women out here don't get into fights, and don't get drunk on the job – at least they're professional.' Being outnumbered didn't scare me; Les and our boat were not that far away.

Felix kept baiting me. 'Women are nothing but trouble. They must know their place.' All standard pontifications used by males across Australia at that time, so if you don't think women have come a long way today, think again!

Like smog above a busy city, a massive brown cloud was moving across the western horizon: it was bats in their thousands heading to the inland swamps for the evening's frivolities, so sunset wasn't far off. As I took in the bat cloud, and the *Jean King* bobbing quietly up and down not far from the trawler's beam, I put the half-drunk beer on the deck and casually inched closer to the back end, then went for the pretentious Boer.

'You build this rig, Felix?'

'No, but—'

I clipped each of his sentences short. 'Wait, you own this boat, Felix?'

'No, bu—'

'Surely you've got a skipper's ticket to drive this thing?'

'No, but—'

At the stern now, I pointed to the *Jean King*. 'Well, I'm Captain Catchlove and I own that boat. Don't *ever* bother applying for a job on it because you haven't got the balls for it and your bad attitude sucks. Bye.' And dived into the water.

As I swam to the dinghy, swung in, and kicked the engine into gear all the prawn blokes could do was gape open-mouthed. Just for a bit of flourish, I flattened the motor and did a few screeching water wheelies around the roped together trawlers so they rocked and twanged up and down uncomfortably against each other in the rollicking wake. On leaving the circle, I stood up, arms to the sky in a V, and I yelled jubilantly, 'Women WILL rule the world!' Stumped and impotent, they could only grip their beers tighter, clutch their dicks with a vengeance, curse me, and say fuck a lot.

Moreover, with my bloke on his back, technically I *was* the skipper of the *Jean King* so I stormed in and told Les how it was too. 'I'm sick of sitting on the outside. That's it, we're off to the Archer River.'

The Bedford grumbled and stirred into action, I stepped out onto the bow, hauled up the 30-pound anchor, battened down the hatches, and smugly steamed past the trawler trilogy. For once, I'd outsmarted 'men' and yelled from the wheelhouse, 'See ya never, boys!'

It might sound a bit wanky, but it felt fantastic. In the years to come, a few of the 'cooks' got even too, got their own skipper's ticket, got their own boats, became skippers of their own destinies and got rid of such blokes and their fear-filled attitudes.

CHAPTER 39

Aurukun Mission

*B*y the next morning, the 500-odd coconut palms that lived on the Archer River's northern bank waved us into one of the richest, unharmed river deltas in Australia, into Wik Munkan territory. So what that it was mid-year, when all the barra were out at sea. So what if our catches would only be enough to keep the sheriff from the door? Who cares, we thought, and drove right in.

The place was as rich as the Nile delta must have been thousands of years ago. Les reckoned it felt like God's country. He was right. With a fully stocked larder of land, sky and sea life, the bonus was a post office, a general store, and non-fisher people just a couple of miles upstream, which meant we could explore an astounding waterway, make land friends, and learn the culture. This new lifestyle was just the go.

In the 1920s the Archer River was where the Aurukun Mission had been established by a biblical mob all awash with stiff white-collar severity and an equivalent kind of dogma. The storm and tempest Presbyterians with Bibles and kiddies tucked underarm, speaking the language of fire and brimstone, preached the hell out of those black earth people – people from a different, much more profound dreamland than theirs. It was all the devil's work, the missionaries pronounced, and lathered and scrubbed 'the heathens' – cut, combed and slicked down their joyous hair; and covered their nakedness with frocks, pants and buttoned-up shirts. Then the Jesus people whipped some white manners into the blackfellas and got their idle hands working, got them down on their dark brown knees planting coconut palms at the foreshore plantation. Ah, now the Christians felt better. Nothing wrong with a bit of force. Jesus H Christ, it saved souls!

The real evil manifested much later when big bad Bjelke and the bauxite barons realised that the area was an untapped money mine. The scoundrels knew just what to do. In God's own state, they introduced specific legislation converting the Wik country status from 'mission' to 'shire' and therefore back under the state's control. After the crooks were reminded, in a condescending addendum, they even granted the real land owners the right to live on their own property. This way, while Comalco milked one of the most prolific bauxite-oozing lands in the world, the Wik mob got buckshee and plenty of brain damage. At least, some said, it was a roof over their heads, another thing the Aboriginals had never lived under.

Then the ambitious premier exploited the people's helplessness by flushing them with social security dollars: that is, flowing cash with no obligation. Such an efficient way to mentally and physically cripple the ancient culture called the Wik Munkan (or to cripple anyone really). Interfering, fiddling and technically fucking with traditional ways always leaves innocent people's self-worth in tatters. 'Dunno what they just give me a free house for, but I get free money eh but. Them govenmint are good fellas.' Which race of people would be immune to that? Perfect really, then just let the beer flow.

The Wiks, back then, were bright, generous folk steeped in bush knowledge, yet there was nothing sweet about the pervasive, bitter genocide that was clearly upon them; it was as stark as a land without trees and animals. When Les and I entered the picture, the last drops of the old mission Aboriginals were still evident. And although the Presbyterians had been a bit heavy-handed, the mission ones were a stronger, sharper mob, inbuilt with self-pride and the desire to work for a living; certainly much better equipped than the non-mission ones, those whom the shire had disenfranchised.

*

Within a couple of weeks a family of gropers took up permanent residence under the *Jean King*. Wherever the boat went, they went too. The two fully matured gropers were like baby *Jean King*s really, with one weighing about 800 kilos and the other around 1000 kilos. Although body-wise not that long, maybe four to five metres, they were about one and a half to two metres thick. Even the two little ones, at around the 400-kilo mark, were simply humungous. And just like James the Bent Diver had said, the fish's massive, gaping mouths were spanned with row upon row of backward-growing needle-like teeth. Often we leant over the side and bristled a fish skeleton across the top of the water. Cautiously, one of the groper would surface, and as it angled in for the kill, its side-on eye would look up at us for a moment. Then with its huge jaw wide open, *swoosh*, the fish frame was gone and the underwater creature tumbled downward, leaving our five-tonne boat rocking in its tail wake, the signature of this olden fish.

The sky teemed with brown kite, a bird that performed extraordinary aerial stunts with awe-inspiring ease. By mimicking their cry then flinging fish guts up into the sky, ten or more would swoop down with outstretched talons, outmanoeuvring, twisting, turning, doing battle with each other until the chunky guts had almost touched the water surface – then the victor would claw the prize up, up and away, whistling his win to the sky kingdom. No wonder we called them kamikaze kites.

With the dawn run done, Les and I decided to visit the mission, to the novelty of a shop, and new friends. The sun was just peeping through the mangroves when we skimmed upstream across the smooth, settled waters, looking, hearing, smelling, feeling, sussing out the rhythmic patterns amongst which we lived. Being canny, the three of us always seemed to be looking at the right spot just as the unexpected happened. *Skip, splink*, a huge manta ray leapt up from the water, flew high into the sky, did a perfect double flip, then vanished back into the water – a sight so astounding, so unique; it was a real wonder.

At the mission landing, our friend Peggy was squatting by a small fire of red-hot stones with about ten or so dead bat bodies lying on paperbark peeled directly off from the tree behind her. As she seared the last of the dead bats' outer skins over the fire, she said, 'You know us Abos, we eat nothing but the best,' so we sat on our heels and watched as she cut the wing membrane near the body, put the little creatures on stones, and covered them with glowing coals. 'Bats only eat honey, flower nectar and ripe bush fruit. Not like the chooks you fellas eat, scratching around in a dirty yard all day.'

There was plenty to talk about, but soon enough Peggy hooked the bats out and onto fresh paperbark, let them cool, then expertly cracked both sides of the backbone and peeled the flesh away. It was soft, delicate and tasted sweet, like smoked ham. After, we lay back, rolled fags and rested for a while.

Reluctantly the three of us left the sandy landing and headed up the half-mile or so of dirt road only to be greeted with circle upon circle of Aboriginals squatting under trees, under houses or out in the piercing sun. Every circle was surrounded by mangy pack dogs and snotty, starving kids. As the distressed little people and dogs begged for attention, the adults in the circle kept playing cards, gambling and drinking. There must have been 50 or 60 mongrel dogs with tails between their legs, so we called Stryder to stay close. The way was lined with deserted, bashed-in government pole houses beneath which grubby Aboriginals either lay out comatose or sat on their haunches coughing, arguing or swearing. Floating past us, shattered, filmy grey ghosts begged: 'Hey bro, you gotta drink? Hey there sis, I give you $200 for a six-pack.' It was social service pay day in Wik Munkan country, and this was the only way they knew how to spend the insidious fortnightly government bribery money.

The whole time, kids – dishevelled, filthy-haired, with bellies distended and ulcerated mouths – hovered round the circles, waiting for their parents to parent them: a wait that would take until all the gambled cash took a day or so's ride up the dirt road to Weipa and was shakily put into the Albatross hotelier's pocket, and then until all that grog made them drunk and exhausted. It was a heavy weight, and a long wait. Then, in only another week or so, the social service money came again, eh but. In a sordid and bitter irony, this was a social *dis*service, a degradation of contagious proportions.

It was also common knowledge that infectious diseases like golden staph, gonorrhoea, and syphilis were also tearing down kids and adults alike. And the bush nurses, the unspoken heroes of the bush, had already been set straight about speaking up. On that score the government threatened any medical staff who stepped out of line with 'speak up and you will be unemployable in Queensland'.

'City people oughta take a proper look, and where're all the poncy solicitors now?' I said despairingly. 'A crime, that's what it is, and no wonder kids are going blind, sleeping among all these diseased, filthy, inbred dogs.'

'How else they gunna get warm at night?' Les knew that one from childhood.

Not before time, we reached the general store. About the size of an average city dweller's double garage, inside was stacked to the ceiling with row on row of tinned food. Using small talk to help settle my sadness, I complimented the new manager on how well stocked the place looked, and told Stryder to wait outside.

The new storekeeper shook his head. 'She's a fine-looking dog, let her stay.' He introduced himself as Bob, and explained that the previous manager had been a shonky white accountant who had just done a runner with $30,000 cash in hand. 'Done it before, ya know. Selfish son-of-a-bitch. They'll never catch 'im.'

Nearby, the old-fashioned cash register drawer, too swollen with cash and cheques to close, lay wide open. Money was spewing all over the mission like a permanent illness. Below the till, a range of healthy pumpkins, potatoes, onions, carrots and turnips lay waiting to be bought.

I pointed to the bloated till. 'I know they got the genocide money today, but how come we're the only ones shopping?'

Bob added up our bill, took the money and mournfully explained that of the $40,000 worth of cheques cashed that morning, only $5000 had been spent on food. 'The rest is out there being frittered away. It's sick alright.' It was a black day all round.

Les said it all: 'Don't give us any of that Abo gamblin' money, mate. It's like them, handled beyond recognition and frayin' at the seams.'

Bob put the crumpled-up, illegible paper notes back and pulled a couple of mint conditions from underneath. 'That Minster for Everything, Russ Hinze, came through yesterdee, laughin' about it all.'

Les told Bob not to get me started, that we didn't want to be there till doomsday.

'You men don't get it, do you? Doomsday is already here.' Feeling sick and useless, I stormed out and sat under the big old grandfather tamarind tree.

Before long Les, with Jenny, who was still decked out in her nurse's uniform, found me brooding away. The happy-go-lucky bush nurse and Les told me we were having a party at the plantation that night, and Jen was bringing her latest beau, Bernie, one of the Bush Pilots Airways newest pilots. The country nurses, with boundless compassion and hearts bigger than gropers, were always welcome on the *Jean King*.

What was the use of me feeling bad about something I could not change? And if it was hurting me, what must it have been doing to the people experiencing it? Realising how lucky I was in the scheme of things, I shrugged off the murky feeling and let my natural enthusiasm take over.

The night did itself proud. The coconut palms whispered suggestively, and the ocean lapped quietly as we lay around in the sand joking and tittering, eating grilled barramundi wings, tossing down drinks and drawing peace from the friendships.

'Under the weather does not fuckin' describe it.' It was the morning after the party and grizzling Les was the worse for wear. 'It's not the rum that makes me sick, it's all that sugar in the coke.' Sure it was! He had just returned from dropping off our friends, and quickly decided that diving overboard would freshen him up. I'd seen Les dive in some tricky situations, but this was not one of them so I never thought twice when I heard his body splash into the river. Instead I made a cup of tea and settled into a book.

Suddenly, from the back deck came his panic-stricken voice: 'Quick! Get out here. I'm hurt!'

Even from the wheelhouse door Les looked a bit possessed; still, that was nothing new. 'Fuck me over, one of the big gropers just tried to drown me!' Short of air and talking like a sped-up record, he rattled on: 'Just hangin' in the water gettin' me head clear when the big one closed his huge mouth right over me bloody waist.' He turned on his side and I saw bright red blood gushing down his thigh and the deep, long, lacerations that ran right across one hip and down; the same on Les's opposite-side ankle. Immediately, I heaped salt in a bowl of tepid water, grabbed fresh towels and the tobacco and went to him.

'I'm shakin' like a fuckin' girl.' Les's chattering shiver was fear, so I dropped a towel over his shoulders.

'Bloody fish got me in a grip, so I rolled to one side and pulled away.' He shrugged off the towel. 'Not only that, he's come in again and grabbed me and started pullin' me down to the bottom.'

I put the towel back over his shoulders, stuck a thick rollie in his mouth, and shoved my cup of hot tea into his hand. He was going a pale jade kind of colour so I murmured, 'Sit, sit,' and pushed him back onto the railing.

Les stood up. 'So I elbowed that groper with full force right on his big ugly fuckin' snout, and gouged at his eyes. Thank fuck he let go.' Smartly, Les had used the old blind eye groper trick. Thanks James, I remember thinking and pushed him down onto the railing again, and started bathing the long gushing wounds. 'And what's more, I know which one it was, because of the thick, long scar across his back. It's the big bastard, for sure!'

Seeing the huge chunks of gouged flesh with blood running from them like a busted dam I said innocently, 'I'm glad the groper took you and not anyone else.' My man stood up again, and looked down at me threateningly. 'I mean, at least with your diving experience, you knew exactly how to save yourself.' He settled, and I sat him back down again.

Les was hyped to the max, he was in murder mode. 'Fuck me dead, I'm gunna kill him!'

'But why, Les? He's only a fish. He doesn't know that he's trying to kill you. Please don't.'

'No! Where I come from it's a tit for a tat, and that's that!'

'But he doesn't come from where you come from.'

'He tried to kill me twice, so now it's my turn.'

From somewhere, two other dopey fishermen appeared on board, naturally urging Les to press on with his brainless revenge.

Who was I, a mere woman, to reason with such blockheads? Les baited up a small hook, snared a lively silver grunter, and rehooked it onto a huge double-bunger, gang-hook weapon, and dropped the squirming bait over the back.

'This fish is probably forty or fifty years old, and he's got family, please.' Might have been even older, could have been the mother, but reason as I might, to the men I sounded stupid.

'This is the way it has to be. This is between him and me.' If the blokes thought I was being sentimental they were very wrong but my kind of logic was never going to win the day – there was no one home in Les's head, and the boyhood days of black and white determination were in full throttle.

I don't even think words like environment, ecology and animal protection had even been verbalised yet, but a terrible sadness came over me as, impotently, I watched as the huge creature signed his/her own death warrant by snagging onto the unforgiving, ugly stainless-steel hooks. Ironically, the fish was so heavy and so large there was no way the three men could pull it into the boat. So we all stood in the dinghy while the ancient amphibian towed our four-metre dinghy, the heavy outboard and four adult human beings around the river. It was like being in a surreal dream. If only we intolerant, all-conquering humans thought for one moment and stopped going off half-cocked all the time, no doubt there'd be a few more animal species still wandering around amongst us.

By then, like ritual witnesses from Dreamtime, a bunch of black people inexplicably manifested on the closest riverbank. Finally, Les started the outboard and towed the heroic fish over and together they helped drag the massive groper onto the shore. Sure enough, there for all to see was a 90-centimetre long scar running from one side of his back to the other. To me, at that moment, the human and the fish were more than even.

Les cocked his tarnished old .303 and aimed. 'You lose, I win,' he said to the flailing creature, and fired two shots into the groper's head. Both glanced off its thick, primordial skull so for more than an agonising hour, the amazing fish lay still, submitting to his last seconds of life, only becoming agitated and flapping about angrily when Les went near him. To everyone there, it was obvious the fish had it in for Les – even the Aboriginals closed in and spoke in language about the situation for a time. Finally, the groper ceased breathing. Les and the fish had both lost; only when one of the two does not kill the other will they have both won.

'Okay, you fellas can fillet him now,' Les said triumphantly to the Aboriginals, and left the scene without looking back.

Inexplicably heartbroken, I watched from the middle of the river as the tribe cut him up. So large were the fillets, taller than a man, that one had to grip each fillet with both hands and, lifting as he went, walk backwards, as another sliced it from the mighty fish's frame.

Once before we had netted a huge, blind barramundi and I regretted her death too. Each time felt like another example of brazen disrespect. I killed fish for a living, and cattle for food, but for certain singular beings, the unusual ones, for some reason I wanted to give mercy too – my own lost one had left an indelible imprint. We call ourselves human *beings*, and every other creature on the planet we call *animals*, arrogantly elevating ourselves to a higher plane, and then give ourselves permission to treat every other 'animal' any way we want to. We human species leave a cruel stamp.

The *Jean King* moved on but the family of groper no longer lived under our hull. Trying to put into words why I missed what I considered to be ancient dwellers of the ocean sounds 'esoteric', but somehow it's about reaching back into our beginnings, not just on the Earth but into the mysterious universe.

With Stryder in tow, we decided to go across to the shore each morning to do some 'homework'. Using the original mariner art of stitching called macramé, we repaired torn diamond triangles in the old nets, tidied up buoys, floats and anchor ropes, stretched new nets from tree trunk to tree trunk, and sewed in the top and bottom ropes.

There were two types of nets – rag or monofilament: rag nets were good, monofilament nets were, and still are, bad and all the barra fishermen used the latter. All nets made of monofilament twine – plastic, that is – should be banned from all types of fishing throughout the oceans and rivers of the world. You see, the plastic does not deteriorate so when a chunk of net gets torn away, or a whole net is lost at sea, it continues to catch fish *forever*. An eternal plastic death-trap. And monofilament catches everything, no matter whether it is a mature five-foot long fish or a tiny, five-inch long baby – it's a goner.

A few natives with their little people and camp dogs usually drifted down on the outgoing tide each day, lit a small fire, speared and cooked a fish or a crab or two, and chatted while we sewed. The birds comfortably discussed things above and, like normal street traffic, a few pigs strolled on by. When the tide was incoming again, the Aboriginals caught a ride back upstream. That way, the clever fellas did without petrol.

One such day, a force beyond reckoning suddenly burst onto the scene. Beside the river's edge I was busily loading the stitching gear back into the dinghy when from out of the shallows right beside me came an unearthly *whooshing* sound of tunnelled energy which swept up, bringing a dam-burst of water with it. Even at arm's length the .303 propped up against a tree was too far away. Still, Les dived for it like an ace World Series cricketer behind the stumps. With volumes of river water still cascading down his muscular four-metre hide, the jaw-snapping croc was already at one of the Aboriginal's dogs. Using a powerful tail jerk, the swift reptile walloped the dog hard and his massive jaws crunched into the unfortunate animal's gizzard. The young healthy croc, together with the still jerking dead dog, spun like an ace roulette wheel and slid back down the soft mud bank. The river closed over both. Rarely in the bush was there such an indefinable time of echoing silence. Gone. Forget running, or climbing a tree, it was done, over, didn't seem to have happened. Les, with gun in hand, hadn't had enough seconds to pull the trigger.

CHAPTER 40

Taking a Stand

*M*y thirtieth birthday snuck up while the *Jean King* was still banned from anywhere Port, up the river of nowhere, with zilch fish in the freezer, nary an intelligent conversation in sight and, to make matters worse, over on the bank stood a bunch of drunken fishermen beckoning me to the brink of madness. As if that wasn't depressing enough, none of us had caught fish for a while, so I'd been setting my own nets and had been out-catching the men. Instead of acknowledging my skills, patronisingly they ridiculed my success.

Looking over at the barra fishermen, I thought, nice people, but if fuck wasn't in every fucking sentence, they weren't up for it; and unless this was a bad taste party with a lot of winning costumes it in, they'd hardly gone out of their way for my birthday bash: all sported scaly, grubby clothes, frizzled-up, neglected hair, salt-brined twigs of chest bristle, nicotine-browned grizzly beards, plus the unsure, knobbly knees that tried to keep all of the above afloat. It should have been hilarious seeing the party guests moving around disguised as tattered hobos but instead it was almost enough to make me want to cry.

From the boat I watched the half-baked lot swaying around, all grinning and waving at me like Bugs Bunny mistakes. Evidently this was way past a very clever cartoon. I'd just finished skinning a croc, my hair looked as though a lawnmower with blunt blades had gone haywire over it and to top that off, my period was just about to arrive. Not the pretty thirtieth picture I'd had in mind, but with nothing else going for it, begrudgingly I dinghied over to meet the fate of an apparently significant birth year.

Enduring awkward one-armed hugs (the other arm on crucial beer-holding duty), bony unhinged bodies and bad-breath kisses, I humoured their cautiously offered birthday wishes, their chatty teeth, grungy, crap-filled fingernails, stubby coolers with more greasy fingerprints on them than ASIO held in total – but frankly I could easily have walked off into the bush with Stryder and never returned.

'Look, love, we've put a leg of lamb on the fire, just for you,' one of them said, proudly pointing to an unattended, billowing fire in the centre of which sat my now carbon black, best tripod camp oven. Another managed to shove a warm beer in my hand. Disgruntled, I poured the foaming ale into my eager pond of instant gratification. Glug, glug, glug. Maybe a few dozen beers would, I considered, turn my view around, and I glugged down some more. The limited conversation hardly warranted words but between breaths and beer I queried the unusual odour in the air. 'That smell! Something's burning?'

We all sniffed up toward the hectic flames.

'How long since anyone checked the roast?'

This intelligent question was met with vacant silence, shrugs and idiot stares. Like babies with their dummies, the men replugged beers into their mouths. I snatched a solid chunk of firewood from the stack and knocked the flaming fire in the four known directions, then kicked the camp oven lid off. Inside, glued to the bottom of my favourite cooking pot, lay a dead piece of unrecognisable, smoking charcoal. Any depression I had now turned to fury.

Rightfully prepared for a burst of wrath, the men hung back. I leapt to the esky and booted its lid to hell and back. Huddled stonily in one corner stood three beers – all that was left of two cartons. Three beers on my goddamned birthday! The blokes cringed and watched anxiously as one beer went in each of my pockets, and the third almost popped its anxious lid before I ripped it asunder. Guz-zzzle, glug, glug. Knowing anything they now did or said would be wrong, the men stood around like stunned mullets, so I gave them a nasty tongue-lashing. 'Thanks for not caring. That burnt offering looks just like you charred no-brainers so why not gobble it all up like you did the beer? Good riddance to you all.'

Stryder and I sped off round the first bend and were out of sight before the party poopers came too. Venting my feelings by screaming out loud, I slowed down, stowed the beers and kept plugging upstream. It wasn't the beer, it was the thoughtlessness, the culture – it was me feeling trapped. Thankfully, the beauty of the land easily drew me in. Eventually I cut the outboard engine, lay back on the nets with Stryder and drifted into sleep. The dream still comes to me now, of being out in a sandy desert, Mum and Dad, Les's dad Kingy and I all sitting in the Canoess: and a black orchid spray on the prow transforming into a small native kid, a little girl, standing outside the boat, looking at us. But where was Les?

Awakening to a late afternoon of flighty grey clouds and Stryder pawing my hand, I travelled back downstream, sipping a beer thoughtfully. With huge toothy jaws spread open like iron rabbit snares, crocs sunbaked casually along sandbars in the late sun, bats still tired tried to get some sleep, native wasps filled their mud hut tombs with drugged-out grubs, and deadly taipan snakes swam alongside me. Each was doing its job. No matter what, this was an exquisite and abundant paradise. Thinking of how funny the whole event must have looked brought my humour back and I laughed out loud. 'Forgive and move on, eh Stryder!'

And the dream, that was another secret I kept inside.

As matters stood, Comalco were still in control, and we were used to being out at sea for long periods of time and thought that being in the right was all the mattered. What's more, working the Archer River's many tributaries meant there never was a dull day. After Les seriously burnt his tongue by using it to test a TX valve's temperature, I worked alone for a while. At night the fallen logs, tangled and torn trees, the oddly angled branches, all took on an eerie shadowy atmosphere that reminded me of the dark forests of Tolkien's Middle Earth. Often the big foam buoys on the river side of the nets were riddled with croc teeth dents. The savvy reptiles were always trying to rip caught fish from the nets. Unfortunately, sometimes they got entangled. We took no joy from shooting anything needlessly, yet extracting the feisty creatures alive was bloody impossible: I know because we tried it. In every case, we always utilised as much of the animal as possible, so the skins were brined ready for curing, the jaws cleaned, and the teeth and claws extracted. From his extensive New Guinea experiences, German Jack insisted that long-term eating of croc flesh produced sterility in men, so we took his advice and committed the meat back to the depths.

Incredibly, the Archer flowed from the west coast all the way across the continent to almost reach the sea off the east coast. Being virtually unexplored by white men, the river was an adventure waiting to happen so we started venturing deeper into the inland river system until finally we were far far away from everyone and everything. But this time the journey had not really been planned, it just seemed to evolve. The further upstream we flowed, the more difficult it became to return home to the *Jean King* every night, so we set up simple overnight camps along the riverbank and just kept going further inward each day. By towing a smaller dinghy, when the obstacles became too great for the big dinghy we left it behind and continued to forge over sandbars, across rock walls and extended stony patches, and up small waterfalls. A couple of times we even hauled the little dinghy overland and relaunched it, as on we pressed. This ultimate taste, the true spirit of exploration, came from being cast out.

One day, instinctively, we left the dinghy and padded softly across a riverbank – the place felt unusual, like a hallowed space, and it made us whisper reverently. 'Listen. Hear that echo? I reckon there's a tunnel below this ground.' The gossamer stream babbled and talked, everywhere vivid green moss lived under quaint gnarled trees – then at the same time, strangely enough, Les and I both decided that it reminded us of Elven Country in *Lord of the Rings*.

Padding along the goblin riverbank, the change in awareness felt like some heightened privilege, then a valley came into being quite unlike anything we'd experienced: the ochre soil, the soft golden grasses, pebble rock caches, and a perfectly carved-out amphitheatre. All the way around the basin lip, like guards, stood massive bark-curling, orange-slashed gums. Even the smallest stood six metres high – and the entire stand grew about two metres in toward the centre of the valley, then shot straight up to the sky. It wasn't just the extraordinary design or the stunning perfection of the scene; it was an immediate sense of sacredness. Automatically we dropped to the ground.

I'll try to water it down, but afterwards, for once, both of us agreed on what we witnessed. Day definitely fell into a kind of twilight, and in the amphitheatre, hearths – or more exactly, small crystal orbs of light – glowed, then over the rim came a guild of beings – like some kind of elders, including women, gifted children, and others from more than just the third dimension. They gathered in groups around the orbs and seemed to be exchanging knowledge, in a language that all implicitly understood. Some indefinable time later we came to and retreated soundlessly. It had been some sort of honour, and both of us knew that even if we returned the following day, the same would not have occurred.

Something had irrevocably altered. For the first time in many weeks, with little discussion, the next day we went all the way down-stream, back to the *Jean King*. Lying up on the roof, with the force of the experience still with us, Les reckoned it was the Star People. I reckoned we would never understand. Stryder (who probably did know) simply wedged herself between us, listened and relaxed into the horizon.

As soon as we woke the following morning, Les made a declaration. 'Upon my honour, woman of the sea, it's time we took a stand! Are ya with me?' By then it was November and we had spent nigh on three months in exile – enough was enough, so I rallied immediately. 'Blood oath I'm with you.' Clearing our name was one thing, and completely relying on other fishermen was another, but more than that, the Comalco lot were also trying to steal our commercial livelihood because Weipa was the only place where we could sell our fish, do banking and receive mail including essential spare parts etc – Weipa was our head office. And so as the *Jean King* slipped down the mighty Archer River to Aurukun Mission, Les and I cooked up our next move. As you know already, when it came to plots and plans, nothing fazed the two of us, but this time the scheme was question-able to say the least, and involved Paddy posting us an urgent, special delivery. Already knowing about our impasse, Paddy was really tickled by our rebellious idea when we explained it over the radio, and agreed without hesitation. He also said that Red was back and sent her love.

With Aurukun being about 100 kilometres south of Weipa, it was a surprise to find that false rumours about us were not only still doing the rounds, but seemed to get refuelled each week: of our thievery, of Les Coles's imminent arrest, of the power and rights that Comalco held over everyone in those parts. All of it was incredible crap and perfect propaganda for the forceful mining corporation to help keep the disliked fishermen on unsure grounds as to their rights – that is, to keep us all on tenterhooks, if you'll pardon the pun.

And like an omen, just as the *Jean King* rocked into Aurukun Mission, we were invited to an Aboriginal 'house opening'. Mistakenly thinking this was some kind of party, we turned up at the right house to see a subdued crowd of Wik Munkan people surrounding a small group of black warrior men, naked except for thin loincloths, and Aboriginal women dressed the same with their well-used bare breasts hanging free. The dancers, all covered in ash-dabbled stripes, were enacting extraordinary dance scenes to the evocative, lingering resonance of the didgeridoo. As the red dust rose from the ancient movements, and the unearthly chanting came through from spirit, the resonance harkened far and wide out into their traditional country. Realising that there was a deliberate intent here, we stood witness to a very important 'welcoming back' ritual. In fact, an Aboriginal had died some weeks before which meant that by decree his home and country automatically became closed to all and sundry. This specific rite of passage honoured that his spirit had decided where it wished to settle, and that his country could now be opened up again to one and all. This was demonstrated when the outdoor ceremony ceased and the front door of the empty fibro house was unlocked and everyone, singing, crying and chanting, trooped deliberately up into the home and flocked through every room. As you will see, the ramifications of proper respect brought about an astonishing opportunity.

Staying busy while we waited for Paddy's important parcel to arrive, we spruced the *Jean King* up inside and out. The key to our quirky plan involved mounting a four-metre high flagpole beside the wheelhouse door and attaching two borrowed big outdoor speakers to our cassette player – crucial ingredients to our strategic return.

Finally, guessing that the package should have arrived, we zipped up to the mission. Finding the butcher's shop actually open for business was like catching a falling star and putting it in your pocket, so while Les pressed on to the post office, I popped into the wrought-iron shed with its dirt floor and tennis-wire windows. A spread of raw, bleeding meat lay naked on the timber bench with a gazillion bush flies holding a corroboree on top of it. The 'butcher' was wrapping up fresh kidneys for Stryder, when my man burst in still tearing open a brown paper package. Raising one clenched fist to the sky, he whooped, 'Now we're armed, we can stand up for our rights.' The black butchers nodded – they knew. 'We have to clear our names, Rob. Being like this isn't free. We've always done the right thing by everyone, let's give 'em our best shot.'

OK, OK, I know you're either going to shake your head incredulously or laugh at our funniness, but Paddy's contribution to us taking a stand included the following: his own personal Eureka Stockade flag, a cleverly acquired skull-and-cross-bones flag, and a cassette recording of 'Waltzing Matilda'.

Goodo – we outlaws were now fully prepared to storm the bastion like proper rebels. And we wanted everyone to witness the event. If we were going to go down, we'd go down fighting the good fight, so back on board the *Jean King* my man called Henry, the Weipa harbourmaster, and asked if the beer at the Palace was still nice and cold.

'Yes,' he laughed, 'it's nearly as cold as the fish in your freezer.'

'Nice to hear it, Captain. You might just want to let the Brown Shirt know we'll be at the Palace tomorrow for the afternoon session to shout him a beer. Might like one yourself, Henry. Matter o' fact, we'll shout the bar, and even have a couple ourselves.' Radio static crackled and buzzed, then faded out.

Strong and clear, Les's blue eyes sparkled at the challenge. 'That'll fuck 'em!' he said with the right amount of pride. For me it was another showdown at the OK Corral and this time it was absolutely OK. In the meantime Les worked at hoisting the witty flags and I stuck like glue to the radio, spreading the word that the *Jean King* was going back to port.

In what turned out to be quite a fateful Friday, we headed for the showdown. Diving in at the deep end, hearts on our sleeves, a daredevil bit of showmanship was underway. With the flags righteously at full mast and symbolic music ready to play, the thrill of taking on Comalco was exhilarating. Pushing into an unruly, white-cap ocean, the jerky waves slapped at the portside, demanding we hold the boat on course. About halfway there, Les noticed a spec on the horizon that I could barely see. He semicircled and studied the miniscule dot through the binoculars. 'Bloody hell, there's two people way too far out, standin' there wavin' something. They're in strife.'

Within the hour, ours plus another dinghy was tied to the back and inside the wheelhouse, two naive teenage boys stood before us wearing only their underwear. Les and I looked over them with blankets, stew and gallons of hot sugary coffee. Stryder lay under the table, letting the boys' feet rest on her back – cleverly earthing them both. The innocent-eyed country lads were just kids really, and had been drifting in the ocean current for three full days. In between mouthfuls of everything, they spilt the beans.

'Me and him were on a good trawler called the *Mettle Maiden* – but Felix, that's the captain, by gosh, talk about a Jekyll and Hyde. Gee, a nice bloke in port but as soon as we put to sea, he wouldn't let us stop work all day. Then every night, without much food, he locked us outside on the deck, eh but. In our undies only! Thanks for the food, Mrs Coles.' Shovel, shovel, slurp. 'Heck, every night he prowled around inside, shovin' a loaded shotgun at us through the window all the time, pointing it and then laughin' hysterical, like a maniac.' The boys' adrenalin came at us from their eyes like electrical currents.

'I'll give him *Mettle Maiden*, I'll iron the cunt out,' Les muttered, and impatiently snatched the radio mike to call up Felix, the very same arrogant Felix who had not that long before used callous, icy standover tactics to try and freak me out. Like any father would, Les wanted to knock the skipper out cold, while I wanted to hug the young cherubs, to rock them, like any mother would, but instead kept filling their plates up with more tucker, and let the story unfold.

After a week of sadistic treatment, the kids became scared for their lives. Convinced that Felix was going to kill them, the boys decided to escape and, while he wasn't looking, deliberately hid some possessions in the dinghy. Still calling the *Mettle Maiden*, Les shook his head at the boys in frustration. 'Now fuck me brainless, tell me once again exactly what did you stash in the dinghy to save your lives?'

'One paddle, our thongs, oh yeah and our transistor radio plus all our favourite music tapes. Then yesterday the paddle snapped in half.' Both were going at the food and drink just like the dingo had.

Les and I just looked at each other, both nodding sideways in disbelief, then up and down for the miracle. Les wanted to punch Felix's lights right out, but now he also wanted to knock the young boys' heads into tomorrow – and didn't fail to give the two a very serious talking to then and there regarding the survival kit they'd packed. Obviously, Les had totally forgotten about our own completely mindless first foray on the high seas.

Knowing that somewhere out there the nasty Dutch Boer was listening but would never respond, Les stopped calling Felix and instead called up the kids' mums and dads.

On the one hand there was the wonderment of having found them at all and the disbelief at their childlike ways and, on the other, a real disgust at Felix for not taking the call then, or ever. This was a bad and twisted man who must have decided that the two boys could just die at sea. How did he ever live with that? From then until we reached Weipa, the two teenagers crashed into deep foghorn-snoring sleep. Although the outcasts were in from the cold, we banished ones still had a stand to make.

Steaming up to the landing that afternoon, we rebels and the good dog Stryder stood proudly beside the two soaring flags: the pirates' standard – the skull-and-crossbones – represented the rightful stand seamen had taken centuries ago against notoriously cruel ocean captains and their torturous ways. It also spoke about the right to freely roam the earth in an 'up yours with a knuckle-bone sandwich' kinda way. The other, emblazoned with the legendary Southern Cross star configuration on a sky-blue background, to many Australians, still arguably the real flag of the Australian nation, was the flag that had historically flown over the most famous Australian uprising of all time, the Eureka Stockade gunfight in 1854. It reflected the true heroism of the early Diggers' rebellion against the pompous, draconian rule of British tyranny, and the same for us with Comalco's arrogant use of power and impenetrable intolerance.

And booming out across the river was 'Waltzing Matilda', to some, Australia's real national anthem. Written in the 1890s, it is the country's most famous song and deals with a poor and starving man who after stealing a sheep from a wealthy landowner, decides that rather than submit to being captured and imprisoned by police, in principled defiance of unjust authorities drowns himself in a pond.

One thing's for sure, there Les, Stryder and I were there on the dot of opening time, saluting and coasting past a pub called the Palace (the People's Parliament) with flags raised at the mast, daring the global corporation of Comalco to take their own stand. And there, headed by Henry the harbourmaster, stood most of the town, stubbies in hand (the real Australian salute), waving, shouting, welcoming us back from our extended exile.

I think you get the picture well enough about fighting to the death for our rights without compromise or fear – well, a bit of fear but no compromise. 'Thank fuck for that!' I blurted, and kept saluting. 'I figured if they did chuck us in those open-air cells where they put the drunks and troublemakers, at least we'd be able see the Southern Cross. Didn't fancy it though.'

Les reached out and shook my hand. 'Me neither. Fancy a few cold beers eh but. That standover merchant was having a severe lend of everyone. Let's park the old girl and go sink a few.'

How we ever came up with such a peculiar yet powerful action is beyond me, but from where I sit today, I still feel the same way. Vive le Révolution!

With the physical distance between Weipa and the rest of the world being considerable, the state-run Fish Board took every opportunity to screw us hardworking, knuckly little fishermen. Once Les and I cut them out altogether by hiring a small light aircraft, reefing out all the seats and stacking it full of frozen product, and flew the load south that way. Ultimately there wasn't much more money in the deal, but it felt better.

'Fuck me over, that bloody Fish Board quoted me $2.40 a kilo for barra on Friday night, and now, two days later, they've dropped that to $2.00. In 48 hours we've lost $800 on the deal. They're snookering us in the money department and I'm goin' up to tear their bloody arms off. Then I want a word with Henry about that arsehole Felix.'

For once, I didn't care. 'I have to be up in town by ten, so I'll drop you off.' My corridor of escape, that is my embezzlement fund, needed establishing.

Because Felix didn't have an official skipper's ticket, apparently the harbourmaster had no legal recourse regarding the whippersnappers being left to die at sea, but I could do something illegal about saving myself. The second that the only bank (the Commonwealth) in town opened its doors for business, I waltzed in with the *Jean King* chequebook, opened up a false account in my mum's maiden name, and calmly deposited $500. While I'm not convinced that the bank is about common wealth, wealth for my future health it certainly was. From that day forward, I took my own stand and vowed that each time Les lashed out I would deposit money into the 'secret-Robyn's-business' escape fund: all the better to get back on my own two feet.

The thing was, in the early days the struggle between us had been a feisty, healthy game. But this wasn't the case anymore. While it should have been an excellent relationship, in the seesaw of emotions, sometimes flowing tears would satisfy Les's ego and cause him to change back, or every now and then it had to be a haymaker to an eye or a slug across the jaw; otherwise it was a dash for the shore or us both silently brooding at opposite ends of our little boat, with me keeping still but still quivering a bit. Somehow, somewhere along the way, the petty arguments had gotten deeper and sadly neither of us had enough wisdom to come back from there. Perhaps unconsciously we were already parting and couldn't confront it. Any which way, the good love between us was getting a bruising. His pain, his suffering, I knew, was far greater than mine, but how to cure it, I hadn't a clue.

One afternoon, all alone and lazing around on deck, flotsam and jetsam of another kind slipped on board, a slippery customer called Selwood Wormwood. Not his real name, of course, but we used to call him Woody: a polished, moon-faced, slicked-up bottle blond, steely sharp kinda bloke who'd been snooping around Weipa for a short while. Rumour was that he'd spent the last decade inside Australia's most infamous slammer for armed robbery – jail time which showed up in his sharp tongue and 'straight to the point' approach.

Woody was always straight with me so I humoured him. Out on the back deck, we sat watching the river life when suddenly he opened up. 'After eight years in the slot, the dirty coppers said if I shelfed the boys they'd let me out. I told 'em where to get off, real quick. No use them thinkin' they had one over me.'

He was a dapper-dan, for sure, and one of the toughest nuts I ever met, yet he had a way with people, always telling a clever joke at the drop of a hat – paradoxically, easily holding a spellbound crowd in the palm of his hand.

'The time I did the robbery, I was livin' like a king. Had girls all round me, champagne, cars, the top-shelf life. Married to a good lookin', smart young sort. We even had kids, and I loved 'em.' It was a unique moment, with him confessing, being so personal. As he wistfully gazed back, his life story just rolled out. 'Mate, there was plenty of money and things were goin' good.'

The way he looked, money still wasn't a problem. 'So what happened to her after, you know . . . ?' I asked.

'After I got arrested? Yep, she came up to Long Bay every weekend, as faithful as, till the day I forced her to face the fact that I was gunna be in there for a long stretch. The girl was still young and needed a man, so I told her not to come anymore, that I wouldn't see her if she did. Tears streamed down her pretty face. I tell ya, darl, my girl cried her heart out that day, pleading her love case.' Woody's expression seemed to come from behind the bars. 'Anyway, she never came back after that day but I heard she got tied up with another bloke, an acquaintance of mine. Even had a kid with him.'

Above us, whistle-blower screeching kites sent down short sharp screams, calling for our attention.

'Twelve years later I got out of the godforsaken hole. So I kidnapped her and kept her hidden for about a week.' I didn't flinch, just kept watching the kites jostling with each other. 'Then one day she says, this ain't right, I've got a husband and kid to look after, so I sez, let's make love one more time just like we used to in the old days, and then I'll take you back. Later I rung and told her bloke I'd bring her back for $20,000 cash.'

I whistled up at the kites and threw a leftover sausage into the sky. 'So you sold your wife for money, Woody. That's pretty bloody ordinary, don't you reckon?'

'Hey, love,' he protested, 'I needed the money, he wanted his wife back and she still loved me. It was a good business deal and no one got hurt.' Even without being able to actually sight the food scrap, the winning kite's claws seized it up just before it sank under the river's surface.

'Speaking of deals,' Woody flowed right on, 'how much fish does your freezer hold, love?' Thinking we'd dropped back into fishing lingo I told him we could carry about 2000 kilos.

'How much dried and pressed marijuana could you carry on board then?' Woody asked this question like it was a joke.

'Many thousands of kilos probably,' I answered laughing, 'unless we smoked it all!' The old days of indulging were gone, but I didn't mind an occasional smoke; in fact, by my philosophy the stuff was much healthier for body and mind than alcohol and should have been legalised.

Woody looked this way and that, then asked if Les and I would like to step into some big money. 'I mean cash, real big cash!'

Still not switched on to where he was leading, I told him it had been an average year, and that we could always do with a big bit of the lovely money.

Suddenly Woody's mouth was talking trapshot style. 'The boys've got a big marijuana crop dried, weighed, vacuum-packed, all ready for pick-up from the east coast. All ya hafta do is slip up a particular river, fill up your freezer, fill up below deck, fill up your forward locker, fill up ya pillowcases, anywhere ya can, and deliver it to Cairns – no strings attached.' He said there was a thousand dollars a kilo hard cash in it for us. 'You'd be back here fishin' three weeks from now and no one would even know.' Our eyes met in mutual understanding but my mind was busy doing a different kind of maths: that 'no one would even know' probably meant the entire east coast Mafia would know, and that 'no strings attached' definitely meant the very reverse.

For sure, we hadn't had our hands on any real money for a few years but it was for sure too that 'the boys' had to be the godfather's boys, and I knew what that meant – so I laughed casually and told him Les and I built our boat to be free.

'Yes love, but love,' Selwood started looking like a kite himself, 'what's wrong with havin' a decent dollar in your pocket? Ya both deserve it.'

Mentally, I did the sums and thinking like 'the mob', I did it by the grands and thous, and it looked pretty startling . . . that's er, $20 thou, $50 thou, or even more thous . . . or 100 grand, even 150 grand, like more big ones than we had ever dreamed of, let alone touched: the size of money we were never going to make fishing, the size of which made my escape fund look like little kids' lunch money.

Woody's eyes stayed steady on me, his beak-like nose sensing the mood. 'Don't say no. Give it some fair dinkum thought and there'd be plenty of the good gear to wrap your head around.'

Unlimited stone and plenty of grands – now that sounded better than grand. The only reason you wouldn't like a joint, I reasoned, was if you'd never had one. Hell, nothing to argue with there, and an escape fund outta this world.

While Woody's jailbait lips twitched on one side, making his eyes go shifty-squint, a lone Brahminy kite dropped from the sky, landed on the far end wharf pylon and momentarily faced us. A Brahminy! Such an uncommon bird to see, particularly alone, with a crest so white, chestnut wings glowing, holding a stance without compromise, he was so poised and unowned. The bird seemed to look directly at me before catching the draught and effortlessly drifting out to sea.

'Out there, Selwood, we come and go as we please. We don't owe anyone. We survive, and keep a pretty tidy plate. That way, doesn't matter who knocks on the door. We like it like that.' Woody never dropped his guard for a second, just shook his head. I shrugged affably. 'Thanks for asking, and by the way, my lips are sealed. Trust me.'

As Woody got up to go, he looked me in the eye again. 'By jeez, Robyn, there's not too many good sorts like you around. I'd snatch ya up, if I could.' He was not the good wood, and I was not a wood duck. In your dreams, I thought, and slipped right on into a fish, fishing and fighting rave so he'd sidle off quick-smart.

CHAPTER 41

Trapped in the Love

So what if bombs got dropped, parliaments fell, coalminers went on strike, electricity was cut, famous people did famous things, or died; other than me, no one up there took one iota of notice. In those years, without television, without daily newspapers, and just a dash of ABC radio, the barra fleet, caring less and less about outside machinations, dashed to and fro across the prolific waters, anchoring up wherever their hearts desired.

Checking nets alone was a blessing in disguise so I always jumped at the chance. But this time a nasty surprise struck: box jellyfish. The soaring, invasive pain rushed toward my heart so intensely that when my mouth opened to scream nothing came out. Box jellies don't attack, they go with the flow, poisoning to death most everything their clammy tentacles touch – in that way they are even more deadly than a premeditated attack from a passing shark. As the fatal serum struck with grave-rolling numbness, I let the fish net fall away, knowing it was imperative to concentrate. For probably less than 60 seconds, the long orange tentacles stayed glued onto my inner arm, like sticky lolly paper does to a grubby hand. As the hair on my head bristled and cold goose bumps made my body shiver uncontrollably, I remembered that rubbing, wiping, or touching the adhesive tentacle injection of deadly poison would only make things worse. My breath got short and shallow, my sight went hazy and I could feel the icy toxic wind going up my veins.

Flicking the clumsy, oversized plastic gloves to the dinghy floor while my eyes tried to pop from their sockets and my face skin spread open back past my ears, little by little I peeled off the lines of orange gel. Somewhere in the clutching agony, I got the outboard going and drove home like the wind, like a woman possessed. At the big boat, Les soaked the blistering gashes in vinegar and for a few days we watched while the furious blisters which had bubbled along my inner arm turned into a long-term scar. Today, the thought of that agonising limbo still brings goose bumps.

Not the best way to start the season yet, there we three were, sitting pretty in the Love River, watching nature's conditions ripen. It was a strong-flowing, one-boat river with a wall of mangroves running along her banks so the fish population was healthy enough, and males, mothers and kids of every variety strolled around like people in a suburban shopping centre: crocs, pigs, cattle, roos, lizards, even the occasional brumby horse appeared. With rain aplenty and a month of bigger-than-big tides, instead of setting nets all the way along the shore, we spread them exclusively around the river mouth. Despite it being the end of the Wet, psychedelic sunsets still backdropped phantasmagorical electrical storms and, as if by the command of a wizard's baton, the ABC classics seemed to strike up and play in tune with the silent lightning rods. While birds too myriad to mention flocked across the electric tango and into squabbling rookeries, fish watched on from below.

Lying back on the roof, we vowed never to tell the outside world the real extent of this extraordinary country we were fortunate enough to have stumbled upon.

One dawn, a two-metre, half-drowned wedge-tailed eagle got trapped in one of the nets. To stop his beak from slicing Les's face to ribbons, I used both hands to hold closed his scissor-sharp beak while we freed him. The drenched, shivering bird stood in the bottom of our dinghy for over half a day, waiting for his saturated spread-out wings to dry enough for take-off. Then he raised his body to the sky, circled us and dissolved into the stratosphere.

On another early morning run, Les blew the breath of life into a comatose turtle's nostrils, bringing the dear creature back from death. The shelled one had been trapped in one of our man-made nets too. See what I mean about plastic monofilament net?

That same day, Les, on a gut feeling, decided to do an unscheduled net run. Because it was an unusual, middle-of-the-day run, we took Stryder too. With box jellies floating in the water by the hundreds of thousands, as usual we wrapped ourselves from head to toe in gawky, stiff wet-weather raincoats, long pants and plastic gloves. As if the tropics weren't humid enough, sitting inside the sweatbox of oversized, clumsy gear made us feel like lumbering, gung-ho firemen on the front line of a major bushfire.

Just after bursting out through the mouth, right away Les picked up on the odd sea conditions, commenting on how unusually big the swell was. Following his gaze out to the horizon, not only were the smooth waves four metres high, but the huge water hills were surging our way like a ceaseless big dipper highway. 'Haven't seen that before and look at the spray flyin' off the crests, too, mate.' Captain Petersen's Law of Storms day was paying dividends.

Overhead puffy, voluminous grey clouds, already doing 30 or more knots, raced above us like ominous dark riders from another realm. Although there had been nothing mentioned on the weather update that morning, that meant nothing either because there was nothing subtle about the signs of the impending cyclone. Surfing the dinghy up and over along the huge rolling waves Les hit it right on the nail: 'Looks pretty fucked. Let's pull the nets quick and get the whole operation upstream.'

At first the nets got stripped of fish and folded in the centre, and the anchors stacked up the front. But the swells became increasingly higher, and wallowing in the bottom of them took the dinghy below sea level, which meant we could not sight any horizon. Rapidly, the brewing clouds scrummed up and the squally rain splattered our faces and blurred our vision. Like a bad-tempered brat, the storm looked hell-bent on yanking up and tossing away our entire livelihood; moreover, our plastic, non-deteriorating diamond-plaited nets would not only be reefed asunder and lost but they would drift aimlessly, killing sea animals *forever*. Such imperatives pushed Les to command, 'We're too slow and it's gettin' dangerous. Just reef the lot in, fish 'nd all.' Stryder scrambled out of the way by balancing on the front skirt of the dinghy.

With the cyclone coming for us like an out-of-control torpedo, and both drenched in sweat, we kept heaving in the living nets fully choked with sharks, catfish, sticks, barramundi, box jelly slime, crabs, salmon – all like us, out of their depth, trapped and flailing about.

'Get faster. The next net's half-adrift already.' With sand anchors piling up in the front and mountains of fish and nets doing the same in the middle, the combined weight was forcing the dinghy to sink lower and lower into the disturbed, fuming sea. As the last net came in all tangled up in poisonous snakes and more catfish, Les said, 'Hurry, just yank the anchor in.' So I did and frantically chucked it up the front. 'No, no, not up the front!' Les yelled too late. With too much weight, all too unevenly balanced, just like that Captain Petersen's Laws of Ballast did as he predicted, and we went down, and the swamped dinghy drank in salt water like it was rapturously thirsty. Everything, all of it, slid into the roller-coaster waves filled with a zillion or two of mindless, grim reaper box jellies which were gumming up the storming viscosity we were now floating in.

I could feel my skin and bones treading water inside the thick, heavy plastic coat and boots, *and* the outside raincoat skin which was treading its own bit of water. My spirit was doing the same, really. Squinting through the stinging rain, land looked about half a mile off. *What the fuck am I doin' out here* ran uselessly through my mind. Even then, with torches, nets, plastic bags of spare thingamabobs, batteries, blubber, gunk and nets straying all around, still one of us lamented, 'Fffffuck, there goes the tobacco too.'

Apparently the umbilical cord of the universe, the crucial plug, had been pulled and we were going down the gurgler. Amongst it all, Les inexplicably managed to rope all the fish-flapping nets back in the dinghy while I somehow found the dinghy's front tie-up rope and doubled it into two harnesses. I tied one thick, chafing loop around me and the other I swooshed through the waves to Les. 'Here, wrap this around ya laughin' gear. Ready, set, swim.' Both roughly roped up to the mass of dinghy, using braveness as a shield, we struck out for the shore towing the dinghy behind us.

As we hauled the heavily laden sunken clutter back to land, from some scary corner of my mind came Tiny Tim's falsetto shrill of *'Tiptoe through the tulips, thru the tulips with me'*. At times the bulky, flim-flam baggage surged past us in the wave mountains, at other times the undertow tried to lasso and tug us backwards. Savvy Stryder sized up the situation and without instruction also struck out for the shore. She did not look back. In the middle, we three tiny beings hung in suspension and pretended we would make it. In the vastness of the universe, I was nothing.

Stryder grinned like a croc when she squelched onto shore. Us too, as water poured out from every orifice, pocket and crevice of our plastic-enveloped bodies. Something must have touched my funny bone because I looked over at Les and in a highbrow accent asked, 'I say, do you swim here often?'

Instead of laughing, Les's jaw cracked open and his eyes riveted onto the sand just two metres from our jetsam landing site. There beside us was a croc slide, a deep crocodile trench carved into the sand, telling us that a big mother crocodile had just freshly dragged her one-metre wide belly across the sand and into the ocean for a quick dip. It was clear that the croc going out must have swum past us as we were going in. After letting a few of only the best swear-words flood out we both got back into the water and, fighting the massive current every step of the way, pulled and pushed the cumbersome, inundated dinghy along the shore and up the banks of the flooding creek. Cleaning the swamped dinghy and the fish-filled nets would have to wait because all of our attention was on saving ourselves and our precious boat.

Valiantly, Les swam to the *Jean King,* manoeuvred it into the riverbank, and held it steady while I bundled Stryder inside and secured the dinghy. We then drove upstream, way way up, wedged the boat tightly in a small tributary, and strapped down the lot as soundly as the fabled traveller Gulliver had been. By the time the cyclone spread its damage along the coast, we were drinking rum, playing bridge and arguing. Like Gulliver, we might have been tied to the land, but our hearts were not in it.

*

As cleverly as we'd read the unstable winds of impending disaster, unfortunately we weren't so clever when it came to ourselves. It was a battle of wills, and I flared up and held on like a tenacious shark when he used bully tactics to stand over me. There seemed to be no reason or logic to his anger, and when finicky baiting followed through with more hurtful accusations, it often led us to a subject too sad to speculate on: of getting off the sea and of sinking the boat deliberately and claiming the insurance money. Skulduggery and insurance companies went hand-in-hand but one thing we both felt with unsubstantiated certainty was that if the boat went down deliberately, when we needed a boat to stay afloat to save our lives, it would go down for sure. Some called that view superstition; we called it respect for the sea.

Suffice to say, I loved the brave spontaneous man in him and hated the bully, and he loved the wild woman and hated the know-all. One of us had been born with love and raised in silent anger and the other raised with love but surrounded by bully boys: it was the same kind of energy in different configurations. If I'd been a man, we probably would have been arch enemies. From fickleness to frustration to fury, striking out like a cornered snake worked for him; and like all habits, the more often one goes there, the deeper it needs to be felt to get release. On a whim, I took to marking the logbook with a red 'X' each time his volatile temper swung my way. Why? An imprint on white paper, a tangible reminder, a diary of deeds? Retrospectively, I'm sure it was a hunch, a map to help show me the way out.

Sand on the ocean bed is the same as sand in the desert – bloody shifty. Back down from Gulliver's Stream, the reality was that the cyclone had locked us into the Love, and until enough sand swept aside from the entrance to give our draught the right clearance, there was no leaving. Classic, isn't it? Locked in the Love by the lashing rage of the very thing we both loved the most – things could not have been more obvious if Queen Elizabeth herself had sent us a telegram.

Fishing slowed down to a fickle few, and the waiting game began. With less than a dozen fish to fillet each day, it wasn't long before we invented a plot, especially since there was plenty of booze, bullets, and time on our idle hands.

Firstly we secured the *Jean King* beside the deepest riverbank edge thereby gaining quick access to the shore while providing maximum shooting range for the game at hand. Then our array of weaponry was serviced: the corroded old Lee Enfield .303 blunderbuss with crooked sights; the very nice Miroko .308 with variable telescopic sights; a Smith and Wesson .22 hand pistol; a Nukill .22 single-shot rifle; and my 1908 Winchester pump-action repeater. As for targets, well, we decided to kill two birds with one stone and use the empty yellow Forex beer cans as we drank them.

By eleven each day, the beer would be cooling down in the freezer, the guns ready for action, and Les'd be on the case: 'Pick your weapon. See ya out the back.'

The more beer drunk, the more empty beer cans to dinghy over to the other riverbank and set up as shooting targets. *Boom, boom.* The rules of engagement included the winner of each round keeping the coldies and food coming, the other zipping to the opposite riverbank and lining up more fresh dead ducks. The more difficult the placement of the wounded cans, the better the challenge, so cans were positioned in tree branches, stood on fallen trunks, burrowed into the sand – and believe me, there were plenty of yella perils to decorate the wilderness shooting gallery. While the actual target positions were ingenious, the amount of beer being quaffed was record-breaking, as right before the tipsy shooting squad, brave cans of emptiness got shot to the shithouse.

'Mate, it's Baz. Heard you was locked in so meet us out the front in your dinghy because we're coming through with twenty cartons for yas.' Handy that, more beer!

We both excelled at target shooting, and for a while the game was the daily highlight, a fun challenge between mates, a six-pack trick. But as the weeks dragged on, the daily beer consumption and the bickering increased. By nightfall of each day's tournament, the war of words was aimed to kill. Feeling trapped, alone and vulnerable in the reptile-infested backwater, the black hours gave nothing away either. Everything was so life-and-death tough, so unrelenting, so inescapable. Shot down in flames by the cruel verbal abuse, one moonless night I lost it.

'I'm warnin' ya, quit fuckin' cryin'. All I said was your mum and dad had no idea 'bout raisin' kids,' he sneered.

The silly nonsense just went on and on so to drown it out I started howling. My well of fear and despair was maudlin drunk and I could not stop the moaning, grieving waterworks. Even the crickets seemed to crank up their droning racket just to get a voice in over our unhappy din. When Les tried to manhandle me, I ducked and recoiled onto the back deck, so he barrelled out, snatched my squirming body and javelined me overboard on the deep side, yelling, 'And good riddance to ya too!'

Down, down through the dim, thin air into the thick, cold, black water with bubbles being the only tangible sense, a squirming at my feet, a slimy unknowable thing, sunken up to the ankles in slurry, then up, up, my adrenalin burst through the surface, then my nostrils, then my mouth guzzling in great gulps of air, my arms reaching out for the boat, me trying to scramble up the impossible side. No helping hands waited. All the lights were switched off. No one was home in there, just a sullen, dark presence. My man deserted me in an emergency. Right then Les broke the 'mateship forever' pledge – an action that was actually more shocking than being thrown overboard. This, then, was the one defining moment that cemented my resolve to leave.

Without any lifeline, I shut my inner fear down enough to stealthily breaststroke around past the boat's stern and stagger up the sinister riverbank. I could have stepped back on board easily but what would Les do to me? And dearest Stryder was there, waiting. Tearless, voiceless, like a zombie, I noisily clattered through the mangroves, down to where the croc slide had been written in the sand. There, drenched through, the sopping-wet clothes clung to my empty shell, and with limbs spread-eagled like an 'X', I lay down on the sand and let go. For once, I did not see the bright and reliable stars but rather the endless blackness in between. In true abandonment, I deserted myself to death and fervently prayed, 'Let the croc come, please, let the death be complete, please, something, please take me. Anything.'

Nothing shivered or quaked, no body to feel, just a colourless void. The ocean sounds, even the deafening crickets, receded. At some time, even the dog left my side. Silently, I screamed for death to invade, for jaws to snap closed, to do me a favour, for Gurumaka, the tall thin spirit thereabouts, for his teeth to bite me in half, that way at least making some being happy. Water swirled up and back, higher each time. Who was it who said you can only save yourself?

Hours later, more muffled, more rote than before, I returned to the boat, unsalvaged. Nothing had come, nothing had changed. Just another day with a secret red 'X' marked on the logbook. It is said that water is a healer but below the surface Les and I were oceans apart. Clearly we were not 'living happily ever after on the sea', instead we were locked in the Love and the paradise of our making was imploding on its own brilliance.

Just because one is stuck in crappy circumstances doesn't mean that every moment is a miserable one. Nature, like a mother with a child at the breast, conversed with us 24 hours every day. We did the same back and always kept an eye, an ear and two nostrils out there in the ocean just over the other side of the sand spit. Hand-washing from the big bucket on the back deck, I used those inner senses to reckon what time of day it was: the sun had a bit of bite to it, the sou'easter had just begun to brush across my face, and my stomach growled for food, so it was bound to be around noon when Les's laughing call came from the roof and his pointed finger went over the sand spit, through the she-oaks, to about 200 metres offshore. There doing zero knots as it battled through the rolling, calm swell trudged a struggling dinghy overflowing with six or seven Aboriginal women, a few chirpy kids, chooks, pumpkins and so forth, all perched on top of stacked tucker cartons: life's necessities bought at the Aurukun store. Flat-out going forward, the working man's vessel was weighed down so much that it was almost taking in water. Easily keeping abreast of the dinghy, a string of folk strolled casually along the shore. Being about one day south from Aurukun, the mob were obviously heading back to tribal country, down around Warwick and Peggy's way.

'Fuck me tricky,' Les pulled off his hat and waved it to them, 'hope they make it before nightfall.' With that, we thought no more about it.

Late the next day, after a beachcomb, we passed the same stand of she-oaks and were ready to launch the dinghy to cross over to the *Jean King* when Stryder crouched low and growled menacingly. She was never one to bark at nothing, and we had not brought a gun, so we both spun around rapidly to see what she was reacting to. Amongst the lengthening tree shadows, leaning on his spears, one leg bent up like a poised brolga, stood a tall, mean-looking blackfella.

'Jesus H, Wes! I was just about to spread you all over that tree,' Les said, recognising him as Peggy's brother. Infectious fun spilt into the dusk as we shook hands and squatted in the sand. 'Looked like you got all the brothers in the whole of Australia in that dinghy yesterday.'

As his black eyes dived into ours, Wes's easy laughter echoed through the country. 'G'day, Les, Rob, Stryd. We seen you fellas yesterday. It's good you still here, only we just run out of outboard fuel further down the track, and need one more full tank to get us there.'

It was better Wes stay overnight and Les take the fuel and him back down the next morning, so on board, we slowly sipped stubbies and let Wes take the floor. 'Me dad always told us boys that while you was busy worryin' about a man's colour, you was just missin' the point. Don't matter what colour ya born, there's good whitefellas 'nd bad whitefellas, same goes for the blacks, yellas 'nd brindles. He reckoned you gotta feel 'em, 'nd how they are in the world. Don't matter if they're on the sea, in the bush, or down the road,' his long spindly hand waved, 'Dad reckoned no way colour made respect, always tellin' us not to miss out on real friends by lettin' silly prejudices get in your eyes.'

Wes sounded just like his dad, who'd reared his sons like all kids should be: no way perfect, but they knew how to listen, how to learn and, if need be, how to apologise without losing face. Moreover, their old man had made sure their knowledge of the bush held them in good stead.

'It's always about how people treat each other,' Les said. How he could say such things when he wasn't applying that principle on the home front was beyond me. 'As long as I can see the Milky Way, I know I'm not dead.'

I cut in. 'Same colour hearts, same colour blood, the same tribe,

I reckon.' For a nice change, the philosophic raves broke to the surface and wove into the harmony. It started getting cold so I tossed
Wes a shirt someone had left on board: a white and blue Canadian
ice-hockey guernsey with a red number 13 emblazoned on the front
and back of the flashy, nylon top. Wes looked so classic that when he
asked to keep it, we readily agreed. When I handed him a joint he
heartily enthused: 'Wow, man, this here sure is paradise.' Seeing him
dressed like that, saying such a thing, the whole scene was so funny
we laughed till we howled. The night, the mood, the men waffling
on, let me drift into my own thoughts.

'Me and Rob love it up here. It's so full like it's pregnant, always
givin' birth, always dyin', all the time, flowing around all of us.'

'Funny eh, back at camp they been talkin' about youse two eh.
They got a kid they wanna give you.'

Startled out of the daydream, I said, 'Who said what?'

'Yeah, our people trust youse two plenty, and there's this little
girl we wanna give you. Her mum's lost down the whitefella trail
and her grandma's gettin' old and already carin' for the little girl's
older brother. Yeah, so what do ya reckon?'

As though this was some everyday request, just like that, Wes
seemed to expect a yes or no right then. The mood changed and we
talked for a while, but there were private questions I badly needed
to ask and not wanting to offend I kissed his cheek, and we left him
up on the roof.

'Let's do it!' Les spoke keenly, from the knowing of his childhood. Kicking the fo'c'sle hatch wide open, he lay back and explained
how it was not an uncommon practice to 'lend' out their kids, but
usually only to other Aboriginals. 'It's a privilege, them givin' us the
choice like that. Later, at some time in the future, the family claims
the kid back.'

Sitting upright, broodily hugging my legs, I asked, 'How do they
even do that? I mean, give 'em away?'

'The mum must be havin' problems – you know, too much western walkabout. Makes sense a lot of the time, to give the kid a fair
chance. Then later, could be two, three, four years down the track,
they come and get 'em.'

'And that's it, they just appear and collect the kid, just like that?'

I clicked two fingers together. 'Gone! Goodbye, good luck, and see ya later alligator?'

He stilled my upturned hand. 'Yeah, Robyn, just like that. But look at all the fun in between. It'd be magic. A real chance. I'm all for it, what do you reckon?'

Didn't he know how unhappy we were? Or maybe he thought this would fix everything. At any rate, we talked for what seemed like a long time and just before sleep stole him away, Les even proposed we get legally married to somehow honour the little girl.

I slid down beside him, spoon-curled and did not sleep. Although he held me close, for my money, Les had rocks in his head.

When dawn light changed night into day, from the dinghy Wesley and Les said their goodbyes to me.

I told Wes his mob were always welcome around us, and to thank them all for the offer of a little one. 'I know it's an honour.' Unblinkingly, I let my dwelling sadness go right at him. 'Tell 'em I've got too much love to give, and that I couldn't stand the pain when they came and took our little girl back. I could never give her away.'

The men looked at each other and nodded as if they understood, but I knew they didn't. The outboard stirred into action. For safety reasons Les told me which direction they were going in and that he'd be back in about three or four hours.

As they pulled away, leaving me alone, good, I thought, and quickly turned away, hoping my straight back would reveal nothing as the king-tide tears flooded down my face. No way could we raise kids when the abuse just kept happening, no way in the world would I let the little one be a party to that. It was just tough shit that right decisions don't always have happy endings.

Soon, the Love unlocked its entrance and we shifted on.

CHAPTER 42

Losing It

*B*ack in the Kirke, day and night, we drove the big aluminium tinny to and fro into the choppy seas. Being ankle-deep in fish blood and live things, the whole enterprise was a slimy, pungent slippery dip. Les stood up the front dealing with fish while I pulled and heaved the full weight of the five-metre dinghy, the heavy 30 hp outboard hanging off the back, the two of us, a few sand anchors, plus a lead battery or two. For a five-foot tall, 50-kilogram woman, the work was demanding – no wonder I had muscles coming out of my muscles.

Then only a couple of months after the Aboriginals offered us one of their little people, suddenly I began feeling rundown and tired. Even when the scatty vaginal bleeding appeared, never in a month of Sundays did I think it was anything other than an inexplicable 'funny' period: a reasonable enough assumption considering that for the past week or so I'd been doing most of the daytime runs alone because Les was halfway through a major service on the main engine.

Only the day before, standing on a small sandbar digging in a net anchor, I'd heard a croc roar, looked up and there it was, facing me a couple of metres away. At about four metres long, he was a healthy young buck. Next thing I remembered was speeding flat-chat downstream in the dinghy. From croc to dinghy, I had flown again. The experience also scared the crap out of me. How ironic: this flourishing land's beauty was everything, yet my soul felt so diminished. Drained and jumpy, finally I confessed to Les.

'Jesus H, you could be pregnant.'

'Yeah, and the Star of David has just risen over Bethlehem,' I said cynically, reminding him that I did not ovulate.

'That's it, you're not workin' nets on your own anymore. You know what happened last time!' He was right, and was also thinking of the number of hours it would take the *Jean King* to get me into port, a time span that could mean the difference between life and death.

Before going out to clear the nets that evening, my bleeding went from a rusty trickle to a thick, clotty flow. And there were other signs, signs that spoke clearly with unusual foreboding. For instance, a rare form of saw sharks, a species older than Aboriginals, appeared. With protruding teeth running up each side of a very thin, long extended bill that comes straight off the shovel-flattened head, saw sharks are a harmless species and only use the two-metre long bill to riffle through the shallow water sands sifting out little critters with their small ray-type mouths. Much, much rarer were the saw sharks which appeared that night – still the same species except with a much thicker, very broad, shorter bill. For sure, unsubtle signs of things yet to come.

Back from the midnight run, we sat talking about how eerie the clear, beautiful night had felt. 'Strange feeling. I just hate it when we have to kill monoliths just to clear the nets. They're so unique.'

Suddenly the radio jumped into life. 'It's the Old Man calling, come in, Les.'

Davey's news was a big worry. The day before, the Boof's deckhand had taken off in a dinghy, heading for Weipa with tucker, water, his dog, a battery radiophone and the promise to stay in contact every two hours. A worried Davey went on to say that the decky, Peter, had not been in touch for hours. 'Didn't see him by any chance, did ja?' the Old Man asked hopefully.

Because we'd been outside mucking around since before midnight and not seen anything didn't stop us from immediately going back out and speeding deeply south, way past where Peter last radioed in from, then spinning back and dashing north, intensely scouring the shoreline, the horizon, and everything between or any movement or any abnormal bump or lump. No one was out there, but plenty of blood was pouring from me though.

Les snapped when I told him. 'I told you somethin' was wrong. And we've got the bloody Bedford stripped apart so we can't leave the river. I'm ringin' Bernie' – the bush nurse's boyfriend from Aurukun – 'he'll fly you straight out to Cairns.' Connecting to Bush Pilots Airways was easy; getting the flight out, not so. 'Bernie, what do ya mean, the plane's fully booked? Mate, this isn't a holiday bookin', it's an emergency. Rob's bleedin' bad.'

The trouble was that by law, Aboriginals came first, and the air-line could not or would not do anything about our dilemma.

Les went mental and started squeezing the mike like it was Bernie's neck, and bellowed down the line, 'Get one of them to wait till tomorrow, or the next day, or whenever. Bernie, fuck the rules, fuck the colour. Bernie, it's our Robbie, man, she could die! Get the cops to get one of . . .'

Les blowing a fuse like that caused Stryder to leap into the river and start paddling to the shore. Her splash made me look up and that's when I saw the boat, tapped Les with the binoculars and shoved them into his hands. He snarled and thrust them to his eyes.

'Bern, there's another way out. Just tell 'em it's tit for fuckin' tat.'

Right outside our front doorstep, the Boof was rolling north, up the coast, obviously out there searching for Peter.

Les rang the Boof, then told me in no uncertain terms to get clothes, get money and to get in the dinghy: 'You're goin'!'

With no choice in the matter, the necessity of mateship ruled and there the Boof and I were, face to face in his wheelhouse, and just as ironically, he was listening to the ABC news:

. . . with state elections days away, and the bitter anti-abortion legislation entering its final stages, the members of all parties will remain locked in debate every night . . . Meanwhile more protesters demanded that Premier Petersen guarantee his government will not demolish the Belview Hotel . . .

As I was about to discover, even the news headlines held more than a hidden political agenda. Boof flicked off the radio. 'Nothin' wrong with Bjelke. It's them bloody greenies. They're a pest to humanity.' How wrong could a whole mainstream generation have been? Thinking very differently than that, I kept my big mouth shut tight, brushed my sea-splattered face and stepped forward to shake his hand. Standing at the helm, he spread one bony arm around my shoulders and kept wrestling the boat against the outside elements.

'S'takin' a bit to keep the boat on course today, a bit like life, eh love?' He held me strongly against his sinewy, stalwart frame. 'Don't worry, girl, I've got ya now, and Les's already given me real strict instructions.' Some unencumbered love shone through and I felt safe then, protected. 'Jesus, one minute I'm protectin' my kid from you, eh, now I'm tryin' to help save your kid. Bloody strange how it works, eh but?'

Boof's words were spot on so I fessed up too. 'Yep. One minute I'm fighting for Les, next minute I'm losing the fight.'

'Don't say that, love. Just keep ya eyes peeled for Peter, the poor bugger. Least you're not out there in nowhere-land, maybe lost forever.' Wanna bet, I thought – feels like it.

In what was a parallel universe, bouncing headlong against the tide made for a rough ride all the way into Weipa.

Hospitals, white coats, anxious whispering outsiders, vibes of illness, echoing tiles, all disinfected and clinically polished, peeking curtains, bent worried backbones with stethoscope necklaces slipping past silently, the swinging doors of life and death: it was enough to give healthy people the creeps.

When the junior doctor struggled with my surname, I cut him off, insisting, 'It's been a long day, just cut to the chase.'

He explained that there was some problem that needed closer attention but that unfortunately he could not legally administer ether so I needed to go to Cairns. 'Now if it is deemed an emergency, we can fly you down for free.'

I might have felt like crap but still, I wasn't going to cop that so I shoved back my sleeves and leant fully across the desk's leather top.

'Listen mister, I've been gushing blood constantly for the past week, and still am. Believe me, my man is not someone you want to tangle with so if you don't want to end up in the emergency ward yourself, get me on the plane quick-smart.' The intern was taken aback and winced a bit as though it hurt to look at me. 'Now how 'bout you phone Bush Bastards, sorry Bush Pilots, and get me outta here.' My little black girl had come in on the wind and now this little one was going out on a wing and a prayer – both storm babies.

Back in Cairns, back where it had all begun, and nothing had changed except me and the type of vessel I was in. No more love-boat of life, smoky, raging bars and laughs aplenty; now it was an inhospitable public ward, alone, in a canoe of fear, and mockingly, my only lifesaver, a stranger in a white coat.

Grim-face, condescending stern eyes behind black-rimmed glasses, was how I saw the doctor who told me I was pregnant. I just knew it, and also knew the shape of my reply – a decision that would stay with me a long time, possibly forever. 'I must have an abortion.'

There, the unnamed had been named, the unborn not to be: it had to be the same as the decision around the little girl the Aboriginals had offered. I could already prophesy the unhappy future of this child – and *thought* I could glimpse the eternal turmoil that this one would go through as he got torn between the two of us: I was already feeling mother love for this unexpected little person, feeling it so profoundly that letting the baby go rather than having him be abused felt paramount.

'Not possible, I'm afraid, what with the anti-abortion debate raging and me running in the next state elections – it's just too risky.' So that was where the automatic smile came from, and I knew all too well about the parliamentary debate being used to distract attention away from destroying some important architectural heritage.

'So? It's not illegal yet, doctor. Besides, my partner and I won't make the grade. He hits me and I won't have the kid being hurt.'

The aspiring politician's eyebrows quizzed up and down at the blunt honesty of my reply. He hesitated a bit then took up my hand and explained that an abortion was absolutely out of the question, however, if by the same time tomorrow I was still bleeding so heavily, 'I will perform a curette, that is, a scraping out of the—'

'I know what it is, and thanks for the tip.'

The doctor's distant, self-important demeanour returned immediately, along with his stiff and formal bedside manner. He called a
passing nurse into the room and issued instructions. 'Get a dressing
gown for the girl. I will return in the morning,' then without a please
or a thank you, swept regally from the room.

Even though the smallest-size dressing gown was way too big
for my diminished frame, wear it I did. From up to down, down to
up, to down the three flights of hospital stairs sadly I trod all day,
encouraging my pregnant blood to pump away. With my own life
all narrowed and bent, so too was my outlook. Inside the frayed
and faded navy-blue gown, I felt old and lifeless, yet still up and
down, down and up I climbed. So much for the vast womb of fish in
which I'd floated for years, now, from my very own precious vessel of
human life, numbly I was about to set afloat one of my own.

Finally back in the ward, filled with the heavy grief of everything, I pulled the privacy curtain around the bed. For one moment,
I thought I saw Stryder. The silly bed sheets were tucked in like a
madman's straitjacket so I tore at them until they were away from
under the mattress, away and free. At last, dressing gown and all,
I climbed inside the sterilised public ward blankets and lay, eyes
closed, watching from inside. It felt like I was in the yellow oversized
raincoat swimming for the shore, only this time I was drifting away
from it. Slumber and sleep, light and flicker, darkness and deeper,
remotely, at some second, thankfully, the ward lights switched off.
Still I lay inside and saw . . . from the full moon only one ray beaming down on the Canoess, the silvery one, and me, beside it, eyes wide
open, hair spread out and lying afloat on the Gulf's sea, my left arm
thatched into the canoe's bark, the glassy, horizonless ocean, waves
of calm passing through me . . . like I had been lying there for an
eternity, certainly a lifetime.

The die was set, the morning came, the curette performed.

A day later, I was back in the ceaseless stream of life, trying to
remember to forget, feeling the wheels within wheels, death within
life, using tequila shots at some corner bar to sting my heart and
bizarrely hearing the radio's blaring siren sounds of a newsflash:

... Today the state government finally succeeded in passing the unpopular anti-abortion legislation. In further news, while members from both sides were inside the house, in the early hours of this morning the Petersen government successfully bulldozed the Belview Hotel to the ground. It was only when members left parliament house and stood facing the final moments of the reverse construction ...

Reverse construction? That was it, how I felt. It was 1979 and heritage architecture from another time had been crunched to the bone, dust to dust, buried by the blind and ignorant while I, with three little ones gone, hid my sorrow by tossing down the peyote punch, hoping it would help my spirit come alive again. Amongst it all I felt such an interminable sadness for the human race. Then a song came on, one they could have been playing just for me:

I don't like you, but I love you, don't wanna spend another day here, oh oh oh you do me wrong now, I love you strong now, you really got a hold on me ...

The radio said it all, and my well of tears silently trickled over the corner bar's carpet and down into the cry river.

And the desperate deckhand's demise, the one who had tried to make it back to his loved one come hell or high water? His dog was found marooned on a beach but the impatient man and his dinghy, never. Obviously he had drowned. And me, another story. A bit like both of them: apparently still alive, a lost outsider now, but drowning too – silently.

Straight from the bar of tequila, turmoil and tears, I flew back to Weipa where my man was not at the airport, not waiting staunchly for me. Rather, later in the day a flushed, scrubby stranger with beer breath apologetically bustled into the wheelhouse where I lay buried in an odd, icy limbo. He mumbled around, unsurely, somehow embarrassed, as though by not knowing what had really happened, the cord between us would remain intact.

It is almost implausible to think that, as though protecting myself and the gone little one in some limited way, I never told Les the full extent of what had gone down. Instead, each wrapped in our own cocoon, we tried to immerse ourselves in the comings and goings of fishing, fish and fighting. My inner light did not go out, it just froze. Maintaining the internal change called for constant focus – keeping it secret was difficult because the true love I had for Les never died – so I carried on externally being the same but I was more pliable now, less spritely and alive; and by deliberately touching my skin, used those tangible ways to remind myself that I was inside my body. And my erratic periods refused to recover too. The whole time was strange and dark.

It wouldn't be the first time that someone in the middle of a nervous breakdown didn't know it.

CHAPTER 43

A Hardening Resolve

'I'm back alright, luvvie!' Her infectious shriek of laughter blew the wheelhouse inside out, and what a lifesaver it was when Big Red's voice boomed over the radio telling us that the yachtie she had left Thursday Island with couldn't 'sail if his life depended on it', and that before turning west-ish at the New Guinea pass, she bailed out, and met up with a Highlands farm owner. 'Yep, nice plantation, lovely coffee, pity he liked native men better!'

Later I rang her from the public phone box so we could talk more privately. For me, the penny dropped, and as it rolled to the darkest corner, my inner voice issued clear instructions: 'Go away and get some.' I simply assumed it meant laughter, but it meant much more. Thank heavens the *Jean King* was once again stalled in port, impatiently waiting for a part to be sent from Sydney. Funny that, funny-good I realised, and pitched to Les for all I was worth.

'Red needs me in Sydney, the poor thing's broken-hearted. I'll only be gone a week and I'll bring back the freezer part too. That way we know it'll be the right part.' The irony of the broken part being for the freezer did not escape my attention either. A little white lie, a bit of 'method in the madness' acting, and I was gone – at last, the first holiday without my 'lover'.

After living the life of a one-man woman, I finally started breaking the mould, first with the lie and then I 'betrayed' him: Big Red, the bright lights of the big smoke, some trendy bar at The Rocks, a live jazz quartet and a sexy boy was all it took. I think my private grief brought on a kind of haunting beauty and the boy was captured by it. And a sweet touch of love attention goes a long way so all night I let his soft vibes sweep over my troubled heart.

'Jeez, you were so easy to talk to last night,' Giovanni's youthful phone call went the next day 'and, and I've never had a girl being so interested in engines before.' The way he said 'girl' made me feel like I was 18 again. As the good medicine surfed across my lingering sadness, his eager, naive approach touched my hibernating tingle font, so I let him remind me about my self, my own loveliness and bright mind. 'I really want to see you again, please, say yes?'

Taking with Red about it, I felt renewed. 'The next thing he'll be telling me about his school days.'

'You mean last year?' We screeched a bit and she told me to be flattered, that he was genuine, a good looker, and had no hang-ups. 'Right now you're 3000 miles away from everyone. It's time you grabbed life by the balls again.' Red was a good friend alright, and her take on it sounded spot on. She selected 'Pink the Town' nail polish and started dabbing my fingernails. 'Go and get some while you can, it will be healthy for you and, besides, nothin' like a young pup to blow away the cobwebs.'

When something outside of the ballpark makes sense, drop the ball and go with it, get out of the park.

A couple of days later, under rafters strung with garlic bundles, calico-swathed cheeses and stringed red chillies, Giovanni and I cared nothing for the checked tablecloth, the flickering candles or the menus of promises, all sautéed in basil and rosemary – for both it was much more natural to share a light entrée, a sip of suburban red, then drive to the borrowed mate's flat and dive straight into the thoughtfully new crisp white sheets.

Even ships in the night still care for precious cargo, so try not to assume that this was only about leading the young colt through the paces of pleasure, and/or remaining entwined for the weekend. Both of us had plenty of genuine feelings and important conversations to share. When my period blood came, it was vivid red and flowed strongly like it should. The man took this in his stride, and we went into a more tender experience than I had ever had. It seemed as it should be, the boy being led to manhood by the older woman, a boy giving an older woman rebirth – a cure doctors should prescribe more often, a life experience which should be cultivated across civilisations.

By the end of the holiday, blinded by infatuation, the man-boy begged me to stay. Right in that moment I'd be telling another lie if I said I didn't want to, but it was not the passion of love that had driven me to him, it was a deeply wounded heart, an echoing still coming from the womb. And I was transformed too because he had shown me that I was ready now, that I knew the way out was necessary. 'Our pathways lead in different directions, but you have been more important in my life than you will ever know,' I explained. 'Thank you, my friend.' I hope he knew.

And it was funny really, because to most people, especially men, my lifestyle was their wishful thinking, something most people do for a holiday, a paradise job in Paradise. Yet the rest of my life was calling me back and Les, fish, fishing and fighting were not included.

Entering the final year of unfinished business with proper intent, I built the escape fund into a decent reservoir of cash, and now when Les's monster habitually arose and stormed through our relationship imposing bewilderment and anguish, I no longer engaged, I just did everything his way or stayed silent, and always marked the logbook with my covert symbol.

Les, on the other hand, had no plans to lose me, or to change anything. Following another night filled with his volcanic temper, and another red X marked in the logbook, Les's trusting blue eyes looked up from the main engine. 'Sorry about last night, love, I just got carried away.' Already that morning another $500 had gone into the secret escape fund. Call it dues, call it compensation, call it fraud, call it what you like, nonexistent notions of how it ought to be are thorny like that – and let me say that while my actions helped give me strength, please understand there was no joy in the method. This man deserved some honour, yet so did I. Everyone has principles but living by them fully is another thing. Isn't life full of contradictions?

Maybe I wanted one last taste of the real us because as the fishing season came to a close, I suggested that instead of going so far down the coast to catch barramundi, we do a spot of mackerel fishing closer to home around Pera Heads. Lazily leaving the engine cover off, Les grinned, scrambled up onto the wharf and called, 'Yeah love, nice call.' Like waiting gangsters, a couple of his cronies sat in the old ute with the engine running, so he scampered off merrily toward them saying, 'I'll be back in a jiffy.'

Now, steaming out, slicing south down the coast, slipping into one or another favourite haunt was just a different place in which to continue the baiting game, the snare of unforgiving habit-ridden accusations, days of sullen silence, and hard work. In the final year, the constant abuse permanently arrived at my lotus blossom core and sex had become a function for his relief, something I just submitted to, then receded from. Too much, too little, not being heard, not understood; either way, the ship was going down and there were no salvage rights.

Nevertheless the *Jean King* was still my wonderful home, so nimbly I adjusted ropes to keep the boat from knocking up against other vessels, and seeing the tide was right, I looped a rope around each one of the empty 44-gallon drums and from the wharf eased two onto the front deck and two on the back. Another way to keep the dwelling sadness of the inevitable decision at a distance was to work my guts out. As I was thinking that this must have been why Les's dad, Kingy, worked like he did, and how he must have felt, the voice of an old friend brought me back: 'Hey, that's no work for a little girl like you, and anyway this is bloke's work. Where's that bloody fella of yours gone to this time?' It was Conj, grinning happily at me.

'Have a guess!' I kept heaving the last 44 down. 'Just help get the drum into position steady, thanks mate.' The man always had a soft spot for me, and had told me as much more than once. In fact, ever since the boat-building days he'd been there for me and I lit up around him too, but the next movement, the real escape needed no entanglements. I'd be going it alone, I'd have to cut and run fast.

All day I worked around the boat until a cold body shiver reminded me that the sun was nearly down, that it was time. One key turn and Wednesday started up, so I backed the *Jean King* away from the wharf, out into the main stream, and chugged across the channel into Turtle Creek. Turtles live between their bottom and top shells, inseparable from its place in between. In this way just like humans and all other beings, it walks between heaven and earth. Thinking like that, I went on . . . we might be connected to all things but I didn't feel too connected to Les . . . and how could I leave without devastating him? How could I go when we were not arguing? How could I leave when we were? How could I leave my life, home, dog and friends? What would I tell my family?

Although the human being is small in size, somewhere within there is a place deeper than a fathomless ocean . . . way below the numbness pain – yes, there it was, alive and so bruised, it was almost a pleasure to greet, a pleasure to stay there, where only I and the pain understood. Knowing I must leave very soon didn't stop jumbled thoughts from coming . . . men hit women, women hit men, men hit men and women hit women, but why, I asked, do lovers hit lovers? Why didn't the human species have the barramundi's hermaphrodite skills of being able to stand in each other's shoes, that ultimate in understanding?

'Why, why, why?' I cried aloud and glanced down at the open logbook, noticing the red Xs, which I'd been penning each time Les's violence flared. Suddenly an apparent pattern jumped off the pages at me and the further I flicked back over the past year or so, the more obvious it was that his violent moods struck regularly every month! Bloody hell! Right before my eyes, there was a red cross marked every 28 or so days, as regular as a woman's period – there, written in red, was another part of the truth as to why his anger was out of my control.

Water was the planet's engine coolant, and it was the same in the case of the human body, comprised as it is of 70 per cent water – water was our engine coolant, only we impregnated it with emotions too. And my man's 70 per cent water had turned red with anger, and kept boiling over *habitually*. While his water was erupting in rage and fury, my heart was bleeding from grief and shame.

This understanding was like a bolt out of the blue – like a

lightening of the load, a physical knowledge that I was not to blame and that it was not possible for me to alter him – it was imperative knowledge to me, and unaccountably an important trigger of my release.

In need of company I burst back across to the other side. Not to Les and his cronies wading around in drink-type company – I needed real companionship. Pequitta's home fit the bill, a place where I was openly welcomed. We spent the night talking about my discovery, about my feelings, about life and its options, about the heart of the matter. At last, I stepped into the light of understanding.

CHAPTER 44

Game Over

*W*ithin the next few days we had slipped the half-day south to Pera Heads. The three or four weeks of fancy-free fishing fell into place so easily and this was proper fishing: mackerel, the gentlemen's game.

My superb heartland was just the same: fresh water glistened down the ochre cliffs, the family of she-oaks, the quirky pandanus tribe, pink cockatoos, wedge-tails, ospreys and sand so fine my feet couldn't wait to feel it – even the air had a delectable flavour about it; all sparkling and good. We were on top of a sea which was clear right to the bottom and literally jumping with gar, queenies and scuttling cuttlefish. There were the plucky little shags too, floating effortlessly on the ocean's skin. It must have felt good to live most of your life in a brisk bath, and be able to pull your favourite food, fresh, from the same source.

The next day the sea was cack green and jumpy, the sky steely grey, a large flock of frigate birds circled over the patch, and the pull to go mackerel fishing was as irresistible as stealing a look at the poker hand you've just been dealt.

Tilling from the back and dropping the lines as we went, Les headed to the grounds. Inside, to secure the oversized fishing gloves onto my hands, I wrapped sprag wire at each wrist. Just like the old days at Bramble Cay, immersed in the picture, together we trawled, talked techniques, baited up, worked the lines, and waited. *Sproing* the line went and the first fish was hooked. To keep the invisible school near the surface meant getting the mackerel on board quick-smart. Two. Three. To keep them striking meant keeping the bait up to them. Four. Five. Like driving with a busted windscreen in a thunderstorm, salt water blurred our vision. Six. To wrestle properly with the fish we dug our knees hard into the back deck railing, leant over and down to the water's surface, double wrapping swiftly, and yelling the play to each other like any team player does. Seven. Line wrapping fish was an art, done in such a way that at the first sign of trouble, one flick of the wrist and all the fishing line entwined around your hands would automatically fall to your feet. Eight. Any blunder and a finger or fingers could be torn off.

As the fish hit fast and furious, we trawled in ever-constant circles around our prey: a bit like how Les and I were with each other, really. For sure, the wind was whistling, the waves dancing, the clouds flying, and the *Jean King* cutting the mustard: working together like this, it felt like the war was over, only now I knew that the peace was just another monthly truce in disguise.

Twang. Nine. The rubber O snapped tightly so I reached out, grabbed the rope and pulled it to me. Judging by the weight and fight in the fish, it was a big one. Beside me, Les was playing the same game. Hunched down, I jettisoned rope between my legs, double-wrapping the Bowden cable, then the piano wire like it was chewy, reefing away until the fish was at the back of the boat. Leaning right over to get a proper grip, I started hauling the good-sized, rainbow-skinned mackerel from the ocean.

Thwack! A massive shark, his jaws fully dislocated for a wider crunch, started shuddering up the mackerel's body. His exposed gums, bulging eyes, his rows of crunching teeth were engulfing my fish. Jarred then shocked, I watched in disbelief as the shark's tenacious, full-strength power went for broke as he kept yanking what was left of the poor boggle-eyed fish into the swirling waters. Being as dumbstruck as the mackerel was one thing, but still being connected by fishing line and therefore to what was left of the torn apart, bleeding mackerel was another. Suddenly my feet were jerked from under me – the immensely powerful shark was tearing me out of the boat too. Frozen by the scene, like an eyewitness all I saw was the churning prop, the macabre grinning shark gorging his way toward *me*, and the engulfing, swirling vortex of the gory ocean depths.

Whack! Like running smack bang into an immovable iron bar, Les's arm slammed me right across the chest, knocking my body full force backwards and I crashed into the freezer. Les's spontaneous strength was almighty. The shark, still looking straight at us, bit off all that he could chew, leaving only the bloodshot, crazy-eyed tattered head of one of the razor gang. At that instant, the spell broke. I flicked the wrapped, scrambled fishing wire from my hands and Les leaped away, snatched up his line again, and kept on pulling in the other fish.

Suddenly plundering pain seared from my fingers up the arm and right across my chest bones. Jittery and dazed, I held out one oversized gloved hand. 'Get this glove off for me. Undo it. Please.'

'Get in fuckin' line,' Les roared as he reefed another 25-pounder into the boat, swung the tiller with one foot, and bent to pull the hook out of the quivering fish's jaw. 'Chuck all the jumbled wire overboard. Get the hooks off the deck, the place's jumpin'. Pull your finger out, mate.'

'Speaking of fingers,' I snarled back, 'I think I've just lost one on the right hand, *mate*!' That stopped him in his tracks. Les looked up sharply so I thrust my right hand at his eyes and emphasised, 'So take it easy pullin' off the glove.'

The day stood still. We spun out of the circle. He unsplined the copper wire and gently extracted my hand from the groper-sized glove. It was already the size of a baseball mitt and the colour of a bruised Thursday Islander, and my face was the opposite colour as the throbbing pain went to work. No fingers had been ripped apart, but a couple were badly dislocated, and my collarbone was already changing colour and going black.

The ocean game was over.

Figuratively speaking, at some time or another, everyone has a gun pointed at them. How they respond is hopefully the very opposite of how I did.

Back in port we anchored up opposite the Palace in Turtle Creek. The Wet was threatening to burst apart, the Palace was bursting with pals and again after drinks-a-plenty, so was Les. Back on board the boat, when his temper rose all tethered up with the familiar accusations, this time Les pulled the .22, and aimed it at my head. So fragile was the tension, so screamingly absurd, to save myself some response had to take place, so I played the most serious game of charades in my life and pretended to capture his uncalled for, pointless madness on film. What in the name of life was I thinking? This was as bloody silly as tiptoeing through the tulips with Tiny Tim, but that's what I did.

Following some survival instinct that my mind invented, I listened to his every breath and watched his every action without distraction as I moved around just like a charade cameraman on set, one arm rolling the pretend film, the other holding the nonexistent camera – all the time saying risky things like, 'If only your mates could see you now, Les, what would they say?' Around and around him I went. 'Ladies and gentlemen, we have here the famous Les, the brave hero' – winding the film – 'if only you could see you now, Les,' I urged softly with one eye closed and the other looking through the pretend view-finder . . . whispering sharply . . . 'Just look, look at yourself now.' Why would such a ridiculous strategy work? This went on for some interminable time before suddenly he flung the pistol down and mumbled, 'Oh . . . oh well, wasn't fuckin' loaded anyway.' Stumbling and grumbling, he slumped onto the lounge and with the gun still at his side eventually nodded off where he lay. I did not. And whether the gun was or was not loaded I did not know either, and what difference did that make anyway? None at all – I had been afraid for my life. Racing to the shore, I found the dog and we stayed on guard in the dinghy through the dark hours.

It was a fortunate second for me when Les embarrassed himself and backed off, when his strutting bravado went arse-up, but whoever – whatever – it was that I had originally loved no longer lived in there. And for obvious reasons, of course, I was scared to death of leaving, but the Les I knew was irretrievable, and in my (and his) philosophy, dying trying was better than living imprisoned by your own fear. It was sink or swim time.

Driving back over to Turtle Creek, still the foreboding made me hesitate. While I sat there feeling completely immobilised, a booming voice came through my mind: *If you stay here then you must love it, if you don't, then go NOW!* It was loud, clear and indelible – and that was it. I went on board, looked him in the eyes and finally the essential words fell from my mouth: 'Today's the day, Les.' After eight years together, I heard myself saying, 'I'm off. Take me to the wharf. I'm booking a flight out.' The deep blue pain of his eyes clutched at my heart.

But he knew, Stryder knew, I knew. The final moment had come. It was a day just like any other day, there was no sign from heaven, no knight in shining armour to swoop me up onto the pure black stallion and away into the glowing twilight. It was just another day in paradise, but it was a reverse day inside of me: a foggy, deep quagmire I could not own anymore. By then my secret escape fund totalled $4500, which by rough calculation was the equivalent dollars' worth of the fish that lay in the *Jean King*'s freezer, so it was even-stevens, fair enough – it was over and out time.

Across the big river and into the ute with Stryder flying in the back, Les and I rode off down the long copper road for the last time, a dusty cloud hanging silently in our wake. In town, the up, up and away forever flight was booked for the next day and paid for – him all amicable and compliant, almost like nothing was different, but everything had changed.

Day was turning into night when we arrived back on board and by then it was all feeling suspiciously easy, like swimming from a swamped dinghy to the safety of the shore, but this time knowing that an invisible croc was coming my way. Every second felt naked, raw to the soul, as I continued to do this unbearable thing: leave my *Jean King*, my way of life, my boat, my ocean, my heart country, my love, my no longer there soul mate. Pale, weighed down with it all, grieving, all the time trying to imbibe the last drops of this precious, luscious land into my soul.

And then there was Stryder, my Stryd, who reached across the known species lines, the dog that knew many things, and knowing she must stay.

Everything had to be left behind. I was going back to the intergalactic transit lounge of life again.

In the midst of the knife-sharp terrible, terrible pain, in the heart of the *Jean King* I was stuffing what felt like unimportant things like photograph albums, favourite books, trinkets, my private belongings into a torn, raggedy duffle bag when Les's angry, tattooed hand snatched a bunch of my hair and dragged me onto the floor. 'How dare you leave! Don't go, I need you. Please don't go, don't go!' he pleaded as he kept thudding my face, scrunching it into the oven door, as I was bashed up against the windowpane. Momentarily, I even submitted to his right to do this, thinking this was the only way to pay the final price – but that was just buying back into the unwritten folklore nonsense too; put plainly that was bullshit, so I stood my ground.

'Les, it's me, your Robyn, let go, please let me go.' My words reached past his blindness because he loved me, and he let me leap away from his grasp. As the red blood warmed my face, adrenalin came running too. 'Right! Now back right off, get away from me. Don't you touch me ever, ever again!' This was not a time to yell or get hysterical, but the warning came with such a force that he stepped away. And tears could not blind the way either because the situation still felt like major danger, so I needed to see every movement, to feel every nuance, to suffer no more harm, I needed to escape quicksmart. With an old duffle bag across my shoulder, I leapt over the back into the dinghy, and was away, swallowed up in the night, a night so black that I could see no horizon.

There was one final look back, a memory I will never erase: of tears streaming down my lover's ruddy face, of a strong warrior ripped open – of Les standing up on the railings with one fierce clenched fist raised skyward, and him calling, reaching through the elements for me in a voice racked with pain, making a declaration from his own depths: 'I LOVE YOU. I'LL LOVE YOU TILL I DIE,' he roared into my being. 'I'LL LOVE YOU AFTER THAT. FOREVER. I LOVE YOU.'

Such an enormous sound bellowed up and out from him that its resonance tore out into the world. It went on until it could no longer possibly reach me and yet I believed I could still hear it even then. As though all the searing lover pain since the beginning of time had been busting to enter the galaxy, the words cleaved right into me like a heavy, thick-bladed Viking axe. The words were true, so true, as true as it was that I loved him back from that very same depth. Embedded in unhealable pain, dashing for life toward unknowable tomorrows, I flew across the breath between heaven and earth.

Perhaps the affair was finished but significantly, one thing had deliberately been left behind – my chain of five silver marlin which lay on top of the compass.

CHAPTER 45

Sailing on Pain

*J*ust for starters, nothing can illustrate the loss of my Stryder, a being so connected to my heart and to life itself. Leaving her was the same as leaving a beloved child behind. The rawness of it all was embedded more deeply than any ocean I ever steamed across the surface of – so I decided, uncleverly, to remain living in the shallows, on the surface of life so to speak. Today it's called living in denial.

I ached inside badly, that is if I let myself, but mostly below the pretence I lived in a bewildering kind of numbness. Maybe that was the way I kept going because I think the real pain manifested in how I lived the next few years out – wandering alone, running from town to town at the least heart-break. Someone once told me that shifting homes in itself is considered to be a traumatic event, and that I was to do many times. And then there was the almost careless choice of men I spent time with. When you think about it, no matter how successful, famous, poor, bent, clever, wretched or accomplished you are, the second our 'lover-love clock' begins to tick, all of us relentlessly storm the world for our opposite – and continue come hell or high water no matter what havoc occurs along the trail. With my standards so weakened, in the midst of desiring strong intelligent lovers, I only chose badly wounded ones and always ended up nursing their hearts. It was a kindness in a way, but how can a cripple heal a cripple? I was just incapable of lifting my game above the bar that had been set.

It was going to take a very close brush with insanity, a fair bit of stumbling, too many rolling-stone lovers and an extraordinary chain of events before the healing would begin. All of which meant I was destined to live an outsider kind of existence for way too long.

And quite a few people shook their heads in disbelief when they heard that I'd left without extracting any money from the boat – but what price does one pay for sanity, and where does one buy it from? Besides, money is only meant to be a unit of energy to fuel one's life with – treat it as your ultimate aim and happiness will not come.

Trapped by a real love of the ocean life and blinded as to my own worth, to say I had stayed for far too long is an understatement, so, dragging a ball and chain of heavy baggage stuffed with unrequited love, I flew, or rather spun out of the Gulf filled with overshadowing sadness, all mixed up with a wild sense of relief and freedom and a quarrelsome male-type anger.

Bunkered down with a good friend in Cairns, two days later neither of us was surprised when Les came hunting for me – as he should have. Hidden from sight, I listened as he tearily declared his innocence and undying love for me, and pleaded for her to help find me, even attempting some pesky intimidation when she declined to do so.

Later we girls sauntered along the sandy, palm-lined shore talking options. I loved north Queensland, it had been home for a long time, but apparently I had to go. Les and I were supposed to last forever and for the past eight years everything had been about the sea, so which road to take to which city or for what reason was very blurred. The world was filled with plenty of pathways, but that didn't mean I knew where to go or what to do, other than to start.

Unguarded and unaccounted for, I wandered loosely down the coast and told no one, not even Mum and Dad. What was there to talk about other than my indescribable circumstances and mixed-up bearings, and why should they be burdened down with that? What the hell was I thinking? Obviously I wasn't. Of course my parents would have offered realistic, honest answers and nurtured my damaged spirit. Why did I never open up to them? Probably embarrassed pride. Maybe holding on to the secret pain was itself some kind of anchor in the unfamiliar 'outside' world. Wrapped up in such blinding feelings, there wasn't much space to think about how anyone else was.

For the following weeks, whether in towns or cities, all around me oblivious strangers rushed about their daily business. Everything looked like a mirage of repetitive apartment blocks towering over long flat beaches and smiles without meaning. The world was faster and more modern, and it was difficult to see where I would possibly fit in. Besides the potency of being nowhere with choices, I was lost not only in thought but physically too, really.

Eventually, from the unsunny Gold Coast, I reluctantly rang old friends in northern New South Wales. Although it had been a long time between calls, they insisted that I come to them immediately. That was all the encouragement I needed to go straight to the bus terminal, buy a one-way ticket and edgily wait out the long hours until the right coach appeared.

Who likes interstate bus depots with their rattling windiness, grubby walls strewn with half-torn, graffiti-mutilated posters and painful, second-rate chairs in untidy rows? This one was no different. It was so B grade, you'd swear the place had been modelled on a badly built tinny outhouse. Anyway, there was a broody edge about the place, with the dubious hodge-podge of lanky cowboys, anxious old ladies fearfully clutching their baggage, and the mishmash of shoddily dressed outsiders with their poker faces.

Finally the passenger coach purred into action and gunned down the highway like a big cat, while I sat and glumly watched the dark, shadowy outside world rip past. On the roadside just before Ballina, there stood my friends, Jack and Bren, and even as they shovelled me into the car, tears from my broken heart bubbled up and out in big, gulping hiccups.

I felt disoriented and strange, and was barely capable of putting any clarity around what had happened. And they knew how volatile Les was but, like proper friends, there was no taking sides. So for a little while, like mother hens, my two friends loved me with as much intelligence as they could. It should have been a pleasure to be there, but it was not.

Restless and with no appetite for food or social life, as I drifted away the two cleverly nudged me down to Melbourne, into the hands of another life-long friend – the lion-hearted Magoochio, or 'Gooch', the man Les and I had asked to be godfather to our firstborn all those years before. He took me into his home and watched over me the same way Jack and Bren had.

In a surprising twist of fate an old friend sprang up: Aileen, a true north Queenslander. You might remember, she and I went way back to the day my ex-husband and I first arrived in Cairns, and we'd been close buddies too. Aileen rode horses and motorbikes like a natural, liked raisin' the dust, drinking Bundy rum and had a great love of literature.

Her right arm was all thin, debilitated and permanently strapped in an iron-padded, thick leather sleeve (today, a condition known as carpal tunnel syndrome). In an attempt to get some intelligent therapy for it, Aileen had come 'down south'. At the same time, my friend was whipping up an arts degree at Melbourne University. Furthermore, the day we found each other, she just happened to be heading over to the Burwood campus to enrol for her second year, so I swung up into her small truck and went along for the ride.

Our destiny was a soothing surprise. The campus was dominated by a double-storey mid-1800s mansion, surrounded by spacious grounds filled with 'elder' trees, no doubt planted in the nineteenth century too. And just being in a place so deeply steeped in history, ideals, philosophies, politics, professors and absent-minded boffins, plus the several huge libraries stacked to the ceiling with books, books, glorious books was spellbinding.

'Since you're here, Catch [my nickname], why not enrol too? Then we'll go and have a few Bundys over at the Yarraville hotel.' Offhandedly Aileen chucked me the application form. 'If you get in, you can come and live with me. Besides, being a "mature age" student means it'll cost you nothin' – mate, for you it's free.'

It was a nice call so I did the simple paperwork and easily rattled off the required 500 word essay. There might not have been much chance of getting in to university, but I did have some good stories, and my father's love of language. Sometimes when you do something without expectation the results can be surprising, so learning that I had passed with flying colours was a big boost.

*

Well then, Melbourne was the very reverse of taking a sea change and, like the locals said, it was best if each day you wore your bathers underneath a winter frock, took a warm jumper, a summer hat, and always carried an umbrella, just in case. By changing my way of life in such a dramatic manner, there was less time to dwell in the past because everything was as new and unpredictable as the city's weather. In fact, in the following years, this unpredictable, impulsive changing of my complete surroundings, friends and work was to become about the only thing you could actually predict about me. Poor Mum and Dad.

Not to mention the taking on of the seriously intellectual life. The way was filled with unknowns, but being so directionless it seemed like as good a place as any to try and mend my heart and life. So there I went, and set up home with Aileen in a windy old house in Balwyn.

However, while 'old school' Melbourne might have been up to its aristocratic bow ties, tiaras and dinner suits in culture, I on the other hand, was up to my elbows keeping a different part of the Aussie culture alive and well – getting on the drink at an unruly truckies' pub in the western suburbs. Mmm: fishermen, truckies, same unwieldy, lawless bunch really, so no wonder I felt at home.

Then it was the first day at uni. Talk about feeling like a country bumpkin just freshly in from the furtherest away sticks. Where had I been all those years? Maybe this was more than I could handle – but no, I reasoned, the 'in' crowd might know more than me, but none of them had ever wrestled a croc, or young Baz Mulligan for that matter. Not even sitting inside windowless, air-tight, stuffy great halls for hours on end mattered, as long as it just kept coming on – so with a good mate by my side I knuckled down and got stuck into Literature, Sociology, English and Philosophy.

The student income was ridiculously small, something like $50 per week, but Aileen and I were old hands and used our wits, drank sherry à la cardboard and merrily lived on the bones of our bums. Up to then, she was the closest girlfriend I'd had since Red so I fell in with her crowd at the Yarraville Hotel: a pub that was a trashy dive really, but all I saw were raunchy truckies filled with plenty of tall tales. As such, by night Aileen and I occasionally snaffled transient lovers from the highway cowboy pool, while by day we dipped fever-ishly into the abundant pond of learned knowledge.

Soon, Les bobbed up searching for forgiveness and me. Wearing real shoes and clumsy city clobber, he looked a bit silly, much like the dodgy drug cops at the Normanby River had. With deep hope reflect-ing from those ocean-blues, he came waving $25,000 cash in my face.

'Come away with me, Robbie. Money's no problem. I want to take you to the Taj Mahal. Let's travel the world together,' he begged. 'I'm a changed man. You're the only one I'll ever love.'

As Melbourne's tricky autumn breeze rustled through the fistful of paper money, I must confess I toyed with the idea. Les had played a good card and the thought of such a grand adventure beckoned, no, nearly seduced me back again. Sure, I loved his inner essence, but the fear of more violence was too great – and I was too crippled to do anything else but say no. When his eyes leaked with unending sadness, I could barely look his way.

Finally Les decided to return north. In a parting gesture, I dropped him off at another ghostly interstate bus terminal. Somehow we ended up on the roof – probably to have a cigarette. I remember thinking that there the two of us were, once more exposed to the swirling, unpredictable elements of nature we had always embraced with fear-less enthusiasm. There was still one burning question, something that, try as I might, I had never been able to fully comprehend, a question that repeatedly gave me anguish: 'Why did you hit me all the time?' A gush of bottled-up, hurt tears burst out. 'Why, Les, why?'

As though preparing for an onslaught of some kind, the man flinched a bit, then his body seemed to straighten up, to pull itself into the present. Les strengthened like a real man and said gamely, 'You were always so much smarter than I was, and I couldn't handle that.'

The first part of his statement was simply not true. Neither of us was smarter than the other. Secondly, it was a shame on him, and such a stupid, stupid irony. Was this the only reason for him so vio-lently destroying our love? I lashed out at his face with all the furious force that ludicrous reason deserved. The man did not defend him-self in any way, but just rebalanced and stood there, ready for more. 'Do it again, Rob, hit me – go on hit me as many times as you want. I'll never hurt you again.'

Instead, I held the knotted-up madness inside and spat out, 'It's too bloody late, Les. Hurting you doesn't help, it changes nothing.' I turned quickly and left the building, all the time feeling his distressed loneliness at my back. Why should I repeat what he had already done, and when did hitting your lover ever end up in understanding?

Not long after that, Gooch went his own way and so did Aileen, when she fell for a truckie who already had a brood of kids and a good wife – so she attended university and was at home less often.

Left more and more to my own devices, I stopped driving across town to the Yarraville, and tried creating a circle of friends closer to home. Most of the students were way younger, so friendships mostly started and stopped at the classroom door. And with precious little money, what was I to do: join a stamp collecting club, play tenpin bowling, become religious and go to church every Sunday? Not bloody likely. Instead I haunted the local hotels, not for the drinking but for the company. Everyone was sociable, but incredibly cliquey, so try as I did, it was quite impossible to meet anyone new.

Getting around in an unfamiliar city on my own might have been gutsy, but I stood out from any crowd, always left alone and the woman in me could not understand why. I mean I didn't even know how to flirt properly: nor did I know that my blunt, uncalled-for opinions were spewing forth all over the place. By then I was in my mid-thirties, had totally blonde shoulder-length hair and, compliments of the sea years, a tanned, trim, muscle-bound body. So, while I must have looked quite outstanding, sometimes my hostile argumentative anger burnt men more easily than dropping a lit match on petrol-soaked timber. Blinded by my own resentment of men, I did not see Melbourne cringe away in my wake and instead felt abandoned, unloved and so alone. Which is how loneliness so easily crept in and nearly stole me away.

As autumn's vibrant cloak faded, Melbourne's sharp wind began stripping the campus trees of their leaves, the winter rain leaked into my rusty Volkswagen, and with the only warmth in our breezy old Victorian home being limited to one little woodfire, my tropical blood started to freeze. To counteract the cold, I piled every bit of clothing

I owned on top of the bed's eiderdown, and slept in whatever I happened to be wearing that day, including shoes and socks – which is where I was hiding when Aileen unexpectedly arrived home one night with a surprise bottle of Bundy.

We were about three-quarters of the way through the second semester and about halfway through the bottle of rum when she sprang her next move on me. 'I'm goin' on the road with Charlie for a few months.' Her affair was love on both sides, so by trucking across Australia while he worked, the two could buy some private time together. Within a few days she had completely vanished.

By then the badly buffeted trees and bushes outside home were naked of leaves, the stagnant pool of water on my car floor was just about deep enough to swim in, and I was following winter's dictate by retreating inwards too. Surrounded by a million indifferent city strangers, the loss of Les, Stryder, my storm babies, my boat and the ocean came raining down in the deepest grieving I ever felt, and with it the grey, empty house closed in over me like a dense, protective fog.

Life just felt too heavy and the truth is I welcomed the intensely sad and lonely part, and let it rise just like some urgent desire. The more I went in there, the more I receded from reality, and the more I gave depression permission to dwell longingly within. As I abandoned university, the Yarraville Hotel and the local scene, no one missed me either, so it was easy to let the agony settle in and become familiar. Feeling twisted and bent, my jaw clamped shut and I ceased talking, showering, sleeping or eating that much, or in any order. Down, down, down I went, into the raw pain of my devastated love force where things like the occasional doorbell or the telephone ringing simply echoed somewhere else, and remained unanswered. Eventually all external goings-on ceased. Nothing, including day and night, held meaning or relevance. All I owned was this pain, it was my friend, it was exclusive, I liked it and chose to live in it, all the time hoping that everyone would forget and I would be forgotten.

Whether the sun warmed some part of this strange planet, or the same stars filled a darkening sky, my mind continued to rest in the almost exotic consciousness of suffering. Ah yes, there it would be, the hurt of hurts, the mesmerising, all-enveloping shadow of selfish indulgence. And to feel the pain to its utmost, to remind myself of how terrible the suffering was, each time I went markedly deeper and deeper. Voluntarily I became an addict of the mirror reverse of that which I most desired. Dangerously I started stalking insanity.

How long I swam around in the womb of perpetual distress, compulsively pushing the pain button trying to get more and more, who knows, but at the least a few weeks vanished. Without doubt it's a bold person who can go to the edge, look directly into the abyss and manage to return, but at some point I did – and realised that a relentless, screeching sound was piercing through the place. Propped up at the kitchen table, all decked out in a faded pink, tacky dressing gown and slippers, it was about midday, and outside on the backyard fence, the noise culprit, a large black and white currawong, stood frantically rocking to and fro, shrieking incessantly and staring me dead in the eye.

For a while I tried to make him go away by tearing open the door and irately flinging a few things at him. Each time, the agitated bird craftily flapped just out of reach, then returned to the fence and cranked up the persistent din again. The bird was completely nuts. Right then, like some clever result to the lost weeks, I thought, 'That's it! Why not just go insane, then "they" can put me in an institution and someone else can look after me forever.'

Realising that I was in grave trouble, I sprung away from the table. The only thing I could think to do was to change something about myself immediately. Hastily donning whatever clothes lay on top of the dishevelled eiderdown, I plunged into the Vee Dub's floor of wallowing water, and sped off to find a hairdresser, any hairdresser. And the hairdresser I found must have picked up on my wavelength because she didn't need much convincing to completely shave my long blonde hair right off.

They say a change is as good as a holiday, and there could be something in that. All I knew was that my pattern of being predictably unpredictable was working when an hour or two later, I stepped back out into a crowd of Friday afternoon shoppers and another typical Melbourne day: that is, even though the sun was beating down and the wind was blowing women's skirts up, it was also raining cats and dogs. Also I was crying my heart out. Walking amongst the crowd of bemused shoppers back to the car, I knew not to stop, and that there was a healing taking place. Just why the tears came there and then I think is unanswerable, but over and above that, at least I had the nous to let them come until there were no more.

Odd as it may be, just like that, the worst of my blackness lifted. I wanted to thank that clever bird, but it was gone – hopefully off elsewhere busily trying to bring some other self-absorbed wallower to their senses. Anyhow I checked the next week's schedule at uni, had a shower, dressed then drove across the city to the Yarraville Hotel for some company. Why is it so difficult to be happy?

No, I was not healed, but close to it. Of course, such deep-rooted, habitual feelings returned, and of course I went back into it again and again, willingly embracing the pain of despair. The thing is there was no one to consult, really. You see, at the beginning of the 1980s there were no wonder pills, government support systems or New-Age workshops to turn to. Yet somehow I decided my condition was curable, and eventually figured out how to outsmart the addiction. To escape the demon, I kept a watch on the murky pattern and stopped it before it went too far, and by putting some discipline around it, by not going in so deeply each time, I notched back the dark feelings and surfaced more quickly each time. Finally I was able to pick the strange stirring when it started and just somehow let it go – in some way not let the feeling even start to hook me in.

What's really interesting is that whether it's anger, sadness, despair or rage you're holding on to, the negative feelings are almost always about something that has already happened and gone past, something that no longer exists, so there is really nothing holding the powerful, unsettling emotions in place other than yourself. And we end up believing that such emotions are part of who we are, part of our character, when they are not.

Look, it's OK to feel sad and lonely every now and then, it's natural – everyone goes through that, just the same way we all go through happiness and joy – but remember *none* of these emotions lasts 24/7. The trick is not to cling on to any of it, because everything changes.

I settled down after that, went back to uni, and when one of the older, unattached truckies asked if he could come over occasionally and just lay beside me at night I agreed. There was no sex, we just held each other, talked for a while and then slept. It was the touch of one body against another, his heart, like a talking drum, beating just under the flesh of my hand, his breathing, the realness of another. After all, we human beings are warm-blooded, social animals, not meant to go without some tenderness from others any more than we can survive without food or water.

You wouldn't think it was such a big call, but there weren't too many ballsy blokes around – good protectors who wouldn't hesitate to go the fisticuffs if need be, men who used their brain, were decent lovers, and capable of pulling their own weight

Unexpectedly my end-of-year uni results included a couple of distinctions, which was pretty good all things considered, and when the last semester was over, I revved up the Vee Dub and headed for Adelaide.

Our home was the family castle and Mum and Dad gave us practical values, stability and uncomplicated honesty. Both brothers were married, had kids and lived much like Mum and Dad did. Since my family didn't know what had really taken place in the Gulf, the way I kept bucking the stereo-life must have confused them somewhat. Yet Mum was/is perpetually bright, well-informed and held a wonderfully biased love for her children – and religiously insisted at celebrations that glasses be raised in memory of absent family. That's because most years I was missing. This time, though, we all came together, and made the most of it. In a pattern which was to become the norm, I was the only one without a partner, but it was enough just to be there eating, drinking, laughing and wrestling with my brothers.

I returned briefly to Melbourne but this time when Aileen left, she went out on the road for good. Feeling unbalanced and without any backup, it only took for the trees outside my bedroom window to suddenly be cut down, and I was gone. Leaving so much potential opportunity scattered in the ashes like that was short-sighted, a real shame.

Back in Adelaide the new threads of life brought a promotions job in the horse racing industry and a good lover. Life was tolerable for a year or two, but there was another voice inside which came from a deeper, more distant place saying something was still missing. When an offer to go deckhand on a 150-year-old racing yacht came up I grabbed it and slipped back up the east coast.

CHAPTER 46

Myriad Turns for the Best

*B*y the time I turned up back in Cairns again, the mid-1980s were in full play. Like a contagious disease, noxious sugarcane fields now spread up the entire, once natural coastline. And to further pump the government coffers, Premier Petersen cunningly offered decent tax breaks to wealthy southerners if they shifted permanently to Queensland. Lured by the tropical lifestyle, it wasn't a difficult sell. The southern exodus was more like an unchecked cattle stampede and many thundered into Cairns. And why not? By then the home-grown marlin fishing industry was internationally recognised as the best in the world, tourism was at its height, and the general building industry was throwing unattractive apartments up quicker than you could make a simple sand castle – all of which lent a savvy, sophisticated air and a very large chunk of new investment riches to the once modest town I had left behind not all that long ago.

So what! The goose might have been laying nonstop golden eggs upon the perpetually effervescent town but the local crowd hadn't changed much. Everything was so luxuriously available that none of us gave two hoots about tomorrow. The hippie era may have been over, but we still thought Cairns was nirvana.

Just to get the lay of the land, for a month or so I stayed at a girlfriend's and sold handmade pearl jewellery at weekly local markets – which was where Shelley, an old friend and an ex-Gulf buddy, found me and how I got to share digs with her and her younger sister. Neatly tucked into the side of a grassy hill covered in native trees and shrubs, their Queenslander (pole home) was private, charming and just made for fun, healthy food, good people and romance. Oh yes, and being painted bright pink on the outside, we called our home the Pink Palace. *And*, just at the bottom of the street ran a healthy, steadily flowing creek.

I was 36 years old, Shelley, with long, ginger hair springing out like spherical firecrackers was about 30, and her little sister, Janet, was in her early twenties. The three of us quickly formed a sister-hood, worked full-time in the straight world, and privately lived like urban hippies. We made conscious choices around food and exercise, and were passionately concerned about environmental topics which today are vital mainstream concerns.

To stay with the pulse, I consumed the dailies and the weekly current affairs magazines, and indulged in political debates with anyone willing enough. My heroes definitely reflect the same – like Chips Rafferty, the Australian actor and lone outspoken critic of Hollywood's dominance over our home-grown film industry; Germaine Greer, the clever academic who made everyone, including me, reassess how we thought; Mahatma Gandhi, the most brilliant activist the world had ever seen; His Holiness The Dalai Lama, the young, embattled leader of Tibet; and the courageous Australian author Frank Hardy, for vocally supporting Vincent LeGarde's mob over their claim for Wave Hill. All were original thinkers giving the establishment a good run for its money, no matter how badly things went against them. Of course I never expected that one day I would meet one of them.

So far I have shared some pretty sad and tough times with you but there is one that is equally worth sharing because it was the reverse, and because it was how I experienced some respite from my inner turmoil. What was even more precious was that I was unaware that love was pursuing me.

While soaking up the grass roots, caring atmosphere of the Pink Palace, I was also playing grade competition squash and doing tai chi, when onto the scene came Mick: a boyishly handsome, lovely young man who was always around our place and who, I noticed, never seemed intimidated by being amongst women only. He was unpretentious, a good tradesman, tamed horses on the home farm, wrote poetry and displayed quite a gift in wood carving. The three of us reckoned he was pretty special, but it was clear that he had a 'thing' for Janet.

The months flew by until one Saturday afternoon when I happened to be home alone and Mick turned up unannounced, suggesting we go for a picnic. 'But Janet's not here,' I replied, to which he just smiled and said, 'I know, let's go anyway.'

So we took an esky of food down to the creek running at the bottom of our street, found a quiet, grassy nook and settled in. How our conversation went or what it was about I cannot remember, it was simply a lovely time. In the end I think Mick just about had to spell out in big capital letters that he was seriously keen on *me*!

Feeling flattered was only part of it. He possessed that unusual kind of shy presence we would all like to have some of, so the fact that he had come to me at all, and the uncontrived nature of how he had come, was why I felt honoured by Mick's declaration. He was 23 years old.

All of what took place after that, until we departed from each other's lives, was a sweet, uncomplicated experience filled with effortless joy. I encouraged his way of being in life, and gave without grasping, while Mick unhesitatingly offered up such innocence that it almost made me hold my breath.

And there must have been a special aura around us because sometimes complete strangers would encourage us. That was unusual in itself, plus I knew there was nothing to change, improve or be. To keep it that way, I never imposed any expectations on him: every time Mick rumbled up on his 900cc sleek black Ducati, he came because he really wanted to. Then off we'd go swimming, dancing or roaming the northern hinterland highways on his swift, shiny racing machine. It was an intoxicating love, and I gladly watched him blossom into manhood. Every time he left, I thanked the Gods who had put him in my pathway.

When Mick decided to ride motorbikes professionally in Brisbane, I decided that he should go unimpeded, so I never asked that fateful question – about whether I could go with him or not – and instead privately began counting down the days. So in the waiting game of love, I held him with even more awareness each night, and if it was possible treasured all the more dearly the passing seconds. The day before I saw him for the last time, the grief broke, rose up and erupted in a loud series of astounding moans and I wept long and hard for this beautiful young man and our inevitable separation – and knew then where Les's sounds had come from on the night I had sped away into the dark horizon.

Our affair lasted no more than about six months – and if you were to question me now, I'd say it was a mistake not to ask if I could have gone with him to Brisbane. Mick gave me something back, he showed that I had some inner beauty, and that also I had the capacity to attract decent men. Even if just once in your lifetime something so tender happens, count your blessings because you have been very fortunate.

How was anything going to match that? I could feel his presence everywhere I went, so it took time, solitude and some hidden grieving before I dropped back into 'normal' society – where, like a strange fish out of water, I now felt out of place once more.

On the one hand there was this candid up-front side to me, but the turbulent undercurrent of my sadness must have been obvious too. Opportunistic men would have seen me coming from miles away.

On the rebound, one of the local sports news reporters and I soon became lovers, and I had sunken all my money into a commercial T-shirt printing venture called 'The Office'. Business seemed good, but the money was disappearing fast and already he was proving to be about as stable as a No. 1 category cyclone. After too many drinks one day, it was no wonder the breathalyser cops chucked me in the slammer for DUI. For once, the law was unwittingly about to do me a greater favour than just licence suspension, believe me. It always pays to remember that sometimes what looks to be a bad experience can flip the other way, and turn into a good one.

And I know, I know, every time I rose from the ashes, another badwood bloke would take me out on a tangent. But please, don't give up on me, because while the uncontrollable chaos rained down like a whirlwind, another action was hurtling in – the effects of which still resound in my life today.

Sunk down in amongst the muddle of rising bills, evaporating money, and the awaiting constraint of losing my licence, one day as I puzzled away at the desk, an overwhelming urge to write to the Dalai Lama came over me. Why then I have no idea, and am glad that every last thing in one's life cannot be explained away logically and in sequence. In fact it would be years down the track before I did remember being fascinated by Tibet and His Holiness as a little kid.

As impulsive as the idea was, so was the letter I wrote right then and there saying that the most positive outcome of the Chinese invasion of Tibet was that now He and His monks could come to the west and teach wisdom to the rest of the world; and that should my services ever be required, all He had to do was ask. Well, the internet didn't exist in 1988 so His address could have been in 'kingdom come' for all I knew, but since I expected no reply anyway, I hurriedly stuck a few token stamps on an envelope and mailed the letter, simply addressed to The Dalai Lama, North India.

In court a few days later, the law took my licence away for six months which meant that the failing 'The Office' doors had to close. On the day of my fortieth birthday, driving illegally, I went around the town shelling out the last bit of money there was paying off outstanding accounts. In comparison, my thirtieth on the banks of the Archer had been a sparkling gala event.

When karmic conditions ripen there is always a result, so just before abandoning Cairns, an envelope with odd overseas stamps turned up. Who, I wondered, would be writing from somewhere called Dharamsala? The letter, unmistakably typed on an old manual typewriter and headed up by two red snow lions holding an eight-spoked wheel toward some pointy mountains, said:

Your letter addressed to His Holiness the Dalai Lama has been received. I have brought the contents of your letter to His notice and He directs me to thank you for your kind thoughts. Your offer of services is much appreciated.

With our best wishes,
Yours Sincerely,
Tenzin Geyche Tethong.

They should have sent a live lightning bolt along with this most significant signpost because I did not register that the way was opening up. There's no denying that the Dalai Lama's wisdom is beyond most of us living on the planet, but in a way he and I were in similar circumstances – I no longer had a place to call home, all my money was gone and I would have to start from scratch all over again.

Still, there was one person who would take me in – Kenny who, with the stature of a quizzical fairybook gnome, bubbled over with humour, generosity and compassion. And he dwelled in Cardwell. Once again, the No. 1 Highway of Life was waiting.

If any town could have been more emerald green, or any ocean more brilliant sapphire blue than Cairns, it was the still unaffected small coastal settlement of Cardwell. There, 200-year-old bamboo groves still flourished by the railway track, the back mountains were in natural balance, and the vigorous, crystal-clear creeks looked to have manifested straight from God's tears.

Getting over my previous partner was easy really: that was just me wandering the earth with an overflowing chalice of love, blindly spilling it everywhere – a statement that pretty much sums up the way I was with would-be lovers. Anyway, I took a leaf from Kenny's book, drank much less alcohol, got into the relaxed lifestyle and melded with his small band of quirky friends.

Motherhood was not something that featured much in my thinking, and I must say that it did roll in like a fresh summer breeze. Still being a parent was usually born when two people came together in love and decided to have children, and since I was contented enough with being single, when I say that the opportunity came straight out of left field, I'm serious.

'Robyn, I want you to look after my kids so you need to come up to Lower Tully.' Really, it was just like that. Beside me and grinning away confidently stood Johnny! Even in a small town with a popula-tion of about 500, he was someone I knew only by vague association. 'I've been watchin' you for a while and you're the right one for them, for sure,' he said, and went on to explain that his kids – Lilly, six,

Carlo, eight, and Marie, nine – had lost their mother following a fatal asthma attack some four years earlier.

Johnny – well, Giovanni Bartollo – born and bred about two hours to the north, was the only son of a first-generation Italian cane farmer, and one of the main bobcat contractors around Cardwell. He must have trusted his perceptions because my only experience of kids was herding the little Normanby River chappies safely away from raging rivers and stealthy crocodiles; and of course, there were my own three storm babies who swam around permanently in my regretful sadness. Sometimes life intervenes in odd ways, and this one struck me as being a big chance to have children all on my own, a way to reconcile my own three, and maybe even dish out some unconditional and upfront kind of love at the same time.

The man seemed kind enough and not too complex, so I didn't bother asking why the previous nanny had left, and instead suggested that only his kids could decide if I was the right one, to which he agreed. So that weekend I went visiting.

Tully might have been only 50 clicks to the north but the town drank Forex like it was a health supplement, harboured an unattractively high redneck ratio, and even though there must have been a few hidden marijuana crops cooking away in the undergrowth, the people were excruciatingly conservative.

From there, I threaded coastwise through an endless carpet of flowering sugarcane farms to Lower Tully, which consisted of an uninhabited beach nicely littered with flotsam and jetsam, a few houses patchily spread over four or five crisscrossing streets, and a population (including dogs, cats and crocodiles) of about 100.

Johnny's fairly new home was a fully furnished, redbrick, tufty lawned, three-bedroom, polished floor affair, with a double garage and, albeit vibrant green, a proper full-length, in-ground swimming pool complete with underwater coloured lighting. Considering that the deal came with a reasonable car and some cash, things were looking up.

Best of all, three little people excitedly hovered around all ready and willing to give as much honest love as I could handle. Me too! And they quickly let me cross the invisible kid bridge directly into their world – so it wasn't at all difficult for us to climb into each others' vacant, enthusiastic hearts. I moved in the next weekend.

Now that's not to say we all lived happily ever after, but the spark between us was authentic. Plus none of it would have worked if Marie, the eldest, hadn't given her approval. Not that I knew it at the time, but she'd already weathered too many nannies, so the surrogate protector role was fully upon the young girl. At first Marie hovered somewhere in between being a grown-up minder and a reserved little girl watching to see if she could trust me. Once that was sorted, Marie let the reins go and became an olive-skinned, gangling nine year old again. Then she, like the other two, quickly dropped any self-consciousness, and took to always hanging around me in a natural loving way, getting hugs, fiddling in my stuff or taking me off into their world – all of which made my world so fulfilling too.

Carlo was the dearest, and the most obviously traumatised by the loss of his mother. The eight year old was hesitant, more mentally scattered, and so tender that I could see he was already a bit lost in life, and feared that later this bewilderment might set him adrift unkindly in the big hard world.

We all blossomed, but Lilly, the youngest, felt like a child of mine, like a reincarnated one, and as she unfolded into a delightful flower, my heart zinged the most for her. She was quick, vibrant, loving and responded in such a way that it was even more of a privilege to be part of their lives. At six years old, Lilly was blonde, freckled, joyous and showed the least evidence of disturbance or memory of her mum.

Our togetherness felt real and strong, and somehow we balanced each other out – and that was after two important events. Firstly, it took a couple of weeks before I grasped that this was a two-way thing and that they had plenty to teach me too. I told them this, that I was committed and confessed that I love them. In turn, they let me in on a few private things, which cleared the air.

Soon after that, the youngest threw an 'I want Daddy' tantrum and would not stop. Within minutes, the little girl I was responsible for was going into breathless convulsions – dying! Seeing that dunking her fighting, struggling body into the pool three times only made her redder and more breathless, I straightened her up and let fly with a three or four strong, stinging slaps across her cheeks.

Lilly snapped out of it instantly, thank God, and afterwards, cradling her tenderly in my arms, with Carlo and Marie sitting closely each side of me, they spoke of how it was for them. In that moment, the right words came for me, and I saw obvious relief lift from their young minds when they grasped that they were not the only kids in the world without a mum, that she still loved them and would always watch out for them. I'd never thought of myself as merely their nanny anyway, but from then, I knew I was their protector and friend, and took the role seriously indeed.

After they went off to school with packed lunches and a kiss every day, I filled the between hours by tampering with the saltwater pool, mowing the lawn and fiddling in the garden like I owned the place, then every afternoon I welcomed them back home. Like any family we shared our woes, did homework together, argued, laughed, cried and shared the jobs out. I made sure they ate plenty of greens before the sweet stuff, and never missed tucking the little chappies into bed with a story – and a kiss. We loved each other simply and life felt normal and right, so we hunkered down contentedly in the Lower Tully swamplands and all my external trappings fell away easily. Whenever the torment of my lost ones came through, I prayed that they were somewhere as good as we four were.

At first Johnny came each weekend, until the birthday party incident that was, when in front of all the neighbourhood kids, he burst in late and stomped about selfishly demanding to be noticed for all the wrong reasons. Everyone froze, all the fun stopped and the uncomfortable party guests quickly straggled away. Johnny, I saw, was the youngest member of the family, so I pulled him aside and tore a few strips off his moody hide, finishing up with, 'If you were my kid, I'd give you a good spanking,' and demanded he go back to Cardwell and leave me to raise his children in a bit of peace for a while. Johnny stomped to his car, deliberately screeched up the empty road and to his credit, aside from phone calls and very irregular visits, left us alone for the next few months. The kids might not have heard our tirade, but as with most children they were psychic like that and knew something had happened. When I explained that he was still grieving for their mum, they just nodded thoughtfully.

Later, it came out from a neighbour that I was just the last in a long string of nannies over the past four years, and that Johnny had even threatened one with a gun. But he didn't scare me – hell, my love for the kids was bold and full, besides better men than him had already tried to bully me and had been unsuccessful!

Following the outburst I visited Johnny's parents, explained what had happened and asked them to set me straight. They had intrepidly emigrated 30 years beforehand from Italy with nothing but a plan, and we now sat in their kitchen overlooking a very tidy sugarcane estate. His mum knew of her son's ways, and readily agreed with my summation. Then, while Johnny's dad sat in the background silently nodding his approval, she took me quite by surprise.

'You know you should be the kids' mother. We've never seen them so happy and healthy, and they love you.' I always admired their honesty, and was really chuffed by her statement. Over the months we became firm friends. Later that year, they even visited my mum and dad in Adelaide – it was like that between us.

Then at the primary school's 'Parents' Night', the headmaster gave his stamp of approval too, saying unexpected things, something like the kids were 'responding more confidently in class, and openly mixing in the playground again'. Apparently all the locals were watching, but without any gauge to tell if I was doing the right thing, my way around them just came from intelligent love, I think.

Through the winter months, *every* night after the kids were asleep I'd prop Gary the pet galah on the pool fence, strip naked and spend hours swimming . . . well, lying under the pool's surface, surrendering into the malleable water's perfect arms. With eyes wide open, the rainbow illumination from the submerged pool lights refracted through, around and into me. Under the Lower Tully sky of cloud, rain, thick blankety stars or total blackness, while Gary perched patiently on guard, I hung in the chamber of healing. Suspended in the silent, soothing limbo, my mind rested from its internal chatter, and the translucent womb of clear essence caressed my deepest, most vulnerable self.

At some time I found – or was it remembered – feelings of betterness and started praying – for myself, for the men in my life, for the Gods to help, and of course for the storm babies. Ultimately, I took to swimming successive laps underwater, feeling into every luxurious stroke, and reaching as far out into the beautiful liquid as I could.

Thankfully it's not possible to fully comprehend and comfortably box everything up into the white coats' lab world, because although this endeavour might sound very clever, it was not of my conscious doing, really. Instead, Gary the Cocky responded by never dozing off or wandering away, while I answered some unidentifiable vital call from my spirit. Somehow we both intrinsically knew that I was taking 'the cure'. Coinciding with this, curious events kept unfolding: vivid night dreams filled with rowdy processions and lamas in robes; me *repeatedly* seeing that the early summer clouds looked like swirling eastern temples; and there was a heightened feeling of awareness which I could not explain so I started joking to those around me that I was 'in training' – whatever that meant.

Unbeknownst to me, this was the present trying to inform me about the future, trying to show me that I was moving on and that my spirituality was rising or, to paraphrase Goethe from the eighteenth century, all manner of unforeseen incidences and material assistance which I could not have dreamt of were streaming in. For instance, I'd never been clairvoyant and never ever bought lottery tickets, yet as the year led toward Christmas, I 'got' that some money was on the way. In Tully one morning, I bought a Lotto ticket which I knew even before I checked it was on the money, and won $3000 dollars! Ostensibly without need of a car, the winnings went on a Gemini station wagon. In training or not, something outside of the norm was fermenting.

The kids and I walked the beach most afternoons, picnicked around the area, always had friends over to swim in the pool, and often sat under the trees at night talking about 'stuff' using some kind of mutual wisdom reasoning. Our joint healing was just about done, and the more our love stabilised, the more I stopped pretending this was some casual job. For their sake, a relationship with Johnny would have been ideal, but neither of us was the slightest bit interested.

With love and devotion like I had, the real question was, should I stay with the children permanently until their high school years were over, or let go, leave at the end of the final school term and get back to my own life?

CHAPTER 47

Awakenings:
Rude and Otherwise

*B*ut 'my' mistake had already been made, one I was unaware of. And it was fatal. Whenever Johnny did visit, the kids ran to me, only wanted to go where I went, and almost exclusively sought my counsel and attention. They stopped needing their father for anything anymore. Thinking he would be proud of the job I was doing, I didn't realise the extent of it, and regrettably Johnny became jealous and brooded over it silently.

The first I knew was when Johnny uncharacteristically started checking up on me via cagey phone calls and making impromptu visits home, visits that felt more like drug raids than fatherly love. Alerted by his wobbly actions, sadly I understood that my devotion question was being answered. Then just before the school year wound up, Johnny, mistaking liquor and nasty language for courage, rang and let loose. Filled with ill-informed, paranoid suspicions about my child-raising ability and using language heavy enough to scare even me, the man finished his 'possessed' rave with a serious threat to come up that very night and bash me – something I couldn't take any more of. Suddenly it was time to go *the next day*.

How does one go about explaining such tangled-up things to beloved kids? It was shocking and undeserved, wrenching my kids' trusting hearts around like that. The two little ones instantly decided to come with me – it took a while before they got that it was not possible, that they were too young to leave. Seeing them go pale and quiet in the understanding of that just beggars description. With a vow that if they ever needed me, their grandmother would always hold my current address, I put them to bed – as if they slept! I rang her, explained why I would be gone in the morning, and through the night stuffed useless possessions into the little wagon. When were these bloody awful lessons in life ever going to give up?

I kept my promise, of always leaving a forwarding address until a few years later, when I dropped in on the grandparents unexpectedly. As I stood to leave she took my hand and said, 'It's better that you forget the kids now, Robyn, just let them go for your own sake.' She was honest like that, so I never got in touch with any of the family again – but that doesn't mean I stopped loving them, especially Lilly.

That following morning is burned into my mind like some merciless, slow-motion home movie: especially from our kitchen window, watching my little ones broken-heartedly lurch off to school (as if that was where they wanted to be), all trying to be brave, with Marie courageously herding them along like wounded cubs, Carlo hesitantly looking back and forward, unable to grasp what was really happening; seeing Lilly sobbing uncontrollably then stumble up the bus steps; seeing them for the very last time. I wanted to rush out, tear them from the bus and hold them like I should have. It was heart-wrenching, more unbearable than anything else that had ever happened to me. How badly they must have felt, I can only imagine.

I cleaned the house so thoroughly it looked like I had never been there, and was gone by lunchtime. Naturally no one was there to say goodbye, but some farmers had lit back-burning fires across their fields. Escaping down the narrow road through the waving flames, my heart turned into ashes. It might have been just another day in paradise, but for me it was a terrible, terrible day.

At the No. 1 highway, I made the fateful decision of which way to go, and turned left and went home to Mum and Dad. The non-stop 5000 kilometre trip to Adelaide took four days and four nights. Amongst the incommunicable grief, and not quite in these exact words, something kept telling me that this was divine timing. To lift some weight from my mind, I invented a game – to take no maps, turn right every time the traffic got too heavy and, for safety reasons, always nestle my wagon amongst the big trucks at petrol stations and nap there. And so keeping the sun on my left in the mornings, and on my right in the afternoons, and trusting to the nights, I rolled south following an uncluttered horizon.

Healing was going to be a deep affair, and would have to wait until I reached Adelaide, so somehow I put the shocking grief aside and cutting through the wide open spaces I skimmed across the ocean of earth. With the purple-blue mountains one side of me, teenage gums sent zebra shadows across the bitumen, and unique pandanus silhouetted against the cloudless, pale skies: flying alongside creeks gouged out by flash floods, ghostly white Brahman cows stared skittishly from the endless pastures in between, as down into sumptuous valleys bound by prehistoric, rolling ranges I went and on and further into the remarkable land of never-never. At some point, feelings of Aboriginal tribal gatherings came, and I 'knew' that such spirits from way before us were still here amongst the rising and falling, wild, wild beauty.

The brilliant moon illuminated the entire journey, so Lady Luck was with me. At about the halfway-home post, just out of West Wyalong, way after the sun had vanished an unforeseen road block forced me southwest-ish along an obscure, quite narrow, high-set side track. Now some might have cursed, it being night-time and not having a map for guidance, that the main highway was impassable and the flood which had made it so – but for me that night the moon filled the universe like a cauldron of shimmering liquid, giving the hours of darkness an almost tangible enchantment. On each side of the narrow dirt road, the fields had flooded into lakes, and as corny as it sounds, I, the only one out there, seemed to float across the inland sea of molten silver. It's a wonder I didn't just slip into overdrive, tilt the spaceship up slightly and pop up and visit the star people – should have. I could have taken my hands from the wheel too, and just let destiny do the driving, because evidently other forces were at work.

A couple of days later, with just the one speeding fine under my belt and the little wagon only working on three cylinders, I surfed down through the Adelaide Hills and into our beachside driveway right on the eve of Dad's seventieth birthday. Once more I took to the willow tree and went searching for some understanding, and tried to forgive myself for the mistake. This suffering was deeper than that of lover loss. This was the most difficult kind of injury – lovers could come and go, but my little ones would never come again.

Somehow, somewhere, at some time we come good and eventually spring back into the tempting fabric of life's possibilities. Trying to settle into the rhythm of existence, I fudged some mundane work in the temp secretary field. To break the monotony I took up driving a different route to and from work each day. It might have seemed like an idle, short-term distraction, but in fact something was driving me somewhere.

As if the signs in Lower Tully hadn't been enough, one after-noon while taking another new route to see if it would lead to my home, I heard a very normal-looking house call out. 'Stop, reverse and look at me,' it yelled. Occasionally I had been able to hear that inner voice guide me, and this time it was loud and definite, so there was nothing imaginary about it. The talking house was at 45 Smith Street, and the sign on the roof read 'Thai Buddhist Meditation Cen-tre'. Strange event – sure it was a nice house, but so what, I thought.

How long it took before *that* penny dropped? Maybe a month or two. Anyhow, one morning I just got in the car and drove straight there. A black crow lifted up and away from the gate when on that normal morning, I stood knocking on No. 45's normal door. Should have picked up on the bird sign, but instead saw two sets of san-dals sat at the entrance, waiting to be walked somewhere, then the wooden door slid quietly open to reveal a dark-skinned, saffron-robed fellow who asked whether I had an appointment or not. That was a pretty normal question, so I shrugged respectfully, and replied, 'You tell me why I'm here because I have no idea!'

'Oh really!' He smiled warmly. 'This is an auspicious day. My name's Sam, come in mate.'

Sam gestured for my shoes to join the patient sandals, quietly ushered me in and closed the door firmly. I liked the position of no return, the home-grown accent and the wafting charcoally incense smell and willingly followed his swishing robes along the shadowy hallway and into the clear light at the other end.

In a semi-dark corner of an unfurnished room, on the floor in the lotus position, sat another fellow, a monk also saffron-robed but Asian looking. Behind him stood a very tall, golden Buddha. Waved to some cushions, I clumsily dropped to the floor, then the seated one closed his eyes, and folded both hands in prayer, so I did the same and let the foreign chanting permeate my mind. After all, this could only be good. Via translation, the seated one enquired about my life thus far. Trusting to the lama's external enquiry and penetrating gaze, my nomad story spilled out. Having only ever tinkered with the notion of past and future lives, still I couldn't help feeling that the monk was penetrating far deeper than just the life I was currently waffling on about. Almost as an afterthought, I remembered to mention the letter from His Holiness.

Through the afternoon, Sam supported the puzzling proceedings by translating, bringing freshly brewed tea, and keeping candles lit around the Buddha. Finally, with eyes closed and hands folded in prayer mode, the lotus monk repeated the verse he had begun with. Good manneredly, I bobbed my head and murmured thanks. The non-appointment was over and I was back in the normal traffic of a normal afternoon.

When Sam rang me a few days later, he offered me an even more abnormal opportunity. Would I like to go on a boat with them? Well, no, not really, but who can resist the unexplainable way? And how hilarious that they wanted to take *me* on the sea! Next thing, we three plus a skipper were ensconced on a tiny yacht sailing up the Port River with a rabble of cheeky seagulls squawking overhead. The main monk was robed in saffron but this time Sam, of all things, had on suit pants, a collared shirt, a tie and lace-up shoes, and both were shading themselves under opened umbrellas! I'd never seen umbrellas on a boat in my lifetime, and most certainly never with a robed one and a suit sitting under them. Suddenly the yacht crunched, then slid to a standstill. Now this was more like it. It was time for Captain Catchlove to come to the rescue.

I lifted the bow by sending the men (and therefore their combined weight) forward, leapt over the side, and leant a shoulder into the hull. As the vessel slowly eased back into the deeper, choppy waters, I got the telegram from the Universe – just like I kept relaunching back into the river of life, maybe there was a place to shelter, a refuge for the soul – perhaps the Buddha was throwing out a lifebuoy. Maybe He could give me a few clues about everything which so far had eluded me.

'Robyn, His Holiness is coming to Australia in two years, and we have been invited to a public meeting that's being held regarding it,' Sam's phone call went, 'and we wondered if you would drive us to it.'

Since I had never returned to the Thai Buddhist Meditation Centre, this time there was no doubt that their request was a sign. Me driving a pale green FJ Holden while waxing lyrical with two robed monks was about as far out as seeing a flying saucer land on Mum and Dad's front lawn – and there were representatives from all the different Buddhist traditions at the meeting, so it felt like I had boarded the flying saucer when, of all people, they voted *me*, the newest-comer in their midst, to be official secretary for the South Australian leg of the Dalai Lama's 1992 tour! And that was how my spiritual awakening, and my first physical contact with a Tibetan Buddhist teacher, came about – all served up on a platter filled with omens, strange events and a fair bit of luck. Imagine an outsider, rolling-stone, fisher kind of girl discovering that in the midst of the eight billion people swarming an obscure planet somewhere out there in the colossal Milky Way, that her teacher was now living Down Under and, in fact, was just around the corner in the next suburb – what a blast!

It was a grand entry alright, and despite the fact that my letter to His Holiness about coming to the west was old news, Tibetan Buddhism was like discovering the key to an eternal treasure chest. So even though back then, 'going all religious' was simply not the done thing, I 'knew' without hesitation. All I'd needed was a few quick miracles. Called the Borderless Doctor, the Buddha was the medicine, the curative remedy of all negative emotions and actions – and hopefully just the antidote for me.

Tibetans reckon that when you first meet up with the teachings, it is not uncommon to cry. They say it's tears of relief at having rediscovered your teacher and the pathway again from your previous life. I did cry copiously but, look, the teachings are so packed with universal, albeit practical, wisdom and deal so meticulously with the very foundations of existence that a few tears are not the price you pay, they're a joy you express.

Additionally, for many years I had been trying to invent an original solution to fix our planet – and now there was a tribe from the remotest of kingdoms who were *demonstrating* the answer: by doing that which we all should be doing – practising forgiveness, compassion and loving kindness toward all living beings, including our 'enemies'.

Life, they said, was as swift as a lightning flash in the sky, and death a sure thing, but when death would come was uncertain, so then, I thought, shouldn't I start practising compassion and forgiveness immediately? And apparently everyone went through endless, repetitious rebirths and only when we practised compassion and wisdom toward all other living beings (not just human ones) would our lives change and ultimately the current fucked-up world model. So then shouldn't I start living the principle? I mean, who, I ask you, who would want to have the life I was having, let alone repeat it? So if reincarnation just happened to be true, maybe it was time to pay serious attention. Moreover, one's wisdom would ultimately arise as a state of total bliss, as the state of enlightenment. Maybe all we Buddhists could attain the enlightenment state and just surf off into the galaxy, leaving the crappy turmoil of Earth behind. But no – to top it all off, there was an astounding pledge to postpone enlightenment and keep returning to Earth again and again until such time as *all* living beings had attained the same mind-blowing state!

The pathway spoke profoundly and with clarity about using immaculate insight to create peace for mankind. And all jokes aside, it not only sounded like the only answer left for our maddened planet, it was undeniably familiar to my heart, mind and soul. There was nothing to resist when the tenet lent such emotional intelligence to the planet and to me, so much so that I was to adopt Buddhist techniques and practices as a normal part of my everyday life thereafter.

Apparently everyone was in the ocean of wanderers, and all carried the same enlightenment seed – including the labelled ones, like gays, blacks, women, white coats – even crocodiles, fish, and *me*. Certainly the terminology sounded nautical, but there was nothing empty about how I felt.

'Er, does this include the bulbous-eyed, ill-fated fish-fanged, abandoned creatures that career at the bottom of our deepest oceans?' I unsteadily asked my root guru – who, because he had already consciously reincarnated to Earth six times, had been bestowed with the honorific title of 'Rinpoche' ('precious one').

He nodded matter-of-factly. 'Of course.' That's when I cried again. 'But why are you crying?'

'Rinpoche, this vow is too difficult, it's just too impossible to achieve.'

Soberly he looked into my eyes. 'Now you understand, Robyn.'

And what treasures were these extraordinary teachers who for me not only held all the answers but additionally dedicated life after life to straightening out us wanderers? Given that Rinpoche had been returning for countable lifetimes already with ungraspable, selfless compassion and the patience of an ancient tree which drops one seed every thousand years – plus he had probably been giving *me* the same profound advice for a few lifetimes too – it looked like I'd better get into it asap. Besides, a project of this dimension would be enough to keep me out of trouble for an eon or two.

Like the labelling or not, I now had a 'religion'. All that was necessary was applying it. Radical change was right up my alley so I slipped under their generous umbrella, took refuge in my teacher, and for the first time stopped unconsciously killing 'things', including cockroaches, flies, worms, snails, mice, rats and fish – after all, they were not only living beings, but that might be me in the next lifetime if I didn't get this one right.

Mum was Christian and when I told her I was a Tibetan Buddhist she said, 'That's lovely, dear, but knowing you that means next thing you'll be off wandering around in Tibet, and it's so dangerous over there, dear. Couldn't you just get involved with the Aborigines instead? That way at least you'll stay here in Australia, and I wouldn't have to worry about you.' I love my mum.

My oldest brother laughed and insisted that I had been a Buddhist all my life. How come he'd never told me? Then over the phone, my younger brother David gasped in shock, 'Bloody hell, Rob, how are you going to get out of that?' He meant well.

Meanwhile, back in Adelaide, being even faintly connected to His Holiness was amazing, so as well as the role of secretary, I took on organising a fundraising event we called the 'World Multicultural Peace Concert', and straight away dropped out of the social scene to single-mindedly zero in on the most important event in my life so far.

Despite how it may seem, every one of us has facets of goodness, and just because I'd been burnt in love didn't mean I was giving up, so in complete opposition to my newfound Buddhist liberation, another wounded warrior was on the scene and he was a tricky handful; plus a friend and I started up a small publishing business too.

However, the more I turned to the tour, the more restless my new man and my new business partner became. Still, if there was one purpose for which I was born, it was to make the fundraising event reach as many people as possible, so I left them both and snatched up the concert reins, and enthusiastically pulled all the strings Adelaide let me.

The event unfolded on Remembrance Day 1990, and when 800 people completely filled the main theatre with excited expectancy, that was reward enough, but the wide and unique range of musical artists was so exceptional that even the uppity aristocratic Adelaidean audience clapped until they all stood up and cried out for more! His Holiness and the Tibetan people deserved that standing ovation.

When I lay down to sleep, I had the most wonderful dream that the Dalai Lama held my hand while row upon row upon row of seated smiling Tibetan monks clapped continuously. What more could I want? Certainly not waking up to a pile of unpaid bills, no money, no food, no fuel, no phone ringing, no nothing really: abruptly I was without even enough cash to buy milk for a coffee. This was not the kind of emptiness the Buddhists had in mind. It was time to go again, but at least I had done something for one of my precious teachers before I hurried off.

My spiritual path was unquestionable, but that didn't solve me. Just because I had found the way did not mean I suddenly became pure. There were plenty of ways to describe how I was behaving – Mum and Dad must have had a few. And please don't think that my parents were weak, they were not at all, but I was too old to be told, so all they could do was watch and respond when I let them. Evidently the experience with Les was still unconsciously messing with me and it showed in how I just gave myself away to any unbalanced bloke out there. Yet trickily, life persisted in bubbling out in such a bright and able way that I was fooled into mixing up open-heartedness with reckless passion.

You could use the standard saying about me running away from myself, or that one about having to love yourself first before you could love anyone else, to describe my behaviour – but I never liked that, or the wanky people who suggested it. No, how about wanting to kick open the doors beyond the average life? How about a driving desire to feel the texture of life without limitation – I mean, nothing's fatal while you're still breathing. And pray tell, which one of us isn't out there searching for the elusive butterfly of authentic lover love?

I spent the next year journeying through the Red Centre to Darwin, across to Kununurra, down to Perth, over the remarkable Nullarbor to Ceduna, up into the legendary Strzelecki Track and on until I finally arrived back in Cairns. In each city I joined the closest library, sought out the local Tibetan Buddhist crowd and earned money the same way I had in Adelaide, by publishing my own tourist directories.

By then His Holiness was touring the southern states and I wasn't there. That hurt. He was my heart teacher, and one of the most profound minds on the planet. I could hardly bear it. After some quick business in Cairns I made just enough cash to pay for the journey to the same place His Holiness was heading to right then – New Zealand.

So there I was, of all places, back in Auckland, the city where Les and I had loved with such a fierce and promising lover love – and it looked like I'd been going round in ever decreasing circles ever since. No one met me there, there was no one to catch up with, no one to guide or answer to, nor was this any kind of tour: I was there to walk with one of my gurus – and did just that. I wanted this connection so badly, I used the tour itinerary like a Bible and gladly followed His profound footsteps across the two islands. I just went by plane, bus, train and feet to wherever he was coming to, turned up early and just waited till He got there. It being 1992 meant there was no big-time security cavalcade or pistol-packing motorbike cops, no barricades or two-way radio guards rudely barrelling everyone here or there – just Himself, a small entourage of monks, and a Maori Christian minister-translator all touring around in a couple of your normal sedan motor vehicles. Whatever happened to our unafraid ways?

Firstly He called at Pipitea, a marae (a sacred Maori ancestral gathering place) in Wellington. This was appropriate enough, considering both nations had things in common – like having been 'displaced', that polite English word used to describe rape, murder and plunder without respite. The Maori also honoured ancestors, dead beings and all living ones as well. Then came the first sight of my most precious heart teacher (in this lifetime anyway). Tears of relief, of joy, of elation, of fortunateness streamed from me and fell onto the sacred grounds of the marae. This day was the most profoundly opposite day to the one when I left my children behind – and the tears that came were part of the cleansing process, because that's when I first began really letting go of the past.

With bowed head, He stepped into the crowd, reached for people's hands and gently took us all as one to the wood carved entrance. Inside, almost within a breath of Him, I listened while two elders, speaking Maori, unfolded the appalling story of their cruel demise. His Holiness did not need a translator to understand. In due course, four grey-haired, elder women, covered from head to toe in black, sang the saddest, most compelling hymn of all – their story and language rolled in from the mists of creation's deepest heart, from where the elephants bury their dead, from where the whales must sing forgiveness of those who slaughter them, from a place where all the universe's mourning gathers. I had heard it before, we all have, even if we don't think so. It was the voice of the God which lives within all us beings in the ocean of wanderers. His Holiness knew, and in Tibetan told exactly the same story back, and of how only forgiveness, loving kindness and compassion could help the harmed ones and their 'enemy' heal – something we all also know of in our true hearts. The Maoris didn't need any translation either. They knew.

Well, windy Welly might have been blowing a gale, but it was Himself who blew me away. But then it got even better. His agenda for the following day included the 'official' welcome attended by the nation's most prominent leaders and their hangers-on.

'It's only for politicians, various dignitaries and the like,' a tour official said gruffly. 'The show is closed to the public, and you're not welcome.' I don't think so!

Still, if the official hadn't said it that way, I wouldn't have gotten shirty and sped in a cab to the town hall the next morning, or swished past the large gathering of well-heeled guests and up the steps of the pristine town hall to the alarmingly large, deep ebony Maori standing on guard, and launched into an impulsive pitch. 'How do you do? My name is Robyn Catchlove and I have done quite a bit of work for His Holiness in Australia and would like to attend this morning's meeting if I may, may I?' Even when the big Maori baulked at the suggestion, grinned kindly enough and attempted to move me aside, I just cut to the chase – after all, I was on a mission. 'So then my man, if you can't, who can?' and strategically slipped the last remaining 'SA Tour Committee' business card I had into his giant hand.

He read it, shuffled apologetically and replied, 'Well sis, that'd be the mayor himself, aye.' So I grabbed the precious business card back and responded firmly, as one would, 'So take me to the mayor!' The lovely Maori, with me in tow, spun heel across the foyer, up the polished split stairs, and into the superior stratosphere of officialdom and there we were facing a chunky mahogany door upon which was inscribed 'THE MAYOR'.

My unlikely-looking guiding angel tapped on the door, shrugged hopefully and vanished smartly. Obeying a muffled call to enter, there standing beside the matching mahogany desk was one silver-haired, red-faced, flustered mayor, black penguin suit and all. Why change a winning stroke, I thought, and launched into the same pitch and thrust said business card into his hand. Seeing that he was having trouble getting the 24-carat gold, double-tiered, clunky chains of office to sit comfortably over his old boys' school tie, I peppered the moment with guile, chuckled, 'Tsk, tsk, tsk,' and went to the job of straightening out the outrageously regal necklace, fussed about his collar and tie, and affectionately brushed the dandruff from his black morning suit.

Whereupon the mayor grinned thankfully, clicked his heels together and declared, 'My dear, not only can you come, you can come on my arm.' He bowed and offered me the crook of his arm, whereupon I curtsied, took his arm, then together, like the reigning king and queen, we stepped from the office and paraded slowly down the hall – which was now fully lined with notable personages – and into the mahogany encrusted room, where the mayor graciously ensured I was comfortably seated, and politely introduced me to several others – as one should.

Shortly after, His Holiness entered the room and the official occasion got underway. While He imbued the significant diplomatic proceedings with graciousness and humour, really this was an affair of state, so there was absolutely no reason whatsoever for me to be there! Afterwards, as the upper crust, ever hopeful of a formal introduction, tittered away quietly, delicately sipped drinks and nibbled petite hors d'oeuvres, the convivial major dutifully did the 'rounds' with the Dalai Lama. As I stood to one side, absent-mindedly congratulating myself for the bit of fun it had been, suddenly he and Him were standing before *me*!

'His Holiness,' the cordial mayor said, 'this is Robyn Catchlove and she has done quite a bit of work for your tour in Australia,' and, as if I didn't already know, he continued, 'and, Robyn, this is His Holiness.'

He took my hand, gazed into my eyes just like the Thai monk had in Adelaide, paused for some seconds, or it might have been an eon, then murmured, 'Thank you, Robyn, thank you, thank you.'

For sure and certain I had been blessed by a most extraordinary man, and it was then that my lifetime(s') commitment to Him and the Tibetan Buddhist teachings really kicked in.

I know that you know His Holiness didn't go back to Dharamasala telling all and sundry that he'd run into Rob down in New Zealand, but the karma mechanics did some good work that fateful day – so in turn I scoffed more than my share of canapés, drank every sweet sherry that came past and made certain to shout myself a cab back to the hostel.

The tour moved to Auckland, so I followed. During a radio interview, the Dalai Lama called the Chinese his brothers and sisters, and explained that He was just a simple monk but would continue to reincarnate again and again for the benefit of all sentient beings. The man had already had 14 fully authenticated conscious rebirths on our childish, bull-headed planet, and there He went committing to do the same once again. After all that had been perpetrated upon Him and His people, if He could forgive the Chinese *and* keep turning up on the planet to remind us about compassion leading to wisdom, it was about time to address my own miniscule story.

That night, fatefully from the city where our love had spoken volumes, I rang Les and opened up about how floating around the ocean in our Tupperware bowl boat with our beloved dog had been. In the end, I let all my feelings loose and howled down the line, 'I forgive you, I forgive you, Les.' The call was so filled with emotion that I expected a similar, just as highly charged comeback. Instead Les tearily spluttered down the line, 'Jezus H, Rob, just when I was getting back on my feet, you had to ring and say that.' Aaaaaaaaah men! But of course he was still suffering badly too.

Back in Cairns, I drove alone to Brisbane. It was just like a big country town then, and West End the only really bohemian suburb, so I took an apartment there. It was a strange time. The people at the local Buddhist centre weren't exactly sociable, the friends I made all went somewhere else after the sun went down and somehow I stumbled onto work at the largest record exchange store in Australia: a place chocked to the hilt with records, posters, rock books, tapes and, unsurprisingly, locked glass cabinets of assorted marijuana accoutrements, silver skulls, and the like – the kind of place you enter at 9am, emerge from at 3pm with a bag full of quirky bargains, and think you've been to a museum.

I was so unrealistically idealistic about saving the Tibetan refugees that one day I found myself spending the last of my food money on photocopying pamphlets about their terrible plight. That's what I mean about living on the surface – how could I save anyone when I couldn't save myself? What was it with all this giving and no receiving? Why did I keep turning the light of consciousness out all the time? It was time to face myself. At another imperative crossroad of my gypsy life I had to go within and try to sort out who I really was, and I went up and down with my inner journey as boldly as I could.

Sitting in the eye of the mind cyclone, in the following months I worked at how to be alone and not lonely, how *not* to give the melancholies permission to turn into depression, how to let the deep longing for a lover be OK in itself without impatiently making another error of judgement. All of my life's negative actions were begging me to transform the experiences and myself. More importantly, I knew the longer that took, the longer it would be before I got to move onto the good bits. Sifting through it all I 'asked' that willpower and wisdom help show me the way.

I'm sure that fine-tuning our crappy habits or attitudes on the inner level is the same as keeping oil, water and petrol up to one's car – it makes us go better. Who of us can say they are always calmly, consistently at peace and at one with the world – not even His Holiness! Most answers are simple and come from nature itself so just acknowledging that you have a spirit is enough: take the time to watch a tree drop a seed and then see a new shoot appear; think that even though you might not be here in the years to come, your spirit certainly will be through your children and their children's children, etc – that's rebirth enough. Remember that all of us, including animals, are just seeking food, safety, the right family life and peace, and treat them accordingly – that's compassion enough. And you don't have to be a Tibetan Buddhist, get a telegram from the Universe, or personally meet His Holiness – just lighten up a bit, forgive yourself and know that compassion, not love, is the greatest equaliser.

Despite Brisbane being my home base, eventually I scored a job with a real estate developer which involved driving massive miles around the mostly empty highways and byways of the western Queensland mining belt for the next year or two. The money was big, but still it was a very solitary, nomadic lifestyle.

Back in Brisbane at a Tibetan Buddhist centre one night, I heard that a certain Rinpoche who lived in Sydney was coming to Brisbane to give teachings. The force of hearing his name triggered me to seek him out, and soon enough there he was, my root guru, filled with joyous laughter and placing a khatag (symbolic, traditional silk scarf) over my head as a blessing. Imagine me having a plan that reached beyond this lifetime, let alone having an actual guide who was willing to remain steadfast in life after life and onward until such time as I attained enlightenment!

My guru, His Eminence Khejok Rinpoche, was the sixth incarnation of the abbot of Dhe Tsang, a monastery first built in the fourteenth century in eastern Tibet. With a young life dotted by various omens and extraordinary displays of what we in the west would call magic, recognising Rinpoche as an incarnation had not been so difficult. But when the Chinese revolutionaries usurped control of the unspoiled kingdom, their mighty axe fell swiftly. On the run-through, his monastery was destroyed, his lamas murdered and, along with millions of his fellow Tibetans, Rinpoche was tossed, at age 24, into a prison camp overflowing with the most extreme of human suffering. There they put him to breaking impossible quarry rocks and emptying filthy toilet pits. Imagine your most loved one suffering this, and my guru even more precious too.

For Rinpoche, being denied the right to help others or to practise his faith was more devastating than any death, be it by execution, hunger, being lost in the snow, murder or escape. In his words, 'Compassion is the spontaneous response of an open heart, and everything in our religion. If we cannot actively work towards others' relief, our lives are empty.'

Karma is so complex that in an ironic turnaround Rinpoche's escape came as a result of saving the life of his very ill prison commandant who, as a 'thank you', allowed him some freedom of movement, and thus the opening to flee for India. As Rinpoche put it, 'When you face a hostile person, think he is simply having a hard time trying to find happiness and avoid suffering. See yourself in him and your anger will melt away.'

After Rinpoche left Brisbane, I went back on the road until Christmas time, then I resigned and speared back down the No. 1 Highway – this time to snappy Sydney town. Rinpoche from my ancestral lineage lived there, and so did my oldest brother and his wife, Chris. One would take care of my inner world, and the other two would nurture my outer life.

CHAPTER 48

From Tinsel Town to Tibet and Back

'This is Sydney, baby, get tough or get out!' That was just about the first phrase I heard in Sydney so there was no mistaking that unlike the old school aristocracy of Melbourne, I was in the cheeky city of the nouveau riche. And I must have taken that statement about getting tough to heart because that's what I did. Seeing money disappear from my hands like carnival fairy floss, I knew it was time to get a job, but without a car that was not going to by easy. At Australia's most famous car yard alley, Parramatta Road, I found a good shitter (ie an unreliable $1000 rust bucket with lots of rego and too many kilometres). When the cruncher (deal maker) and I, the woody (the easy mark), finished bartering away at the price, he asked if I knew anything about cars.

'Not a bloody thing,' I admitted jokingly.

'Good,' he said, 'that means you'd be perfect sellin' them. When can you start?'

They used to say that if you were still on a car yard after three months, you deserved long service leave. They were right, and for a woman who couldn't find a good man, I certainly had the gift of the gab when it came to selling cars. It was a pretty radical living for a woman in the mid-1990s and who would have believed me if

I'd told them I was Tibetan Buddhist too?

And it was definitely a jungle out there, with all kinds of cars, bikes, buses, wagons, vans and big trucks chundering up and down the bitumen as if they were running late for a dire emergency – not to mention the mangled bunch of multi-language personages called customers; the 30 knot gales, the pissing down rain, the freezing cold winter, the 40 degree Gobi Desert mirage-like heat or the full inferno summer sun waves bouncing straight off the car panels in a delirium. Additionally, the men I worked with were like fishermen and truckies, only slicker, more arrogant and much richer.

So, for ten hours a day, six days a week, I, usually the only Australian and always the only woman, worked in the car game surrounded by a pack of other salesmen all of whom were trying to outsmart me. It was fun at the beginning but the more successful I became, the more difficult the other salesmen made it for me. Was I ever going to come to my senses?

My pub of choice was in Balmain until halfway through one loud boozy Friday night when I noticed that all the patrons looked and sounded like deranged escapees – so I got up and left, which forever after put an end to pubs being where I went to socialise.

Amid this surreal backdrop, in 1996 His Holiness lobbed into Sydney to confer the rare and complex Kalachakra Initiation upon a crowd 4000 strong. And no, he did not give me a quick call to say, 'Hey there, Rob.' Instead, Horden Pavilion at the old Sydney Showgrounds burst into being – me helping paint snow lions on His golden throne, unrolling magnificent hangings, crawling aloft to straighten curtains; tidying the marigold flower pots, and sweeping His entranceway clean every day. Still, not bad for a used car salesman, eh?

Then His Holiness was in the building, smiling and bowing lower than the bowing audience, surrounded by the golden lamas who chanted a song of sound vibration, a sea of harmonic syllables which washed through our consciousness like soft lapping waves. Him sitting mere feet away from the splendid, intricate sand mandala, and for a week teaching the cosmology of the Universe to a potpourri of people from every corner of our spinning globe.

The Dalai Lama left an indelible imprint and then He was gone, and I was back selling anything from junky, rust bucket Russian

Ladas to immaculate 1970s Chevy Impalas. That was after I had sat every dawn in meditation on the trail of enlightenment. Being the only woman selling used cars on the stretch, or possibly even in Sydney, was more than just a challenge, it was hard bloody work, and by then bad manners, abrasive rudeness and nasty manipulation by the blokes was the norm.

But, like a bull terrier, I refused to be beaten by their pack bullying and for a few years fought for 'my rights', steadily made big bucks and kept reminding myself that they had never wrestled a crocodile. Call it fighting the good fight if you like but, really, I was wrestling with something much more difficult – myself. Being resilient and nimble was all well and good, but work was a horror stretch and I became more silent and unhappy with every bulging pay packet. Adjectives like 'strong' and 'tough' sound flattering but really 'brittle' and 'shrill' is closer to the mark – whatever description, somehow I was in the boxing ring again.

Don't get me wrong, it wasn't a lack of friends, but 99 per cent of them were women – single, good-looking, well-informed, smart at business, funny, generous – but still women. The only thing missing amongst us was male energy – not necessarily as lovers even; just men who could influence our viewpoints would have been a relief. As strange as it sounds, I'm a man's woman, and I missed the real ones, so eventually I stepped back quite a bit. It meant being on my own, but now I understood not to be lonely about it – not to dwell self-indulgently in what is just a mood not a fact.

By then I owned an investment apartment and was living (and still am today) in a big garage behind the home-cum-art studio of good friends. My home is filled with plants, swanky lamps, tasty rugs and lots of sixties décor, but there's no air conditioning, no wall-to-wall synthetic carpets, and no boxed-up tiny rooms designating what should or shouldn't go on in them. Most days I plunge my fingers into the veggie patch, talk to the chooks, and in early spring, across the cow skin floor rug glistening iridescent snail trails appear randomly. The trappings of 'soft' society mean nothing, provided the double-roller door stays up most nights so I can stay in touch with the splendid Milky Way. And I let go of cigarettes, and made friends with alcohol too, only sipping the lovely elixir on occasions.

At home in Adelaide one year, while having a cup of tea with Mum, it dawned on me that an apology might be in order for not having lived the 'standard model daughter' life, for not getting married and settling down close by in the brick veneer with the 2.5 kids, the one dog and the two Volvos. 'Sorry for living such an unpredictable wandering life,' I said lightly, thinking that would be enough. She stayed silent, and the comment hung in the air uncomfortably, so I fumbled on. 'I hope I haven't disappointed you too much. I just tried to do my best with the kind of life that's come along. Don't worry Mum, it's been a surprise to me too.'

She sighed deeply, gazed off into the distance, and then spoke. 'It would have been alright if it had been one of your brothers, but not from our daughter. You've lived such a man's way of life.' That comment was a bit of a shock. 'Sometimes I never knew where you were for months on end, or whether you were alive or dead or had even been eaten by a crocodile, but Dad and I never gave up hope and never stopped loving you.' Mum kept talking and led me to their bedroom. 'I think everyone's life is written at birth, and we knew you had to do what life intended.' From a bottom drawer, my darling mum carefully withdrew a delicate, hand-crocheted, simply perfect, white baby's gown all properly preserved and sealed in a special plastic bag. The exquisite, tiny little piece of art was obviously all her own handiwork. 'Through all these years I saved this for the time when my own daughter's baby would be christened.'

The gown and Mum's hidden feelings completely stunned me. We reached out, held each other and cried. Every woman has secrets of the heart and she was no different. That day she became more than just my mum, she became a woman in her own right, and from then on my deepest confidante in life. In fact most days I put in a quick thank you to whoever for the mum and dad I managed to draw.

Despite being unhappy at work there was one very good reason to keep tripping the car yard boards – Rinpoche was going home to Tibet, and said that I, along with other students, could come too. The trip filled me with barely containable excitement, but given the Chinese track record, imprisonment or even worse was not out of the question. Let me explain: death, for proficient Tibetan Buddhist practitioners, is just another state of consciousness – more like taking a welcome holiday from the maddened world – and although I'm not that clever, whatever was to happen, at least I would be with my teacher and in the heart of my true belonging, so I went willingly.

Flying 30,000 feet above the Arafura Sea at 800 kilometres per hour, the plane flew through a sky that looked like a futuristic ice age with its clouds of soft rolling waves, jagged icebergs and swirling castles. Directly below I could see the ocean on which my *Jean King* had done six knots per hour flat-chat some 15 years earlier. I might have been a trillion lifetimes away from that, but I was still fishing, only this time my body was just catching up with where my soul already was – the same as the time in Adelaide when destiny sent me knocking on the unknown door of the 'talking' Thai Buddhist Meditation Centre. For me, this was *the* journey.

As the plane sped on, vivid memories came and went: flashes of a previous life in robes; another of chanting in a dim, damp monastery, and another of offering a khatag to a lama seated beside a rocky cliff, and me in this life as a 10-year-old girl poring over Tibetan history books in libraries – apparently the Land of Snowy Mountains had been chanting me home for further back than I could possibly have recognised.

And so to Sichuan province in China where many millions of people lived, all of whom appeared to be visiting the sweltering city of Chengdu at the same time that our gathering of 100 or so students of Rinpoche's were. Then us wheeling out and away toward the alluring, sacred land of dharma, unique stupas (burial monuments), classic monasteries, whitewashed homes and the long-haired, bronze Tibetans, to the place I had been tied to since I was a child. Our overladen, chain-wheeled, cranky buses staunchly crawled up the single-lane, dirt mountain roads, over the mighty Mekong, past alpine forests, beside gushing streams, and on toward the Gyalrong region. At Tiger Skin Pass, over 5500 feet above sea level, our multicoloured prayer flags (wind horses) joined the already fluttering cache waving across the rolling mountain tops: good, now the prayers to benefit all living beings could spread out into the known and unknown galaxies – and on we pressed into the heart of compassion, to my teacher's historic monastery.

At Rinpoche's birthplace, as we climbed up to a tiny, tiny monastery propped on a hill's edge, the sharp, cleansing tang of juniper pine incense literally engulfed us before clouding up into the bluest sky. Seeing the pyre of smoke spiral into nothingness, feeling the swirl of inquisitive ruddy-faced Tibetans and a growing gladness at heart, inexplicable tears came. One of our group, a tall, kindly man, put an arm around me and said, 'I understand tears. I have some to shed myself.' When the group of pilgrims sat inside the monastery paying respect, I parked myself amongst the Tibetans – now that felt better.

Two and a half bumpy bus days later, we were literally at the end of the dirt track and at the entrance of Dhe Tsang monastery. There were no flushing toilets, no phones, no television sets, no radios, no computers – unbelievably there was me, straight from the nasty battlefields of 'trust me' auto alley, standing in the enchanted kingdom which levitated just on the edge of the pure lands.

Greeted by more billowing clouds of juniper smoke, two rows of yellow-hatted lamas carrying a golden parasol and blowing conch shells welcomed Rinpoche into his ancestral home. Inside, the astonishing vibrancy and uniqueness of spectacular frescoes and drapery, century-old wall hangings, the art pieces and carpets were just staggering, and constituted mountainous evidence of Rinpoche's persistent efforts to repair the damage the cultural revolution had done to this place of peace.

Behind the cluster of buildings we visitors set up tents, lit small fires, brewed tea and got to know each other. Each morning, we sat in meditation or joined the locals and circumambulated the place, feeling the beauty of the land as we went. No wonder those fortunate enough to have come from other lands fell under its spell.

And speaking of spells, amongst the heady days, the tall man, the one who had come to my teary rescue, fell under my gaze more often than not. He and I joked a lot and at the same things, and just liked each other – nothing more. It had been years since a good man responded like that, so all my suspended joy bubbled up and over, just like good champagne. When he said, 'You're special, you're helping me to laugh again,' I felt the same in return.

We visitors and the sea of the local Tibetans gazed at each other in gentle curiosity. None of us needed translators: the languages were completely different but we understood each other easily. I liked their deep black eyes, toothless smiles, weather-beaten, antique faces and humble style. Despite all the great difficulty, poverty, hunger and imprisonment within their own land, still these people took joy from us being there: this in itself was a true teaching and sometimes their humbleness made me just cry.

Although the monastery and surrounding countryside completely matched any magical picture you might have conjured up, it would be wrong to assume everything was fine. It was profusely clear, right then and there, that the Tibetans themselves were suffering badly from the absence of simple medical care, proper and constant food, real education, money and, most of all, they were suffering the suppressed deepest grief of their lost spiritual teachers and teachings. I swear it was enough to touch the most cynical heart.

And how could one not be affected by the futility of what had happened, and not see the destruction that was everywhere, including the smashed-up remnants of ancient hermitage cells still standing silent witness to the consequences of the 'red revolution'. No film or painting or story can describe how it must have been. What was cultural about the irrational killing of retreat hermits, simple monks who no doubt had been praying for the ill-intending Chinese militias even as they forged rampantly down the cul-de-sac road one half-century earlier?

For us lucky ones, what unfolded was a week of extraordinary ceremonies and blessings, and Rinpoche demonstrating that tangible compassion could be sustained through actual centuries. Sitting beside the locals, we watched lamas wearing bright brocade costumes and handmade masks perform ritual dances; gasped as a three-storey high, 18-metre wide thanga (traditional cloth scroll painted with enlightened beings) unfolded; and celebrated when the main hall, all drenched in colour and treasures, overflowed with high lamas, monks, guests, students, locals and wild warrior men with curved knives stuck into knee-length boots.

You know how good holidays always take on special qualities? Well this one seemed like an iridescent dream, like a brief glimpse into a time and place I wanted to stay in forever. In amongst it, a more personal experience was happening: 'the man' and I were drawn to each other, always staying close at hand, at least within arm's reach, always feeling completely at ease together. When some chirpy Tibetan women giggled softly between themselves about us, I stumbled and became unsure. Finding privacy sitting amongst tiny deity flowers behind the monastery, I realised that love had come again. He found me there, and together we sat beside the ruined but still standing hermitage cottages. Somewhere, the lamas kept chanting, the cymbals clashed and the timing drums throbbed.

'This is the nicest illusion I have ever known. In some uncanny familiarity, I feel like a lover to you,' I explained, more to get something off my mind than expecting something in return.

Although taken aback, the man treated my 'outing' with genuine kindness. 'Maybe in a past lifetime,' he answered. But what about in this one, I thought. 'To have an attractive woman say such a thing is unexpected, but I love my wife and my four teenage kids very much.' In some time, not now, I thought, maybe we can become as one.

I was glad to have spoken honestly, and his explanation lightened me – now I could refocus on the real purpose of the journey. And there was my teacher standing beside walls so blackened by 500 years of smoke and incense offerings that we had to hold lit candles up to see the ancient paintings of Buddhas, consorts and wrathful deities. When someone asked why he had more female students than male, he answered, 'Because women suffer more!' He is a modern man, my Rinpoche.

Still, 'the man' and I naturally gravitated to each other. One afternoon under the most vivid blue sky in the universe we sat on top of the dreamtime mountain overlooking a world from another time. 'You are wonderful. What do you want?' he asked.

'Why not share what's happening to us here in this magical place, then let it evolve into a deep and long friendship?' Our attraction had been accidental, and mutual, and that was enough. Later in the afternoon, white butterflies lifted and filled the valley below.

At night a big bonfire was lit, and the Tibetans sang folk songs. All the humour and music made everyone's heart feel a bit drunk, so like old friends we laughed, mingled, hugged each other and for a twilight moment let the truth of their plight go. Sometimes they leapt into the middle of the deep circle and mimed a story, so for a bit of Aussie culture, I took up the centre and did a fair rendition of 'Waltzing Matilda'. It brought plenty of laughs but, as you know, the song does speak about oppression of the poor and hungry, and so it was on the goods.

Long after we outsiders were tucked into the latest technologically lightweight, whizzbang sleeping bags, the Tibetans kept echoing a particular tune which sounded like waves of sad longing rising and falling eternally. You could tell it came from their inconsolable hearts.

Then we were leaving Dhe Tsang. As the tears came I lingered and bowed and touched the humble, tender people again and again – I would never forget them. In this wild affair called life it had been a most significant experience.

From the high mountain pass, we dipped down the other side into steep valleys where less fortunate Tibetan men, women and children stood in quarries chipping rocks with blunt hand axes. Without relief, nor roof, nor hat, nor fridge, and working under an intense inferno of dust and burning sun, they were in conditions impossible for any creature. This I would never forget either. Further on through the dense haze, we passed lime factories with bilious streams of dirty cloud continuously issuing forth from numerous smokestacks. From the pure lands we had come down to the hell realms.

A couple of days later, the group was on the airport road to the fabled, once forbidden capital of Tibet, Lhasa. Halfway there Rinpoche stopped the bus. He led us through the weedy paddocks to a most inconspicuous mudbrick house. Inside was the stupa of Atisha, the famed teacher who came up from India 1000 years ago to teach Buddhism. As we walked back past, I shivered and began to sob, and a vision came: of being there as a small child in some former time, watching helplessly while relatives of some kind were forcibly taken away – and me not being able to save them or stop whoever was taking them away. Maybe here was some explanation for my fighting for the underdog.

'The man' came, surrounded me, and for the remaining bus trip just sat close and let me be with it. That any man cared in such a manner was new, and that my ways did not disturb him meant just as much – maybe I was not such a bad person after all. How long does it take to forgive yourself? When, for the first time, we drove past Lhasa's famous Potala Palace, home of the Dalai Lama, he cried openly too because seeing it was one of his dreams in life. For me, a man like him was rare.

Lhasa might have been swathed in Himalayan mist, but it was covered with smog too. Same amongst the inhabitants, where armed Chinese soldiers mixed in with the olden people wrapped in yak garb and spinning hand-held prayer wheels, the maroon-robed lamas and the sky of sapphire and there they were, the clouds – clouds exactly like I had seen in Lower Tully a trillion years ago; and the most sacred of all, 1000-year-old Jokhang Temple surrounded by crowded alley-ways and a bustling marketplace. Everywhere were seething beggars and poverty enough to stun, and broken minds, errant, cheeky kids, wheelers and dealers, swashbuckling warriors from Kham with red ribbons plaited in their long black hair and sturdy silver-handled daggers hanging from yak belts, malas swinging from devoted pilgrims' hands, and dotted in between it all, a melting pot of travellers from the world over – not to mention turquoise, red coral, amber, jewels, zhees (rare gemstones which Tibetans say fall from the sky), uncountable Buddha statues, trinkets, thangas, texts, cloth to die for, and my Rinpoche . . . Who would not be captured by it all? The Lhasaians warmed easily to me, and it was true that I felt at one with them, and so just like them, I bought and wore a black gypsy-style man's hat.

Everyone who goes to Lhasa visits the fabled 1300-year-old Potala Palace. Winding uphill to the side entrance was a market-place strewn with crystal skull caps, ornate daggers, ritual drums, big chunks of natural stones, and hand-carved leather shoes and belts all covered in symbols. The richness of their wares was nothing in comparison to the golden-roofed, main home of the previous 10 Dalai Lamas with its ad infinitum of solid gold, silver and bronze holy

deities; ancient text written in gold, secret seals of diplomatic importance, and mandalas encrusted with turquoise, pearls, rubies and
diamonds, plus the legendary 14-metre high lifelike stupa-tombs of
previous incarnations of His Holiness. And just like the history that
surrounded Tibet, most of it was shrouded in dank, grimy conditions
with brazen soldiers strolling around either carrying loaded guns or
hiding inside monks' robes pretending that they were fooling us.

Then we were up on top of the roof at the top of the world where
golden snow lions with silk khatags in their jaws stood guarding the
cardinal points, and where as a lonely little boy, His Holiness the
fourteenth often used to come and peer out over his own people. At
least up here, I thought, He could get some space, light and vision.

The entire experience was exotic and swayed before me continuously. With 'the man' beside me, it was even more so, and I prayed
that it would not stop.

The day we visited Sera-Mey Monastery, as the bus navigated
through the gouged-up, filthy dirt streets, we watched passively
when a man brutally beat his wife – Buddhist or not, none of us were
game to stop him. At the monastery, where once many thousands of
monks lived and trained, now a mere 200 resided. In a small tree-
grove courtyard we watched them debate wisdom topics regarding
the very essence of being, while in the narrow laneway behind, a band
of street urchins tried to kickbox each other into painful submission.

Bending down to give a beggar some money, Rinpoche tapped
me on the shoulder. 'Robyn, don't think you're doing her a favour.'
My brow creased questioningly. 'She's doing you one by spending
a lifetime showing you how fortunate you are.' Ever since that, no
matter how little or large, I always give and remember what's really
taking place.

In the midst of it all, 'the man' lightened up and talked about the
life of being a happily married 'father and husband' and how it went
with the loneliness of the man within. 'You think I am not strong
because we don't make love – you think less of me.'

'I love you for what you are, not for what you could give me, so
it's quite the opposite. One of the reasons for my love is that you do
keep the integrity of your marriage within our own pretty amazing experience.' Our soul familiarity was unexpected – so that for a

moment or two in this life, we drifted on a velvet cloud. It was like a personal secret, something no one could know or take away.

Fancy having to go all the way to Tibet to find the man I would have remained with until death. Cosmic jokes are like that. How many happily married men and women, I wondered, have that secret love, that person whom they do not make love to or leave their families for, but hold in the privacy of their heart?

Even the best things are impermanent, and so was the trip. My gratitude and thanks to Rinpoche seemed lame and inadequate. He slipped a khatag over my head, patted my hand lightly, smiled enigmatically and said he would be home in Sydney soon. He knew everything – he knew that day, the next and into my next life.

It all sounds a bit too rosy, but I make no excuse about that. It's always important to have a bit of enchantment in life. And despite the heavy car yard years, at least I still had the capacity to rise above it. I hadn't just visited Tibet, I had entered another realm where Rinpoche and 'the man' had given me the best tools in life – a clear enough pathway and a calmer pride about who I was.

CHAPTER 49

The Best Bit

*B*ack in Australia, for the first few weeks my external life just ran on automatic pilot. Sure I walked the boards, did deals, earned the dollars and made light with the friendly faces – but internally something altogether different was going on. Each night from sleep until waking, came intense dreaming like never before. Filled with visions and continuous teachings, the images burned so brightly, it appeared that I rested inside my body, rather than fell into the common, unconscious sleep state.

Genuinely hoping that 'the man's' remaining years would be filled with personal reward, family love and success, still I couldn't help mourning for that which could not be ours – but this time I used the dharma as an ally, and understood that there was no rush or need to change anything – everything was as it should be. As Rinpoche put it: 'Given that we have countless lives, a singular experience of a painful nature is as small as a teardrop in the ocean. There is no reason to allow emotions to affect the constant state of awareness you are in.' Thinking like this made me feel more honourable, and I began to truly transform.

That's the thing, no matter what else, transforming is something which no one else can do for you. I know it's a rave but it's called inner work, and that sounds a bit New Agey too – but both men and women should be doing it on some level all the time. Really, if you're holding anger, resentment, sadness or even fear around a person or circumstance (and who isn't?), those kinds of attitudes will never change that story to your liking. To be free, the only choice is to start looking at it from a different angle, to start changing that which you can – your own self.

The winter rain lessened, yet the wind was sharp and pushy. Soon pink blossoms appeared on the almond trees, and the daily skies once again became splattered with small families of galahs, rowdy know-all cockatoos and long-beaked egrets. I was a spunky, blokey kind of woman, but still had an unnecessarily fierce streak of independence. At the close of every day I wound up 100 motor car windows, locked 100 motor car doors, put 100 motor car keys away, pulled the solid iron bar gates across the car yard entrance and drove home. Every morning I meditated on the cycles of life, death and rebirth, and tried to develop compassion for all sentient beings – especially the ones I disliked, like the hard, bullying, cowardly men I still worked with.

Sure, there must be easier ways, but look as I did, those doors were never really open for me. There is a reason that your life is like it is. If there are eight billion people in the world, there are eight billion different ways to find peace and eight billion different ways to lighten up.

Sometimes my intangible, invisible desire for love also danced a merry flame and burned like a wild bushfire. I ached, the flame stirred, then in defiance I would remember and laugh at the understanding that I was suffering for something that did not exist – so if it did not exist, why pretend that it should? You might even say that I mistook passion for love, but that is only partly true – I'm sure all women give a drop or two of pure essence to whoever they make love with, so I suspect it was just overwhelming goodness that turned my love into longing. But love cannot come until it does. In the world of dharma we expand any experience of suffering to encompass all those in the world who are in that same experience and pray that they all cease to suffer too.

'The man' rang every now and then. Always at some subtle point within our conversations some intrinsic intimacy that could only be ours would fleetingly open up, but we knew. There was also a longing to dissolve amongst the humble people who had touched my heart, entered my stream of consciousness and woven me into their source.

Hoping to fix my unhappy workplace, finally I moved on, and toward the end even managed a small yard for Harry, who was as classic as the Hollywood movie set office we worked from: the grimy shell of a ramshackle old home complete with the shabby black leather lounge, and walls covered in big tits calendars, a framed and signed footy guernsey, and a bad taste painting done by Harry's kid.

Cogitating away at my desk one morning, finally I realised that underneath my exterior bravado, below all the big dollars and fiery will, there lay nearly as much bitter unhappiness as I had carried in grief when I left the Gulf. This realisation was the most important part of my transformation, a crucial acknowledgement, and it was vital that I shift the stuckness just how I did – by right away snatching up my bag and loudly declaring that I was 'off'. While Harry stood there scratching his balls, looking confused and repeatedly muttering, 'Fuck love, ya can't fucken go on a fucken Sunday, what'll we f—', without a backward glance I squeezed through the tight-knit line of best value, fully guaranteed, immaculate condition, deal of the century cars, and was gone. Unpopular? Highly. Necessary? Utterly.

At home I lifted up the garage's big roller doors, looked into the sky and yelled, 'That's it, I give up. Please send me everything.'

I stopped trying to force my life into submission and just let it come to me – finally, I surrendered. Instead of dreaming or thinking about how it might be at some future date, I gave up everything I didn't like about me and my life – which was pretty much everything, including the use of my sharp clever tongue which had supported whoever I thought I was – and stood by and watched what happened, almost like a spectator. There was plenty of beauty within, I just needed to give it a chance. You're in a life, so why not live on its most daring edge, why not get to the nitty-gritty of your own self? That way at least you have the time to see the signs and can learn to trust yourself a bit more.

So I lived on the smell of an oily rag, and watched and waited. This was *not* New Agey, this was me applying the wisdom I kept wishing others would apply to me. And there was plenty of amassed emotional baggage that had to go too. So when a very clever, energetic healing modality surfaced, where by letting go of negative emotions and old stories you heal your heart and any physical pain at the same time, I used it to fix me, and in the process became a practitioner myself.

Getting off life's rat-race wheel and opening up like that has been the greatest adventure (so far). Really, life is so profoundly unexplainable, why dislike it so much and be unhappy? Why not feel the most positive you can about whatever it brings? Simple as it may be, I reckon the only reason we are all here is to help each other, including the white coats, and that when we all actually comprehend that every land and all the waters in between are precious, then every creature inclusively, every tree, bush, weed, rock and flower becomes precious too. This is not a religion or a dogma, but I do suspect it might just be a necessary universal truth.

Travelling is not necessary either, but it does settle your mind about places you are drawn to: therefore against advice from friends and family I sold my investment apartment and returned to Tibet twice more, swam in the blessed Lake Manasarovar, circumambulated the most sacred of mountains, Mount Kailash, went to India and very nearly got married in the US of A.

Sitting with Rinpoche in retreat on a mountain edge above a fertile valley just outside of Kathmandu one morning, he said, 'Robyn, your father.' After racing into the city, I found a telephone and listened as Mum explained that Dad, although still lucid, was in palliative care and dying.

Immediately I went back to Rinpoche, but of course he knew already. 'Better for your father you here in sacred place. I do prayers now, you go Big Stupa, light candles for him.' (The Big Stupa is a very sacred ancient Buddhist site in Kathmandu.)

'Ah, there you are, bird's nest,' I heard my darling dad say when he came to me that night in a clear vision, so I told him not to wait for me, to go when the lamas in maroon came for him. The next day while I sadly arranged my flight back home, my Rinpoche and his monastery of lamas in southern India performed a special cleansing ceremony: Dad died at the same time, so he must have pretty special karma from thousands and thousands of kilometres away in

Adelaide. It was experiences like that which confirmed the profound nature of Tibetan Buddhism. You might not have come to your spiritual pathway yet, but it is in every man and woman and is the place we all end up seeking – after all, who amongst us has not called out for their God at some moment in time?

Anyone who says there's no proof of life after death hasn't done the study and is just having an opinion because there's evidence aplenty. I'll never stop missing my dad, but with the concrete knowledge I have about reincarnation, I don't cling on to the sadness. He's definitely out there somewhere lighting up other people's lives.

Sydney is like living in a Jerry Seinfeld, snappy Jack Russell kind of town, so it keeps me sharp, laughing and always on my toes as I stumble on through life just like everyone else. Every morning I meditate on life, the universe and everything, but mostly I revel in the nature of that which is around me, keep a lookout for my next career and occasionally hold my own hand, and feel the lovely unfamiliarity of that.

Having now spent more years living alone than otherwise, feeling the warmth and protection of another's love is rare indeed. Maybe my lover karma is up, but I hope not. My mum, God love her, always reckons he's just around the next corner, but the 'right man' has not come along yet and I don't *need* him to. The life we live is no coincidence – it is an astonishing tool from which to learn how to live with an open heart. In amongst this constant awareness, I know not to be afraid of lover love, that if it comes again to embrace it fully – and my story is not over yet, so whether he finds me or not, there's plenty of music in my life what with my precious teacher, my darling mum, friends I would never swap and three good godsons.

There's another bonus too because there are two breathtaking little girls, my landlords' children, who have lived around me since their births. Just the other day Mimi, aged nine now, and Eliza, aged seven, rushed into my garage wanting the answer to a very important question. 'Who are you, Robyn, who are you?' they fluttered around asking urgently. It was a good question which had taken years for them to get to. 'You're not our nanny or our granny, and you're not an aunty, so who are you?' In fact I had begun to wonder myself just exactly how they saw me. The three of us tossed a few options around, and easily came up with a definition which I reckon covers the lot – lifelong friend – and then they both contentedly veered off elsewhere. Even though secretly I like to think I'm the girls' natural godmother, it means that some way or other I have had a taste of both motherhood and grandmother-hood – and been very fluky in that regard.

Life is a love story, not just an adventure, even if it's learning to love which comes your way, so as for my ex-lovers, why would I not stay friends with them, considering that which is most intimate has taken place and what I have learned from them? You see, even if your marriage goes the distance, at some stage the relationship changes from lover to deep companionship, doesn't it?

As it turned out, the Korean bathhouse, just like me, was not destroyed, but instead had undergone a serious renovation. I went there not long ago. The baths were more bland and corporate, it cost more to get in, the tiled Roman orgy wall was gone, and the steaming waters were not as deep. Since writing this book, both of us had changed, but I reckon I'm richer in spirit, have a great belly laugh, am happy, strong and lucky for everything that has happened in my life because it has led me to today.

I also bumped into Les recently. He is old now, silver-haired, a bit bent-up, and he's been married for a few years. Heart tears still fell, so he held me close and said, 'It doesn't matter any more, Rob. Don't worry about it.' In all this time, I rarely thought of how his life must have felt, and it was true, whatever had happened was over and we still loved each other. Always keep in mind that if you have ever loved and then 'lost' someone, don't worry, somewhere in the mix you still love them and they you.

My Rinpoche says if you want to know about your past lives, have a look at how your present life is panning out – and if you want to know about your future lives, look at how you are living the one you are in now. So then from birth until death no matter what, love does drive everything, but we need to mix in a bit of compassion and forgiveness not just for others but for ourselves too, right?

Oh, and by the way, two of my lovers and I took a vow to meet up in the next lifetime – I'll let you guess who they might be.